25 Years of the TRIPS Agreement

IEEM AND INTERNATIONAL INTELLECTUAL PROPERTY LAW

The involvement of the Institute of European Studies of Macau (IEEM) in matters of intellectual property is based on annual conferences that take up topical issues of intellectual property from a comparative perspective with a particular focus on Asia and Europe. The first of these conferences was held back in 2000, and has meanwhile become an annual event complemented by an Intellectual Property School and IP Master Classes. All three venues serve as a platform for academic teaching and discussion on intellectual property awareness and the proper place and function of intellectual property law in the context of society and public interest.

From the very start, the intellectual property conferences, the IP Law School and the Master Classes have enjoyed the support, assistance and commitment of Mr. Gonçalo Cabral, who is an advisor to the Government of Macau, of Ms. Maria do Céu Esteves, past president of the IEEM, and the IEEM's current president Dr. José Luís de Sales Marques. The latter was also instrumental in setting up an IEEM chair for intellectual property law at the Maastricht University in 2004, thereby further contributing to IEEM's academic commitment to the field of intellectual property law. During the five years of its existence, this chair was held by Anselm Kamperman Sanders.

The conference papers, as revised and updated, are edited by Christopher Heath and Anselm Kamperman Sanders as an IEEM Intellectual Property Series the volumes of which are listed at the end of this book.

25 Years of the TRIPS Agreement

Past, Present, Future

Edited by

Christopher Heath

Anselm Kamperman Sanders

INSTITUTE OF EUROPEAN STUDIES OF MACAU
澳 門 歐 洲 研 究 學 會
INSTITUTO DE ESTUDOS EUROPEUS DE MACAU

Wolters Kluwer

Published by:
Kluwer Law International B.V.
PO Box 316
2400 AH Alphen aan den Rijn
The Netherlands
E-mail: international-sales@wolterskluwer.com
Website: www.wolterskluwer.com/en/solutions/kluwerlawinternational

Sold and distributed by:
Wolters Kluwer Legal & Regulatory U.S.
7201 McKinney Circle
Frederick, MD 21704
United States of America
Email: customer.service@wolterskluwer.com

ISBN: 978-94-035-2883-0

e-Book: ISBN 978-94-035-2884-7
web-PDF: ISBN 978-94-035-2885-4

Summary of Contents

When TRIPS was concluded, many understood the agreement to embody a new gold standard of IP protection that made not only reforms to the Paris and Berne Conventions, but also further IP agreements unnecessary. The ubiquitous sprawling of specific IP agreements, and especially the inclusion of IP chapters in bilateral and multilateral free trade agreements has proven this wrong. Obligations to protect IP rights can now be found in bilateral and multilateral trade agreements, and can be enforced before domestic courts, the WTO and before investor-state tribunals. IP has become far more pervasive in society than ever before. For good, better, or worse?

TRIPS has led to a number of issues in the context of international law: the relationship between GATT and TRIPS (e.g. freedom of transit), the relationship between the Paris and Berne Conventions with TRIPS (whether rights specified under Paris and Berne were actionable by way of WTO dispute resolution; what the most-favoured nation obligation meant in the context of Berne and Paris), the relationship between the WTO and WIPO (settled by way of an agreement), the direct applicability of TRIPS (not uniformly answered). These issues were partly dealt with by agreements, partly by dispute settlement decisions and partly by decisions of national courts. Increasingly the WTO panels and Appellate Body have been accused of judicial activism in allowing for non-trade obligations and concerns to factor into accepted defences to WTO disputes. Whereas TRIPS flexibilities are certainly more pronounced as compared to the other WTO covered agreements, it has taken a health crisis and

Preface

The TRIPS Agreement as an integral part of the World Trade Organisation started with the promise to replace unilateral threats of trade sanctions by a comprehensive multilateral framework including a mechanism for dispute settlement. The price to pay were levels of IP protection that did not reflect a desirable balance between rights and limits: Those representing the public interest were notably absent from the negotiating table.

In the following 25 years, both the promise and the main achievement of TRIPS were eroded by the multilateral approach giving way to a new bilateralism through free trade agreements, and by the waning support for the dispute settlement mechanism that at the time of writing is all but paralysed.

The contributions of this book highlight the development of the TRIPS Agreement in the last 25 years in the different areas of intellectual property law covered by the agreement.

The editors gratefully acknowledge the continuing support of the Institute of European Studies (ieem) in Macao and its president Dr. Sales Marques in the publication of the ieem series on intellectual property law.

The Editors

Table of Contents

About the Authors and Editors

Prof. dr. Peter L.H. Van den Bossche, LL.M is Director of Studies of the World Trade Institute (WTI) and Professor of International Economic Law at the University of Bern, Switzerland. Since 2018, he serves as President of the Society of International Economic Law. From 2009 to 2019, he was a Member of the Appellate Body of the World Trade Organization (WTO) and served as chairman of the Appellate Body in 2015. He is an honorary professor at Maastricht University, the Netherlands (since 2018), and a visiting professor at the University of Geneva (since 2018), at LUISS Guido Carli University, Rome, Italy (since 2016), at the Universidad San Francisco de Quito, Ecuador (since 2016), and at the College of Europe, Bruges, Belgium (since 2010). Since 2020, he is Editor of the *World Trade Review*, Cambridge University Press. Van den Bossche is the author (with Werner Zdouc) of *The Law and Policy of the World Trade Organization*, 4th edition (Cambridge University Press, 2017), 1077 p.; and (with SHAN Wenhua) of the Chinese edition of this book (Law Press - China, 2020), 1151 p. Van den Bossche is also the author (with Denise Prévost) of *Essentials of WTO Law* (Cambridge University Press, 2016), 302 p.

Christopher Heath (1964) studied law at the Universities of Konstanz, Edinburgh and the LSE. He lived and worked in Japan for three years, and between 1992 and 2005 headed the Asian Department of the Max Planck Institute for Patent, Copyright and Competition Law in Munich. Christopher Heath, who wrote his Ph.D. thesis on Japanese unfair competition prevention law, is a Member of the Boards of Appeal at the European Patent Office in Munich and extra-curricular professor at the University of Maastricht.

He can be reached by e-mail at blitzblitzblau@web.de

Anselm Kamperman Sanders (1968) is Professor of Intellectual Property Law, Director of the Advanced Masters Intellectual Property Law and Knowledge Management (IPKM LL.M/MSc), and Academic Director of the Institute for Globalization and International Regulation (IGIR) at Maastricht University, the Netherlands.

He acts as Academic Co-director of the Annual Intellectual Property Law School and IP Seminar of the Institute for European Studies of Macau (IEEM), Macau SAR, China and is Adjunct Professor at Jinan University Law School, Guangzhou, China.

Anselm holds a Ph.D. from the Centre for Commercial Law Studies, Queen Mary University of London, where he worked as a Marie Skłodowska-Curie Fellow before joining Maastricht University in 1995. For the UN he was member of the expert group for the World Economic and Social Survey 2018. Anselm sits as deputy judge in the Court of Appeal in the Hague, which has exclusive jurisdiction on patent matters.

He can be reached by e-mail at a.kampermansanders@maastrichtuniversity.nl

Jens Hillebrand Pohl (1975) teaches and writes about Law and Geoeconomics. He is a founding Co-Director of the CELIS Institute, an independent nonprofit, nonpartisan research enterprise dedicated to promoting better regulation of foreign investment in light of security and public order concerns. He is also a doctoral fellow of the Institute for Globalization and International Regulation (IGIR) and a lecturer of law in the Department of International and European Law at Maastricht University, the Netherlands. He is qualified in New York, England and Ireland and holds an LL.M. from Harvard Law School.

Natale Rampazzo (1971) is Senior researcher, Italian National Research Council – Institute for Research on Innovation and Services for Development (CNR-IRISS) in Naples. He studied law at the Universities Federico II-Naples (Full degree), Salerno (PhD), Luiss-Rome (Master) and LMU-Munich (LL.M.) with a focus on innovation law, data protection and consumer rights. 2017–2019 he worked at the MPI for Innovation (Munich) on the topics of geographical indications.

He can be reached by email at natale.rampazzo@cnr.it

Xavier Seuba (1977) is Associate Professor of Law, Vice-Dean of the Law and Political Science Faculty of Universitat Oberta de Catalunya and Director of the Diploma on Patent Litigation in Europe of the Center for International Intellectual Property Studies (CEIPI), University of Strasbourg. Xavier Seuba has worked for several international organizations (WIPO, WHO, UNHCHR, IDB, UNCTAD, EUIPO) and governments in the context of international treaty negotiations and also in normative and policy reform impacting intellectual property, pharmaceutical regulation and innovation policies. He has also acted as arbiter in patent-related disputes and is a member of the WIPO Arbitration and Mediation Center. He holds a PhD from Universitat Pompeu Fabra (Barcelona) and is Co-Rapporteur of the Global Health Law Committee, of the International Law Association.

Marketa Trimble (1973) is the Samuel S. Lionel Professor of Intellectual Property Law at the William S. Boyd School of Law at the University of Nevada, Las Vegas, where she also serves as a Supervisor of the Intellectual Property Law Concentration. She specializes in international intellectual property law and publishes extensively on issues at the intersection of conflict of laws/private international law and intellectual property law, particularly patent law and copyright law. She has taught in the Munich Intellectual Property Law Center and the Munich Summer Program of the George Washington University School of Law. Before she embarked on her academic career, she worked as a lawyer in civil service in Europe. She holds a JUDr. and a Ph.D.

from the Faculty of Law of the Charles University in Prague and a JSM and JSD from Stanford Law School.

She can be reached by e-mail at marketa.trimble@unlv.edu.

Guy Tritton is an intellectual property barrister who practises at Hogarth Chambers, London. He has appeared in the English High Court, Court of Appeal, Supreme Court, Court of Justice of European Union, European Patent Office, the Trade Mark Registry, VAT Tribunal and Crown Court. He has a scientific background having a Natural Science degree (Durham, Physics, Maths, Computing). He is a visiting lecturer at the University of Maastricht and also CEIPI, Strasbourg. He is the chief author of *Tritton on Intellectual Property in Europe* (5th edition, 2018, Thomson Reuters) – a book often cited in Advocate-General's Opinions. He also sits as an adjudicator in disputes between animal health and infant nutrition companies, both of which industries have their own self-regulatory codes.

Peter K. Yu is Regents Professor of Law and Communication and Director of the Center for Law and Intellectual Property at Texas A&M University. Born and raised in Hong Kong, he previously held the Kern Family Chair in Intellectual Property Law at Drake University Law School and was Wenlan Scholar Chair Professor at Zhongnan University of Economics and Law in Wuhan, China. He served as a visiting professor of law at Bocconi University, Hanken School of Economics, Hokkaido University, the University of Haifa, the University of Helsinki, the University of Hong Kong and the University of Strasbourg.

CHAPTER 1

To the End of History and Back Again: A Critical Look at the Political Promise of TRIPS

Jens Hillebrand Pohl

> *The promise given was a necessity of the past: the word broken is a necessity of the present*
>
> Niccolò Machiavelli

A. INTRODUCTION

When the Agreement on Trade-Related Aspects of Intellectual Property Rights (TRIPS Agreement) was concluded in 1994,[1] many understood the agreement to embody a new gold standard of intellectual property (IP) protection that rendered unnecessary, not only reforms to the major multilateral IP treaties – the Paris and Berne Conventions – but also further international agreements on intellectual property ('IP agreements').[2] The ubiquitous sprawling of specific IP agreements, and especially the inclusion of IP chapters in bilateral and multilateral free trade agreements (FTAs) has proven this expectation wrong. Obligations to protect IP rights can now be found in FTAs and can be enforced before domestic courts, the World Trade Organization

1. Annex 1(C) to the Agreement Establishing the World Trade Organization, signed at Marrakech on 15 April 1994. The official text is accessible at www.wto.org/english/docs_e/legal_e.htm.
2. *See, e.g.*, William Cornish and Kathleen Liddell, 'The Origins and Structure of the TRIPS Agreement', in H. Ullrich et al. (eds.), *TRIPS plus 20: From Trade Rules to Market Practices* (MPI Studies on Intellectual Property and Competition Law, 2016), 23–27; Kirsty Thomas, *Assessing Intellectual Property Compliance in Contemporary China* (Palgrave Series in Asia and Pacific Studies, 2017), 5–7.

(WTO) and investor-State arbitral tribunals.[3] At the same time, IP has become far more pervasive in society than was ever the case before, whether for better or for worse.[4]

What has been gradually happening in this field over the course of the past few decades is important, because it undermines the fundamental premise of TRIPS – and hence the settlement of conflicting interests that underlies it, between States, but also, ultimately, between producers, owners, users and consumers of IP.[5] This settlement is being unravelled as the balance of powers between owners and users and among States, non-State actors and individuals is shifting.[6] That is an evolution pointing towards a – possibly not too distant – future of uncertainty, re-alignment and renewed conflict between significant socio-economic interests and between State and non-State political actors, where critical technology, critical data and other strategic IP assets will be playing a central role.

Setting forth this argument, the present chapter retraces the origins of TRIPS and the aspirations of its framers. It argues that TRIPS failed to introduce a dynamic solution to the evolving problem of IP protection. Instead, the continuous balancing and weighing of opposing policy interests – of owners versus users of IP – was left to be battled out in different competing fora and through parallel and overlapping international treaty-based initiatives, which continue to this day to elaborate the paradigm established by TRIPS. The chapter analyses the future relevance of that paradigm in light of the existential challenges currently facing globalisation and the multilateral trading system, and explores the ascendance of non-State IP rule makers on the international plane.

Part B dives into the political history of TRIPS and situates it within the broader evolution of the global IP regime. TRIPS was conceived as the IP agreement to end all IP agreements; an elegant wrap-around solution that ensured that the essence of the Paris and Berne Conventions could be accepted by the very countries that resisted reform of those conventions. It promised expanding trade and an end to unilateralism. On top of that, it promised a transparent, efficient, independent and strictly inter-State enforcement mechanism. As shall be elaborated, all these promises have been broken.

3. *See further*, the various contributions in Christopher Heath and Anselm Kamperman Sanders, *Intellectual Property and International Dispute Resolution* (Wolters Kluwer, 2019), in particular Christopher Heath 'The Direct Application of International IP Agreements Before National Courts', and Peter K. Yu 'The Pathways of Multinational Intellectual Property Dispute Settlement'.
4. *See further* on this topic the various contributions in Joseph Drexl and Anselm Kamperman Sanders, *The Innovation Society and Intellectual Property* (Edward Elgar, 2019). For a still relevant but also evolutionary overview of the debates surrounding the role of IP in the new knowledge economy and knowledge society, *see*, e.g., Kenneth Carlaw et al., 'Beyond the Hype: Intellectual Property and the Knowledge Society/Knowledge Economy', 20(4) *Journal of Economic Surveys* (2006), 633–90.
5. Christopher J. Buccafusco and Jonathan S. Masur, 'Intellectual Property Law and the Promotion of Welfare', in Ben Depoorter and Peter Menell (eds.), *Research Handbook on the Economics of Intellectual Property Law*, Vol. I – Theory (Edward Elgar, 2019) 98 .
6. For more on this topic, *see* Daniel Gervais, 'The Internationalization of Intellectual Property: New Challenges from the Very Old and the Very New', 12 *Fordham Intellectual Property, Media and Entertainment Journal* (2012), 929–90, and by the same author 'Country Clubs, Empiricism, Blogs and Innovation: The Future of International Intellectual Property Norm Making in the Wake of ACTA', in Mira Burri and Thomas Cottier (eds.), *Trade Governance in the Digital Age* (Cambridge, 2012), 323–43.

Part C asks why. The first and overarching argument is that TRIPS was not designed to continuously adapt in response to changing international consensus, in turn driven by underlying commercial, technological and societal trends. The WTO regime, of which TRIPS forms an integral part, foresees neither an executive organ nor a 'legislature', and its dispute settlement system (DSS) expressly discourages judicial activism. With the arguable exception of the role of WTO case law, legal evolution and adaptation had to occur outside the existing WTO framework. Secondly, the framers of TRIPS could not envisage the emergence of quasi-legal norms that transcend national borders, set by private actors with global operations, such as the GAFAs (Google, Amazon, Facebook and Apple), the BATs (Baidu, Alibaba and Tencent), Xiaome and Samsung, to name some of the most influential. This transnational private ordering of IP protection is more directly and often more effectively enforced than IP agreements or national IP law. As a result, the relative importance of TRIPS has been eclipsed by developments outside its framework, which is precisely the opposite of what TRIPS was meant to achieve.

Part D concludes by reflecting on the future relevance and legacy of TRIPS in an age of de-globalisation and resurgent economic nationalism.

B. THE POLITICAL PROMISE OF TRIPS

According to established historiography, TRIPS emerged as a settlement of a long drawn-out disagreement between net IP exporting and importing countries by incorporating international commitments on IP protection under the ambit of international trade as a means of securing the compliance of such commitments (section I). While its early success is undeniable, this settlement has run its course (section II); it has been unravelling as a result of a failure to adapt to commercial, technological and societal changes, which will be further explored in Part C.

I. TRIPS: The History from the Beginning to the End

The history and pre-history of the TRIPS Agreement is well documented.[7] From its nineteenth century origins up until 1995, the protection of IP on the international plane had predominantly evolved in parallel with the regulation of international commerce.[8] IP protection at the national level in the form of patent, copyright and trade mark law – itself a relative novelty at the time – became a focal point of diplomacy as trade expanded in the first half of that century and global competition for ideas

7. *See generally* Cornish and Liddell, *supra* note 2. For the negotiation history of the TRIPS Agreements, *see* Daniel Gervais, *The TRIPS Agreement: Drafting History and Analysis* (4th edn, Sweet and Maxwell, 2012); J.C. Ross and A. Wasserman, 'Trade-Related Aspects of Intellectual Property Rights', in T.P. Stewart (ed.), *The GATT Uruguay Round: A Negotiating History 1986–1992* (Kluwer Law and Taxation, 1993), 2241–334. For a comprehensive review of the history of the concept of intellectual property, *see* the various contributions of Oren Bracha (ed.) *The History of Intellectual Property Law,* Vols. I–II (Edward Elgar, 2018).
8. *See generally* Peter Drahos and John Braithwaite, *Information Feudalism: Who Owns the Knowledge Economy?* (Earthscan, 2002), ch. 7–9; John M. Curtis, 'Intellectual Property Rights and International Trade: An Overview', CIGI Papers 3 (May 2012), 6–8.

intensified.[9] The policy rationale of such protection was increasingly recognised by various nations,[10] and it became apparent that effective IP protection at the national level required either some degree of international policy cooperation, coordination and harmonisation of standards,[11] or the imposition of protective barriers to cross-border IP transactions.[12] As this was the heyday of the age of classical liberalism, it is unsurprising that the cooperative approach prevailed.[13]

Early attempts at international policy coordination in the area of IP protection eventually paved the way for some of the very first multilateral treaties on any specialised subject matter.[14] The Paris Convention for the Protection of Industrial Property of 1883[15] and Berne Convention for the Protection of Literary and Artistic Works of 1886[16] followed an earlier slew of bilateral, regional and multilateral treaties that attempted to regulate these subject matters on a more piecemeal basis.[17] These major conventions pioneered what would become a trend of the second half of the nineteenth century towards 'general treaties' or 'unions' – or what today would be termed 'multilateral treaties' – on diverse topics ranging from postal and telegraphic transmission, railway transport, weights and measures, and industrial workers' rights.[18]

Notably, international trade defied this trend and followed instead a parallel evolutionary pattern.[19] The particular character of the various States' economic

9. For an excellent history of the road to the Berne Convention, *see* Catherine Seville, *The Internationalisation of Copyright Law: Books, Buccaneers and the Black Flag in the Nineteenth Century* (Cambridge, 2006), 41 *et seq*. With respect to the history of patent diplomacy pre-Paris, *see* Peter Drahos, 'The Universality of Intellectual Property Rights: Origins and Development', in *Intellectual Property and Human Rights* (World Intellectual Property Organization, 1999), 13–41.
10. Seville, *supra* note 9, 52 *et seq*.; Drahos, *supra* note 9, 18 *et seq*.
11. Cornish and Liddell, *supra* note 2, 12–13; Seville, *supra* note 9, 24–25; Drahos, *supra* note 9.
12. Seville, *supra* note 9, 22–24. A notable early example of a conditional trade-barrier approach is the British International Copyright Act of 1838 which laid down a principle of international reciprocity in granting copyright to foreign works.
13. Indeed, the cooperative approach appears to have emerged as a compromise position with free-traders at the time largely supporting the anti-patent movement, arguing for the abolition of patents. *See* Fritz Machlup and Edith Penrose, 'The Patent Controversy in the Nineteenth Century', 10(1) *Journal of Economic History* (1950), 1–29, 5.
14. Rochelle Cooper Dreyfuss, 'Intellectual Property Law and the World Trading System', in Andreas Lowenfeld (ed.), *International Economic Law* (2nd edn, Oxford, 2008), 338; Lassa Oppenheim, *International Law: A Treatise*, Vol. I (2nd edn, 1912), §§ 581–84.
15. Paris Convention for the Protection of Industrial Property of 20 March 1883, as revised at Brussels on 14 December 1900, at Washington on 2 June 1911, at The Hague on 6 November 1925, at London on 2 June 1934, at Lisbon on 31 October 1958, and at Stockholm on 14 July, 1967, and as amended on 28 September 1979.
16. Berne Convention for the Protection of Literary and Artistic Works of 9 September 1886, completed at Paris on 4 May 1896, revised at Berlin on 13 November 1908, completed at Berne on 20 March 1914, revised at Rome on 2 June 1928, at Brussels on 26 June 1948, at Stockholm on 14 July 1967, and at Paris on 24 July 1971, and amended on 28 September 1979.
17. Among the first bilateral copyright treaties are the British treaties with Prussia (1846), France (1851), Belgium (1854), Spain (1857) and Sardinia (1860). *See further* Seville, *supra* note 9, 49–52; Drahos, *supra* note 9, 18 *et seq*.
18. Oppenheim, *supra* note 14, §§ 581–96.
19. There was no equivalent to the great international conventions of the latter half of the nineteenth century in the area of international trade. One important factor contributing to this was the lack

interests and the individual circumstances and conditions upon which these interests depended left trade matters to be settled, if at all, through the conclusion of bilateral treaties of friendship, commerce and navigation (FCN treaties).[20] IP protection came under the scope of early FCN treaties only to the extent that the latter covered property protection in general.[21] Explicit references to IP in FCN treaties emerged after the First World War and became more common in FCN treaty practice after the Second World War.[22] Similarly, both the GATT and the Havana Charter included provisions expressly applicable to IP protection.[23] Yet, none of these treaties, or types of treaties, included detailed, material provisions of IP protection.

Fundamentally, an important difference in perspective concerning the characterisation of IP protection and the relation between IP protection and trade existed between advocates of international IP protection and free traders. A key argument underpinning the major IP conventions was that inadequate protection of the IP rights of foreigners tended to make it difficult to attract industrial technology and was thus – in contemporary parlance – a distortion of, and (unjustified) barrier to, international trade and investment.[24] Only by coordinating policy – ideally to the extent of harmonisation – could this trade distortion and barrier be overcome. By contrast, for the negotiators of trade agreements, it was not the absence of IP protection, but *IP protection itself* that constituted a barrier to trade, albeit a justified barrier.[25] This point of view is clearly evident in the Havana Charter and the GATT.[26] These differences in perspective may also have complicated and possibly delayed the amalgamation of IP protection within the international trade regime that emerged after the Second World War with the GATT.[27]

---

of interest in multilateral trade cooperation by Great Britain, which pursued a unilateral policy of free trade. *See further* Andrew G. Brown, *Reluctant Partners: A History of Multilateral Trade Cooperation, 1850–2000* (University of Michigan, 2003), 49–65.

20. Oppenheim, *supra* note 14, § 581. For a recent study on FCN treaties, *see* John F. Coyle, 'The Treaty of Friendship, Commerce and Navigation in the Modern Era', 51 (2) *Columbia Journal of Transnational Law* (2013), 306–11.
21. Coyle, *supra* note 20, 304, 341; also, Pratyush Nath Upreti, 'Intellectual Property, Investment and the World Trade Organization (WTO): A Historical Account', TTLF Working Papers No. 57, Stanford-Vienna Transatlantic Technology Law Forum (2020) (in Christophe Geiger (ed.), *Research Handbook on Intellectual Property and Investment Law* (Edward Elgar, 2020)).
22. Upreti, *supra* note 21, 2.
23. *See*, notably, Articles XII.3(c)(iii), XVIII.10, and XX(d) GATT 1947; also United Nations Conference on Trade and Employment, Final Act and Related Documents, E/CONF.2/78, United Nations publication, Sales No. 1948.II.D.4. (Havana Charter) Articles 21.3(c)(i), 45.1(a)(v), 46.3(e)–(f), and 49.1(a)(ii).
24. Cornish and Liddell, *supra* note 2, 12; for the role of IP protection as a barrier to or facilitator of trade, *see generally* Henning Grosse Ruse-Khan, 'IP and Trade in a Post-TRIPS Environment', in H. Ullrich, *supra* note 2, 163–83, 165.
25. Ruse-Khan, *supra* note 24.
26. *See supra* note 23.
27. Jerome H. Reichmann, 'Intellectual Property in International Trade: Opportunities and Risks of a GATT Connection, 22 *Vanderbilt Journal of Transnational Law* (1989), 747–891, 756 *et seq.*

1. *Evolution and Crisis*

The major conventions of Paris and Berne were products of their time. Although they were revised and updated in the decades following their conclusion, they embodied not only the evolutionary state of national IP legislation of the late nineteenth century but also an earlier age of treaty practice; one where good faith of the contracting parties was paramount and where diplomacy was the chief policy instrument of international relations.[28] This manifested itself in two ways. First, the major conventions aspired neither to a final and comprehensive settlement of the international legal treatment of IP, nor to a path towards harmonisation of IP rights across the contracting States.[29] Rather, the conventions set forth some basic substantive guarantees, while primarily providing a common *procedure* that facilitated the acquisition of foreign rights.[30] Secondly, in keeping with then-prevailing treaty practice, the conventions did not contemplate an internal compliance mechanism.[31] Enforcement was left to general international law on inter-State dispute settlement, notably arbitration.[32]

This type of arrangement already represented a groundbreaking achievement and was surely sufficient for as long as the contracting parties shared a strong similarity or reciprocity of interest. Aspiring, mostly industrialising, mostly European, nation States competed fiercely in the technology race of the time and joined the conventions out of a desire to protect domestic inventions, innovations and ideas from being 'stolen and exploited commercially in other countries'.[33] Nowhere was this intense competition more readily on display than at the great international expositions in London (1851, 1862), Paris (1855, 1867, 1878, 1889), Vienna (1873), Philadelphia (1876), and Chicago (1893).[34]

The nineteenth century treaty-making approach became increasingly inadequate to ensure compliance as trade continued to expand.[35] Over time, the balanced reciprocity of interests among the contracting parties to the major conventions faded.[36] As the members of the family of nations grew, notably as a result of decolonialisation in the 1950s through 1970s, the interests of net IP exporting, industrialised countries diverged ever more from those of net IP importing, mostly newly independent,

28. For an insightful reflection, *see* Douglas M. Johnston, *The Historical Foundations of World Order: The Tower and the Arena* (Martinus Nijhoff, 2008), 640 *et seq.*
29. Dreyfuss, *supra* note 14, 334–49. Also, Peter-Tobias Stoll, 'Introduction I', in Peter-Tobias Stoll, Jan Busche and Katrin Arend (eds.), *WTO – Trade-Related Aspects of Intellectual Property Law* (Martinus Nijhoff, 2009), 1–9.
30. Dreyfuss, *supra* note 14.
31. *Ibid.*
32. *Ibid.*
33. Kirsty, *supra* note 2, 4.
34. *See* Petra Moser, 'How Do Patent Laws Influence Innovation? Evidence from Nineteenth-Century World's Fairs', 95 *American Economic Review* (2005), 1214, 1216.
35. Drahos, *supra* note 9, 22 *et seq.*; Cornish and Liddell, *supra* note 2, 22 *et seq.*
36. Susan K. Sell, 'Intellectual Property as Trade Issue: From the Paris Convention to GATT, 13(4) *Legal Studies Forum* (1989), 407–22, 409 *et seq.*; Cornish and Liddell, *supra* note 2, 15, 22; Kirsty, *supra* note 2, 4; also J. Hillebrand Pohl, 'Dispute Settlement Under the WTO Regime', in Heath and Kamperman Sanders, *supra* note 3, 75 *et seq.*; *cf.* Andreas F. Lowenfeld, 'Dispute Resolution in the GATT, 1948–94', in Lowenfeld, *supra* note 14, 150, 153.

developing countries, notably in Latin America.[37] The latter resisted what they perceived as neoimperialist attempts to impose higher production costs and consumer prices as a result of increased IP protection and, in particular, advocated a loosening of protections for foreign-held patented technology.[38]

This divergence of interests coincided with a wave of expropriations that took place in 'Third World' countries in the shadow of Cold War rivalry between the Western nations led by the United States and the Soviet Union.[39] This mirrored the rise to prominence of the 'Group of 77' non-aligned developing nations,[40] culminating in the 1975 attempt to bring about a 'New International Economic Order' through the adoption by the UN General Assembly of the Charter of Economic Rights and Duties of States.[41] Although the Charter was eventually adopted,[42] the attempt to overthrow, or at least radically re-define, the international capitalist system, ultimately failed.

The struggle between North and South, industrialised and developing nations – paralleled by the disconnect between net IP exporting and importing countries – manifested itself through contracting States increasingly failing to comply with the spirit and terms of the Paris and Berne Conventions.[43] Newly industrialised and industrialising developing countries, notably the 'Four Asian Tigers' – South Korea, Taiwan, Hong Kong and Singapore – became associated with free-market, export-oriented economic policies with a light-touch approach to IP protection.[44] The inadequacy of the major conventions to deal with the evolving needs for IP protection and provide a minimum 'level playing field', compounded by the lack of robust and utile enforcement mechanisms, led the net IP exporting nations to push

37. *See supra* note 36.
38. Dreyfuss, *supra* note 14, 339 *et seq.*; Sell, *supra* note 36, 409 *et seq.*; Cornish and Liddell, *supra* note 2, 22.
39. For a contemporaneous historical account, *see* J. Frederick Truitt, 'Expropriation of Foreign Investment: Summary of the Post World War II Experience of American and British Investors in the Less Developed Countries, 1(2) *Journal of International Business Studies* (1970), 21–34.
40. Jennifer Bair, 'From the Politics of Development to the Challenges of Globalization', 4(4) *Globalizations* (2007), 486–99, 489 *et seq.*; Andreas F. Lowenfeld, 'The Responsibility of Host States to Foreign Investors: Customary International Law', in Lowenfeld, *supra* note 14, 491.
41. *See supra* note 40; *also,* Robert W. Cox, 'Ideologies and the New International Economic Order: Reflections on some recent literature', 33(2) *International Organization* (1979), 257–302.
42. UN General Assembly, *Charter of Economic Rights and Duties of States : resolution/adopted by the General Assembly*, 17 December 1984, A/RES/39/163.
43. Gustavo Bravo, 'From Paris Convention to TRIPS: A Brief History', 12(1) *Journal of Contemporary Legal Issues* (2001), 445–49, 448; Autar Krishan Koul, 'Negotiating the Intellectual Property in International Trade and the Uruguay Round of Multilateral Trade Negotiations under GATT, 26(3) *Foreign Trade Review* (1991), 157–79, 159 *et seq.*; Richard A. Morford, 'Intellectual Property Protection: A United States Priority', 19(2) *Georgia Journal of International and Comparative Law* (1989), 336–42, 337; Michael G. Harvey, 'Industrial Product Counterfeiting: Problems and Proposed Solutions', 2(4) *Journal of Business & Industrial Marketing* (1987), 5–13, 5.
44. *See generally* Edgardo Buscaglia and José-Luis Guerrero-Cusumano, 'Quantitative Analysis of Counterfeiting Activities in Developing Countries in the Pre-GATT Period', 35(2) *Jurimetrics Journal* (1995), 221–31; David I. Wilson, 'A Trade Policy Goal for the 1990s: Improving the Adequacy and Effectiveness of Intellectual Property Protection in Foreign Countries', 1(2) *Transnational Lawyer* (1988), 426 *et seq.*, 440 *et seq.*; Jared R. Margolis, 'Counterfeit Combat', 19(4) *Brief* (1989), 17–37,

for reform.[45] However, attempts at updating the conventions and strengthening their protections through negotiations for their amendment was met with resistance by mostly net IP importing countries in the developing South.[46]

2. *The Uruguay Round and the Birth of TRIPS*

At the time the crisis in the international IP regime was unfolding, a different sort of crisis had beset the multilateral trading system. While the IP regime chiefly suffered from a lack of substantive protections, the overarching structural shortcoming of the multilateral trade system was the absence of an effective dispute settlement mechanism.[47] These twin issues – of IP protection and dispute settlement – became the core negotiation items in the Uruguay Round (1986–1993) of GATT negotiations, with other priorities being the reduction of protective services regulations and investment-control practices.[48] By casting the absence of effective IP protections as a precondition to barrier-free trade, or, which is equivalent, as a barrier to trade, the traditional IP perspective prevailed over the earlier trade-policy understanding that IP protections constituted a justified exception to free trade.[49]

To underscore the need for reform of the international trade architecture, the United States began to vigorously enforce its domestic trade remedies on the basis that the GATT enforcement system was inadequate.[50] In 1988, Section 301 *et seq.* of the U.S. Trade Act of 1974 was amended to authorise trade remedies against 'unfair' trade practices of other countries.[51] This included lax enforcement of IP rights, an area which was anyway considered outside the scope of GATT.[52]

45. Dreyfuss, *supra* note 14, 339 *et seq.*; Sell, *supra* note 36, 409 *et seq.*; Cornish and Liddell, *supra* note 2, 22. For a detailed discussion on the shortcomings of the enforcement mechanism of the Paris Convention, *see* Hans Peter Kunz-Hallstein, 'The United States Proposal for a GATT Agreement on Intellectual Property and the Paris Convention for the Protection of Industrial Property', 22(2) *Vanderbilt Journal of Transnational Law* (1989), 265–84, 279 *et seq.*
46. *See supra* note 45.
47. Rochelle Cooper Dreyfuss and Andreas F. Lowenfeld, 'Two Achievements of the Uruguay Round: Putting TRIPS and Dispute Settlement Together', 37(2) *Virginia Journal of International Law* (1997), 275–334, 276 *et seq.*; on the shortcomings of the old GATT dispute settlement system, *see also* Pohl, *supra* note 36, 69–79.
48. Ernest H. Preeg, *Traders in a Brave World: The Uruguay Round and the Future of the International Trading System* (University of Chicago, 1995), 46–63; John H. Jackson, 'Managing the Trading System: The World Trade System and the Post-Uruguay Round GATT Agenda', in Peter B. Kenen (ed.) *Managing the World Economy: Fifty Years After Bretton-Woods* (Institute for International Economics, 1994), 131–51, 132 *et seq.*
49. Grosse Ruse-Khan, *supra* note 24 p. 165; Reichmann, *supra* note 27 pp. 756 *et seq.*
50. Lowenfeld, *supra* note 36, 158 *et seq.*; Morford, *supra* note 43, 337; Pohl, *supra* note 36, 78.
51. 19 U.S.C. §§ 2411–20 and 2242. The Act authorised the US government to take action where 'the rights of the United States under any trade agreement is being denied' including where 'an act, policy, or practice of a foreign country violates, or is inconsistent with, the provisions of' such agreement or 'is unjustifiable and burdens or restricts United States commerce'.
52. Steven R. Phillips, 'The New Section 301 of the Omnibus Trade and Competitiveness Act of 1988: Trade Wars or Open Markets', 22(3) *Vanderbilt Journal of Transnational Law* (1989), 491–580, 505; Judith Hippler Bello and Alan F. Holmer, 'The Heart of the 1988 Trade Act: A Legislative History of the Amendments to Section 301', 25(1) *Stanford Journal of International Law* (1988), 1–44, 40 *et seq.*

The successful conclusion of the Uruguay Round negotiations resulted in the Marrakesh Agreement of 1994 of which the TRIPS Agreement and Dispute Settlement Understanding (DSU) constitute integral parts.[53] The basic mechanism by which the TRIPS Agreement solved the IP protection crisis was by incorporating the principal procedural and substantive provisions of the Paris and Berne Conventions (Article 2), introducing uniform national treatment and most-favoured-nations treatment clauses (Articles 3 and 4), extending the application of specific IP protection beyond patents (Articles 27–34), trade marks (Articles 15–21) and copyright (Articles 9–14) to a range of other IP products, such as industrial designs (Articles 25–26), circuit layouts (Articles 35–38), undisclosed information of commercial value (Article 39), and geographical indications (Articles 22–24). Together with provisions on enforcement and dispute settlement (Articles 41–61, 63–64), these provisions constitute the core 'wrap-around' solution by which the framers of the TRIPS Agreement were able to (a) integrate the essence of core international IP protection treaties, most notably the Paris and Berne Conventions, into the multilateral trading system, (b) extend the substantive protections of such treaties, (c) extend the scope of application of IP protections to a broader field of IP products, and (d) provide a transparent, efficient, independent and strictly inter-State dispute settlement mechanism.

The prospect of membership in the newly created WTO, for which adherence to the TRIPS Agreement is an absolute condition, ultimately persuaded the very countries who had resisted reform of – or who had never even signed or ratified – the Paris and Berne Conventions ultimately to cede ground.[54] The promises of increased trade and an end to unilateral trade remedies (by the United States) apparently outweighed the perceived costs and difficulties for developing countries of maintaining a strongly pro-property IP protection regime.[55] Moreover, the TRIPS Agreement promised to spur technological innovation, not least in developing countries, and to facilitate technological knowledge transfer.[56] If this did not convince the most ardent sceptics, then at least many saw in TRIPS a gold standard, that would once and for all satisfy the demands of the pro-property advocates.[57] The monolithic nature of the WTO framework, to which amendments require unanimity among a near universal membership, surely helped to convey the promise that no further demands for higher levels of IP protection would be on the horizon.[58]

II. The Broken Promise

If the Paris and Berne Conventions were children of their time, so was TRIPS. In his classic 1989 essay, Francis Fukuyama famously portrayed Western liberal

53. Article II.2 of the Agreement Establishing the World Trade Organization, signed at Marrakech on 15 April 1994.
54. *See generally* Hanns Ullrich, 'The Political Foundations of TRIPS Revisited', in Ullrich, *supra* note 2 pp. 88 *et seq*.
55. *See supra* note 54.
56. *See* Daniel J. Gervais, '(Re)implementing the Agreement on Trade-Related Aspects of Intellectual Property Rights to Foster Innovation', 12(5) *Journal of World Intellectual Property* (2009), 348–70, 350; Ullrich, *supra* note 54 p. 99.
57. Dreyfuss, *supra* note 14 pp. 363 *et seq*.
58. *Cf.* Dreyfuss, *supra* note 14 *ibid*.

democracy and market economy as an 'end of history' paradigm.[59] According to this highly influential narrative, capitalist democracies have triumphed definitively over ideologically competing politico-economic 'constitutions' to the point that future conflicts within and between societies will have to be worked out within the framework of the Western paradigm.[60]

In an eerily similar fashion, the entry into force of the TRIPS Agreement on 1 January 1995 seemed to promise an 'end of history' in the sense of providing a global 'constitution' for transnational IP protection, within the framework of which future legal evolution would take place.[61] Once united, it would be unthinkable that international IP law could again be decoupled from international trade law; these would continue to evolve in symbiosis within the TRIPS framework.[62] Once established, the DSS of the WTO would provide the exclusive forum for settling any differences on an inter-State basis as to the interpretation and application of international IP protection insofar as the TRIPS Agreement was applicable.[63] And, once in place, the TRIPS Agreement would guarantee continued good prospects for expanded trade (the 'carrot') and discontinued use of unilateral trade remedies (the 'stick').[64]

Yet, 25 years later all these promises have been broken. What happened?

First, substantive IP law has continued to evolve after the conclusion of the TRIPS Agreement. Far from being the 'IP agreement to end all IP agreements', this evolution has only exceptionally occurred by means of an amendment to the original TRIPS Agreement and has predominantly not even been multilateral in a WTO sense.[65] In fact, the legal evolution has occurred through several different channels and has led to a significant fragmentation of international IP law.[66] One source of

59. Francis Fukuyama, 'The End of History?', 16 *The National Interest* (1989), 3–18. Also, by the same author *The End of History and the Last Man* (Free Press, 1992).
60. For in-depth analyses, *see generally*, e.g., Howard Williams, David Sullivan and E. Gwynn Matthews, *Fukuyama and the End of History* (2nd edn., University of Wales, 2016); Chris Hughes, *Liberal Democracy as the End of History: Fukuyama and Postmodern Challenges* (Routledge, 2012).
61. *See*, e.g., Thomas Cottier, 'Working Together Towards TRIPS', in Jayashree Watal and Antony Taubman (eds.) *The Making of the TRIPS Agreement: Personal Insights from the Uruguay Round Negotiations* (World Trade Organization, 2015), 79–94, 81.
62. For a discussion situating 'traditional' international IP law within a wider, multi-dimensional, international-law approach to IP law, *see* Henning Grosse Ruse-Khan, 'Intellectual Property and International Law', in Irene Calboli and Maria Lilla Montagnani (eds.) *Oxford Handbook on Intellectual Property Research* (Oxford University Press, 2020).
63. The non-exclusive jurisdiction of the WTO DSS over claims based on the Paris and Berne Conventions are discussed in Ernst-Ulrich Petersmann, 'Justice as Conflict Resolution: Proliferation, Fragmentation, and Decentralization of Dispute Settlement in International Trade', 27(2) *University of Pennsylvania Journal of International Law* (2004), 273–366.
64. *See*, e.g., Charan Devereaux, Robert Z. Lawrence and Michael D. Watkins, *Case Studies in U.S. Trade Negotiation*. Vol. 1 (Peterson Institute, 2006), 64 *et seq*.
65. Since entering into force on 1 January 1995, the TRIPS Agreement has been amended once. WTO members approved the amendment on 6 December 2005 in order to make permanent the waiver included in the WTO General Council decision on the implementation of paragraph 6 of the 2001 Doha Declaration on the TRIPS Agreement and public health originally adopted in 2003. The amendment took effect on 23 January 2017 and replaced the 2003 waiver for members who have accepted the amendment.
66. *See generally* Grosse Ruse-Khan, *supra* note 24 p. 170 *et seq*.; Julian Rotenberg, 'Intellectual Property and the Risks of Fragmentation' Society of International Economic Law (SIEL), Sixth

legal development is WTO case law, with a moderate number of cases having been decided on the TRIPS Agreement.[67] A second and more important source has been the proliferation of 'TRIPS Plus' provisions in bilateral or multilateral FTAs concluded outside the WTO framework, in WTO accession agreements, or in bilateral investment treaties (BITs).[68] The protection of IP rights in investment treaties also signals the decoupling of international IP law from international trade law.[69] The result of this process – which is frequently described as a 'spaghettification' of international IP law – is a complex and opaque landscape of, in part, overlapping, and, in part, interlocking (e.g. through MFN clauses) obligations owed to different countries in respect of different types of IP rights.[70] This evolution is the very opposite of the uniform 'level playing field' that the framers of the TRIPS Agreement advocated and envisioned.[71] Moreover, with the exception of the Doha Declaration and the subsequent sole amendment of the TRIPS Agreement,[72] the legal evolution of international IP protection has uniformly steered in a pro-property direction.[73]

Second, the promise of a transparent, efficient, independent and strictly inter-State dispute settlement system has eroded, mainly for two reasons. One reason is the emergence of the investor-State dispute settlement (ISDS) under BITs or other bilateral or multilateral international investment agreements (IIAs), such as investment chapters in FTAs, as a new adjudicatory remedy, available in parallel to

Biennial Global Conference, 2018 (available at SSRN: https://ssrn.com/abstract=3209859).

67. As of 1 June 2020, there had been 42 requests for consultation since the establishment of the WTO citing the TRIPS Agreement (out of a total of 595 WTO cases or 7%). Of these, 14 cases were withdrawn following a mutually agreed solution (settled), eight cases had been determined in favour of the complainant, eight cases remained in consultations, five cases had been determined in favour of the respondent, three cases had panels composed, one case had a panel requested, one case had a panel report under appeal, one case had proceeded to enforcement, and one case had a panel lapsed. Source: https://www.wto.org.
68. With respect to FTAs, BITs and other IIAs, *see generally* Anselm Kamperman Sanders, 'Intellectual Property, Free Trade Agreements and Economic Development', 23(4) *Georgia State University Law Review* (2007), 893–912. With respect to WTO accession agreements, *see* C. Deere, *The Implementation Game: The TRIPS Agreement and the Global Politics of Intellectual Property Reform in Developing Countries* (2009), 155 et seq.
69. *See generally* Christopher Heath and Anselm Kamperman Sanders (2019) 'Investor State Dispute Settlement (ISDS) in the Field of Intellectual Property Law and Beyond', in Heath and Kamperman Sanders, *supra* note 3, 5–10; Grosse Ruse-Khan, *supra* note 62 and by the same author: 'From TRIPS to FTAs and Back: Re-Conceptualising the Role of a Multilateral IP Framework in a TRIPS-Plus World', in Fabian Amtenbrink, Denise Prévost, Ramses Wessel (eds.) *Netherlands Yearbook of International Law 2017* (2018), 61 *et seq.*; *The Protection of Intellectual Property in International Law* (Oxford University Press, 2016), 486; and 'Protecting Intellectual Property under BITs, FTAs, and TRIPS: Conflicting Regimes or Mutual Coherence?', in K. Miles and C. Brown (eds.), *Evolution in Investment Treaty Law and Arbitration* (Cambridge University Press, 2011), 485–515.
70. *See supra* notes 68–69.
71. *See supra* note 45.
72. *See supra* note 65. On the Doha Declaration, *see generally* Frederick M. Abbott, 'The Doha Declaration on the TRIPS Agreement and Public Health: Lighting a Dark Corner at the WTO', 5(2) *Journal of International Economic Law* (2002), 469–505.
73. Ullrich, *supra* note 54 pp. 109 *et seq.*; Peter K. Yu, 'The Non-multilateral Approach to International Intellectual Property Normsetting', in Daniel J. Gervais (ed.) *International Intellectual Property A Handbook of Contemporary Research* (Edward Elgar, 2014), 83–120, 95 *et seq.*

WTO dispute settlement.[74] This has resulted in international IP disputes no longer being strictly inter-State matters, as the tobacco plain packaging cases have shown,[75] but has opened the path towards IP rights as quasi-property rights under international law, owed directly by States to individuals.[76] The criticism levelled against ISDS, notably concerning procedural transparency,[77] also undermines the political expectations of dispute settlement under TRIPS.[78] A second and, again, more important reason for the broken promise of efficient and independent dispute settlement is the crisis in, and finally the breakdown of, the WTO DSS in 2019.[79] During almost 25 years of operation, the DSS proved – even to its detractors – to be both efficient and fiercely independent.[80] Although frequently criticised for delays in issuing panel and Appellate Body reports, the DSS case cycles were subject to significantly shorter time lines than other international courts or tribunals.[81] Moreover, its compulsory and exclusive jurisdiction served to prevent a proliferation of competing fora for settling trade disputes.[82] As just discussed, this aim has been undermined with the emergence of ISDS as an alternative adjudicative remedy. The causes for the de facto suspension of the DSS have been discussed extensively,[83] but for present purposes it suffices to note that the inability of the WTO framework to envisage a mechanism

74. *See* in general the various contributions in Heath and Kamperman Sanders, *supra* note 3.
75. *Philip Morris Asia Limited v. The Commonwealth of Australia*, PCA Case No 2012-12, Award on Jurisdiction and Admissibility of 17 December 2015; *Philip Morris Brands Sàrl, Philip Morris Products S.A. and Abal Hermanos S.A. v. Oriental Republic of Uruguay*, ICSID Case No. ARB/10/7, Award of 8 July 2016.
76. *See* Amnon Lehavi and Amir N. Licht, 'BITs and Pieces of Property', 36(1) *Yale Journal of International Law* (2011), 115–66. While quasi-property rights are rights properly so called only under domestic law, international responsibility for the protection of foreigners, notably for expropriation, ensures that such rights become akin to international rights vested in individuals. For example, denying a foreigner protection of an invention under domestic law can lead to liability for indirect expropriation under an international investment agreement, such as in Eli *Lilly and Co. v. The Government of Canada*, Final Award, 16 March 2017. *See* Daniel J. Gervais, '*Lilly v. Canada*: Lessons for International Property Law and Policy', in Heath and Kamperman Sanders, *supra* note 3, 169 *et seq.*, and Anselm Kamperman Sanders, 'Intellectual Property as Investment and the Implications for Industrial Policy', in Heath and Kamperman Sanders, *supra* note 3, 145 *et seq.*, 147–50. The scope and content of such 'intellectual quasi-property rights' is a result of the application of not only (standard) expropriation clauses but also other investment protection standards and the *de facto* multilateralisation of international investment law resulting from the application of most-favoured-nations clauses, which ensure that a host State treats foreign investors of one State no less favourably than investors of another State.
77. *See* Heath and Kamperman Sanders, *supra* note 69, 10–20.
78. *See* Pohl, *supra* note 36, 89–92.
79. *See* Petros C. Mavroidis, Matteo Fiorini, Bernard M. Hoekman, Maarja Saluste, Robert Wolfe, 'WTO Dispute Settlement and the Appellate Body: Insider Perceptions and Members' Revealed Preferences', 54(5) *Journal of World Trade* (2020), 667–98; Henry Gao, 'Disruptive Construction or Constructive Destruction? Reflections on the Appellate Body Crisis', in C. Lo, J. Nakagawa, T. Chen (eds.), *The Appellate Body of the WTO and Its Reform* (Springer, 2020); Pohl, *supra* note 36, 83–89, 92–95.
80. Pohl, *supra* note 36, 84.
81. *Ibid.*, 87, 91.
82. *Ibid.*, 80.
83. *See, e.g.*, Mavroidis et al., *supra* note 79.

for the continuous updating of the TRIPS Agreement, short of an amendment of the Marrakesh Agreement, resulted in an institutional imbalance whereby the Appellate Body increasingly had to address policy issues or politically sensitive legal issues that lacked the consensus support of the WTO Members.[84]

Third, the promise of an end of unilateral trade remedies and of expanded trade has also turned out to be false. The trade policy agenda of US President Donald Trump first announced in 2017[85] set forth a fourfold strategy under the telling headings (a) 'Defending Our National Sovereignty Over Trade Policy', i.e. unshackling from the WTO multilateral trading system,[86] (b) 'Strictly Enforcing U.S. Trade Laws', i.e. return to unilateral trade remedies,[87] (c) 'Using Leverage to Open Foreign Markets', i.e. embarking on a geoeconomic approach to international trade policy,[88] and (d) 'Negotiating New and Better Trade Deals', i.e. a review of existing and future trade agreements.[89] In the years that have followed, this policy agenda has been put into practice, triggering a range of unilaterally imposed trade measures, often referred to as the 'Trump Tariffs', which have developed into the ongoing US–China Trade War.[90] With the WTO enforcement mechanism in practice being suspended, these developments come close to representing the abandonment of the multilateral trading system.[91]

Yet that is not all. While the 'stick' of unilateralism is thus back, it could still – potentially – again be stowed away if a new settlement is reached among the great trading nations and a new global consensus is found. The same does not apply to 'carrot' of increased trade; that is a promise that cannot be repeated. Unlike in the 1990s when the United States could – and did – deliver on a promise of expanded trade as the dividend of the Uruguay Round,[92] the current economic reality is that the United States represents a significantly smaller share of world gross national product (GDP) and possesses significantly less relative consumer-spending power

---

84. *See* Ernst-Ulrich Petersmann, 'Between "Member-Driven Governance" and "Judicialization": Constitutional and Judicial Dilemmas in the World Trading System', in Lo et al., *supra* note 79, 15–41; and by the same author 'The "Crown Jewel" of the WTO Has Been Stolen by US Trade Diplomats – And They Have No Intention of Giving It Back', in Denise Prévost, Iveta Alexovičová and J. Hillebrand Pohl (eds.), *Restoring Trust in Trade: Liber Amicorum in Honour of Peter Van den Bossche* (Hart, 2018), 105–18.
85. President of the United States (2017) 2017 Trade Policy Agenda and 2016 Annual Report.
86. *Ibid.*, ch. I.II.B.1.
87. *Ibid.*, ch. I.II.B.2.
88. *Ibid.*, ch. I.II.B.3.
89. *Ibid.*, ch. I.II.B.4.
90. *See* Marcus Noland, 'U.S. Trade Policy in the Trump Administration', 13(2) *Asian Economic Policy Review* (2018), 262–78; Craig VanGrasstek, 'The Trade Policy of the United States Under the Trump Administration' Robert Schuman Centre for Advanced Studies Research Paper No. RSCAS 2019/11, 2019 (available at SSRN: https://ssrn.com/abstract=3330577).
91. Chad P. Bown and Soumaya Keynes, 'Why Trump Shot the Sheriffs: The End of WTO Dispute Settlement 1.0', Peterson Institute for International Economics Working Paper No. 20-4, 2020 (available at SSRN: https://ssrn.com/abstract=3577935).
92. *See* Jill A. Holman, 'Is the Large U.S. Current Account Deficit Sustainable?', 86(1) *Economic Review* (2001), 5–23, 6 *et seq.*; William A. Lovett, 'The WTO: A Train Wreck in Progress', 24(1&2) *Fordham International Law Journal* (2000), 410–26, 411 *et seq.*

than in the mid-1980s.[93] A country that still struggles with high levels of consumer debt left over from the Great Recession and a historically high income inequality, the United States is not in a position to unleash a global import spree.[94] Even if such a policy were politically opportune,[95] a return to the halcyon days of trade peace and low tariffs could inconceivably boost world trade as it once did, simply because the spending power of the US middle class has once and for all (or at least for a foreseeable future!) been exhausted.[96]

C. REASSESSING THE 'END-OF-HISTORY' NARRATIVE

We have seen that the promise of the TRIPS Agreement as an 'end of history' paradigm for international IP protection has been defenestrated through a combination of legal fragmentation, the loss of reliance on WTO dispute settlement, resurgent unilateralism and the demise of the United States as 'importer of last resort'. We now need to ask: what caused the promise to be broken?

To answer that question, one may identify both proximate and ultimate causes. While the ultimate causes are to be found in commercial, technological and societal

93. *See*, inter alia, James Manyika, Jan Mischke, Jacques Bughin, Jonathan Woetzel, Mekala Krishnan, and Samuel Cudre, 'A New Look at the Declining Labour Share of Income in the United States'. McKinsey Global Institute. Discussion Paper, 2019 (available at: https://www.mckinsey.com/featured-insights/employment-and-growth/a-new-look-at-the-declining-labor-share-of-income-in-the-united-states#); Robert J. Gordon, 'Revisiting U.S. Productivity Growth over the Past Century with a View of the Future', in D.S. Prasada Rao and Bart van Ark (eds.) *World Economic Performance: Past, Present and Future. Essays in Celebration of the Life and Work of Angus Madison* (Edward Elgar, 2013), 317–62; William R. Emmons, 'Don't Expect Consumer Spending to Be the Engine of Economic Growth It Once Was', *The Regional Economist*, Federal Reserve Bank of St. Louis, 2012 (available at: https://www.stlouisfed.org/publications/regional-economist/january-2012/dont-expect-consumer-spending-to-be-the-engine-of-economic-growth-it-once-was); C. Fred Bergsten and Arvind Subramanian, 'America Cannot Resolve Global Imbalances on Its Own' *Financial Times*, Op-Ed, 2009 (available at: https://www.piie.com/commentary/op-eds/america-cannot-resolve-global-imbalances-its-own); Shahid Yusuf, 'The Past and Future of Export-led Growth'. The World Bank Growth and Crisis Blog, The World Bank Institute, 2010 (available at: https://web.worldbank.org/archive/website01601/WEB/PAST_AND.HTM).
94. *See supra* note 93; also, Barry Z. Cynamon and Steven Fazzari, 'Inequality, the Great Recession and Slow Recovery', 40(2) *Cambridge Journal of Economics* (2015), 373–99.
95. *See*, e.g., Phil Levy, 'Rebuilding a Bipartisan Consensus on Trade Policy', Chicago Council on Global Affairs, 2019 (Available at: https://www.thechicagocouncil.org/sites/default/files/report_rebuilding-bipartisan-consensus-on-trade-policy_20190417.pdf); Michael Pettis, 'Is Peter Navarro Wrong on Trade?', *China Financial Markets*, 2 February 2017, Carnegie Endowment for International Peace (available at: https://carnegieendowment.org/chinafinancialmarkets/67867).
96. *See supra* note 93; also, James McBride and Andrew Chatzky, 'The U.S. Trade Deficit: How Much Does It Matter?', Council of Foreign Relations, 2019 (available at: https://www.cfr.org/backgrounder/us-trade-deficit-how-much-does-it-matter); Robert E. Scott and Elizabeth Glass, 'Trans-Pacific Partnership, Currency Manipulation, Trade, and Jobs', Briefing Paper #420, Economic Policy Institute, 2016 (available at: https://www.epi.org/publication/trans-pacific-partnership-currency-manipulation-trade-and-jobs/); C. Fred Bergsten, 'The U.S. Trade Deficit and China', Testimony before the Hearing on US-China Economic Relations Revisited Committee on Finance, United States Senate, 29 March 2006, Peterson Institute of International Economics (available at: https://www.piie.com/commentary/testimonies/us-trade-deficit-and-china).

changes over the course of the intervening 25 years,[97] which are beyond the remit of legal analysis and beyond the scope of this chapter to explore, the proximate cause is simple: the TRIPS Agreement and the legal regime it established failed to adapt to these changes, due to an institutional inability to bypass protracted stalemate in trade negotiations.[98] Specifically, the TRIPS Agreement, and indeed the entire WTO legal architecture, was not designed to continuously adapt autonomously in response to changing international consensus (section I), and the framers of the TRIPS Agreement could not envisage the coming transnationalisation of IP law (section II).

I. The WTO's Seed of Self-Destruction

Circa 1986, on the eve of the Uruguay Round, few would have imagined the great rise of China – a China that in less than 30 years would become the largest economy in the world, overtaking the United States in terms of GDP at purchasing power parity.[99] Yet, one could have foreseen – and surely *did* foresee – continued trends in trade patterns (albeit more moderate), in technological innovation and in societal interests and values.[100] What was surely not foreseen was a questioning of the trajectory towards further liberalisation, let alone of the Western paradigm of liberal democracy and market economy.[101]

97. *See generally* Peter A.G. van Bergeijk, *Deglobalization 2.0: Trade and Opennesss During the Great Depression and the Great Recession* (Edward Elgar, 2019), 81–110; Joseph E. Stiglitz, 'Trump and Globalization' 40 *Journal of Policy Modeling* (2018), 515–28; Harold James, 'Deglobalization: The Rise of Disembedded Unilateralism', 10 *Annual Review of Financial Economics* (2018), 219–37; and by the same author 'Deglobalization as a Global Challenge'. CIGI Papers No. 135, 2017 (available at: https://www.cigionline.org/publications/deglobalization-global-challenge); also, Judith Goldstein and Elisabeth van Lieshout, 'Is there a Future for Multilateral Trade Agreements?', in Andreas Klasen (ed.) *The Handbook of Global Trade Policy* (John Wiley, 2020), 173–200.
98. For similar arguments, *see* Bernard Hoekman and Petros C. Mavroidis, 'Preventing the Bad from Getting Worse: The End of the World (Trade Organization) As We Know It?' Robert Schuman Centre for Advanced Studies Research Paper No. RSCAS 2020/06, 2020 (available at: https://ssrn.com/abstract=3531704 or http://dx.doi.org/10.2139/ssrn.3531704): pp. 20 *et seq.*; Robert McDougall, 'The Crisis in WTO Dispute Settlement: Fixing Birth Defects to Restore Balance', 52(6) *Journal of World Trade* (2018), 867–96, 887 *et seq.*; Valbona Muzaka and Matthew Louis Bishop, 'Doha Stalemate: The End of Trade Multilateralism?', 41(2) *Review of International Studies* (2015), 383–406.
99. As of April 2020, the International Monetary Fund estimates China's GDP by purchasing power parity to amount to $27,804,953 million, compared to a global total of $138,352,382 million. By comparison, the United States' GDP was estimated to $ 20,289,987 million and the European Union's to $ 18,377,114 million. International Monetary Fund, 'World Economic Outlook Database, April 2020', 2020 (available at: https://www.imf.org).
100. Graeme B. Dinwoodie; Rochelle C. Dreyfuss, 'Designing a Global Intellectual Property System Responsive to Change: The WTO, WIPO, and beyond', 46(4) *Houston Law Review* (2009), 1187–234, 1190 *et seq.*
101. Indicative of the *Zeitgeist* is Gary Clyde Hufbauer and Barbara Kotschwar, 'Future Course of Trade Liberalization'. Paper for The World Bank 'Challenges for the Twenty-First Century'. Peterson Institute for International Economics, 1998 (available at: https://www.piie.com/commentary/speeches-papers/future-course-trade-liberalization); *see also* Peter Van den Bossche and Werner Zdouc, *The Law and Policy of the World Trade Organization* (4th edn., Cambridge University Press, 2017), 3–33.

The Uruguay Round negotiations followed a pattern of previous negotiation rounds dating back to the initial round of GATT negotiations ending in 1947 and continued over the course of the six subsequent rounds between 1949 and 1979, of 'locking in' incremental gains in trade liberalisation, while keeping static the over-arching guarantees on non-discrimination and equality of economic opportunity.[102] Indeed, the aim of trade liberalisation, as the negotiation variable, is evident in the preamble of the GATT which sets forth the twin proximate aims of 'substantial reduction of tariffs and other barriers to trade and to the elimination of discriminatory treatment in international commerce'.[103] While the latter was meant to be 'eliminated', the former was destined for a process of 'reduction'. Trade liberalisation was thus an existential character trait of both the GATT and the WTO. Neither were conceived to serve the role of a more neutral forum for international trade diplomacy; in fact, it was for such purpose that UNCTAD was created in 1964.[104]

The negotiators of the WTO Agreement expected the pattern of locking in incremental gains through trade negotiation rounds to continue after the creation of WTO.[105] In that sense, the WTO was not meant to be an end-state or a 'mission accomplished', even though it was initially envisaged that the system of multilateral trade negotiations would be made permanent within the new organisation.[106] Indeed, there were plenty of 'other barriers to trade'[107] to tackle in the decades to come. There was surely no desire to contemplate a 'WTO legislative assembly' or some similar dynamic internal mechanism through which liberalisation would be potentially rolled back.[108] Nor was there any appetite - or indeed a need - for handing over decision-making power or executive authority to such an international organisation or endow it with supranational 'life'.[109] The experience of the GATT as a 'member driven' process was understood as a great success, which the negotiators did not jeopardise.[110]

The hesitance towards giving the WTO political autonomy is mirrored in the anxiousness of its framers that the DSS would not provide *de facto* rulemaking.[111]

102. For a good overview, Andreas F. Lowenfeld, 'Evolution of the GATT and GATT Law', in Lowenfeld, *supra* note 14, 48-71.
103. Preamble to the GATT 1947. An almost identical formulation appears in the preamble to the Marrakesh Agreement.
104. John Toye () 'Assessing the G77: 50 Years After UNCTAD and 40 Years After the NIEO', 35(10) *Third World Quarterly* (2014), 1759-74; *See also* UNCTAD, *UNCTAD at 50: A Short History* (UNCTAD, 2014), 88 *et seq.* (available at: https://unctad.org/system/files/official-document/osg2014d1_en.pdf)
105. Van den Bossche and Zdouc, *supra* note 101, 93.
106. *Ibid.*
107. GATT preamble. *See supra* note 103.
108. Indeed, the suspicion towards voting for decision-making, seeing it as a potential threat to their vital interests. *See* Mary E. Footer, 'The Role of Consensus in GATT/WTO Decision-making', 17 *Northwestern Journal of International Law & Business* (1996), 653-80, 662.
109. The utility of instituting an executive body has been argued in the literature. *See* Debra P. Steger, 'The Future of the WTO: The Case for Institutional Reform', 12(4) *Journal of International Economic Law* (2009), 803-33, 818 *et seq.* On the reluctance by the GATT Contracting Parties to agree to supranational elements, *see* Van den Bossche and Zdouc, *supra* note 101, 86 *et seq.*
110. Van den Bossche and Zdouc, *supra* note 101.
111. The main worry was, however, not of judicial activism of the Appellate Body, but of individual 'rogue panels' whose reports could not be blocked by the WTO membership. Indeed, the

Not once, but twice does the DSU stipulate that the dispute settlement body 'cannot add to or diminish the rights and obligations provided in the covered agreements'.[112] It has more recently been echoed in criticism against the Appellate Body 'cogent reasons' case law on judicial precedent.[113]

It is unsurprising, therefore, not only that the WTO would exist in a dynamic socio-economic and politico-economic environment, but also that any adaptation of international trade law to such dynamics would have to occur by means of: (a) modifications to the WTO legal framework through the continuous process of multilateral trade negotiations, (b) the reformulation of the WTO legal framework *ex post facto* through case law, subject to the interpretation that such case law does not 'add to or diminish' the original agreement, but merely clarifies the meaning it was supposed to have all along, or (c) legal evolution occurring outside the WTO legal framework (including FTAs, as discussed under Part B.II). Indeed, with the exception provided by WTO case law in the area of TRIPS,[114] the last of these avenues prevailed, with legal evolution occurring through the 'spaghettification' of international IP law discussed above. The Uruguay Round succeeded in creating a static architecture, which is the WTO, but deliberately failed to establish a dynamic process to respond to the twists and turns of international consensus and the underlying commercial, technological and societal forces that informs such consensus.

II. The Nation-State Bias

The TRIPS Agreement, the WTO, and the GATT all follow the centuries-old Western legalist tradition of invoking the language of 'the Law' to socially control the relations between nominally sovereign and equal 'nation States' as the principal global actors.[115] The potential limits of this tradition, or even the existence of a serious challenger,

Appellate Body was introduced late in the Uruguay Round negotiations as an 'afterthought' to provide a solution to the rogue panel problem. *See further* Pohl, *supra* note 36, 81; also, Robert Howse, 'The World Trade Organization 20 Years On: Global Governance by Judiciary', 27(1) *European Journal of International Law* (2016), 9-77, 25.

112. Articles 3.2 and 19.2 of the DSU.
113. *See* Statements by the United States at the Meeting of the WTO Dispute Settlement Body (18 Dec. 2018) paras. 89, 113; cf. James Bacchus and Simon Lester, 'Of Precedent and Persuasion: The Crucial Role of an Appeals Court in WTO Disputes', 74 *Free Trade Bulletin* (2019), Herbert A. Stiefel Center for Trade Policy Studies, Cato Institute (available at: https://www.cato.org/sites/cato.org/files/2019-09/FTB_74.pdf). On the Appellate Body's understanding of precedent, *see* Van den Bossche and Zdouc, *supra* note 101, 57.
114. *See supra* note 67.
115. Koskenniemi reminds us that in spite of the oft-invoked references to Westphalia, modern international law predates the momentous events that took place in Münster and Osnabrück in October 1648, as German academics began to adopt the discourse of natural law as a 'language of secular statecraft' a few decades earlier. Martti Koskenniemi, 'Between Coordination and Constitution: International Law as a German Discipline', 15(1) *Redescriptions* (2011), 45-70, 46 *et seq.*; *see also* Ernst-Ulrich Petersmann, *International Economic Law in the 21st Century: Constitutional Pluralism and Multilevel Governance of Interdependent Public Goods* (Hart, 2012), 47 *et seq.*

must have been well-nigh impossible to imagine at the time of the Uruguay Round negotiations.[116]

Globalisation – a word that was not in common use at the time[117] – would open up dynamics and opportunities for political interaction between States, on the one hand, and non-State and infra-State actors, on the other, i.e. outside traditional State-to-State relations.[118] At the same time transnational economic and intellectual activity would enable the intra-State and extra-State cooperation, conflict and projection of power – and thus both influence over politico-economic processes and socio-economic control – affecting individuals at the domestic level.[119]

This process which is captured by the concept of 'transnationalisation' of the law[120] renders, not necessarily obsolete, but certainly incomplete, the legal ordering of IP protection established by the TRIPS Agreement.[121] Transnational norms based on contract and unilaterally adopted by private actors with global operations, such as the aforementioned GAFAs and BATs, as well as YouKu, Xiaome, Huawei, WeChat and Samsung, to name some of the most influential, today provide an important avenue of legal evolution.[122] Actors such as these and others unilaterally impose IP rules

---

116. Although the idea of transnational enterprises as non-State polities did not escape the imagination of legal scholars pre-1995, it seems to mostly have belonged to the genre of 'legal science fiction'. *See*, e.g., P. A. Reynolds, 'Non-State Actors and International Outcomes', 5(2) *British Journal of International Studies* (1979), 91–111; Bernard Mennis and Karl P. Sauvant, *Emerging Forms of Transnational Community; Transnational Business Enterprises and Regional Integration* (Lexington Books, 1976). Nevertheless, anything like private 'law-making' activity in the sense discussed below, such by social media and internet platforms, obviously did not yet exist.
117. The word 'globalisation' was popularised in Theodore Levitt, 'The Globalization of Markets', *Harvard Business Review* (May 1983). The widespread usage of the word is associated with the 1990s, *see* Google Books Ngram Viewer: https://books.google.com/ngrams.
118. *See generally* Gregory C. Shaffer and Terence C. Halliday, 'With, Within, and Beyond the State: The Promise and Limits of Transnational Legal Ordering', in Peer Zumbansen (ed.) *Oxford Handbook of Transnational Law* (Oxford University Press, 2020); Gregory Shaffer, 'Theorizing Transnational Legal Ordering', 12(1) *Annual Review of Law and Social Science* (2016), 231–53.
119. Marcel Kordos and Sergej Vojtovic, 'Transnational Corporations in the Global World Economic Environment', 230 *Procedia – Social and Behavioural Sciences* (2016), 150–58, 154; A. Claire Cutler, *Private Power and Global Authority: Transnational Merchant Law in the Global Political Economy* (Cambridge University Press, 2003), 236 *et seq.*; *see also* generally Christoph Knill and Dirk Lehmkuhl, 'Private Actors and the State: Internationalization and Changing Patterns of Governance', 15(1) *Governance: An International Journal of Policy and Administration* (2002), 41–63.
120. Thomas Duve, 'Transnationalization of Law and Legal Scholarship: Intellectual and Institutional Challenges', 44(1) *International Journal of Legal Information* (2016), 28–34, 30; Peer C. Zumbansen, 'Transnational Law: Theories & Applications', 14 May 2020, TLI Think! Paper 15/2020, available at SSRN: https://ssrn.com/abstract=3601385 or http://dx.doi.org/10.2139/ssrn.3601385. The term was first conceptualised by Philip Jessup, *Transnational Law* (Yale University Press, 1956).
121. *See generally* Reto M. Hilty, 'Intellectual Property and Private Ordering', in Rochelle C. Dreyfuss and Justine Pila (eds.) *Oxford Handbook of Intellectual Property Law* (Oxford University Press, 2018), 898–930; *see also* Paul Street, 'Stabilizing Flows in the Legal Field: Illusions of Permanence, Intellectual Property Rights and the Transnationalization of Law', 3(1) *Global Networks* (2003), 7–28.
122. Such private 'law making' has been referred to as 'platform law'. *See* David Kaye, *Report of the Special Rapporteur on the Promotion and Protection of the Right to Freedom of Opinion*

and policies much like a State imposes laws. This is achieved not only (a) through licensing contracts concerning technology, brands and copyrighted content, and other contractual arrangements, such as click-wrap contracts,[123] private international law,[124] and various 'soft law' instruments, such as terms of reference and community guidelines,[125] but also through (b) the *design* of technological infrastructure, i.e. so-called 'compliance by design' or applying a systematic approach to integrating regulatory requirements into manual and automated tasks and processes,[126] (c) automated (algorithmic) decision-making by means of artificial intelligence,[127] and (d) internal corporate complaint and appeal mechanisms, e.g. the Facebook Oversight Board (Facebook's 'Supreme Court').[128]

This private ordering of IP protection transcends national borders and is more directly and often more effectively enforced than IP agreements or national IP law, given the unilateral determination by the IP owner of the fora for settling IP disputes and its wielding of the power to deny service to the IP user.[129] Since these 'norm setters' often enjoy a monopolistic or otherwise near-supreme market power, there is nothing remotely resembling a balance of power between norm setter and norm taker.[130]

It would be premature to claim that the relative importance of the TRIPS Agreement has been eclipsed by the *transnational private ordering of IP protection*, but it is certainly no exaggeration that this development tends towards the precise opposite of what the TRIPS Agreement was meant to achieve: more legal fragmentation, less transparency, less procedural and substantive rights of the individual in the case of dispute, and a new form of 'unilateralism' in power relations.

D. CONCLUSION: BACK TO A POST-GLOBAL FUTURE?

In examining the historical currents that gave birth to the TRIPS Agreement and the experiences that have unfolded in the quarter of a century thereafter, the present chapter has discussed the ever-evolving problem of IP protection – finding a durable settlement of the conflicting interests between those who own and those who use

---

and Expression, U.N. Doc. A/HRC/38/35, 2018, para. 1; also, Sonia Katyal and Leah Chan Grinvald, 'Platform Law and the Brand Enterprise', 32(3) *Berkeley Technology Law Journal* (2018), 101–47; Molly K. Land, 'The Problem of Platform Law: Pluralistic Legal Ordering on Social Media', 2019 (available at SSRN: https://ssrn.com/abstract=3454222 or http://dx.doi.org/10.2139/ssrn.3454222).

123. Graeme B. Dinwoodie, 'The International Intellectual Property System: Treaties, Norms, National Courts, and Private Ordering', in Daniel Gervais (ed.) *Intellectual Property, Trade and Development: Strategies to Optimize Economic Development in a TRIPS Plus Era* (Oxford University Press, 2007), 61–114, 101; also, Land, *supra* note 122, 6.
124. Dinwoodie, *supra* note 123, 100 *et seq.*
125. *Ibid.* Also, generally, Grosse Ruse-Khan, *supra* note 62.
126. *Ibid.*
127. *Ibid.*
128. *Ibid.*
129. This novel topic is addressed by Orit Fischman Afori, 'Online Rulers as Hybrid Bodies: The Case of Infringing Content Monitoring', *University of Pennsylvania Journal of Constitutional Law* (2020) (available at SSRN: https://ssrn.com/abstract=3580004).
130. *Ibid.*

IP. By the measure of that objective, the TRIPS Agreement has been a true success for much of its lifespan. However, as this chapter has argued, TRIPS was always a fragile settlement and never more so than presently.

Although the TRIPS Agreement is still firmly situated as a central node of international IP protection, its autonomy (and relevance) has increasingly been chipped away by a growing web of specific IP agreements, notably FTAs, which has led to complexity and opacity. Moreover, first by the rise of ISDS and later by the breakdown of the WTO DSS, the primacy of its once-formidable international enforcement mechanism has been challenged. The causes of these developments must be attributed, in part, to the design of the TRIPS Agreement and, in part, to trends of transnationalisation that must have defied the wildest expectations of its framers.

TRIPS was made to be difficult to amend. This assured net IP importing countries who worried about further demands for IP protection from net IP exporting countries. Yet, it did not worry those who pushed for further trade liberalisation. After all, they could look back at almost 50 years of continuous, incremental reductions of trade barriers under successive rounds of GATT negotiations and were justified in expecting that this trend would continue following the establishment of the WTO. Alas, that expectation was soon frustrated.

However dynamically the TRIPS Agreement might have been designed, it would not have been able to address the transnationalisation of IP law. The very idea of transnationally active non-State polities founded on capital mobilisation and private-law transactions is one that State-to-State agreements, like TRIPS, are ill-equipped to regulate. Moreover, the power exerted by the likes of the GAFAs and the BATs is not only based on capital resources, but crucially on market power and indeed monopolistic market power. Nobody is *legally* obliged to use Amazon or Spotify; nonetheless, many find themselves *economically* so obliged. Increasingly, high-street book shops or music shops (remember those?) are a thing of the past, and only the online alternatives remain for anyone who would like to read or listen to music, for example. In the markets where they operate, these new global champions typically face no competitor with a directly substitutable product offering; indeed, they are sectorial *monopolists*. Then again, the problem that this entails is rather a matter of competition law and policy, than one of IP protection. Or so it would seem.

This leads us to question the future relevance of the TRIPS Agreement as paradigm of international IP protection. 'History' did not end with TRIPS, as has been argued in these pages; evolution continued, and the settlement of 1995 soon started to wither away. In important respects, we find ourselves back in an environment not unlike that which preceded the TRIPS Agreement.

So, is there a chance for a 'TRIPS 2.0'? Surely the road to a new global settlement between owners and users and a new universal consensus among States seems today a very long one indeed. Nevertheless, one can detect signs that the trend of transnationalisation may also have begun to reach its limits; it too is surely no 'end of history'. As the case of Huawei has illustrated,[131] the new global champions depend crucially on the architecture of the Western liberal order, notably the guarantees

131. For an overview of the geoeconomic battle over the involvement of Huawei in the construction of 5G networks, *see* Kavé Salamatian, 'Trump Against Huawei: Geopolitical Stakes of 5G', 177–178(2–3) *Hérodote* (2020), 197–213; Chris Stokel-Walker, 'Banning Huawei from 5G

and freedoms of cross-border enterprise: free movement of services and capital, recognition of foreign legal entities, contracts and arrangements, of judgments and arbitral awards, and, above all, free movement of data.[132] As States and non-State actors are chipping away at the authority of the Western liberal order, they are also chipping away at the branch they are sitting on.

It will be interesting to watch in the coming years the continued trajectory of geoeconomic policies. The presence of monopolistic and sometimes State-owned, State-subsidised, or State-influenced IP behemoths, such as the GAFAs, BATs, and others, is increasingly met by concerns about control of critical resources and strategic assets.[133] Notable in this regard is the recent heightened attention in the United States, the European Union and many other countries to national security threats against access to critical technologies (including artificial intelligence, robotics, cybersecurity, quantum-, nano- and bio-technologies, and pharmaceuticals),[134] critical infrastructures (including virtual infrastructures, communications, media, data processing and storage),[135] critical inputs (notably energy)[136] and control of sensitive information (including personal data).[137] Since 2020, the EU has its own screening framework for foreign direct investments to defend against external geoeconomic threats.[138]

In what is perhaps an ironic twist of history, it seems that with the demise of Western liberalism, the – older – Westphalian doctrine of pragmatism, realism and power politics stands ready to re-emerge from the shadows.

Infrastructure', 242(3228) *New Scientist* (2019), 1; Christopher Balding and Donald C. Clarke, 'Who Owns Huawei?', 2019 (available at SSRN: https://ssrn.com/abstract=3372669).

132. *See* François Heisbourg, 'War and Peace After the Age of Liberal Globalisation', 60(1) *Survival: Global Politics and Strategy* (2018), 211–28, 215; *Cf.* André Barrinha and Thomas Renard, 'Power and Diplomacy in the Post-Liberal Cyberspace', 96(3) *International Affairs* (2020), 749–66.
133. *See*, e.g., European Commission, A New Industrial Strategy for Europe, 10 March 2020, COM(2020) 102 final; European Commission (2020) Guidance to the Member States Concerning Foreign Direct Investment and Free Movement of Capital from Third Countries, and the Protection of Europe's Strategic Assets, Ahead of the Application of Regulation (EU) 2019/452 (FDI Screening Regulation), Communication from the Commission, C(2020) 1981 final.
134. *See*, e.g., 50 U.S. Code § 4565(a)(6).
135. *See*, e.g., 50 U.S. Code § 4565(a)(5).
136. *See*, e.g., 50 U.S. Code § 4565(a)(4)(B)(iii)(I).
137. *See*, e.g., 50 U.S. Code § 4565(a)(4)(B)(iii)(III).
138. Regulation (EU) 2019/452 establishing a framework for the screening of foreign direct investments into the Union, 19 March 2019, OJ L 79, 21/3/2019.

CHAPTER 2
TRIPS in the Context of International Law

Anselm Kamperman Sanders

A. INTRODUCTION

The Agreement on the Trade-Related Aspects of Intellectual Property Rights (TRIPS) was signed in Marrakesh as part of the Agreement on the Establishment of the World Trade Organisation (WTO) that started operating on 1 January 1995. It heralded a new way to approach intellectual property rights, which until that time were not considered trade-related as such, but rather instruments for domestic policy to stimulate innovation and creativity. In their more basic forms IPRs fulfil three basic functions: the 'creation of competitive markets' for human, industrial and intellectual creativity that is novel or original, where consumers can make rational choices about which goods or services to buy; 'insurance' to innovators, safeguarding the fruits of their labour from abuse by free-riders; and a 'commercial gateway' through which innovators can exploit and benefit from their creations.

The TRIPS Agreement tries to strike a balance by ensuring 'that measures and procedures to enforce intellectual property rights do not themselves become barriers to legitimate trade', which also encompasses the transfer and dissemination of technology.[1]

The TRIPS Agreement therefore relies on both pre-existent norms on intellectual property law, as well as its incorporation in the multilateral trade agreements that are part of the WTO. As such, intellectual property became subject to the rules on dispute settlement, the Dispute Settlement Understanding (DSU) applicable to the constellation of WTO agreements covering the General Agreement on Tariffs and Trade (GATT 1994), General Agreement on Trade in Services (GATS), Technical Barriers to Trade (TBT), and Sanitary and Phytosanitary Measures (SPS).

The TRIPS Agreement for the first time put IPRs in the context of multilateral trade agreements. The reasoning was that only a harmonised level of intellectual

1. Articles 7 and 8 TRIPS Agreement.

property (IP) protection would ensure a level playing field in international trade, while on the other hand lacunae in the scope of IP protection and enforcement would lead to trade distortions. It sets minimum standards of protection of IPRs, including their subsistence and enforcement. It recognises intellectual property as one of the key elements in international trade next to the WTO agreements on goods and services, and other trade barriers. Although the WTO was established by its Members to effectuate an agenda of trade liberalisation, and the permitted exceptions thereto, it is clear that the TRIPS Agreement, in reinforcing the position of intellectual property rightholders, provides and defines legitimate barriers to trade. Its principal aim is not to reduce barriers to trade in the way that, for example GATT aims to reduce tariff barriers and customs duties. Naturally, IPRs also have limitations and boundaries, not least the problems that may arise due to the considerable market power that IPRs provide to their owners. IPRs may thus create obstacles to legitimate trade.

In tandem, Articles 7 and 8 TRIPS provide a strong basis for the shaping of intellectual property policy in a manner conducive to social and economic welfare. This is also reflected in the Preamble to the Marrakesh Agreement that contains an expression of the overall goals of the WTO:

> 'Recognising that their relations in the field of trade and economic endeavour should be conducted with a view to raising standards of living, ensure full employment and a large steadily growing volume of real income and effective demand, and expanding the production of and trade in goods and services, while allowing for the optimal use of the world's resources in accordance with the objective of sustainable development, seeking both to protect and preserve the environment and to enhance the means for doing so in a manner consistent with their respective needs and concerns at different levels of economic development.'

In framing innovation policy to effectuate the intricate link between sustainable development and technological progress, one has to approach intellectual property as a complex adaptive system that is seen in light of other international obligations, such as, *inter alia*:

- The Universal Declaration of Human Rights (UDHR);[2]
- The UNESCO Convention for the Safeguarding of the Intangible Cultural Heritage (ICH);[3]
- The United Nations Framework Convention on Climate Change (UNFCCC);[4]
- The Convention on Biological Diversity (CBD)

Intellectual property law does not exist in a legal vacuum. It is interdependent on the existence of the rule of law, most notably where enforcement of intellectual property

2. *See* in this respect WIPO/OHCHR, *Intellectual Property and Human Rights* (WIPO, 1998)
3. *See* M. Torsten and J. Anderson, *Intellectual Property and the Safeguarding of Traditional Cultures – Legal Issues and Practical Options for Museums, Libraries and Archives* (WIPO, 2010), online: https://www.wipo.int/edocs/pubdocs/en/tk/1023/wipo_pub_1023.pdf.
4. A. Taubman and J. Watal, *The WTO TRIPS Agreement – A Practical Overview for Climate Change Policymakers* (WTO, 2010), online: https://www.wto.org/english/tratop_e/trips_e/ta_docs_e/8_3_overviewclimatechange_e.pdf. *See also* D. Shabalala, *Climate Change, Technology Transfer and Intellectual Property: Options for Action at the UNFCCC* (Diss., 2014), online: https://dalishabalala.files.wordpress.com/2014/10/shabalala-climate-change-tech-transfer-and-ip.pdf.

is concerned, and it also interacts closely with other branches of public and private law, with public law most notably where, *inter alia*, the acquisition and registration of IPRs, administrative and criminal enforcement, and taxation are concerned, and with private law when, *inter alia*, contracts, labour agreements, incorporation of undertakings, and torts are concerned. As a property right, intellectual property is a possession subject to the protective regime against interference by the state, meaning that it is considered to be an investment that can be subject to investor-state dispute settlement,[5] or subject to domestic or even international protection as a human right to property entitlement.[6] Through the TRIPS Agreement, intellectual property has been framed as a trade issue, which prompts the question as to whether WTO law and adjudication is limited to trade issues only, or whether the TRIPS Agreement should be read in the context of international law. In other words, can WTO panels, the Appellate Body (AB) and Dispute Settlement Body (DSB) also approach intellectual property as a complex adaptive system, or is there a strict confinement to the WTO covered agreements?

B. INTERNATIONAL CONVENTIONS AND MULTILATERAL TREATIES

I. Industrial Property

The genesis of the modern[7] concept of industrial property[8] lies in the abolishment,[9] during the reign of James I in England, of exclusive privileges and monopolies that kings would grant in exchange for sums or tributes. The Statute of Monopolies, enacted in 1623, declared all monopolies void, with the exception of inventions.[10]

5. *See* the cases *Philip Morris Asia Limited v. the Commonwealth of Australia*, (UNCITRAL PCA Case No. 2012-12); *Philip Morris v. Uruguay* (ICSID Case No. ARB/10/7); and *Eli Lily v. Canada* NAFTA (ICSID Case No. UNCT/14/2).
6. *See* for example *Anheuser-Busch Inc. v. Portugal*, no. 73049/01, European Court Human Rights (Grand Chamber), Judgment (Merits and Just Satisfaction) of 11.01.2007, Reports of Judgments and Decisions 2007-I.
7. Although Venice was the first state to adopt a patent law on 19 March 1474, it was not in order to put an end to unlawful monopolies, but in order to reward and incentivise inventors and entice them to bring technology to Venice.
8. S. Ladas, *Patents, Trademarks, and Related Rights – National and International Protection* (Harvard University Press, 1975).
9. The 1602 English case of *Darcy v. Allein*, Noy. 178; Web. P. R. 7; *see* M. Fisher, 'Darcy v. Allen', in C. Heath and A. Kamperman Sanders (eds.), *Landmark Intellectual Property Cases and Their Legacy* (Kluwer Law International, 2011), 63–82.
10. 21 Jam. I, c. 3, with Section 6 dealing with patents granted in the future:

    'Provided also and be it declared and enacted, that any declaration before mentioned shall not extend to any letters patent and grants of privilege, for the term of fourteen years, or under, hereafter to be made, of the sole working or making of any manner of new manufactures within this realm, to the true and first inventor and inventors of such manufactures, which others at the time of making such letters patents and grants shall not use. So as also this be not contrary to the law, nor mischievous to the State, by raising prices of commodities at home, or hurt of trade, or generally inconvenient; the said fourteen years to be accounted from the date of the first letters patent or grants of such privileges hereafter to be made, but that the same shall be of such force that they should be if this Act had never been made and of none other.'

The principles contained in this legislation have been adopted all over the world. The justification for the retention of a patent for invention lies in the fact that inventions provide a technical solution to a technical problem, which by its very nature is comprised in an idea, or information. Since such information on technical solutions to technical problems is non-rival and non-exhaustible, it must be considered a public good to which the principles of the free market (supply and demand determine price) cannot be applied. In other words, there is no market for such ideas, as there is no scarcity once the idea is shared. The only way to create a form of scarcity is to keep such information secret. In a competitive economy, however, information is crucial for the functioning of a free market economy. The only way to create a competitive market for technology that comprises teachings on technical solutions to technical problems, is to create a legal monopoly for inventions. These teachings must be novel, meaning that they are new and not yet part of the public domain. In order to foster competition, the patentee has to make the invention public, and can only claim an exclusive right to use for a limited period of time. In this way, the inconvenience to the state and the free market economy that is caused by the grant of a monopoly is offset by the fact that society will receive access to new technical knowledge that can be applied, assigned or licensed, used to improve upon existing technology, or used as a basis to find alternative solutions. On this basis, the patent system serves as an incentive to innovate, a means to recoup investments in research and development, and to disclose information obtained in the patent bargain.[11] Based on economic considerations analogous to patent protection, legislation protecting industrial designs or models was enacted from 1787 onward.[12]

In a free market economy, the price of products and services is determined by supply and demand. This also means that information is important, and trade marks are capable of conferring the origin of goods or services. The use of trade marks enables consumers to make a rational choice in terms of what to buy and what not to buy, and to assess the quality or qualities of the goods or services offered under such a mark. This means that trade marks allow for the creation of diversified markets for products and services, where multiple traders are in competition for sale of those goods or services to consumers. In order to fulfil this function, a trade mark must confer the commercial origin of a good or a service.[13] Protection of this basic function of the trade mark then entails the prevention of consumer confusion when another uses, in the course of trade, the same or similar sign in relation to the same or similar goods or services for which the mark is registered (or used).[14]

Analogous to the enactment of trade mark laws, the protection of commercial names, indications or appellations of origin and the repression of unfair competition was developed nationally, but through the increase of international trade relations following the first industrial revolution (1760–1840), industrial property rights also became barriers to international trade, with national law placing limits on protection

11. All patent applications are published 18 months after filing, irrespective whether the application results in a granted patent.
12. Once more first in England, 27 Geo. III, c. 38.
13. A. Kamperman Sanders and S.M. Maniatis, 'A Consumer Trade Mark: Protection Based on Origin and Quality', *EIPR* [1993] 406–15.
14. *See* Art. 16(1) TRIPS.

for foreigners. Treaties of commerce, or bilateral trade arrangements, did not prove satisfactory either, as their application was too cumbersome and uncertain.

The Paris Convention for the Protection of Industrial Property, concluded in 1883, introduced the non-discriminatory principle of national treatment, while recognising the independence of rights. It also established the principle of priority. For trade marks the priority period of six months allows the claimant to rely on the first date of filing in one of the member states to the Paris Union in other member states, thus overriding the first-come-first-served principle of national registries. Priority in respect of patents allows the claimant during a period of twelve months from the time of first filing in one of the member states of the Paris Union to rely on the fixation of novelty and state of the art on the priority date. The Paris Convention was soon enhanced by the Madrid Agreement for the Repression of False or Deceptive Indications of Source on Goods in 1891.

The Paris Convention has thereby allowed the proliferation of industrial property acquisition and exercise in a global market place. Enterprises can much more easily and strategically determine where the conditions are most optimal for their business operations.

Where owners have been placed in a position of advantage, many developing industrial economies, however, feel that this advantage serves foreign nationals and enterprises in particular. Local investment and the transfer of technology may not occur if the technological needs of a nation are served through importation, and the standard of living of the population may not rise as a result. Since studies[15] confirm that IPR-intensive industries contribute significantly to GDP[16] and employment,[17] and that these industries are also capable of paying higher wages, it is evident that the attraction and development of IPR-intensive industries is of prime importance for a nation's welfare and economic progress. Understandably developing countries are critical of what they perceive as foreign-held commercial monopolies.

The development of protection of industrial property was further expanded by special treaties, most notably in the field of geographical indications of origin - the Lisbon Agreement for the Protection of Appellations of Origin and their International Registration (1958, with the Geneva Act of the Lisbon Agreement of 2015 making it easier for trade mark systems to enter), but also the Patent Cooperation Treaty, which placed the World Intellectual Property Organisation as the agency (and incidentally the only self-funded agency of the UN) in charge of providing international search reports to patent applicants wishing to register in multiple jurisdictions. The World

15. EPO-EUIPO, *Intellectual Property Rights Intensive Industries and Economic Performance in the European Union*. Industry-level Analysis Report, October 2016, Second edition, online: https://euipo.europa.eu/ohimportal/en/web/observatory/ip-contribution.
    See similarly the USPTO and Economics and Statistics Administration, *Intellectual Property and the U.S. Economy: 2016 Update*, online: https://www.uspto.gov/sites/default/files/documents/IPandtheUSEconomySept2016.pdf.
16. EPO-EUIPO, *Intellectual Property Rights Intensive Industries and Economic Performance in the European Union*. Industry-level Analysis Report, *Ibid*. concluding that the contribution of IPR-intensive industries to the EU GDP is EUR 5.7 trillion, or 42%, with the patent-intensive industries taking EUR 2 trillion, or 15%.
17. EPO-EUIPO, *Intellectual Property Rights Intensive Industries and Economic Performance in the European Union*. Industry-level Analysis Report, *Ibid*. Concluding that the contribution of IPR-intensive industries to EU employment is 38%.

Intellectual Property Organization (WIPO) also provides arbitration for domain name disputes, but it is also possible to address the WIPO Arbitration and Mediation Center for the settlement of other IP-related international disputes.

Other legislative developments where the United Nations has been the prime driver for creating obligations have ended up at WIPO, rather than the WTO. In fact, a counter-movement is visible in that UN members increasingly seek to protect non-trade values through international conventions. In the Preamble to the 2001 Universal Declaration of Cultural Diversity (UNESCO Convention), the United Nations Educational, Scientific and Cultural Organization (UNESCO) defined the concept of culture as follows:

> 'Culture should be regarded as the set of distinctive spiritual, material, intellectual and emotional features of society or a social group, and that it encompasses, in addition to art and literature, lifestyles, ways of living together, value systems, traditions and beliefs' (UNESCO, 2001, Preamble, fn. 2).

The UNESCO Convention entered into force on 18 March 2007 and provides a framework for states to engage in protective measures to safeguard the diversity of cultural expressions and folklore against the influences of globalisation and free trade.

The protection of Traditional Cultural Expressions (TCE) and Traditional Knowledge (TK) covers specifically the role and place of cultural heritage collections and TCE and TK databases. In the context of WIPO,[18] ongoing work is done to deal with defensive and positive protection of TCE and TK. Since for positive protection one has to define 'rightholders' according to entitlement, and award exclusive rights in relation to subject matter already in the public domain, this is not easily done. More promising is the work on defensive protection, which may take the guise of protection against misappropriation by parties that have no connection to the TCE or TK, or in benefit-sharing agreements. Such benefit-sharing agreements are so far foreseen between undertakings and states that are sovereign over genetic resources that form the basis for further inventions.

II. Authors' Rights

The **Berne Convention for the Protection of Literary and Artistic Works**, concluded in 1886, complements the Paris Convention. In respect of its basic principles, national treatment is also guaranteed. It further establishes that no formalities are required to obtain protection, and that there is independence of rights. The Convention also provides for the protection of the moral rights[19] of authors, which includes the right to object to any mutilation, deformation or other modification of, or other derogatory action in relation to the work that would be prejudicial to the author's honour or reputation.[20] Copyright was first created as the economic right to control copy under

18. *See* the work of the WIPO Intergovernmental Committee on Intellectual Property and Genetic Resources, Traditional Knowledge and Folklore, online: https://www.wipo.int/tk/en/igc/.
19. Article 6*bis* Berne Convention. Note that the USA joined the Berne Convention in 1988 and made a reservation in respect of moral rights.
20. For a practical application *see* A. Bertrand, 'Shostakovich and John Huston: The French Supreme Court on Copyright, Contracts and Moral Rights', in Heath/ Kamperman Sanders (eds), *Landmark*

the British Statute of Anne,[21] in an attempt to regulate the printing industry, while simultaneously recognising the public nature of the grant by vesting the right to copy in authors, rather than publishers. By contrast, the continental legal systems recognised authors' rights as 'works of the mind' that have an economic and moral component. The latter formed the basis for the Berne Convention.[22]

Technological progress has continuously challenged the application of authors' rights, most notably in the realm of protection of performers, producers and broadcasting organisations,[23] phonograms,[24] software,[25] integrated circuits,[26] the internet,[27] and audio-visual performances.[28] In contrast to industrial property rights, the rights conferred by copyright affect not only persons acting in a commercial capacity, but also private citizens. Furthermore, the rights created in relation to the internet, most notably the right of communication to the public, is not subject to exhaustion. Exhaustion is the principle that upon the first commercial exploitation (or first sale), the IP rightholder can no longer object to the further commercialisation (or onward sale or distribution) of the work. This because the rightholder could control the supply and price during this first transaction and is deemed to be appropriately compensated as a result. In an online setting, however, acts of communication invariably result in the making of a copy of the work. This is a reproduction for which the rightholder is not compensated, and hence the copyright system has been adapted to allow for the control of and compensation for access to the work.[29] This, however, severely constrains commercial and non-commercial actors alike from transferring any digital work. The onward sale of legally purchased e-books or other media contents without the authorisation of the rightholder has thus become an act of copyright infringement. The concentration in suppliers of legal digital contents, as well as in platform providers for digital sales has severely undermined citizens' trust in and acceptance of the copyright system.

The world of copyright protection has been a quickly expanding one. With every new commercial activity related to copyright works, a new commercial actor has emerged and been granted protection. This has resulted in the protection of rights related to authors' rights, *inter alia*, in the Rome Convention for the Protection of Performers, Producers of Phonograms and Broadcasting Organizations and

Intellectual Property Cases and Their Legacy (Kluwer Law International, 2011), 1–12.

21. Copyright Act 1710, 8 Ann. c. 21.
22. A. Sterling and T. Cook, *World Copyright Law* (4th edn., Sweet & Maxwell, 2015).
23. 1961 Rome Convention for the Protection of Performers, Producers of Phonograms and Broadcasting Organizations.
24. 1971 Convention for the Protection of Producers of Phonograms Against Unauthorized Duplication of Their Phonograms.
25. Albeit only partial for original selection and arrangement of data through article 10 TRIPS under copyright, whereas the EU has a *sui generis* database right contained in Directive 96/9/EC on the Legal Protection of Databases.
26. 1989 Washington Treaty on Intellectual Property in Respect of Integrated Circuits (not in force, but largely implemented through Article 35 of the TRIPS Agreement.
27. 1996 WIPO Copyright Treaty and WIPO Performances and Phonograms Treaty.
28. 2012 Beijing Treaty on Audiovisual Performances.
29. J. Reinbothe and S. Von Lewinski, *The WIPO Treaties on Copyright* (Oxford University Press, 2015).

the Brussels Convention Relating to the Distribution of Program-Carrying Signals Transmitted by Satellite.

The 1996 WIPO 'Internet Treaties', comprising the WIPO Copyright Treaty (WCT) and the WIPO Performances and Phonograms Treaty (WPPT), have re-defined copyright for the digital age. This last true technology-driven adaption of the IP system in an international context came as a direct response to the third industrial revolution. These changes are outside of the WTO TRIPS framework: the creation of the right of communication to the public, and the recognition of Digital Rights Management (DRM) and Technological Protection Mechanisms (TPM) as relevant in the context of copyright.

Since 1996, the rate of harmonisation has slowed down, seeing only the inception of the Beijing Treaty on Audiovisual Performances, and the Marrakesh Treaty to Facilitate Access to Published Works for Persons Who Are Blind, Visually Impaired or Otherwise Print Disabled. This may in part be attributed to the fact that although WIPO has remained the traditionalist's venue for intellectual property development, the WTO TRIPS Agreement has been perceived as being the more relevant international instrument, largely due to the fact that it is a minimum standards agreement and the fact that the WTO's dispute settlement mechanism provides for true enforcement possibilities ... if only on paper.

C. INTELLECTUAL PROPERTY IN THE CONTEXT OF INTERNATIONAL TRADE

Under the 1994 Agreement on Trade-Related Aspects of Intellectual Property Rights (TRIPS Agreement), the principles of national treatment, independence of rights, priority and/or automatic protection also bind those WTO Members not party to the Paris or Berne Conventions. In addition, the TRIPS Agreement imposes an obligation of 'most-favoured-nation treatment', under which advantages accorded by a WTO Member to the nationals of any other country must also be accorded to the nationals of all WTO Members.[30] Unlike the Paris and Berne Conventions, the TRIPS Agreement also provides minimum standards for the protection and enforcement of IPRs, which to this day remains a very relevant issue.[31]

Under the Agreement Establishing the WTO, disagreements over the interpretation and implementation of the TRIPS Agreement are subject to conflict resolution under the DSU. This is an intra-state adjudication mechanism in which the DSB provides for: 1) consultations and mediation; 2) the establishment of a Panel that will present its findings and conclusions to the DSB; with the possibility for 3) an appeal to the AB that may uphold, modify or reverse the Panel's legal findings and conclusions. In the context of the DSU, countervailing measures involving IPRs have become an accepted practice for retaliatory measures.[32]

30. J. Malbon, C. Lawson and M. Davison, *The WTO Agreement on Trade-Related Aspects of Intellectual Property Rights* (Edward Elgar, 2014).
31. OECD-EUIPO, *Trade in Counterfeit and Pirated Goods: Mapping the Economic Impact* (OECD/EUIPO, 2016).
32. R. Vargas Amaral, *Cross-retaliation in IP Rights: Addressing Member Asymmetries and Compliance at the WTO* (Wolf Publishing, 2012).

The inclusion of minimum standards for protection and enforcement of IPRs in the Uruguay round of trade negotiations was commonly understood to be a balancing act: promoting industrialised country interests in return for greater access by developing countries to markets for their goods in agricultural products.[33] The history of TRIPS brings up four narratives[34] in this regard: 1) the bargain narrative, in which the agreement was considered the product of a compromise between developed and less-developed countries; 2) a coercion or imperialistic narrative, in which the TRIPS Agreement is portrayed as an unfair trade document that has been imposed upon developing countries; 3) an ignorance narrative in which less-developed countries are portrayed as countries that did not understand the importance of intellectual property; and 4) a self-interest narrative, according to which less-developed countries agreed to and/or benefit from stronger intellectual property protection because it was found that such protection is necessary for knowledge development. All four narratives are not mutually exclusive, and therefore it has been suggested that in the implementation of the TRIPS Agreement in the context of the global trading system, it is more useful to speak of a 'calibration narrative'. A 'calibrated innovation policy' is then one where the implementation of the TRIPS Agreement should go hand in hand with technology capacity building, education and institutional capacity building, and access to innovation venture capital.[35]

It must be noted that the number of WTO disputes involving intellectual property have been rather limited in number and overall balanced in taking into consideration the interests of IP rightholders, competitors, and society.[36]

Yet in the aftermath of the WTO Agreement, trade negotiations did not result in further progress in terms of establishing a veritable development policy.[37] Instead, developing countries began to react against higher IP standards,[38] which at the WTO resulted in the Doha Declaration on TRIPS and Public Health.[39] Ultimately the WIPO Development Agenda,[40] the result of pressure from civil society and developing countries, is the only tangible set of recommendations that tied into the so-called Millennium Development Goals at the time.[41] The Development Agenda has resulted

33. D. Gervais (ed.), *Intellectual Property, Trade and Development* (2nd edn., Oxford University Press, 2014).
34. P. Yu, 'TRIPS and Its Discontents', 10 *Marquette Intellectual Property Law Review* (2005), 369.
35. D. Gervais, 'TRIPS and Development', in *Intellectual Property, Trade and Development* (Oxford University Press, 2007), 5–12.
36. *See* J. Pauwelyn, 'The Dog that Barked But Didn't Bite: 15 Years of Intellectual Property Disputes at the WTO', 1 *Journal of International Dispute Settlement* (2010) 389–429, available at DOI: doi.org/10.1093/jnlids/idq001.
37. A. Kamperman Sanders and D. Shabalala, 'Intellectual Property Treaties and Development', in D. Gervais (ed.), *Intellectual Property, Trade and Development* (Oxford University Press, 2007), 41–72.
38. ICTSD, *The Global Debate on the Enforcement of Intellectual Property Rights and Developing Countries* (ICTSD, 2009) with contributions by C. Fink, 'Enforcing Intellectual Property Rights: An Economic Perspective'; and C. Correa, 'The Push for Stronger Enforcement Rules: Implications for Developing Countries'.
39. WT/MIN(01)/DEC/2 (2001), adopted 14 November 2001.
40. WO/GA/31/11 of 27 August 2004.
41. *See* A. Kamperman Sanders, *The Development Agenda for Intellectual Property – Rational Humane Policy of 'Modern-day Communism'*, Inaugural Lecture (Maastricht University, 2005), DOI: 10.26481/spe.20050520aks.

in closer cooperation between the WTO and the United Nations agencies WIPO[42] and the World Health Organization (WHO).[43] The Development Agenda remains relevant today in that it was established that WIPO should:

> '[a]pproach intellectual property enforcement in the context of broader societal interests and especially development oriented concerns, with the view that "the protection and enforcement of intellectual property rights should contribute to the promotion of technological innovation in the transfer and dissemination of technology, to the mutual advantage of producers and users of technological knowledge and in a manner conducive to social and economic welfare, and to balance the rights and obligations", in accordance with Article 7 of the TRIPS Agreement.'[44]

WIPO has continued to work on the charting and formulation of flexibilities in the IP system,[45] technical assistance, and technology transfer.[46] Equally, the UN's 2015 Resolution 70/1 'Transforming our World: the 2030 Agenda for Sustainable Development' resulted in 2017 in the establishment of the Technology Bank for Least Developed Countries, based in Gebze, Turkey.[47]

Ultimately, from a legal perspective, increasing the absorptive capacity of developing countries starts with legal empowerment.[48] This means ensuring that the population in a jurisdiction can rely on the rule of law to make investments and to be able to participate in commercial life on a level playing field that is free from corruption. In this context, it is also important to point out that there is a correlation between competitiveness, innovation and the strength of protection and enforcement of IPRs.[49] It is therefore important to realise that these developments primarily take place outside the WTO, although they have a direct impact on the way in which the TRIPS Agreement is understood. This is especially visible in the discussion on the

---

42. The WTO-WIPO Agreement, Article 4 provides:
    'The International Bureau [WIPO] shall make available to developing country WTO Members which are not Member States of WIPO the same legal-technical assistance relating to the TRIPS Agreement as it makes available to Member States of WIPO which are developing countries. The WTO Secretariat shall make available to Member States of WIPO which are developing countries and are not WTO Members the same technical cooperation relating to the TRIPS Agreement as it makes available to developing country WTO Members.'
43. *See Promoting Access to Medical Technologies and Innovation – Intersections between public health, intellectual property and trade* (WTO-WIPO-WHO, 2012).
44. The 45 Adopted Recommendations under the WIPO Development Agenda, Cluster F: Other Issues, 45. Online: https://www.wipo.int/ip-development/en/agenda/recommendations.html#f.
45. *See* the WIPO database on Flexibilities in the IP System, available at https://www.wipo.int/ip-development/en/agenda/flexibilities/index.html.
46. *See* https://www.wipo.int/ip-development/en/agenda/.
47. *See* UN A/RES/71/251, Resolution adopted by the General Assembly on 23 December 2016 – Establishment of the Technology Bank for Least Developed Countries. *See* https://unohrlls.org/technologybank/.
48. Commission on Legal Empowerment of the Poor, *Making the Law Work for Everyone* (UNDP, 2008).
49. *See* World Economic Forum Competitiveness Reports and Indices, online: www.reports.weforum.org.

Coronavirus disease (COVID-19) vaccine patent waiver.[50] Discussion on the waiver is after all very much informed by the WHO's analysis of the pandemic and the realisation of governments that the response to the pandemic has been too slow. The issue is now being addressed through a 'Trilateral cooperation on intellectual property and public health' in which the WHO, WIPO and the WTO cooperate.[51]

I. Public Health – The Most Contentious TRIPS Issue?

Although many minimum standards in the field of industrial property were set in the TRIPS Agreement, several matters were not resolved. A number of these issues have been addressed by the inclusion of negotiation mandates on the most controversial topics, being: 1) patentable subject matter in relation to plant-related and biotechnological inventions (Article 27(3)(b) TRIPS), and 2) that of establishing a multilateral system for the registration of geographical indications of origin (Article 23(4) TRIPS).

The first issue deals with the question of whether plant and animal inventions should be covered by patents, and how to protect new plant varieties.

The second issue of geographical indications deals with the creation of a multilateral register for wines and spirits; and extending the higher (Article 23 TRIPS) level of protection beyond wines and spirits is being actively discussed in the WTO context. On both these issues, the WTO members remain divided.[52]

There is one issue, however, that really highlights the differences in points of view on intellectual property as a mechanism for sustainable innovation. This is related to Article 5A of the Paris Convention, which recognises the freedom of member states to grant a compulsory licence to prevent abuse that may result from 'not operating' according to the invention or not operating on reasonable terms.[53] Traditionally, this has been understood as a use of the patent to monopolise imports, while limiting the introduction and spread of the use of the patented technology in a country. Thus, failure to operate or insufficient operation is a legitimate reason for government action. The problem, however, is that the Paris Convention does not define 'failure to operate', leaving it up to Member States to decide whether domestic demand can be served by imports or whether local production is required. What is clear is that when the patent holder abuses his patent right, a compulsory licence may very well be justified. Article 5A(3) of the Paris Convention makes it clear that the compulsory licence is the main instrument to deal with patent abuse, as forfeiture or revocation of the patent is the last resort in case a compulsory licence is proven to be ineffective against the abuse after a period of two years. In short, the Paris Convention provisions provide the basis for the TRIPS provisions that further clarify a number of points.

Limitations can be found in Article 31(d), (e) and (g) of the TRIPS Agreement. For example, a compulsory licence may not be exclusive, as that would restrict the

50. *See* in this respect https://www.wto.org/english/tratop_e/covid19_e/trade_related_ip_measure_e.htm.

51. https://www.wto.org/english/tratop_e/trips_e/who_wipo_wto_e.htm.

52. *See* WTO Module XI, *Current TRIPS Issues*, available at https://www.wto.org/english/tratop_e/trips_e/ta_docs_e/modules11_e.pdf.

53. P. Roffe and C. Spennemann, *Resource Book on TRIPS and Development* (Cambridge University Press, 2005), online: https://www.iprsonline.org/unctadictsd/ResourceBookIndex.htm.

patent holder himself, and the licence may not be freely transferred except with the share of the business or goodwill of the part of the business over which the licence is exercised.

Particularly important is the obligation on the granting authority to withdraw the licence on reasoned request when the circumstances which led to the grant cease to exist and are unlikely to recur. In making this decision, regard must be had to the legitimate interests of the licensee who has made investments during the term of the licence to produce the patented product or implement the patented process.

Furthermore, Article 31(f) of TRIPS provides that production under a compulsory licence must be 'predominantly for the supply of the domestic market', the exception being compulsory licences issued in the context of competition law (TRIPS Article 31(k)). Article 8 of the TRIPS Agreement provides a further elaboration of these grounds by mentioning state measures to protect public health and promote public interests in sectors vital for their socio-economic and technological development.

As regards the interpretation of public health measures, matters were and are still not fully crystallised. A 1998 attempt by the WHO to clarify the TRIPS provisions for the national ministries of health[54] was met with resistance from the US and the European Union, as they felt that intellectual property is the exclusive domain of WIPO and the WTO. After pressure from the African group in the WTO following the AIDS crisis, however, the Doha Declaration on the TRIPS Agreement and Public Health[55] of 14 November 2001 establishes that all WTO members have the autonomy to determine what constitutes a case of national emergency or other circumstances of extreme urgency where public health is concerned. In addition, the question of involuntary use or transfer (compulsory licensing – TRIPS Article 31) for essential pharmaceuticals for least-developed country members of the WTO without production capacity is addressed through the introduction of a new provision (Article 31*bis* TRIPS followed by an Annex, and Appendix to the Annex) to the TRIPS Agreement. This amendment to TRIPS entered into force on 23 January 2017 and allows for a notification procedure[56] though which patented pharmaceuticals can be produced and exported to least-developed country members to the WTO under a compulsory license. Members that have not yet ratified this will continue to benefit from paragraph 6 of the Doha Declaration, which reads:

> 'We recognize that WTO members with insufficient or no manufacturing capacities in the pharmaceutical sector could face difficulties in making effective use of compulsory licensing under the TRIPS Agreement. We instruct the Council for TRIPS to find an expeditious solution to this problem and to report to the General Council before the end of 2002.'

54. G. Velasquez and P. Boulet, *Globalization and Access to Drugs: Perspectives on the WTO/TRIPS Agreement* (WHO, Geneva, 1998).
55. https://www.wto.org/english/thewto_e/minist_e/min01_e/mindecl_trips_e.htm.
56. *See* WTO TRIPS Council 'Notification Under Paragraph 2(c) of the Decision of 30 August 2003 on the Implementation of Paragraph 6 of the Doha Declaration on the TRIPS Agreement and Public Health – Canada' (2007) WTO Doc. No. IP/N/10/CAN/1, available at: https://www.wto.org/english/news_e/news07_e/canada_notification_oct_e.doc.

Many developed countries have indicated that they would be willing to allow production of essential medication for least developed countries (LDCs).[57] It remains questionable whether these systems will be useful at all if there are already generics available on the world market. It is after all much more cost-effective to allow for the importation of existing generics, than to scramble to set up a production line for them.[58] In fact, even in case of developed nations wishing to issue a compulsory licence, this will usually concern drugs that are available at lower cost elsewhere.[59]

A closely related issue of contention is the reading of Article 39(3) TRIPS on the protection of confidential information, raising the issue of the nature of protection of marketing approval information supplied to regulatory authorities. In essence, this is clinical trial test data submitted to regulatory authorities to obtain marketing authorisation for pharmaceutical products or self-propagating plant-genetic material. This so-called data exclusivity, when treated as a right of intellectual property implies that third parties wishing to enter the market upon patent expiry are faced with the hurdle that they must replicate all efforts that the originator faced when generating and submitting the data. One can argue that this replication is either a form of reducing asymmetric market failure so that the costs of market entry are also evened,[60] or a waste of resources and an unnecessary hold-up leading to an artificial extension of the patent monopoly.[61] It has been argued[62] that the grant of a compulsory licence should be accompanied by an obligation of the patentee/registration holder of the marketing approval to give consent to the use of data necessary for the registration

57. For this purpose the EU has adopted Regulation (EC) No. 816/2006 of the European Parliament and of the Council of 17 May 2006 on compulsory licensing of patents relating to the manufacture of pharmaceutical products for export to countries with public health problems, ELI: https://data.europa.eu/eli/reg/2006/816/oj This Regulation allows pharmaceutical manufacturers operating on EU territory to respond positively to a request from a country outside the EU to produce a medicine for them even if it is patented in the country of production. This system has so far not been used.
58. *See*, for example Médecins Sans Frontières Canada, *Neither Expeditious, Nor a Solution: The WTO August 30th Decision is Unworkable* (Toronto, MSF Canada, 2006), available at https://msfaccess.org/neither-expeditious-nor-solution-wto-august-30th-decision-unworkable.
59. *See* for example the Permit of 18 March 2020 (22nd of Adar, 5780) to the Israeli State to Exploit an Invention Pursuant to Chapter Six, Article Three of the Israel Patents Law 5727-1967 for the importation of Kaletra (lopinavir 200mg/ritonavir 50mg) for the sole purpose of medicinal treatment of covid-19 patients. *See* https://www.keionline.org/32503 for a copy and translation of this permit.
60. This is the reading in most developed countries, and thus part of their international trade and investment arrangements. *See* M. Pugatch, *Intellectual Property and Pharmaceutical Data Exclusivity in the Context of Innovation and Market Access* (International Centre for Trade and Sustainable Development, 2004); and M. Pugatch 'Intellectual Property, Data Exclusivity, Innovation, and Market Access', in P. Roffe, G. Tansey, and D. Vivas-Eugui (eds.), *Negotiating Health: Intellectual Property and Access to Medicines*, (Earthscan, London, 2006), 97-132.
61. C. Correa, *Protection of Data Submitted for the Registration of Pharmaceuticals: Implementing the Standards of the TRIPS Agreement* (South Centre, 2002), online: https://www.who.int/medicines/areas/policy/protection_of_data.pdf.
62. V. Junod, 'Legal Analysis: The Interface Between Patent Protection and Data Exclusivity - The Issue of Compulsory licensing in the Public Interest under Swiss Law', *Public Eye*, 29 January 2019, available at https://www.publiceye.ch/fileadmin/doc/Medikamente/ValerieJunod_Legal-Analysis-CL_20190129.pdf.

of the generic product marketed under a compulsory licence.[63] Refusal to grant such a waiver would mean that the registration holder is abusing its dominant market position which ought to lead to intervention by the competent competition authority. This is, however, not a solution that has been tested.[64]

The SARS-CoV-2 (COVID-19) pandemic has raised the issue of access to pharmaceuticals once more, and there has been a call for a general patent waiver for the production of vaccines.[65] At present, the issue of TRIPS flexibilities has to be viewed not only in light of the Doha Declaration itself, but also by taking into consideration several UN resolutions including from the Human Rights Council, the World Health Assembly, the UN Millennium Development Goals, the WHO Global Strategy and Plan of Action on Public Health, Innovation and Intellectual Property,[66] and the UN Sustainable Development Goals 2015.[67] Pertinent in this light are the 'Human Rights Guidelines for Pharmaceutical Companies in relation to Access to Medicines' describing the human rights responsibilities of the pharmaceutical industry. Regarding 'TRIPS flexibilities' such as compulsory licences, this responsibility is formulated as follows:

> 'The company should respect the letter and spirit of the Doha Declaration on the TRIPS Agreement and Public Health (2001) that recognizes a State's right to protect public health and promote access to medicines for all ...The company should not impede those States that wish to implement the World Trade Organization Decision on Implementation of paragraph 6 of the Doha Declaration on the TRIPS Agreement and Public Health (2003) by issuing compulsory licences

63. D. Gervais, 'The Patent Option', 20 *North Carolina Journal of Law and Technology* (2019), 357–403, available online at SSRN: https://ssrn.com/abstract=3266580.
64. *See* in fact a failed attempt at legislative action in Switzerland: https://www.parlament.ch/en/ratsbetrieb/amtliches-bulletin/amtliches-bulletin-die-verhandlungen?SubjectId=47410.
65. Waiver from Certain Provisions of the TRIPS Agreement for the Prevention, Containment and Treatment of Covid-19. Communication from India and South Africa, 2 Oct 2020 (IP/C/W/669); and the revised proposal for a waiver from certain provisions of the TRIPS Agreement. Communication by the African Group, the Plurinational State of Bolivia, Egypt, Eswatini, Fiji, India, Indonesia, Kenya, the LDC Group, Maldives, Mozambique, Mongolia, Namibia, Pakistan, South Africa, Vanuatu, the Bolivian Republic of Venezuela, and Zimbabwe, 25 May 2021 (IP/C/W/669/Rev1), available at https://docs.wto.org/dol2fe/Pages/SS/directdoc.aspx?filename=q:/IP/C/W669R1.pdf&Open=True.
66. *See* the ambitions of the trilateral cooperation in the joint WTO, WIPO, and WHO report *Promoting Access to Medical Technologies and Innovation. Intersections between public health, intellectual property and trade.* (WTO, WIPO, WHO, Geneva, 2012). https://www.wto.org/english/res_e/booksp_e/pamtiwhowipowtoweb13_e.pdf.
67. Goal 3.8: Achieve universal health coverage, including financial risk protection, access to quality essential health-care services and access to safe, effective, quality and affordable essential medicines and vaccines for all. Goal 3.B: Support the research and development of vaccines and medicines for the communicable and non-communicable diseases that primarily affect developing countries, provide access to affordable essential medicines and vaccines, in accordance with the Doha Declaration on the TRIPS Agreement and Public Health, which affirms the right of developing countries to use to the full the provisions in the Agreement on Trade-Related Aspects of Intellectual Property Rights regarding flexibilities to protect public health, and, in particular, provide access to medicines for all.

> for exports to those countries, without manufacturing capacity, encompassed by the Decision.'[68]

Legislative action at national level is furthermore recommended 'in a way that facilitates the prompt and expedient use of a compulsory licence or government use for non-commercial purposes of a patent, including criteria to determine the remuneration for the right holder. As the Doha Declaration notes, governments should retain the freedom to determine the grounds under which compulsory licences are issued.' After the WTO cases *EC – Asbestos*[69] and *Australia – Tobacco Plain Packaging*[70] the flexibility of WTO rules in respect of public health was affirmed, and yet the 2021 discussions on the WTO patent(s) waiver, which would amount to a temporary setting-aside of the compensatory and other regulatory provisos for compulsory licensing, have immediately brought to light the practical shortcomings of the current system. Given the fact that combating the SARS-CoV-2 pandemic requires new vaccines, patents will only become public after 18 months from filing. Once they have become public the question is whether they contain all necessary information to produce a vaccine. This means that ancillary know-how may also have to be transferred as well. And all of this in tandem with the necessary clinical test data submitted to regulatory authorities. The WTO TRIPS rules have not yet fully captured the complexity of an innovation system that is not fully trade and market-driven. To combat the SARS-CoV-2 pandemic, and future pandemics, collective investment will be required, prompting national and international discussions on walk-in rights for governments in case of publicly funded research, possibly leading to radically changed perspectives on ownership positions in public-private partnerships. If after all, the public (government) funder were to obtain ownership rights commensurate with the investment, and by law retain a corresponding say in the subsequent dealings with a downstream product in case of a public health crisis, the instrument of compulsory licensing may not be necessary. Furthermore, advance purchase agreements have proven to be an effective instrument for the offset of risks for corporate producers. These may also

---

68. The Guidelines contain the following two articles with direct reference to the Doha Declaration:

    'Par. 27: The company should respect the letter and spirit of the Doha Declaration on the TRIPS Agreement and Public Health (2001) that recognizes a State's right to protect public health and promote access to medicines for all.

    Par. 28: The company should not impede those States that wish to implement the World Trade Organization Decision on Implementation of paragraph 6 of the Doha Declaration on the TRIPS Agreement and Public Health (2003) by issuing compulsory licences for exports to those countries, without manufacturing capacity, encompassed by the Decision.'

    See https://www.who.int/medicines/areas/human_rights/A63_263.pdf and https://www.who.int/medicines/areas/human_rights/A63_263.pdf.
69. WT/DS135/AB *European Communities — Measures Affecting Asbestos and Products Containing Asbestos* (adopted on 5 April 2001).
70. WT/DS435/R, WT/DS411/R, WT/DS458/R, and WT/DS467/R, bundled as WT/DS467/23 Australia - Certain Measures Concerning Trademarks, Geographical Indications and Other Plain Packaging Requirements Applicable to Tobacco Products and Packaging - Report of the Panels (adopted on 30 August 2018). On the case *see* W. Meier-Ewert, 'The WTO Disputes Regarding Tobacco Plain Packaging: Selected TRIPS Findings from the Panel Stage', in C. Heath and A. Kamperman Sanders (eds.), *Intellectual Property and International Dispute Resolution* (Kluwer Law International, 2019), 211–44.

be accompanied by much stronger entitlements to compel licensing in case rapid upscaling of production is required.

At the WTO, however, the submissions by India and South Africa to the TRIPS Council in 2020 and subsequent revisions in 2021 on proposals for a waiver from certain provisions of the TRIPS Agreement[71] demonstrate that the response to COVID-19 is not a matter for which consensus can be found quickly. Rather, the communication from the European Union on urgent trade policy responses to the pandemic[72] suggests that, although everyone wants to be seen to support global relief efforts, equitable access to vaccines and other medical products does not happen overnight. This because the compulsory licensing mechanisms turn out to be a rather blunt and one-sided instrument that do not address a highly complex problem of increasing actual production and distribution. The complexity is not only due to the lack of clarity on the exact scope of the necessary patents subject to the waiver. Patents filed in relation to COVID-19 vaccines are after all only published 18 months from filing. Any such action must also be accompanied by a transfer of know-how that needs be absorbed by knowledgeable staff capable of operating an actual production facility. Furthermore, ancillary and coordinated action must take place in terms of the production and shipment of raw materials, vials, hypodermic needles, packaging, refrigeration, and other logistics. Furthermore, where TRIPS is concerned, the waiver measures may also have to be extended to copyright in relation to scientific works and any confidential information relevant to the endeavour of meeting current needs. Since the combat of SARS-Cov-2 in all its mutations is likely to require a long-term effort, data mining and further R&D efforts require prolonged access to test results and genomic sequencing, meaning that patented test kits and equipment may also be caught in the ambit of the waiver initially proposed by India and South Africa. Furthermore, the waiver proposes to have an initial term of three years. This proposal is based on a notion that the TRIPS Agreement must be read in context of obligation of WTO members to meet wider public interests in terms of human rights, healthcare, and sustainable development.

The EU's Communication is much narrower in scope, and focuses on the formalities related to compulsory licensing, namely a temporary reprieve from the requirement to negotiate with the rightholder, the method of setting an adequate remuneration for the rightholder once a compulsory licence is granted, and the procedural requirements for notification of the measure to the TRIPS Council under Article 31*bis* and the Annex to the TRIPS Agreement. It will not be easy to reconcile the positions, as the EU, while arguing that there are sufficient flexibilities within the TRIPS Agreement, seeks at most to clarify the meaning and application of existing provisions within the narrow confines of established principles of trade.

Within the WTO, the Development Agenda, being the Doha Round of trade negotiations with the aim of improving the trading prospects of developing countries, was launched in November 2001 and is the way in which the WTO membership can move forward with a focus on special and differential treatment. So far there

71. *Supra* note 65.
72. Communication of the European Union, *Urgent Trade Policy Responses to the COVID-19 Crisis: Intellectual Property*, 4 June 2021 (IP/C/W/680), available at https://docs.wto.org/dol2fe/Pages/SS/directdoc.aspx?filename=q:/IP/C/W680.pdf&Open=True.

has not been a breakthrough in negotiations, and the current deadlock resulting from the United States' refusal to agree to new AB members - a means to address concerns whether AB panellists have interpreted agreements too expansively; have issued opinions on issues not relevant to the case on appeal; the timeliness of AB proceedings, treatment of AB decisions as precedents, and whether AB jurists should be able to finish cases after their terms have expired - is described in greater detail elsewhere in this volume.[73] Apart from a failure to arrive at a single undertaking that all parties can agree to, the current conflict is also the result of a long-standing difference of view on the openness of the WTO system to other norms of international law. From time to time there are attempts to establish clear linkages, such as was the case between the TRIPS Agreement and the CBD concerning sovereignty over biological resources.[74] So far this has merely resulted in an observer status of the CBD at the WTO.[75]

D. WTO LAW SELF-CONTAINED AND CLOSED OR OPEN?

In the section above, it has been argued that intellectual property law, including the TRIPS Agreement, serves a public interest by stimulating innovation and the creative arts. In this context intellectual property does not exist in a vacuum and is subject to interpretation, both when it comes to its strengthened application (think for example of criminal enforcement in cases of economic crime[76]), but also to limitations or application in the context of issues of public health and wider interests of social and economic development, as expressed in Articles 7 and 8 of the TRIPS Agreement. Together with the importation by reference of the Paris Convention, and the non-derogation from obligations under the Berne Convention, Rome Convention and the Treaty on Intellectual Property in Respect of Integrated Circuits,[77] this implies an opening of the WTO law and jurisprudence to outside norms. The current stand-off in terms of reform of the WTO system, however, shows that the United States is not keen on open norms.[78]

What is clear is that the WTO's organisational dealings are limited to the 'conduct of trade relations among Members',[79] and that the competence of the WTO panels, the AB and DSB is limited to disputes brought pursuant to the consultation

73. *See* the contributions by J. Pohl, 'To the End of History and Back Again: A Critical Look at the Political Promise of TRIPS'; and P. Van den Bossche, 'The TRIPS Agreement and WTO Dispute Settlement: Past, Present and Future' to this volume.
74. WTO, 'Draft Decision to enhance mutual supportiveness between the TRIPS Agreement and the Convention on Biological Diversity', Communication from Brazil, China, Colombia, Ecuador, India, Indonesia, Peru, Thailand, the ACP Group, and the African Group, TN/C/W/59 (19 April 2011).
75. *See* https://www.cbd.int/incentives/coop-wto.shtml.
76. In this context *see* for example G. Urbas, 'Criminal Enforcement of Intellectual Property Rights: Interaction Between Public Authorities and Private Interests', in C. Heath and A. Kamperman Sanders (eds.), *New Frontiers of Intellectual Property Law* (Hart Publishing, 2005), 303-22.
77. *See* Article 2(1) and (2) TRIPS.
78. *See* the contributions by J. Pohl, 'To the End of History and Back Again: A Critical Look at the Political Promise of TRIPS'; and P. Van den Bossche, 'The TRIPS Agreement and WTO Dispute Settlement: Past, Present and Future' to this volume.
79. Article II, Marrakesh Agreement.

and dispute settlement provisions of the WTO covered agreements.[80] This means that the only jurisdiction a WTO panel has is to decide whether a WTO treaty obligation has been violated.

The question is therefore to what extent non-trade concerns, as well as rules and principles that WTO members have agreed to or are bound by in addition to their WTO obligations, can provide a defence to WTO claims.

In academic terms, the discussion on open norms is best captured by the debate between Professors Steger and Trachtman on the one side, and Professor Pauwelyn on the other.[81]

Steger and Trachtman argue that international law can inform the interpretation of WTO provisions, but WTO panels can never apply anything but the WTO-covered agreements. This includes any defences that can be raised in relation to a WTO claim,[82] and so all need to be limited to provisions in the WTO agreements themselves. Pauwelyn on the other hand argues[83] that general international law can be applied in cases where the WTO treaties are silent (rules on the burden of proof, private counsel, non-retroactivity, error in treaty formulation, etc.), and where international law is invoked as a defence of a claim of a WTO violation. Steger points to the risk that in doing so, the panels, the AB and DSB risk violating Articles 3(2), 7(1) and 19(2) of the DSU where this results in the extension or diminution of the 'rights and obligations provided in the covered agreements'. Inconsistencies between rules in other international agreements should, according to Steger, therefore, be resolved by

---

80. Dispute Settlement Understanding (DSU) Article 1.1, with the agreements listed in Appendix 1 stating:

    Agreements Covered by the Understanding

    (A) Agreement Establishing the World Trade Organization

    (B) Multilateral Trade Agreements

    Annex 1A: Multilateral Agreements on Trade in Goods
    Annex 1B: General Agreement on Trade in Services
    Annex 1C: Agreement on Trade-Related Aspects of Intellectual Property Rights
    Annex 2: Understanding on Rules and Procedures Governing the Settlement of Disputes

    (C) Plurilateral Trade Agreements

    Annex 4: Agreement on Trade in Civil Aircraft
    Agreement on Government Procurement
    International Dairy Agreement
    International Bovine Meat Agreement

    The applicability of this Understanding to the Plurilateral Trade Agreements shall be subject to the adoption of a decision by the parties to each agreement setting out the terms for the application of the Understanding to the individual agreement, including any special or additional rules or procedures for inclusion in Appendix 2, as notified to the DSB.

81. J. Pauwelyn, J. Trachtman, and D. Steger, 'The Jurisdiction of the WTO is Limited to Trade', 98 *Proceedings of the Annual Meeting (American Society of International Law)* (31 March – 3 April 2004), 135–46, available at https://www.jstor.org/stable/25659908.
82. *Ibid.*, at 139.
83. J. Pauwelyn, *Conflict of Norms in Public International Law: How WTO Law Relates to Other Rules of International Law* (Cambridge University Press, 2003), 478–86, and 'Interplay Between the WTO Treaty and Other International Legal Instruments and Tribunals: Evolution After 20 Years of WTO Jurisprudence', in C. Côté, V. Guèvremont, R. Ouellet (eds.) *Proceedings of the Québec City Conference on the WTO at 20* (Presses de l'Université de Laval, 2018), available at SSRN: https://ssrn.com/abstract=2731144 or https://dx.doi.org/10.2139/ssrn.2731144.

negotiation among the members of the WTO.[84] Practice and reality, however, show that Pauwelyn's view is prevalent,[85] if sometimes only tacitly[86] so.[87]

Former WTO Director-General Pascal Lamy[88] has stated that the WTO is part of the international legal order as a *sui generis* system of trade law, but also that 'the WTO, far from being hegemonic, as it is sometimes portrayed to be, recognises its limited competence and the specialisation of other international organisations. In this sense the WTO participates in the construction of international coherence and reinforces the international legal order.'[89] He further points to the first WTO dispute, an environment-related dispute (*US – Gasoline*),[90] where the Appellate Body articulated an important principle of WTO law, namely that 'the GATT is not to be read in clinical isolation from public international law' and has to be read according to the customary principles of interpretation of public international law.[91] This means that the standard principles of the Vienna Convention on the Law of Treaties, and specifically its Article 31, must be used in that the terms of treaties are to be given 'their ordinary meaning, in their context and in the light of the Treaty's object and purpose'. In this interpretation, Lamy also notes that: 'The WTO, its treaty provisions and their interpretation, confirms the absence of any hierarchy between WTO norms and those norms developed in other forums: WTO norms do not supersede or trump other international norms.'[92]

Pauwelyn states in his book on *Conflict of Norms in Public International Law*:[93]

> 'In the event of conflict involving WTO provisions, WTO provisions may not always prevail, including before a WTO panel. The Trade obligations in the WTO treaty are of the "reciprocal type". They are not of an "integral nature" Hence, WTO provisions can be deviated from as between a limited number of WTO members only, as long as this deviation does not breach third party rights. Affecting the economic interests of other WTO members does not amount to breaching their WTO rights.'

84. Pauwelyn et al., *supra* note 81, at 144–46.
85. J. Pauwelyn, 'How to Win a WTO Dispute Based on Non-WTO Law? Questions of Jurisdiction and Merits', 37 *Journal of World Trade* (2003), 997–1030, available at SSRN: https://ssrn.com/abstract=478021.
86. G. Shaffer, 'The New Legal Realist Approach to International Law', 28 *Leiden Journal of International Law* (2015), 189–210, available at DOI: https://doi.org/10.1017/S0922156515000035.
87. *See* the Panel Report, *EC — Approval and Marketing of Biotech Products*, WT/DS291 (adopted on 21 November 2006), which references to the Cartagena Protocol to the Convention on Biodiversity and the precautionary principle contained therein. *See* G. Shaffer and M. Pollack, 'A Structural Theory of WTO Dispute Settlement: Why Institutional Choice Lies at the Center of the WTO Case', 41 *NYU Journal of International Law and Politics* (2008), 1–101, available at SSRN: https://ssrn.com/abstract=1090293.
88. P. Lamy, 'The Place of the WTO and Its Law in the International Legal Order', 17 *European Journal of International Law* (2006), 968–84, available at https://doi.org/10.1093/ejil/chl035.
89. *Ibid.* at 977.
90. *US – Gasoline* (1996); Appellate Body Report, *United States – Standards for Reformulated and Conventional Gasoline*, WT/DS2/AB/R, Adopted 20 May 1996.
91. Article 3.2 of the DSU also instructs panels and the AB to do so.
92. Lamy, *supra* note 88, at 978.
93. Pauwelyn, *Conflict of Norms*, *supra* note 83, at 491.

This indeed means that in case of a conflict, human rights treaties, climate accords, or other international norms on labour standards may prevail over WTO law. It is only that WTO panels cannot enforce compliance with these specific non-WTO norms, nor can a claim be based upon them.[94] They can, however, form a source of applicable law and a valid defence against claims of infringement of WTO norms.[95]

In *Mexico – Corn Syrup* (2001), an anti-dumping case, the AB considers the extent to which external factors need to be assessed, while citing the case *United States – 1916 Act*:[96]

> 'First, as a matter of due process, and the proper exercise of the judicial function, panels are required to address issues that are put before them by the parties to a dispute. Second, panels have to address and dispose of certain issues of a fundamental nature, even if the parties to the dispute remain silent on those issues. In this regard, we have previously observed that "[t]he vesting of jurisdiction in a panel is a fundamental prerequisite for lawful panel proceedings." For this reason, panels cannot simply ignore issues which go to the root of their jurisdiction – that is, to their authority to deal with and dispose of matters. Rather, panels must deal with such issues – if necessary, on their own motion – in order to satisfy themselves that they have authority to proceed.'[97]

In other words, Pauwelyn's views may be controversial, but they sufficiently persuasive and cannot be dismissed outright. As Lamy himself noted: 'The effectiveness and legitimacy of the WTO depend on how it relates to norms of other legal systems and on the nature and quality of its relationships with other international organizations.'[98]

Historically, intellectual property law has not been merely a trade issue. Rather, it serves to promote human intellectual and industrial creativity and recognises both individual and societal interests. At the inception of the modern patent system, the 1623 English Statute of Monopolies clearly frames any letters patent as a privilege that should be: 'not contrary to the law, nor mischievous to the State, by raising prices of commodities at home, or hurt of trade, or generally inconvenient'.[99]

---

94. *See* in this respect Appellate Body Report *Mexico — Tax Measures on Soft Drinks and Other Beverages*, WT/DS308/AB/R (adopted 24 March 2006); *Mexico – Soft Drinks (2006)* para. 56: 'We see no basis in the DSU for panels and the Appellate Body to adjudicate non-WTO disputes. Article 3.2 of the DSU states that the WTO dispute settlement system "serves to preserve the rights and obligations of Members under the covered agreements, and to clarify the existing provisions of *those agreements*"'.
95. Note that J. Pauwelyn's own position reflects this point of view, *supra* note 83, at 491. Conversely, *see* G. Marceau, 'Conflicts of Norms and Conflicts of Jurisdiction: The Relationship Between the WTO Agreement and MEA's and Other Treaties', 35 *Journal of World Trade* (2001), 1081–131.
96. Appellate Body Report, *United States – Anti-dumping Act of 1916*, WT/DS136/AB/R, WT/DS162/AB/R, (adopted 26 September 2000).
97. Appellate Body Report, *Mexico – Anti-Dumping Investigation of High Fructose Corn Syrup (HFCS) from the United States*, WT/DS132/AB/RW (adopted 21 November 2001): *Mexico – Corn Syrup (2001)*, para 36.
98. Lamy, *supra* note 88, at 977.
99. *See supra* note 10.

I. Intellectual Property Rights Covered

In respect of intellectual property, the 'openness' of the TRIPS Agreement itself equally allows for a more expansive reliance on outside norms. This works both for claims and defences; through importation by reference of *inter alia* Berne and Paris Convention norms, claims for breach of WTO norms can be enlarged, but the available defences are also supplemented by non-WTO norms. Article 1(2) TRIPS provides: 'For the purposes of this Agreement, the term 'intellectual property' refers to all categories of intellectual property that are the subject of Sections 1 to 7 of Part II.' These are: 1) copyright and related rights; 2) trade marks; 3) geographical indications; 4) industrial designs; 5) patents; 6) layout designs (topographies) of integrated circuits; and 7) undisclosed information. Through the importation by reference, however, trade names are included as well through Article 8 of the Paris Convention,[100] as are alternative forms of IP protection. In *US – Section 211 Appropriations Act* (2002), the AB, in overruling the Panel, affirmed that such alternatives would be covered by the TRIPS Agreement:

> 'The subject of Sections 1 through 7 of Part II deals not only with the categories of intellectual property indicated in each section title, but with other subjects as well. For example, in Section 5 of Part II entitled "Patents", Article 27(3)(b) provides that Members have the option of protecting inventions of plant variety rights by sui generis rights (such as breeder's rights) instead of through patents. Under the Panel's theory, such sui generis rights would not be covered by the TRIPS Agreement. The option provided in Article 27(3)(b) would be read out of the TRIPS Agreement.'[101]

The Paris Convention also mentions the utility models as objects of protection,[102] but these only feature in the context of priority.[103] Similarly, repression of unfair competition[104] is covered, albeit that the subject matter is expressed through a general clause worded: 'Any act of competition contrary to honest practices in industrial or commercial matters constitutes an act of unfair competition', and a non-exhaustive list of prohibited acts.[105] The TRIPS Agreement does not set minimum standards in this respect,[106] and so only the basic principles of national treatment and most-favoured-nation treatment (MFN) can arguably be the bone of contention in a TRIPS claim. It is therefore conceivable that in case principles of national treatment or MFN are not observed in the context of the treatment of domain name disputes,[107] that this could give rise to a TRIPS complaint, because this is subject matter that can very

100. Art. 8 Paris Convention: 'A trade name shall be protected in all countries of the Union without the obligation of filing or registration, whether or not it forms part of a trademark.'
101. Appellate Body Report, *United States – Section 211 Omnibus Appropriations Act of 1998*, WT/DS176/AB/R (adopted 1 February 2002), at para. 335.
102. Article 1(2) Paris Convention.
103. Article 4 Paris Convention.
104. Articles 1(2) and 10*bis* Paris Convention.
105. Article 10*bis*(3) Paris Convention.
106. Panel Report, *Indonesia – Certain Measures Affecting the Automobile Industry*, WT/DS54/R, WT/DS55R, WT/DS59/R, and WT/DS64/R (adopted 23 July 1998), para. 14.275.
107. *See* similarly the recognition of domain names as IP subject matter, and thus as property, albeit subject to limitations, ECtHR 18 September 2007 *Paeffgen. GMBH v. Germany*, n. 25379/04,

well be brought within the realm of repression of unfair competition – the creation of the risk of confusion – and therefore be trade-related. In this context, the pre-WTO GATT jurisprudence[108] is leading, rather than the body of national interpretation and application of the principle of national treatment under the pre-existing intellectual property regimes.[109] In the first case on the matter, *US – Section 211 Appropriations Act (2002)*, the AB noted that the principle of national treatment had been the cornerstone of the Paris Convention and other international intellectual property conventions, but that the language of TRIPS Article 3(1) is similar to that of Article III(4) of GATT 1994, and that therefore the case law concerning Article III(4) of the GATT 1994 'may be useful in interpreting the national treatment obligation in the TRIPS Agreement'.[110]

Likewise, in *EC – Trademarks and Geographical Indications (US)* (2005),[111] the panel pointed out that Article 3 TRIPS prohibits not only measures that *de iure* discriminate between the nationals of a WTO Member and foreign nationals, but also *de facto* discriminatory measures. The question was whether requirements for non-EU nationals wishing to register a geographical indication under EC law to demonstrate the certification of an equivalent of geographical indication protection outside of the European Union were TRIPS-compliant. The US argued:

> '[J]urisprudence on Article III:4 of GATT 1994 offers useful guidance on the interpretation of article 3:1 of the TRIPS Agreement. The broad and fundamental purpose of Article III is to avoid protectionism in the application of tax and regulatory measures. This is easily extrapolated to the TRIPS Agreement in which the national treatment obligation is intended to avoid protectionism with respect to the protection of intellectual property rights.'[112]

The only caveat put in place is that:

> '[t]he scope of the national treatment obligation in Article 3.1 of the TRIPS Agreement also differs from that of the national treatment obligation in Article III:4 of GATT 1994, as it is subject to certain exceptions in Articles 3.1, 3.2 and 5, one of which is inspired by the language of Article XX of GATT 1994.'[113]

The difference is expressed in that the exceptions provided for in the pre-existing IP treaties, sometimes allowing for reciprocity, are imported by reference, which

CE:ECHR:2007:0918DEC 002537904, with case comment by A. Kamperman Sanders, 1 *European Human Rights Cases* 16-01-2008, No.17, pp. 156–61.

108. *See* P. Van den Bossche and W. Zdouc, *The Law and Policy of the World Trade Organization* (3rd edn., Cambridge University Press, Cambridge, 2013), 962–68.
109. For concurrence of GATT and TRIPS, *see* C. Heath, 'The Most Favoured-Nation Treatment and Intellectual Property Rights', in C. Heath and A. Kamperman Sanders, *Intellectual Property and Free Trade Agreements* (Hart, 2007), 127–56 at 127.
110. *US – Section 211 Appropriations Act* (2002), *supra* note 101, para. 242.
111. Panel Report, *European Communities – Protection of Trademarks and Geographical Indications for Agricultural Products and Foodstuffs, Complaint by the United States,* WT/DS174/R (adopted 20 April 2005).
112. *Ibid.*, para. 7.107.
113. *Ibid.* paras 7.221 and 7.247.

also makes TRIPS a *lex specialis* in the wider sphere of WTO law.[114] Once more this demonstrates that in case of defences there is more openness to outside norms in WTO adjudication, even though they are often rooted in exceptions provided for by IP treaties that are pre-existing.

Matters are, however, not always so clear cut, as in the reliance on GATT jurisprudence in *Canada – Pharmaceutical Patents*,[115] to define 'discrimination' in the context of Article 27 TRIPS to limit the freedom of Members to provide for exceptions to patentability provided for under Article 30 TRIPS.[116]

Less clear is the status of *sui generis* legislation that primarily addresses market failures in relation to achievements of sweat of the brow, such as the EU's Database Directive,[117] which operates based on reciprocity. This is generally held not to be subject matter that falls within the scope of Articles 3 and 4, and footnote 3 of the TRIPS Agreement that limits its application of national treatment and MFN obligations to 'use of intellectual property rights specifically addressed in this agreement'.

II. Defences

Where interpretation on the scope of rights covered is concerned, including possible defences to a TRIPS dispute, domestic legislation as well as international obligations should be taken into consideration in a WTO dispute settlement. An example can be found in the way in which the application of the law against unfair competition has been used to suppress speech. In the case of *Hertel v. Switzerland*[118] the European Court of Human Rights (ECtHR)[119] upheld the application of provisions of unfair competition law outside of a traditional competitive relationship setting. The ECtHR also sought to define the limits to the application of the law against unfair competition in articulating the proportionality test to be applied considering Article 10 of

114. S. Frankel, 'The Applicability of GATT Jurisprudence to the Interpretation of the TRIPS Agreement', in C. Correa (ed.), *Research Handbook on the Interpretation and Enforcement of Intellectual Property under WTO Rules* (Edward Elgar, Cheltenham, 2010), Vol. II at 3.

115. Panel Report, *Canada – Patent Protection of Pharmaceutical Products*, WT/DS/114/R (adopted 7 April 2000) at para. 7.98:
'In considering how to address these conflicting claims of discrimination, the Panel recalled that various claims of discrimination, de jure and de facto, have been subject of legal rulings under GATT or the WTO. These rulings have addressed the question whether measures were in conflict with various GATT or WTO provisions prohibiting variously defined forms of discrimination. As the Appellate Body has repeatedly made clear, each of these rulings has necessarily been based on the precise legal text in issue, so that it is not possible to treat them as applications of a general concept of discrimination.'

116. *See* G. Dinwoodie and R. Dreyfuss, 'Diversifying without Discrimination: Complying with the Mandate of the TRIPS Agreement', 13 *Michigan Telecommunications and Technology Law Review* (2007), 445–56, at 450: 'Under a normal meaning of the term 'discrimination' treating different cases differently is not discrimination'. Available at SSRN: https://ssrn.com/abstract = 1001264.

117. Directive 96/9/EC of the European Parliament and of the Council of 11 March 1996 on the legal protection of databases, which in Article 11 contains a reciprocity clause.

118. ECtHR 25 August 1998 *Hertel v. Switzerland*, no. 59/1997/843/1049, available at https://hudoc.echr.coe.int/ENG?i = 001-59366.

119. For a more detailed overview *see* A. Peukert, 'The Fundamental Right to (Intellectual) Property and the Discretion of the Legislature', in C. Geiger (ed.), *Research Handbook on Human Rights and Intellectual Property* (Edward Elgar, 2016), 132–48.

the Convention for the Protection of Human Rights and Fundamental Freedoms,[120] recognising the state's wide margin of discretion in such matters.[121] Such a wide margin of appreciation on the imposition of limits to the application and enjoyment of IPRs due to human rights obligations[122] is then also a sound principle when it comes to the adjudication of TRIPS disputes, provided that the WTO members to the dispute are bound by such norms.[123]

E. PROLIFERATION OF BILATERAL AND FTA ARRANGEMENTS

Away from the multilateral framework, bilateral agreements have always been concluded between nations wishing to regulate their trade relationships. The EU, NAFTA, Mercosur, Trans-Pacific Partnership (TPP, a.k.a. Comprehensive and Progressive Agreement for Trans-Pacific Partnership, CPTPP), CETA, etc. all have the objective to eliminate or reduce tariffs and liberalise trade.

Liberalising trade has been the cornerstone of globalisation, and many nations have tried to cement their trade relations in trade agreements, many of which contain provisions on intellectual property. These provisions display the national and domestic interests of industries based in the dominant users of these agreements. The USA and the EU in particular, two of the most IP-sensitive traders, have specific interests represented in their trade deals. They have concluded many agreements with various trade partners. In terms of IPRs, both entities place emphasis on enforcement, but the USA's focus has been on copyright (DMCA) and high-tech, whereas the EU's focus has been on pharma and geographical indications of origin.

Apart from the application of international norms, the question can be raised as to whether the bilateral relations between the WTO members that are party to a dispute should play a role in the adjudication of disputes.

---

120. The ECtHR was called upon multiple times to carry out such an exercise in relation to intellectual property in the following cases: ECtHR 26 May 2005, *Dima v. Romania*, no. 58472/00, CE:ECHR:2005:0526DEC005847200; ECtHR 11 January 2007 *Anheuser-Busch Inc. v. Portugal*, no. 73049/01, CE:ECHR:2007:0111JUD007304901, with a case comment by A. Kamperman Sanders, 44(4) *European Human Rights Cases* (2007), 421–37.
121. For a full description of the case and its implications *see* A. Kamperman Sanders, 'Unfair Competition Law and the European Court of Human Rights – The Case of Hertel v. Switzerland and Beyond', 10 *Fordham Intellectual Property and Entertainment Law Journal* (1999), 295–319.
122. *See* the number of copyright cases on the boundaries of the freedom of expression in: Council of Europe, *Freedom of expression in Europe Case-law concerning Article 10 of the European Convention on Human Rights* (2007 Council of Europe), available at https://www.echr.coe.int/librarydocs/dg2/hrfiles/dg2-en-hrfiles-18(2007).pdf. For a further overview *see* C. Geiger and E. Izyumenko, 'Shaping Intellectual Property Rights Through Human Rights Adjudication: The Example of the European Court of Human Rights', 46 *Mitchell Hamline Law Review* (2020), 527–612, available at https://open.mitchellhamline.edu/mhlr/vol46/iss3/3.
123. *See* H. Wager and J. Watal, 'Human Rights and International Intellectual Property Law', in C. Geiger (ed.), *Research Handbook on Human Rights and Intellectual Property* (Edward Elgar, 2016), 149–72.

I. TRIPS-Plus Obligations

Not content with progress within the WTO Doha round, many nations pursued bilateral agreements containing TRIPS-Plus provisions.[124]

TRIPS-Plus obligations can be qualified as follows: 1) a reinforcement of certain interpretations or readings of TRIPS provisions; 2) the inclusion of subject matter not included in the TRIPS Agreement (Most notably the WCT and WPPT and national expressions thereof, such as the Digital Millennium Copyright Act);[125] and 3) imposing specific policy choices, such as national exhaustion on counterparties. The USA, as the most dominant user of bilateral trade agreements, has imposed the principle of national exhaustion on trade partners. The US Supreme Court has, however, overturned its national system of national exhaustion in two recent cases,[126] raising the question as to whether bilateral trade partners, like Singapore, can now return to their previously held policy, meaning before the US-Singapore FTA, of international exhaustion.

An even more far-flung initiative was the (failed) IP-specific Anti-Counterfeiting Trade Agreement (ACTA).[127] The ACTA negotiations were concluded, after 11 rounds, in October 2010 in Tokyo. On 1 October 2011, Australia, Canada, Japan, Morocco, New Zealand, South Korea, Singapore and the United States signed the agreement during a ceremony in Tokyo. The member states of the European Union, as well as Switzerland and Mexico, were represented at the ceremony but did not sign. Ultimately the secrecy surrounding the negotiation process[128] did not result in a positive public perception of the treaty. Upon the release of the official text, there was pressure to stop the negotiations as late as 2010,[129] with many European MPs asking critical questions: (i) when would the Commission make all negotiating documents public; (ii) whether the chairperson and coordinators of the INTA committee had access to the negotiating documents; (iii) why a secretive forum was chosen rather than a more transparent multilateral venue such as WIPO; and (iv) why was there an apparent mismatch between access to ACTA documents by industry lobby groups and lack of access by parliamentarians and public interest organisations.[130] In Mexico,

124. C. Heath and A. Kamperman Sanders (eds.), *Intellectual Property and Free Trade Agreements* (Hart Publishing, 2007).
125. *See* Chang-Fa Lo, *WTO-Plus in Free Trade Agreements*, Asian Center for WTO and International Health Law and Policy Book Series Vol. 2 (Angle Publishing, 2010).
126. *Kirtsaeng v. Wiley*, 568 U.S. 519, 133 S. Ct. 1351 (2013) - Copyright; and *Impression Products, Inc. v. Lexmark International, Inc.*, 581 U.S. ___ (2017) - Patents.
127. *See* A. Kamperman Sanders, 'The EU and its IP policies: ACTA and third countries', in P. Roffe and X. Seuba (eds.), *The ACTA and the plurilateral enforcement agenda Genesis and Aftermath* (Cambridge University Press, 2015), 259–72.
128. *See* the leaked documents online: www.keionline.org/acta.
129. *See* 'Lawmakers call for halt to ACTA deal', 5 October 2010, online: www.euractiv.com/en/infosociety/lawmakers-call-halt-acta-deal-news-498442.
130. Ad 1): Written Question E-2079/10 by Morten Messerschmidt (EFD) to the Commission; Ad 2) Written Question E-0147/10 by Alexander Alvaro (ALDE) to the Commission; Ad 3) Written Question E-0147/10 by Alexander Alvaro (ALDE) to the Commission; Ad 4) Written Question E-1391/10 by Andreas Mölzer (NI) to the Commission.

similar issues[131] were raised in the Senate, resulting in a strong rejection of ACTA on 7 September 2011.[132]

On 27 January 2012, 22 EU member states (UK, Austria, Belgium, Bulgaria, Czech Republic, Denmark, Finland, France, Greece, Hungary, Ireland, Italy, Latvia, Lithuania, Luxemburg, Malta, Poland, Portugal, Romania, Slovenia, Spain, and Sweden) signed ACTA. The five remaining member states - Cyprus, Germany, Estonia, the Netherlands, and Slovakia - did not. Aside from ratification at member state level, ACTA also had to pass the European Parliament to satisfy all requirements in relation to this mixed agreement. In the run-up to ratification, ACTA was hotly debated. The Commission on International Trade of the European Parliament (INTA) commissioned a study[133] on ACTA's compatibility with the EU's international obligations, most notably WTO-TRIPS, and the EU *Acquis*.

ACTA was rejected by the European Parliament on 4 July 2012 by 478 votes to 39, with 165 abstentions. However, the trade of third parties with remaining ACTA states will continue to be influenced by the treaty, and so the agreement has the potential to affect the multilateral trading system and casts a negative shadow on the progress of multilateral negotiations[134] around intellectual property law. The latter point is relevant in the context of the unstated ambition of ACTA states to influence not only future multilateral negotiations, but to use the treaty as a template for regional and bilateral agreements as well. Indeed, the ACTA negotiations have been described as a 'new kind of international IP lawmaking', as the agreement places its members in plurilateral framework with strong enforcement obligations, but without matching limitations and exceptions.[135] This would have put ACTA members in a strong negotiating position with third parties where the rights of IP owners are concerned. Since ACTA does not foresee the establishment of a secretariat or permanent institutional mechanism, the implementation, future development, or accession of new members remain subject to bilateral consultations, which will remain confidential and secret until parties decide to share information with parliaments and civil society alike.

II. Bilateral Relations and WTO Disputes.

Under the DSU it is possible for parties to an FTA to waive their right as WTO Members to initiate WTO dispute settlement proceedings when they adopt an alternative option in that FTA, such as a 'mutually agreed solution' (MAS) amounting to a choice of

131. Resolution of the Mexican Senate, 5 October 2010, online: www.senado.gob.mx/index.php?ver=sp&mn=2&sm=2&id=5264&lg=61.
132. Resolution of the Mexican Senate, 6 September 2011, online: www.senado.gob.mx/sgsp/gaceta/61/3/2011-09-06-1/assets/documentos/GrupoPlural_ACTA.pdf.
133. INTA study for the European Parliament DG EXPO Policy Department, The Anti-Counterfeiting Trade Agreement (ACTA): An Assessment (European Parliament, Brussels, 2011). *See* www.europarl.europa.eu/studies. The present author has contributed to this study.
134. 'Minutes of Meeting Held in the Centre William Rappard on 26–27 October 2010' Council on Trade-related Aspects of Intellectual Property, IP/C/M/64, 17 February 2011, par 453.
135. *See* K. Weatherall, *ACTA as a New Kind of International IP Law-Making*, (9 January 2010, PIJIP Research Paper no. 12, American University Washington College of Law, DC).

forum clause.[136] However, there has been a clear preference to bring disputes to the WTO, even if they could have been adjudicated under the relevant FTA.[137]

This may be because the DSU confers jurisdiction on a panel over the questions of measures adopted by one or more Members in establishing an FTA as well as subsequent consistency of the FTA with WTO provisions.[138]

In *Peru – Agricultural Products*[139] the question was raised as to whether it is possible to waive one's WTO rights in an FTA.[140] In 2011, Guatemala agreed in an FTA with Peru that Peru may maintain its Price Range System in respect of certain agricultural products. Yet, in 2013, Guatemala challenged the exact same Price Range System as a violation of Peru's WTO commitments although the FTA also contains a dispute settlement clause stating: 'In the event of any inconsistency between this Treaty and the [WTO] agreements … , this Treaty shall prevail to the extent of the inconsistency, unless otherwise provided in this Treaty.' Based on this notion, Peru, which incidentally had not yet ratified the FTA whereas Guatemala had, raised the defence that Guatemala had not only recognised Peru's maintenance of the Price Range System, but through the conclusion of the FTA has also waived its rights to initiate WTO dispute settlement proceedings. In bringing these proceedings, so Peru argued, Guatemala had breached principles of good faith under the DSU Articles 3.7[141] and 3.10.[142] The AB held that 'relinquishment of rights granted under the DSU cannot be lightly assumed', and that 'any such relinquishment must be made clearly'[143] by means of a mutually agreed solution (rather than a waiver) that covers the settlement of the specific dispute.[144] Peru's defence was dismissed and the Price Range System itself was held to be inconsistent with Article 4(2) of the Agreement on Agriculture and Article II(1)(b) of the GATT.[145] Despite the dismissal of Peru's defence, it has

136. *See* for example Article 28(4) of the Comprehensive and Progressive Agreement for Trans-Pacific Partnership (CPTPP), although WTO Panels may still assume jurisdiction, *see* Panel Report, *Argentina – Poultry Anti-dumping Duties*, WT/DS241/R (adopted 19 May 2003); and Appellate Body Report, *Mexico – Taxes on Soft Drinks*, WT/DS308/AB/R (adopted 24 March 2006).
137. C. Chase, A. Yanovich, J. Crawford and P. Ugaz, 'Mapping of Dispute Settlement Mechanisms in Regional Trade Agreements: Innovative or Variations on a Theme?' (WTO Staff Working Paper, 2013) ERSD-2013-07, available at: https://www.wto.org/english/res_e/reser_e/ersd201307_e.htm.
138. Appellate Body Report, *Turkey – Restrictions on Imports of Textile and Clothing Products*, WT/DS34/AB/R (adopted 19 November 1999).
139. Appellate Body Report, *Peru – Additional Duty on Imports of Certain Agricultural Products*, WT/DS457/AB/R and Add.1 (adopted 31 July 2015); Panel Report, *Peru – Agricultural Products*, WT/DS457/R (circulated 27 November 2014).
140. J. Mathis, 'WTO Appellate Body, *Peru – Additional Duty on Imports of Certain Agriculture Products*, WT/DS457/AB/R, 20 July 2015', 43 *Legal Issues of Economic Integration* (2016), 97–105, available at http://www.kluwerlawonline.com/abstract.php?area=Journals&id=LEIE2016005.
141. 'Before bringing a case, a Member shall exercise its judgement as to whether action under these procedures would be fruitful. The aim of the dispute settlement mechanism is to secure a positive solution to a dispute. A solution mutually acceptable to the parties to a dispute and consistent with the covered agreement is clearly to be preferred. …'
142. 'It is understood that requests for conciliation and the use of the dispute settlement procedures should not be intended or considered as contentious acts and that, if a dispute arises, all Members will engage in these procedures in good faith in an effort to resolve the dispute. …'
143. Appellate Body Report, *Peru – Agricultural Products*, *supra* note 139, para. 5.25.
144. *Ibid.*, footnote 106.
145. *Ibid.*, sections 5.3.1 and 5.3.2.

been argued that that the forum selection clauses of the CETA[146] and the CPTPP[147] may satisfy the requirements for waiving rights under the DSU.[148]

Still, when considering disputes between members, the WTO panels and AB will have to take into consideration matters that are dealt with in an FTA or other agreement between the parties. In line with the case law of the WTO, the jurisdiction will also extend to issues of consistency of FTAs with TRIPS provisions although such provisions may also affect the jurisdiction through a forum selection clause or other means of dispute settlement agreed to between the parties.

F. CONCLUSION

After the first 25 years of TRIPS, many issues remain unresolved and contentious. This is most visible in relation to the protection of public health and the environment. The extent to which flexibilities that the WTO covered agreements provide to members in terms of their policy freedom is likely to dominate the discussion on the amount of weight WTO panels and the AB have to give to non-WTO norms.

In the wider context of WTO law, the openness to non-WTO norms for claims in disputes is limited, although in the case of the TRIPS Agreement, the importation by reference of prior treaty obligations may enlarge the subject matter at issue in a dispute beyond those expressly mentioned in the TRIPS Agreement itself. When it comes to defences, however, the SARS-CoV-2 pandemic, like the AIDS pandemic before it, has highlighted the tension between trade-related interests and public health once more. It is important to note that in the wider WTO context, TRIPS is *lex specialis*. Even though moral rights have been excised from the TRIPS obligations, intellectual property as a legal construct serves wider policy objectives and is not merely a trade issue. This means that the scope for non-WTO norms as defences to a claim for breach of TRIPS obligations is broad. After all, intellectual property serves to promote human intellectual and industrial creativity and recognises both individual and societal interests. Articles 7 and 8 of the TRIPS Agreement also express the notion that the promotion of societal interests provides the very justification for the protection of IPRs. The WTO agreements seek to serve such wider societal interests through the promotion of trade but need to find legitimacy through their relationship with norms of other legal systems and other international organisations. Where the global community is in need of urgent action in relation to health and the environment, the TRIPS obligations should be read in conjunction with the UN's Sustainable Development Goals and all other legal instruments that promote these goals. Ultimately, the development of a global inclusive trading system requires sustainable development with an open eye for technology transfer, capacity building, and the promotion of global societal welfare.

146. CETA Article 29(3).
147. CPTPP Article 28(4).
148. J. Pauwelyn, 'Interplay between the WTO Treaty', *supra* note 83.

CHAPTER 3

TRIPS in the Field of Copyright

*Marketa Trimble**

A. INTRODUCTION

The Agreement on Trade-Related Aspects of Intellectual Property Rights (TRIPS) was a milestone in international copyright law. Although its substantive law provisions were arguably not as groundbreaking in copyright law as they were in patent law, TRIPS was a springboard for further intellectual property (IP) law negotiations at the multilateral, plurilateral, and bilateral levels. TRIPS coincided with the emergence of the internet as a global medium that permanently changed the copyright law landscape; not only did the internet create new challenges for copyright law but it also contributed to the expansion of the numbers and types of stakeholders invested in the future of copyright law. Additionally, as have other areas of IP law, copyright law has been affected by its incorporation into trade negotiations and has been critically scrutinised with respect to its ability to serve a multitude of interests in diverse countries.[1]

This chapter reviews the copyright law-specific contributions of TRIPS, including its substantive copyright law provisions and the interpretations that World Trade Organization (WTO) Panel reports have provided for some of the provisions. The chapter further explores how copyright law has developed outside of TRIPS; it focuses on international copyright law negotiations that resulted in the conclusion of the World Intellectual Property Organization (WIPO) treaties and on other international

---

* Samuel S. Lionel Professor of Intellectual Property Law, William S. Boyd School of Law, University of Nevada, Las Vegas. The author thanks for comments and suggestions JUDr. Adéla Faladová, and for their research support Professor Jeanne Price and Professor Youngwoo Ban of the Wiener-Rogers Law Library at the William S. Boyd School of Law at the University of Nevada, Las Vegas, and Miriam Shumway (JD '20). The author is indebted to Gary A. Trimble for his invaluable editing suggestions.

1. Ricketson and Ginsburg, *International Copyright and Neighbouring Rights: The Berne Convention and Beyond* (2nd edn., Oxford/New York, 2005), 135, para. 4.02.

negotiations that led to the conclusion of numerous free trade agreements. Finally, the chapter offers an outlook on the current copyright law landscape; it presents the structural and substantive issues that have arisen in the landscape since the TRIPS negotiations and suggests the paths that copyright law might take in the future.

B. TRIPS AGREEMENT AND COPYRIGHT LAW

I. Copyright Law in TRIPS

TRIPS contains six articles that address copyright law specifically; other TRIPS provisions, such as the provisions in TRIPS Parts I, III, and V (the general provisions, the provisions on the enforcement of IP rights, and the provisions on dispute settlement), apply to all IP rights covered by TRIPS, including copyright. Even though only six copyright-specific articles were incorporated into TRIPS, their inclusion was a significant achievement for international IP law, in part because their inclusion made other TRIPS Parts (which enhanced the enforceability of IP rights in national legal systems and provided for a much-desired enforceability of IP-related treaty obligations internationally) applicable to copyright.[2]

TRIPS Part II, Section 1, which concerns 'Copyright and Related Rights', begins with a clause in Article 9(1) that incorporates Articles 1–21 of the Berne Convention ('Berne').[3] The incorporation is not only a formal recognition of the major building block on which the TRIPS copyright-related provisions were built; the incorporation makes compliance with Berne mandatory under TRIPS and makes the WTO dispute settlement mechanism applicable to disputes concerning countries' violations of Berne. Commentators have emphasised that this arrangement 'giv[es] teeth to a convention that was until then very difficult to enforce';[4] Section II, below, discusses the strength of the 'teeth' in practice.

The Berne incorporation provision makes an exception in the case of Berne's article on moral rights.[5] The United States, which was otherwise a major driving force behind TRIPS, objected to incorporating moral rights into TRIPS;[6] the United States introduced moral rights with a limited scope in its Copyright Act in 1990[7] – reluctantly, and only after the United States became a party to the Berne Convention in 1989. The moral rights statute in the US Copyright Act does not fully implement

2. Anell, 'Foreword', in Kennedy, *WTO Dispute Settlement and the TRIPS Agreement: Applying Intellectual Property Standards in a Trade Law Framework* (Cambridge, 2016), ix-xii, at x and xi. On the 'attractions of the GATT dispute settlement mechanism' *see*, e.g., *ibid.*, 18–28.
3. The incorporation of the Berne Convention also covers 'the jurisprudence relating to the interpretation of those provisions ... discussions, resolutions and reports at or provided to various conferences of the Berne Convention ... and state practices based on the Berne Convention.' Malbon, Lawson and Davison, *The WTO Agreement on Trade-Related Aspects of Intellectual Property Rights* (Cheltenham, 2014), 244, para. 9.02. *See also US – Section 110(5) of US Copyright Act* (2000), WTO, WT/DS160/R, para. 6.66.
4. Gervais, *The TRIPS Agreement: Drafting History and Analysis* (4th edn., London, 2012), 244, para. 2.135.
5. Berne Convention, Article 6*bis*.
6. Gervais, *supra* note 4, 246, para. 2.136.
7. Visual Artists Rights Act; 17 U.S.C. § 106A; H.R. Rep. No. 514, 101st Cong., 5-10 (1990).

the Berne requirements; the US position has been that other provisions of US law, including claims that can be made under US state law, provide additional protection that supplements the moral rights statute in the Copyright Act.[8]

Originally, TRIPS negotiators contemplated including Berne's moral rights in the TRIPS incorporation provision and permitting countries to file reservations regarding moral rights, but negotiators eventually excluded moral rights from the incorporation provision with the understanding that the provision should not lead to a diminishment of moral rights in countries that had already implemented the Berne minimum standard for moral rights by the time the countries concluded TRIPS.[9]

Two TRIPS provisions address subject matter protected by copyright: Article 9(2) formulated a principle - which was already well-recognised in some national copyright laws at the time of the TRIPS negotiations - that copyright protection extends only to expressions and not to ideas; in addition to excluding ideas, the provision excludes from copyright protection 'procedures, methods of operation or mathematical concepts as such.' Article 9(2) evolved from a proposal that Japan originally submitted for inclusion in TRIPS Article 10 (which addresses computer programs and databases).[10]

TRIPS was the first international treaty to provide copyright protection for computer programs, but the subject was not new; by the early 1990s dozens of countries had already protected computer programs through copyright - either by legislation that included computer programs in the definition of protectable subject matter or through court interpretations that extended national copyright law to cover computer programs.[11] Nevertheless, the use of copyright law to protect computer programs was not preordained; decades of debates preceded TRIPS in which a sui generis form of protection competed with the protection by copyright law.[12] In the end, TRIPS Article 10(1) took the path of copyright protection for computer programs as literary works.[13] Brazil and a group of 14 developing countries proposed a solution that would have left to countries the option to select the type of protection, but the proposal did not receive sufficient support.[14]

8. H.R. Rep. No. 609, 100th Cong., 2d Sess. 32-40 (1988).
9. Gervais, *supra* note 4, 245, para. 2.135.
10. Gervais, *supra* note 4, 253, para. 2.140.
11. Gervais, *supra* note 4, 261, para. , 2.152 ('Twenty-two countries mentioned [computer programs in their laws] explicitly by 1992, and a total of 54 protected computer programs when case-law is included in the calculation.').
12. For example, the 1978 Model Provisions on the Protection of Computer Software (drafted by the International Bureau of the WIPO) were designed to implement a sui generis protection. 'Copyright', 14(1) *Monthly Review of the World Intellectual Property Organization* (January 1978), 6–19.
13. In retrospect a participant in the negotiations remarked, 'What could or should have been the focus of much more discussion was the question of how to protect software.' *Carl*, Evaluating the TRIPS Negotiations: A Plea for A Substantial Review of the Agreement, in The Making of the TRIPS Agreement: Personal Insights from the Uruguay Round Negotiations (*Watal & Taubman* eds.), Geneva, 2015, 99–122, at 109.
14. Tarragô, 'Negotiating for Brazil', in Watal and Taubman (eds.), *The Making of the TRIPS Agreement: Personal Insights from the Uruguay Round Negotiations* (Geneva, 2015), 239–56, at 248.

TRIPS settled one issue that was associated with the copyright protection of computer programs but it left another issue unsolved. The settled issue was the protection of object code. In countries where computer programs had received copyright protection before TRIPS, debates arose as to whether copyright should protect not only source code but also object code. Critics argued that source code, which is human readable (since it is written in a human-readable programming language) should be protected, but object code, which is generated by a machine from source code (object code is only machine readable, as it consists of zeros and ones), was not the type of expression that copyright was designed to protect. Judges struggled with the question of the copyrightability of object code as well,[15] and TRIPS finally answered the question by providing for the protection of both source code and object code.

The issue that TRIPS did not address was the protectability of computer programming languages; the importance and complexity of this issue, particularly for object-oriented programming, have been highlighted in recent disputes in *SAS Institute Inc. v. World Programming Ltd.* and *Oracle America, Inc. v. Google LLC.*[16] A Japanese proposal that would have excluded computer programming languages from copyright protection was not included in the final TRIPS text.

A sui generis form of protection had also been contemplated for databases, which are referred to as 'compilations of data' in TRIPS. Article 10(2) mandates the minimum protection that databases must receive, which appears to be set at the level that in some countries is the level of copyrightability; the phrasing of the provision resembles the US test for the copyrightability of compilations.[17] The protection that databases receive must not extend to the underlying data, but data themselves might be protected by copyright to the extent that the data are copyrightable works on their own.[18] TRIPS thus accommodates some systems, such as the system implemented in the European Union, that provide for sui generis protection in addition to the protection given under copyright. Under the 1996 EC Database Directive, copyright law and the sui generis law protect different aspects of databases and result in different terms of protection, which are applicable to the different aspects.[19] TRIPS also allows countries to maintain other means of protection for non-copyrightable features of databases, such as protection under misappropriation doctrines.

The digital age was reflected not only in the TRIPS provisions on computer programs and databases, but also in TRIPS Article 11, which covers rental rights. Copyright owners were concerned about the unauthorised copying that occurred

15. E.g., *Computer Edge Pty Ltd v. Apple Computer Inc.*, [1986] HCA 19, High Court of Australia, 6 May 1986.
16. *SAS Institute Inc. v. World Programming Ltd*, CJEU, C-406/10, 2 May 2012; *SAS Institute Inc. v. World Programming Ltd* [2013] EWCA Civ 1482 (21 November 2013); *SAS Institute Inc. v. World Programming Ltd.*, 64 F.Supp.3d 755 (E.D.N.C. 2014); *SAS Institute Inc. v. World Programming Limited*, 874 F.3d 370 (4th Cir. 2017), cert. denied; *SAS Institute Inc. v. World Programming Ltd.* [2018] EWHC 3452 (Comm) (13 December 2018); *Oracle America, Inc. v. Google LLC*, 886 F.3d 1179 (Fed. Cir. 2018), cert. granted 140 S.Ct. 520 (2019).
17. *Feist Publications, Inc. v. Rural Telephone Service Company, Inc.*, 499 U.S. 340, 348 (1991); 17 U.S.C. 101 ('compilation').
18. TRIPS, Article 10(2), second sentence.
19. Directive 96/9/EC of the European Parliament and of the Council of 11 March 1996 on the legal protection of databases.

when copies were rented; the concerns became pressing because digital technologies improved copy quality to the point at which reproductions could be made with negligible loss from the original quality.[20] Rental rights provide copyright owners additional control over copies of their works and an additional income stream. Article 11 made rental rights mandatory for commercial rentals of computer programs, with the exception of rentals where computer programs are 'not the essential object of the rental', such as rentals of automobiles.[21] Countries have the option of providing rental rights for cinematographic works, but they must institute these rights if the rentals of cinematographic works lead to 'widespread copying' and result in material impairment of the reproduction right under copyright.[22]

Commentators have explained the difference between the approaches to computer programs and cinematographic works by the differences in rental practices between the two types of works: while rentals have been blamed for the unauthorised copying of computer programs, rentals have been a form of authorised distribution of cinematographic works.[23] The United States in particular called for separate treatment for cinematographic works, which led to the inclusion in TRIPS of the criteria that countries should follow to determine whether they must implement rental rights for cinematographic works. Critics note that the test will be difficult to apply in practice; Professor Gervais called the provision 'one of the less desirable provisions of the Agreement.'[24] In some countries rentals of cinematographic works seemed to have caused the same problems as rentals of computer programs; as an Indian negotiator recalled, rental shops and small 'video parlours' were a significant problem for India's film industry,[25] which welcomed the idea of rental rights, and India implemented rental rights for cinematographic works after TRIPS was concluded.[26]

One point that TRIPS does not address is whether the copies referred to in the rental rights provision include both tangible and intangible copies or only tangible copies. Commentators assume that the provision was intended to cover only tangible

20. Malbon, Lawson and Davison, *supra* note 3, 253, para. 11.01 ('The primary reason for the introduction of this right was the development in the 1990s of sophisticated copying technologies which permitted the fast and accurate copying of films in both video and digital format and computer programs.').
21. TRIPS, Article 11, first and third sentences.
22. TRIPS, Article 11, second sentence.
23. Gervais, *supra* note 4, 272, para. 2.166. The different treatment of computer programs and cinematographic works is difficult to justify if some products, such as video games, are considered to consist of not only a computer program but also of a cinematographic or audiovisual work. Commentators have debated whether video games should enjoy protection as cinematographic or audiovisual works. *See* Ramos et al., *The Legal Status of Video Games: Comparative Analysis in National Approaches* (WIPO, 2013) 10. The Court of Justice of the European Union acknowledged that 'videogames ... constitute complex matter comprising not only a computer program but also graphic and sound elements' and if the elements 'are part of its originality, they are protected, together with the entire work, by copyright...' *Nintendo Co. Ltd v. PC Box Srl*, CJEU, C-355/12, 23 January 2014, para. 23. *See also* Matsui, 'Does It Have to Be a Copyright Infringement?: Live Game Streaming and Copyright', 24 *Tex. Intell. Prop. L.J.* (2016), 215.
24. Gervais, *supra* note 4, 270, para. 2.165.
25. Sagar, 'Copyright: An Indian Perspective', in Watal and Taubman (eds.), *The Making of the TRIPS Agreement: Personal Insights from the Uruguay Round Negotiations* (Geneva, 2015), 341–49, at 344.
26. Sagar, *supra* note 25, 345.

copies; they infer this from the only indication of the state of mind of the negotiators on the issue – the Agreed Statements to the WIPO Copyright Treaty (WCT), according to which the WCT rental rights provision refers 'exclusively to fixed copies that can be put into circulation as tangible objects.'[27] In hindsight the lack of clarification as to the types of copies that are covered by rental rights seems to be a fundamental omission in TRIPS, particularly in light of recent disputes regarding the applicability of copyright doctrines to intangible copies.[28]

TRIPS addressed the issue of term of copyright protection when the term is not measured according to a number of years following the death of an author (a number of years post mortem auctoris – 'p.m.a.'). This might be the case when copyright vests directly in a legal entity rather than in a natural person or in other cases where the term is not measured with respect to the death of an author – for example, in cases of works made for hire under US law.[29] For such cases Article 12 mandates that the term be no less than 50 years from the publication of a work; it allows countries to grant shorter terms for photographic works and works of applied art. Originally some negotiators proposed that computer programs be grouped with works that could have a shorter term but this proposal was not incorporated into the final text.[30] The exception concerning photographic works was made irrelevant for the WCT's signatory countries by WCT Article 9.

TRIPS Article 13 formulates the three-step test for limitations and exceptions to copyright. The provision is significant not because of the test itself – the test follows the language of Berne Article 9(2) – but because of the scope of the rights to which it pertains. While Berne Article 9(2) concerns the limitations and exceptions to only the reproduction right, the text of TRIPS Article 13 places no limits on the rights it covers. As is discussed in Section B.II, below, a WTO Panel report provided a much-needed interpretation of Article 13, though the full scope of the provision might still be debated.[31]

The final copyright-specific TRIPS Article, Article 14, concerns neighbouring (or 'related') rights; Article 14 provides for the protection of performers and phonogram producers as concerns performances and phonograms, and broadcasters as concerns broadcasts. TRIPS did not incorporate any of the provisions of the older international treaties concerning performers and phonograms – i.e. the 1961 Rome Convention[32] and the 1971 Geneva Convention;[33] during the TRIPS negotiations both of these Conventions had significantly fewer contracting countries than did the Berne

27. Agreed Statement Concerning Articles 6 and 7 of the WIPO Copyright Treaty. *See* Gervais, *supra* note 4, 271, para. 2.166.
28. E.g., *Usedsoft GmbH v. Oracle International Corp.*, CJEU, C-128/11, 3 July 2012; *Capitol Records, LLC v. ReDigi, Inc.*, 910 F.3d 649 (2d Cir. 2018), cert. denied.
29. Gervais, *supra* note 4, 274, para. 2.173.
30. Gervais, *supra* note 4, 273, paras. 2.168 and 2.169.
31. *See* Report of the Panel, WT/DS160/R, 15 June 2000, para. 6.82, p. 28.
32. International Convention for the Protection of Performers, Producers of Phonograms and Broadcasting Organisations, Rome, 26 October 1961 (the 'Rome Convention').
33. Convention for the Protection of Producers of Phonograms Against Unauthorized Duplication of Their Phonograms, Geneva, 29 October 1971 (the 'Geneva Phonograms Convention').

Convention, and importantly the United States was not, and still is not, a party to the Rome Convention.[34]

A chronic tension that remained in the TRIPS negotiations was the difference in the nature of the protection of performer and phonogram rights, which are covered by copyright in the United States but by neighbouring rights in civil law countries. Article 14 was therefore a compromise that in some respects corresponds to Rome Convention protections but in other respects provides fewer protections.[35] Article 14 sets the minimum term of protection at 50 years from the unfixed performance or from the fixation of the performance for performers and producers, and at 20 years from the broadcast for broadcasters.

Two copyright law provisions were proposed but eventually not included in the final text of TRIPS. The first provision would have defined the term 'public';[36] the definition was subsequently included in WCT Article 8 and in Article 10 of the WIPO Performances and Phonograms Treaty (WPPT), which both contain provisions on the right of communication to the public. The second proposed provision would have covered transfer of rights;[37] however, countries could not agree on the provision. As a negotiator recalled, the provision 'raised difficult questions concerning the law applicable to the determination of authorship and the validity of contractual agreements that did not comply with the requirements of the country where protection was claimed.'[38]

II. Copyright Law Disputes under TRIPS

The inclusion of IP rights in the WTO framework did result in disputes under the WTO dispute settlement mechanism; as of 15 March 2020, 42 requests for consultations citing TRIPS have been filed under the mechanism. Of the 42 requests, nine referred to one or more of the six copyright-specific TRIPS provisions discussed in Section I above, and one of the nine requests, which was filed in 1996, was the very first TRIPS-related request for consultations.[39] Additional requests, even when they did not refer expressly to the copyright-specific provisions, might have concerned copyright

34. Staff of H. Comm. on the Judiciary, 95th Cong., Performance Rights in Sound Recordings (Comm. Print 1978), pp. 7 and 496–588; Ulmer, 'The Rome Convention for the Protection of Performers, Producers of Phonograms and Broadcasting Organizations', 10 *Bulletin of the Copyright Society of the U.S.A.* (1962), 90, 99–100.
35. Gervais, *supra* note 4, 303–04, para. 2.202; Goldstein & Trimble, *International Intellectual Property Law: Cases and Materials* (5th edn., St. Paul, MN, 2019), 384.
36. Gervais, *supra* note 4, 309–10, paras. 2.208–2.210.
37. Gervais, *supra* note 4, 310–11, paras. 2.211–2.213.
38. Wager, 'Copyright: A Nordic Perspective', in Watal and Taubman (eds.), *The Making of the TRIPS Agreement: Personal Insights from the Uruguay Round Negotiations* (Geneva, 2015), 321–39, at 326.
39. *Japan – Measures Concerning Sound Recordings*, WTO, WT/DS28/1, Request for Consultations by the United States, 14 February 1996. For a list of all TRIPS-related disputes *see* Disputes by Agreement, WTO, https://www.wto.org/english/tratop_e/dispu_e/dispu_agreements_index_e.htm?id = A26#selected_agreement (last visited 24 February 2020).

law; for example, some of the requests concerning TRIPS enforcement provisions covered several types of IP rights, including copyright.[40]

Of the nine disputes filed as of 15 March 2020 that were based on requests for consultations that referred to copyright-specific TRIPS provisions, two disputes have not been formally concluded, four were terminated with mutually agreed solutions, and three resulted in Panel reports.[41] One of the Panel reports did not address copyright law; although the request for consultation mentioned TRIPS Article 10, the dispute and the report concerned EU measures for the protection of trade marks and geographical indications.[42] The other two reports interpreted TRIPS's copyright-specific provisions.

The first dispute that resulted in a Panel report specific to copyright law was a dispute that was brought to the WTO in 1999 by the European Union (then the European Community). *United States – Section 110(5) of the US Copyright Act* concerned section 110(5) of the US Copyright Act and the so-called 'homestyle' and 'business' exceptions that it created for public performances and public displays of works. The first exception is limited by the means used for performances and displays ('a single receiving apparatus of a kind commonly used in private homes');[43] the second exception is confined to businesses of a certain size and with defined means that are used for performances.[44] The request for consultation alleged noncompliance with Berne Articles 11 and 11*bis*[45] as incorporated by TRIPS Article 9(1), but in the end the interpretation and application of the three-step test in TRIPS Article 13 became the core of the Panel's report.

The main significance of the Panel report for copyright law is the Panel's interpretation of TRIPS Article 13 and the Panel's clarification of the interplay between Article 13 and Berne. The European Communities argued that TRIPS Article 13 could not be used to limit rights under Berne because Article 13 should apply only to rights that were added by TRIPS.[46] Because, their argument went, section 110(5) concerned rights in Berne Articles 11 and 11*bis*, TRIPS Article 13 could not be used to justify the exceptions in section 110(5).[47]

The Panel sided with the United States, which argued that TRIPS Article 13 is not limited to rights introduced under TRIPS.[48] The Panel concluded that the standards in Berne and TRIPS are not different because Berne Article 11 and 11*bis*(1) also had exceptions to rights – the so-called 'minor exceptions' that were never added to Berne,

---

40. E.g., *European Communities – Enforcement of Intellectual Property Rights for Motion Pictures and Television Programs*, WTO, WT/DS124; *Denmark – Measures Affecting the Enforcement of Intellectual Property Rights*, WT/DS83.
41. *European Union (formerly EC) – Protection of Trademarks and Geographical Indications for Agricultural Products and Foodstuffs*, DS290 (Panel report); *China – Measures Affecting the Protection and Enforcement of Intellectual Property Rights*, DS 362 (Panel report); *United States – Section 110(5) of US Copyright Act* (arbitration award).
42. *European Union (formerly EC) – Protection of Trademarks and Geographical Indications for Agricultural Products and Foodstuffs*, DS290.
43. 17 U.S.C. § 110(5)(A).
44. 17 U.S.C. § 110(5)(B).
45. Request for Consultations by the European Communities and Their Members, WTO, WT/DS160/1, 4 February 1999.
46. Report of the Panel, WTO, WT/DS160/R, 15 June 2000, 27, para. 6.75.
47. *Ibid.*, 15, para. 6.34.
48. *Ibid.*, 28, para. 6.80.

but that countries agreed to tolerate, as stated in the Report to the 1948 Brussels Conference (the Conference that added public performance rights to Berne).[49] The Panel viewed the Report as context for Berne and took the 'minor exception' doctrine into account,[50] concluding that TRIPS Article 13 'clarifies and articulates the standards applicable to minor exceptions under the Berne Convention.'[51]

Upon establishing the relevance of TRIPS Article 13 to the dispute, the Panel assessed whether section 110(5) was compliant with the three-step test. The Panel first clarified its interpretation of the appropriate standard for the three steps. The importance of the Panel's interpretation transcends the case; because of the similarities in the tests in TRIPS Articles 13, 17, and 30, the Panel's holding will likely influence the interpretation of the other tests when they are applied to trade mark and patent rights in the future.[52] Secondly, applying the three-step test in this case the Panel concluded that the homestyle exception met the requirements of Article 13 but that the business exception did not.[53]

The second copyright-specific dispute that resulted in a Panel report was *China – Measures Affecting the Protection and Enforcement of Intellectual Property Rights*, which was a dispute based on a 2017 request for consultations from the United States.[54] The copyright-specific matter was a US complaint in response to China's denial of copyright protection to works of authorship that had not been authorised for publication or distribution in China.[55] The request for consultations also concerned two other sets of measures: criminal procedures and penalties that TRIPS Article 61 requires countries to provide 'at least in cases of willful trademark counterfeiting or copyright piracy on a commercial scale', and measures pertaining to the disposal of goods that are confiscated for infringing IP rights.[56]

The complaint concerning China's denial of copyright protection was based on an allegation that the Chinese Copyright Law was inconsistent with Berne provisions on national treatment and the prohibition of formalities as incorporated in TRIPS, and also with TRIPS Article 14 and other TRIPS provisions.[57] Much of the argument revolved around the interpretation of the Chinese statute, the meaning of which the

49. General Report, Records of the Conference Convened in Brussels 5–26 June 1948, reprinted in Ricketson and Ginsburg, *supra* note 1, 256–70, at 263.
50. Kennedy, *supra* note 2, 195.
51. Report of the Panel, WTO, WT/DS160/R, 15 June 2000, 28, para. 6.82.
52. For an earlier report on the test under TRIPS Article 30 *see Canada – Patent Protection of Pharmaceutical Products*, WTO, WT/DS114/R, 17 March 2000. The Panel in *United States – Section 110(5) of the US Copyright Act* referred to this Panel decision once – *see* Report of the Panel, WTO, WT/DS160/R, 15 June 2000, 58, fn 202.

    On comparisons of the three-step tests in IP treaties *see*, e.g., Christie and Wright, 'A Comparative Analysis of the Three-Step Test in International Treaties', 45 *International Review of Intellectual Property and Competition Law (IIC)* (2014), 409–33.
53. Report of the Panel, WTO, WT/DS160/R, 15 June 2000, 69, para. 7.1.
54. For an in-depth analysis of the dispute *see* Yu, 'The TRIPS Enforcement Dispute', 89 *Nebraska Law Review* (2011) 1046.
55. Report of the Panel, WTO, WT/DS362/R, 26 January 2009, 3, para. 2.4.
56. *Ibid.*, 2–3, paras. 2.3 and 2.4.
57. *Ibid.*, 4, para. 3.1(c).

United States and China disputed. The Panel determined that the Chinese Copyright Law did deny copyright protection to certain works.[58]

China referred in its defence to Berne Article 17; the article, which is also incorporated in TRIPS, provides that Berne does not affect the right of any country's government to limit the 'circulation, presentation, or exhibition of any work.'[59] The Panel agreed with China that the right of a government under Berne Article 17 'clearly includes censorship for reasons of public order'[60] and that a government's right is not limited to the three particular types of actions. However, the Panel concluded that Article 17 does not authorise the denial of 'all copyright protection in any work'[61] and held that the Chinese statute was inconsistent with the national treatment provision in Berne Article 5(1) as incorporated into TRIPS, and also with TRIPS Article 41(1).[62]

The number of copyright-specific, or even copyright-related, disputes in the 25 years of TRIPS might seem sparse, putting into question the effectiveness of the dispute settlement mechanism. However, the effectiveness of the mechanism must be evaluated comprehensively, and the evaluation must lend appropriate weight to the fact that the existing disputes provide guidance, together with some degree of deterrence. Both of the reports mentioned above provided important interpretations of Berne and TRIPS provisions. As for the actual effectiveness of the dispute settlement mechanism in the two disputes, only one of the two reports discussed above led to changes in the law of the responding country. China amended its Copyright Law effective in April 2010; the United States has not yet amended its Copyright Act to comply with the Panel report in *United States – Section 110(5) of the US Copyright Act*.

The fact that the conclusions of the report in *United States – Section 110(5) of the US Copyright Act* have not been implemented by the United States in the 20 years since the publication of the report suggests that the 'teeth' that TRIPS was to provide, including the teeth for Berne, might not be as strong as commentators have suggested.[63] Nevertheless, even in this case there are indications that the Panel report, the arbitration award that followed, and other enforcement attempts might not have been forgotten. In December 2019 the Commission of the European Union expressed its concern regarding the United States' lack of implementation of the report in the Commission's IP law 'watchlist.'[64] In February 2020, the United States filed a status report with the WTO in which it stated that '[t]he U.S. Administration will work closely with the U.S. Congress and will continue to confer with the European Union in order to reach a mutually satisfactory resolution in this matter.'[65]

58. *Ibid.*, 17, para. 7.50.
59. Berne Convention, Article 17; Report of the Panel, WTO, WT/DS362/R, 26 January 2009, 30, para. 7.120.
60. Report of the Panel, WTO, WT/DS362/R, 26 January 2009, 30, para. 7.126.
61. *Ibid.*, 31, para. 7.127.
62. *Ibid.*, 33, para. 7.139, and 40, para. 7.181. After the Panel reached its conclusion under Berne Article 5(1), the Panel concluded that it was unnecessary to rule on the claims under Berne Articles 5(2) and 14, and TRIPS Article 61. *Ibid.*, 35, para. 7.153; 36, para. 7.160; and 40, para. 7.185.
63. *See* above I.
64. Report on the protection and enforcement of intellectual property rights in third countries, European Commission, SWD(2019) 452 final/2, 8 January 2020 (correcting SWD(2019) 452 final of 20 December 2019), 10.
65. Status Report by the United States, WTO, WT/DS160/24/Add.179, 18 February 2020.

The inclusion of IP rights in the larger trade context opened the possibility for IP rights to be affected by WTO arbitration awards that may concern IP rights, including copyright. In 1999, in a WTO dispute that was unrelated to TRIPS, Ecuador became the first country to request authorisation from the WTO Dispute Resolution Body to suspend TRIPS obligations in retaliation for a respondent country's noncompliance with a Panel decision; Ecuador sought the suspension of TRIPS obligations with respect to the European Communities.[66] Similarly, in 2007 Antigua and Barbuda requested authorisation to suspend its obligations under TRIPS, and also its concessions and obligations under GATS, in retaliation for the United States' noncompliance with a Panel report in a dispute concerning online gambling and betting. The requested suspensions would have affected various IP rights, including copyright and related rights.[67]

In both cases the Arbitrators agreed that TRIPS rights may be subject to an authorised suspension in retaliation for noncompliance with a WTO Panel decision, but they expressed skepticism regarding the practicalities of implementing suspensions.[68] A suspension would need to affect only the nationals of the respondent country; however, copyright and neighbouring rights may have multiple right holders with different nationalities, making it impossible to isolate the effects of a suspension to only the nationals of the respondent country.[69] The Arbitrators also warned that while nothing in the WTO rules appeared to prevent them from authorising a suspension of the requested TRIPS obligations, the rules and the authorisation did not protect the authorised countries from being potentially found in violation of other treaties - or even in violation of TRIPS vis-à-vis third countries - once the authorised countries implemented the suspension.[70]

Although in both cases the Arbitrators determined that the complainant countries could request that the Dispute Settlement Body authorise the TRIPS suspensions, in neither case did the complainant country suspend their TRIPS obligations. In the first case the parties reached a mutually agreed solution;[71] in the second case Antigua repeatedly threatened to implement the suspension but has not yet done so.[72]

66. *European Communities – Regime for the Importation, Sale and Distribution of Bananas*, Decision by the Arbitrators, WT/DS27/ARB/ECU, 16, para. 65(i).
67. *United States – Measures Affecting the Cross-Border Supply of Gambling and Betting Services*, Decision by the Arbitrator, WT/DS285/ARB, 21 December 2007, 77, para. 5.6.
68. *Ibid.*, 77, para. 5.10 ('We also note that the suspension of obligations under the TRIPS Agreement may involve more complex means of implementation than, for example, the imposition of higher import duties on goods, and that the exact assessment of the value of the rights affected by the suspension is also likely to be more complex.').
69. *European Communities – Regime for the Importation, Sale and Distribution of Bananas* (*supra* note 66), 29–30, paras. 141–44. The ownership of copyright may also change according to the law applicable to the issues of ownership.
70. *Ibid.*, 31–32, para. 152.
71. *European Communities – Regime for the Importation, Sale and Distribution of Bananas*, Notification of a Mutually Agreed Solution, WTO, WT/DS27/98, 12 November 2012.
72. E.g., *United States – Measures Affecting the Cross-Border Supply of Gambling and Betting Services*, Communication from Antigua and Barbuda, WTO, WT/DS285/26, 25 April 2013; *Miles*, Storm-Battered Antigua Asks U.S. to Settle 12-year Old WTO Bill, Reuters, 29 September 2017, https://www.reuters.com/article/us-usa-antigua-wto/storm-battered-antigua-asks-u-s-to-settle-12-year-old-wto-bill-idUSKCN1C4165 (last visited 24 February 2020).

In the third case in which a complainant country requested retaliation in the form of suspension of IP rights – Brazil in *United States – Subsidies on Upland Cotton*[73] – the Arbitrator also agreed that Brazil could retaliate against the United States by suspending its TRIPS obligations,[74] and Brazil even obtained an authorisation to retaliate. The Brazilian strategy was effective, as the United States and Brazil reached an agreement in the dispute in 2014;[75] Brazil's success might be explained by the size of the Brazilian market and also by its approach to the retaliation. One commentator pointed out that the case has shown that '[t]he most effective step in the retaliation procedure can be the publication of the list of targets, rather than the actual harm.'[76] The US audiovisual industry was among the IP rights owners that Brazil intended to target.

C. DEVELOPMENTS OUTSIDE OF TRIPS

I. WIPO Treaties

With the exception of TRIPS Article 13, the importance of TRIPS in the area of copyright law was eclipsed by subsequent treaties that countries concluded within WIPO.[77] The two most significant treaties that followed TRIPS have been the WCT and the WPPT. While the content of these two treaties looks similar to the content of TRIPS, a closer examination reveals important differences that show the progress that countries had achieved within WIPO since the TRIPS negotiations.

The most significant difference, as compared to TRIPS, was that countries negotiated the WCT and the WPPT while considering issues raised by the internet and the new 'digital agenda.' Though TRIPS did institute some changes that were prompted by the digital age (protection for computer programs and databases, and rental rights), TRIPS did not consider copyright issues arising out of the internet.

In hindsight it might seem perplexing that the TRIPS negotiators did not consider internet-related copyright issues; however, it is important to remember that TRIPS was signed in April 1994 and the negotiations were completed in the very early days of the internet. In January 1994, a *New York Times* article, which opened with the question 'Has the Internet been overhyped?', reported that at that time only about 2.2 million computers were 'capable of communicating directly with other computers on the Internet.'[78] Swedish Ambassador Lars Anell, who had chaired the TRIPS negotiations, recalled that he had not heard of the internet at the time of the TRIPS

73. Decision by the Arbitrator, WTO, WT/DS267/ARB/1, 31 August 2009, 122, para. 5.230, fn 468.
74. *Ibid.*, 124, para. 6.5.
75. Memorandum of Understanding Related to the Cotton Dispute, WTO, WT/DS267, 1 October 2014, available at https://ustr.gov/sites/default/files/20141001201606893.pdf (last visited 26 February 2020).
76. Kennedy, *supra* note 2, 348.
77. For a nuanced view of TRIPS's role in the development of international IP law *see*, e.g., Okediji, 'Back to Bilateralism? Pendulum Swings in International Intellectual Property Protection', 1 *University of Ottawa Law and Technology Journal* (2003–2004), 125 at 130 and 146–47.
78. Lewis, 'Doubts Raised on Number of Internet Users', *The New York Times*, 10 August 1994, https://www.nytimes.com/1994/08/10/business/business-technology-doubts-raised-on-number-of-internet-users.html (last visited 25 February 2020).

negotiations in 1991 and 1992, even though he was also Sweden's representative to CERN – the birthplace of the world wide web (WWW).[79] It was Tim Berners-Lee, a British scientist working at the European Organization for Nuclear Research (CERN, which is within a short drive of the WTO in Geneva), who in 1989 proposed and in 1992 published a summary paper on the WWW; in 1993 CERN announced that it was making the WWW software freely available to all.[80]

The WCT and the WPPT, which were adopted in December 1996, reacted to internet-related issues.[81] Although in 1996 the internet was still largely a US medium, with 66% of internet users located in the United States at the time, it already had approximately 36 million users and a quarter of a million websites worldwide.[82] In addition to the WCT's provisions on the protection of computer programs and databases, and the WCT's and WPPT's provisions on rental rights, the WCT and the WPPT provided for a right of communication to the public and for obligations concerning technological measures for the protection of works and obligations regarding rights management information.[83] Although the provisions were phrased in a media-neutral manner, the provisions, including their definition of the 'public', were designed to function in the internet environment. Countries also clarified in an Agreed Statement on WCT Article 1(4) that 'the storage of a protected work in digital form in an electronic medium constitutes a reproduction.'[84]

There are differences between the parallel provisions in the WCT and TRIPS. The WCT makes it clear that computer programs are to be protected 'whatever may be the mode or form of their expression'; although the wording is different from the wording in TRIPS, under an Agreed Statement on the issue the protection is 'on a par with the relevant provisions of the TRIPS Agreement.'[85] The WCT rental rights provision covers not only computer programs and cinematographic works, as does TRIPS, but also phonograms.[86] As opposed to the coverage provided by TRIPS, the WCT does not permit countries to provide a shorter term of protection for

---

79. Anell, *supra* note 2, 368.
80. Berners-Lee, Cailliau and Groff, 'The World-Wide Web', 25 *Computer Networks and ISDN Systems* (1992), 454–59, at 458; Gillies and Cailliau, *How the Web Was Born: The Story of the World Wide Web* (Oxford, 2007), 261.
81. For a detailed description of the WCT and WPPT content and the genesis of their provisions *see* the WIPO Copyright Treaty (WCT) and the WIPO Performances and Phonograms Treaty (WPPT), International Bureau of WIPO, undated, available at https://www.wipo.int/export/sites/www/copyright/en/activities/pdf/wct_wppt.pdf (last visited 2 March 2020).
82. Internet Growth Statistics, available at https://www.internetworldstats.com/emarketing.htm (last visited Jan. 10, 2020); Total Number of Websites, available at https://www.internetlivestats.com/total-number-of-websites/ (last visited 10 January 2020). By 2019 the internet had 4.5 billion users, who represented about 58.8% of the world population, and over 1.7 billion websites. It was estimated that North American internet users accounted for about 7.2% of internet users in the world in 2019. *Ibid.*
83. WCT, Articles 8, 11, and 12; WPPT, Articles 10, 14, 18, and 19.
84. Agreed Statements concerning the WIPO Copyright Treaty, 20 December 1996, available at https://www.wipo.int/treaties/en/text.jsp?file_id=295456 (last visited 2 March 2020).
85. WCT, Article 4; the Agreed Statement concerning Article 4 in Agreed Statements concerning the WIPO Copyright Treaty, 20 December 1996, available at https://www.wipo.int/treaties/en/text.jsp?file_id=295456 (last visited 2 March 2020).
86. WCT, Article 7.

photographic works.[87] TRIPS referred to the agreement among countries to disagree about the nature of the exhaustion of rights (whether exhaustion should be national or international)[88] but it did not provide for the right to distribute; the WCT includes a provision on the distribution right.[89] An Agreed Statement to WCT Articles 6 and 7 explained that the right of distribution and the right of rental apply only to copies in tangible objects.[90] One proposal that did not appear in the final version of the WCT was a proposal for an extension of the term of copyright to 70 years p.m.a.[91]

The WPPT specifies the rights that countries are to accord to performers and producers of phonograms with respect to unfixed and fixed performances. Unfixed performances should be protected against unauthorised fixation, broadcasting, and communication to the public;[92] for fixed performances the WPPT outlines the rights of reproduction, distribution, rental, and making available to the public.[93] The WPPT also includes a provision on moral rights of performers,[94] and sets the term of protection of copyright at 50 years from the end of the year of the fixation of the performance for performers, and 50 years from the publication or fixation of the phonogram for producers.[95] The provision on limitations and exceptions uses the language of the three-step test.[96] In addition to the provisions on the protection of technological measures and rights management information, the WPPT contains a provision on a right to remuneration for broadcasting and communication to the public.[97]

Before the WCT and the WPPT came into effect in March 2002 and May 2002 respectively, another important event occurred in WIPO: in 1998, WIPO modernised its governance structure and replaced its ad hoc committees, which were established for specific areas of IP law and for other purposes, with standing committees, one of which became the Standing Committee on Copyright and Related Rights (SCCR).[98] The SCCR has been the central point for multilateral negotiations in the areas of copyright and neighbouring rights.

The work of the SCCR resulted in the conclusion of two additional copyright treaties – the 2012 Beijing Treaty and the 2013 Marrakesh Treaty.[99] The Marrakesh Treaty was the first of the two treaties to become effective (in September 2016), and its adoption and ratifications were driven by the overwhelmingly accepted and positive social goal that the Treaty seeks to promote: access to published works by

87. WCT, Article 9.
88. TRIPS, Article 6.
89. WCT, Article 6.
90. Agreed Statements concerning the WIPO Copyright Treaty, 20 December 1996, available at https://www.wipo.int/treaties/en/text.jsp?file_id=295456 (last visited 2 March 2020).
91. Ricketson and Ginsburg, *supra* note 1, 153, para. 4.28.
92. WPPT, Article 6.
93. *Ibid.*, Articles 7-14.
94. *Ibid.*, Article 5.
95. *Ibid.*, Article 17.
96. *Ibid.*, Article 16.
97. *Ibid.*, Article 15.
98. The Governance Structure of WIPO, Memorandum of the International Bureau, WIPO, A/32/INF/2, 20 February 1998, p. 8. Ricketson and Ginsburg, *supra* note 1, 149, para. 4.19.
99. Beijing Treaty on Audiovisual Performances, Beijing, 2012; Marrakesh Treaty to Facilitate Access to Published Works for Persons Who Are Blind, Visually Impaired, or Otherwise Print Disabled, 2013.

the blind and otherwise visually impaired or print disabled persons. Nevertheless, the Treaty negotiations were more controversial than the subject, the goal, and the overall acceptance of the Treaty might indicate.

The Marrakesh Treaty was the first treaty to regulate exceptions and limitations to copyright without providing any new rights to copyright owners, and some copyright owners were understandably concerned that the Treaty would become a Trojan horse for subsequent treaties granting further copyright exceptions and limitations in national laws. The discussions in the SCCR since the Treaty was signed suggest that the concerns were warranted to some degree, although it may take a considerable amount of time before countries agree on further treaties on exceptions and limitations.

Two additional major concerns regarding the Marrakesh Treaty centered on the scope of the exceptions and limitations in the Treaty. The first concern was whether the Treaty would remain within the confines of the three-step test; the final wording of the Treaty preamble reaffirmed 'the importance and flexibility of the three-step test' and further referred to the test in two footnotes.[100] The second concern, voiced by copyright owners, was that accessible-format copies could be misused for copyright-infringing purposes; the Treaty definition of these copies is broad and covers not only materials in Braille but also audiobooks in specially accessible formats.[101] This concern about potential misuse of assistive technologies (in a different context) was also apparent recently in a lawsuit that seven members of the Association of American Publishers filed in a US court against a company that provided 'Audible Captions' to audiobooks.[102] The text of the Marrakesh Treaty also raises some complex choice-of-law questions related to the cross-border exchange of copies; however, the negotiators did not address those questions.[103]

The Beijing Treaty, which came into force in April 2020, provides for the protection of performers with respect to both their unfixed and fixed audiovisual performances. It resembles the WPPT because it provides the same types of rights as does the WPPT; it also includes articles on limitations and exceptions, term of protection, and the protection of technological measures and rights management information.[104] A Beijing Treaty provision that has no parallel in the WPPT is the provision concerning transfer of rights.[105]

As of early 2020 the SCCR agenda included several topics; protection for broadcasting organizations in light of new technological developments has been discussed by the SCCR since 1998, and the SCCR's plan has been eventually to conclude a

100. Marrakesh Treaty, Article 4(4), fn 5, and Article 5(4)(b), fn 8.
101. *Ibid.*, Article 2(b).
102. *Chronicle Books LLC et al. v. Audible Inc.*, No. 19-cv-7913, dismissal order issued (S.D.N.Y. Jan. 14, 2020).
103. For a discussion of choice-of-law issues and the Marrakesh Treaty *see* Trimble, 'Marrakesh Puzzle', 45(7) *International Review of Intellectual Property and Competition Law (IIC)* (2014), 768–95.
104. Beijing Treaty, Articles 5–11 and 13–16.
105. *Ibid.*, Article 12. On the difficulties of the negotiations of Article 12 of the Beijing Treaty *see* von Lewinski, 'The Beijing Treaty on Audiovisual Performances', 6 *Auteurs & Media* (2012), 539–46.

WIPO Treaty on the Protection of Broadcasting Organizations.[106] The SCCR has also discussed limitations and exceptions for libraries and archives, for educational and research institutions, and for persons with disabilities not included in the Marrakesh Treaty.[107] Other topics of interest to the SCCR have included the effects of the digital environment on copyright, including in the area of digital music services,[108] the resale right (based on a proposal from Senegal and Congo), and the protection of theatre directors' rights (based on a proposal from the Russian Federation).[109]

II. Free Trade Agreements

The conclusions of the Beijing and Marrakesh Treaties were heralded as significant victories in international negotiations because of the difficult circumstances following the negotiations of the Anti-Counterfeiting Trade Agreement (ACTA). ACTA, a multilateral treaty that several countries, led by the United States, negotiated between 2008 and 2011, generated a degree of tension unprecedented in international copyright negotiations; although ACTA was signed in 2011 by a number of countries and the European Union, only Japan ratified it, and ACTA never became effective.[110] In copyright law, ACTA focused on enforcement, including enforcement against copyright infringements on the internet, which contributed to wide public interest in and outcry against ACTA that was fueled by some powerful internet intermediaries.

In general, critics vilified ACTA because of the level of secrecy under which it was negotiated; although all negotiations, including international treaty negotiations, require some degree of confidentiality in order for parties to establish and maintain negotiating power, the secrecy surrounding ACTA was extreme when compared to that of the negotiations of other IP law treaties. Further exacerbating the public's negative perception of the overt secretiveness of the treaty negotiations was the fact that the early drafts of ACTA seemed to be available to only selected stakeholders, and that the drafts appeared to provide benefits to rights owners without sufficiently balancing copyright with other rights. Public opposition to the treaty reached a level never before seen in IP law, and perhaps in any area of law; public demonstrations were held against ACTA in a number of places in the world.[111]

---

106. Report on the Standing Committee on Copyright and Related Rights (SCCR), WIPO, WO/GA/51/5 Rev., 19 September 2019, 2, para. 5.
107. *Ibid.*, 2–3.
108. Proposal for Analysis of Copyright Related to the Digital Environment, WIPO, SCCR/31/4, 1 December 2015.
109. Report on the Standing Committee on Copyright and Related Rights (SCCR), WIPO, WO/GA/51/5 Rev., 19 September 2019, 3–4.
110. On ACTA and its origins *see* Yu, 'TRIPs and Its Achilles' Heel', 18 *Journal of Intellectual Property Law* (2011), 479 at 511–14.
111. Lee, 'ACTA Protests: Thousands Take to Streets Across Europe', BBC, 8 March 2012, https://www.bbc.com/news/technology-16999497 (last visited 2 March 2020); Jolly, 'A New Question of Internet Freedom', *The New York Times*, 5 February 2012, https://www.nytimes.com/2012/02/06/technology/06iht-acta06.html (last visited 2 March 2020); Wessels, 'Demonstrations against ACTA in US, Japan, Canada and Europe', Foundation for a Free Information Infrastructure, 8 June 2012, https://blog.ffii.org/demonstrations-against-acta-in-the-us-japan-canada-and-europe/ (last visited 2 March 2020).

With the failure of ACTA it seemed unlikely that countries could in any reasonable time thereafter agree on, and convince the public to accept, another international agreement on IP law, and particularly copyright law. The Beijing and Marrakesh Treaties were therefore beacons of hope for the future of international copyright law, even though it was clear that any and all future negotiation topics would face a steeper path to an international treaty.

ACTA stands out in the history of international IP law because of its failure and also because of the momentous public mobilisation against it; however, ACTA did fit into a line of bilateral and multilateral trade agreements that incorporated IP-specific provisions, including provisions concerning copyright law.[112] The North American Free Trade Agreement (NAFTA), which the United States, Canada, and Mexico began to negotiate and concluded before TRIPS was concluded, included copyright provisions that 'borrowed concepts and language from drafts of the TRIPS Agreement.'[113] Other bilateral and multilateral trade agreements followed suit, often reaching beyond the minimum standards in TRIPS and creating TRIPS-plus regimes.

Most free trade agreements refer to IP rights or include IP-specific sections. Of the 304 regional trade agreements that were notified to the WTO and were valid as of 15 March 2020, more than 200 contained some provisions on IP rights, and more than 100 included specific provisions on copyright and neighbouring rights.[114] Goldstein and Hugenholtz have noted that US-initiated trade agreements usually have a separate chapter with detailed provisions on IP rights, but EU-initiated trade agreements 'commonly refer to existing international conventions and rarely contain explicit substantive norms.'[115] US-initiated FTAs do feature detailed sections on IP rights while other FTAs, such as those concluded by the European Union and China, only include a brief reference to parties' international IP rights obligations and/or provide several sections on IP rights.[116] The Comprehensive and Progressive Agreement for Trans-Pacific Partnership (CPTPP), signed in 2018 without the United States, incorporates the Trans-Pacific Partnership text, which was originally negotiated with the United States, and CPTPP's IP rights chapter therefore follows the structure of detailed US FTA chapters.

---

112. ACTA was accompanied by legislative initiatives in the United States – the Stop Online Piracy Act (SOPA) and the PROTECT IP Act (PIPA) – which were both introduced in Congress in 2011.
113. Goldstein and Hugenholtz, *International Copyright: Principles, Law, and Practice* (4th edn., Oxford, 2019), 75, §3.4.2.1.
114. Regional Trade Agreements Database, http://rtais.wto.org/UI/PublicMaintainRTAHome.aspx (last visited 15 March 2020. As of 15 March 2020, the WTO Regional Trade Agreements Database provided information for 287 trade agreements. *Ibid.*
115. Goldstein and Hugenholtz, *supra* note 113, 75, §3.4.2.
116. *See also*, e.g., Australia–Hong Kong Free Trade Agreement, 26 March 2019, Chapter 14, available at https://www.dfat.gov.au/trade/agreements/in-force/a-hkfta/a-hkfta-text/Pages/a-hkfta-chapter-14-intellectual-property (last visited 15 March 2020). For an example of an FTA with less comprehensive IP law provisions *see* Free Trade Agreement between the Government of the People's Republic of China and the Government of Georgia, 13 May 2017 ('China-Georgia FTA'), Chapter 11. For an example of an EU trade agreement with more comprehensive IP law provisions *see* Comprehensive and Enhanced Partnership Agreement between the European Union and the European Atomic Energy Community and their Member States, of the one part, and the Republic of Armenia, of the other part, 24 November 2017 ('EU-Armenia FTA'), Chapter 7 ('Intellectual Property'), available at https://eur-lex.europa.eu/legal-content/EN/TXT/?uri=CELEX:22018A0126(01) (last visited 15 March 2020).

In their sections on copyright law,[117] US-initiated trade agreements contain provisions on the right of reproduction,[118] the right of communication to the public,[119] including the making available to the public[120] (accompanied by a clarification stating that the provision applies only to tangible copies),[121] the transferability of economic rights,[122] the protection against circumvention of technological measures[123] and against removal and alteration of rights management information,[124] and the rights of performers and producers of phonograms.[125] For limitations and exceptions the agreements repeat the three-step test.[126] In line with post-1998 US law, the agreements, with the exception of NAFTA, mandate that the copyright term, including the term for photographic works, be extended from the internationally mandated 50 years

117. Other provisions of the trade agreements concern copyright, such as the general provisions and the provisions on IP rights enforcement measures.
118. E.g., North American Free Trade Agreement ('NAFTA'), Article 1705(2); US-Australia FTA ('Australia'), Article 17.4(1); US-Chile FTA ('Chile'), Article 17.5(1); US-Bahrain FTA ('Bahrain'), Article 14.4(1); US-the Dominican Republic-Central America FTA ('CAFTA-DR'), Article 15.5(1); US-Mexico-Canada Agreement ('NAFTA 2.0'), Article 20.58; US-Korea FTA ('Korea'), Article 18.4(1); US-Colombia Trade Promotion Agreement ('Colombia'), Article 16.5(2); US-Jordan FTA ('Jordan'), Article 4(10); US-Panama Trade Promotion Agreement ('Panama'), Article 15.5(1); US-Peru Trade Promotion Agreement ('Peru'), Article 16.5(2); US-Singapore FTA ('Singapore'), Article 16.4(1).
119. E.g., NAFTA Article 1705(2)(c); Australia, Article 17(5); Chile, Article 17.5(2); Bahrain, Article 14.5; US-Morocco FTA ('Morocco'), Article 15.6; US-Oman FTA ('Oman'), Article 15.5; Colombia, Article 16.5.
120. E.g., Australia, Article 17.4(2) and 17.5; Chile, Article 17.5(3); Bahrain, Article 14.4(2) and 14.5; CAFTA-DR, Article 15.5(2) and 15.6; NAFTA 2.0, Article 20.59 and 20.60; Korea, Article 18.4(2); Morocco, Article 15.5(2); Oman, Article 15.4(2); Colombia, Article 16.5(3); Panama, Article 15.5(2); Peru, Article 16.5(3); Singapore, Article 16.4(3).
121. E.g., Australia, Article 17.4(2), fn 17-12; Chile, Article 17.6(3), fn 10; NAFTA 2.0, Article 20.60, fn 54; Peru, Article 16.5(3), fn 10.
122. E.g., Australia, Article 17.4(6); Chile, Article 17.7(1) and (2); CAFTA-DR, Article 15.6(6); NAFTA Article 1705(3); NAFTA 2.0, Article 20.66; Korea, Article 18.4(6); Morocco, Article 15.5(7); Oman, Article 15.4(6); Colombia, Article 16.7(3); Panama, Article 15.5(6); Peru, Article 16.7(3); Singapore, Article 16.4(6); Bahrain, Article 14.4(6); Jordan FTA, Article 4(14); TPP, Article 18.67; Colombia FTA, Article 16.7.
123. E.g., Australia, Article 17.4(7); Chile, Article 17.7(5); Bahrain, Article 14.4(7); CAFTA-DR, Article 15.6(7); NAFTA 2.0, Article 20.67; Korea, Article 18.4(7); Morocco, Article 15.5(8); Oman, Article 15.4(7); Colombia, Article 16.7(4); Jordan, Article 4.1(13); Panama, Article 15.5(7); Peru, Article 16.7(4); Singapore, Article 16.4(7). NAFTA did not include this provision.
124. E.g., Australia, Article 17.4(8); Chile, Article 17.7(6); Bahrain, Article 14.4(8); CAFTA-DR, Article 15.6(8); NAFTA 2.0, Article 20.68; Korea, Article 18.4(8); Morocco, Article 15.5(9); Oman, Article 15.4(8); Colombia, Article 16.7(5); Panama, Article 15.5(8); Peru, Article 16.7(5); Singapore, Article 16.4(8). NAFTA did not include this provision.
125. E.g., Australia, Articles 17.4 and 17.6; Chile, Article 17.6; Bahrain, Articles 14.4 and 14.6; CAFTA-DR, Article 15.7; Korea, Articles 18.4 and 18.6; Morocco, Articles 15.5 and 15.7; Oman, Articles 15.4 and 15.6; NAFTA, Article 1706; NAFTA 2.0, Article 20.62; Colombia, Article 16.6; Jordan, Article 4(11) and (12) and 4.1(11) and (12); Panama, Articles 15.5 and 15.7; Peru, Article 16.7(8); Singapore, Articles 16.4 and 16.5.
126. E.g., Australia, Article 17.4(10)(a); Chile, Article 17.7(3); Bahrain, Article 14.4(4); CAFTA-DR, Article 15.5(10)(a); NAFTA, Article 1705(5); NAFTA 2.0, Article 20.65(1); Colombia, Article 16.7(8); Jordan, Article 4.1(16); Peru, Article 16.7(8).

p.m.a. to 70 years p.m.a.[127] The agreements obligate countries to ensure that their government agencies not acquire and use infringing software.[128]

The copyright sections in the various US-initiated agreements exhibit some differences; since NAFTA the agreements have evolved, reflecting progress in negotiations at the international level and developments in US law.[129] For example, as regards the application of the three-step test, the US-Chile FTA, which was signed in June 2003 and became effective on 1 January 2004, declares in a footnote that countries may extend the existing exceptions and limitations under the test 'into the digital environment' and 'devise new exceptions and limitations that are appropriate in the digital network environment.'[130] The US-Australia FTA, which immediately followed the Chile FTA (being signed in May 2004 and effective on 1 January 2005), and some other subsequent FTAs[131] do not include the permissive footnote found in the Chile FTA and expressly prohibit countries from 'permit[ting] the retransmission of television signals (whether terrestrial, cable, or satellite) on the Internet without the authorization of the right holder or right holders, if any, of the content of the signal and of the signal.'[132] It is notable that the US-Australia FTA was signed after the US Supreme Court heard the *Aereo* case in April 2004 but before the Court decided the case in June 2004; the case concerned the unauthorised retransmission of television signals on the internet.[133]

Critics of IP law provisions in FTAs criticise the agreements for raising the minimum standards of IP protection above the minimum prescribed in the TRIPS and WIPO treaties, thereby locking countries into stricter IP protection than international law requires and constraining the flexibilities maintained by IP treaties. The copyright law sections in the FTAs provide examples of this phenomenon: beginning with the US-Chile FTA, the United States has successfully raised the minimum term of protection to 70 years p.m.a. in its FTAs, and to a minimum of 75 years from publication in NAFTA 2.0 for terms calculated other than on the basis of the life of a person.[134] The term of 70 years p.m.a. also appears in FTAs concluded by the European Union.[135] The EU-Armenia FTA, for example, mandates for the signatories

127. E.g., Australia, Article 17.4(4); Chile, Article 17.5(4) and 17.6(7); CAFTA-DR, (4); NAFTA 2.0, Article 20.63; Korea, Article 18.4(4); Morocco, Article 15.5(5); Oman, Article 15.4(4); Colombia, Article 16.5(5); Panama, Article 15.5(4); Peru, Article 16.6(5); Singapore, Article 16.4(4). NAFTA provided for a copyright term of only 50 years p.m.a. and excluded from the copyright term provision photographic works and works of applied arts. NAFTA 1705(4).
128. E.g., Australia, Article 17.4(9); Chile, Article 17.7(4); Bahrain, Article 14.4(9); CAFTA-DR, Article ...(9); Korea, Article 18.4(9); Morocco, Article 15.5(10); Oman, Article 15.4(9); Colombia, Article 16.7(6); Jordan, Article 4.1(15); Panama, Article 15.5(9); Peru, Article 16.7(6); Singapore, Article 16.4(9).
129. The 1985 US-Israel FTA included one general article on IP rights. Israel FTA, Article 14.
130. The footnote specifically mentions narrow exceptions for temporary reproductions necessary for transmissions 'in a network' but expressly excludes 'computer software' from these exceptions. Chile, Article 17.7(3), fn 17.
131. E.g., Bahrain FTA, Article 14.4(10)(b); CAFTA-DR, Article 15.7(10)(a); Colombia FTA, Article 16.7(9).
132. Australia, Article 17.4(10)(b). *See also* CAFTA-DR, Article 15.5(10)(b).
133. *American Broadcasting Companies, Inc. v. Aereo, Inc.*, 573 U.S. 431 (2014).
134. NAFTA 2.0, Article 20.63(b)(i).
135. E.g., EU-Japan FTA, Article 14.13; EU-Armenia FTA, Article 218.

the principle of national or regional exhaustion of IP rights, including copyright,[136] and the adoption of the resale right.[137]

Other examples of higher minimum standards in the copyright law provisions of US-initiated FTAs concern technological protection measures. Countries must provide for criminal penalties for violations of technological protection measures,[138] and the civil and criminal offences created for the protection of the measures must be 'separate ... and independent of any infringement under the [country's] copyright law.'[139] Possible exceptions to the provisions are enumerated in the FTAs.[140] These provisions in the FTAs expand the succinct language found in WCT Article 11 and WPPT Article 18.

Under Berne Article 20, which is also incorporated into TRIPS in TRIPS Article 9(1), special agreements may also 'contain other provisions not contrary to [Berne]', and the provisions of some FTAs do address matters outside the scope of existing international copyright law treaties – for example, the FTAs include provisions concerning the hierarchy of authorisations for phonograms,[141] the transferability of copyright,[142] the collective management of copyright,[143] the safe harbour for internet service providers,[144] and the promotion of public awareness regarding IP rights.[145]

D. CHALLENGES FOR NATIONAL COPYRIGHT LAWS AND THE INTERNATIONAL COPYRIGHT REGIME

As the previous sections of this chapter have shown, in the past three decades at both the international and national levels, copyright law has evolved; but for a variety of reasons copyright law has not accommodated all of the new technological developments and economic and social needs. The following sections discuss the recent developments that have shaped the current landscape of copyright law – the

136. EU-Armenia FTA, Article 211. *Cf.* EU-Canada FTA, Article 20.4 (leaving to the countries the determination of the exhaustion principle that they adopt).
137. EU-Armenia FTA, Article 122. In some other FTAs that the European Union has concluded the FTAs include only a provision regarding the exchange of views and information regarding the resale right. *See*, e.g., EU-Japan FTA, Article 14.15.
138. E.g., Australia FTA, Article 17.4(7)(a); Chile FTA, Article 17.7(5)(a); Panama FTA, Article 15.5(7)(a); Peru FTA, Article 16.7(4)(a); Singapore FTA, Article 16.4(7)(a).
139. E.g., Australia FTA, Article 17.4(7)(d); Peru FTA, Article 16.7(d); Panama FTA, Article 15.5(c).
140. In the United States a split exists among US circuit courts on whether a violation of the technological protection measure requires a nexus with a related infringement of copyright. *See Chamberlain Group, Inc. v. Skylink Technologies, Inc.*, 381 F.3d 1178 (Fed. Cir. 2004); *MDY Industries, LLC v. Blizzard Entertainment, Inc.*, 629 F.3d 928 (9th Cir. 2010).
141. E.g., Australia, Article 17.4(3); Chile, Article 17.7(1); CAFTA-DR, Article 15.5(3); Bahrain, Article 14.4(3); Panama FTA, Article 15.5(3); Peru FTA, Article 16.7; Colombia FTA, Article 16.7; TPP, Article 18.61; NAFTA 2.0, Article 20.61; Korea, Article 18.4(3); Morocco, Article 15.5(4); Oman, Article 15.4(3); Colombia, Article 16.7(1); Panama, Article 15.5(3); Peru, Article 16.7.
142. *See supra* note 122.
143. TPP, Article 18.70; NAFTA 2.0, Article 20.69; China-Australia FTA, Article 11.19; EU-Japan FTA, Article 14.16; China-Georgia FTA, Article 11.15; EU-Armenia FTA, Article 223.
144. E.g., Australia FTA, Article 17.11(29); Bahrain FTA, Article 14.10(29); CAFTA-DR, Article 15.11(27); Chile FTA, Article 17.11(23); TPP, Article 18.81 and 18.82; NAFTA 2.0, Article 20.88; China-Australia FTA, Article 11.20; CETA (EU-Canada FTA), Article 20.11.
145. EU-Japan FTA, 17 July 2018, Article 14.7.

structural issues that have formed the backdrop for copyright law policy and negotiations, and the substantive issues that have emerged for copyright law to address at the international and national levels.

I. Structural Issues

1. *The Fragmentation of International Copyright Law Negotiations*

In an era in which many international relations are on thin ice, some countries have used their negotiating leverage to seek advancements in their copyright or other IP interests through bilateral or plurilateral agreements rather than through multilateral treaties. Ricketson and Ginsburg remarked that 'the tendency to bilateralism may simply be a transitory phase',[146] but the fact that 15 years have passed since they made the remark suggests that the phenomenon has some durability. The Marrakesh and Beijing Treaties did raise optimism regarding the future of the multilateral process and copyright law, but that optimism has been tempered by the fact that the conclusion of both of the treaties represented 'low-hanging fruit' - the Marrakesh Treaty because of its widely accepted socially desirable goal, and the Beijing Treaty because of its pre-negotiated focus.[147]

TRIPS-plus instruments have generated numerous concerns: FTAs have contributed to a proliferation of rules that have made the international IP landscape increasingly fragmented and complex,[148] undermining legal certainty[149] and perhaps even creating a risk of new barriers to trade.[150] The fragmentation is problematic not only because of the multiplicity of the resulting rules but also because of the multiplicity of parallel negotiations at different levels and in various venues.[151] Negotiating trade treaties bilaterally or plurilaterally gives economically strong developed countries greater leverage because they face no serious opposition when they deal with weaker trade partners, whom they can pressure into less favourable trade terms than would have been negotiated in international agreements.[152]

146. Ricketson and Ginsburg, *supra* note 1, 175, para. 4.56.
147. Goldstein and Trimble, *supra* note 35, 389 ('Indeed, most of the countries that negotiated the 1996 WIPO Performances and Phonograms Treaty had been inclined at the time to include audiovisual performances within the 1996's treaty's scope, but stumbled on the issue of transferability of rights.').
148. Dinwoodie and Dreyfuss, *A Neofederalist Vision of TRIPS: The Resilience of the International Intellectual Property Regime* (Oxford/New York, 2012), 147.
149. Okediji, 'Legal Innovation in International Intellectual Property Relations: Revisiting Twenty-One Years of the TRIPS Agreement', 36(1) *University of Pennsylvania Journal of International Law* (2014), 191 at 196.
150. Ruse-Khan, 'IP and Trade in Post-TRIPS Environment', in Ullrich et al. (eds.), *TRIPS Plus 20: From Trade Rules to Market Principles* (Heidelberg, 2018), 163–83, at 164.
151. Hilty, 'Ways Out of the Trap of Article 1(1) TRIPS', in Ullrich et al. (eds.), *TRIPS Plus 20: From Trade Rules to Market Principles* (Heidelberg, 2018), 185–210, at 191; Drahos, 'BITs and BIPs: Bilateralism in Intellectual Property', 4 *Journal of World Intellectual Property* (2001), 791 at 798.
152. Dinwoodie and Dreyfuss, *supra* note 148, 148; Reichman, 'Reframing Intellectual Property Rights with Fewer Distortions of the Trade Paradigm', in Dreyfuss & Ng (eds.), *Framing Intellectual*

Commentators have pointed out that the United States in particular has used FTAs to impose its own legal norms onto other countries, with the result that the laws of those countries have become more like US law.[153] While there might not be anything intrinsically wrong with US law, critics have warned that not all aspects of the laws of developed countries are necessarily optimal, either internationally or even for the developed countries themselves.[154] When countries replicate laws that are imposed by external agreements into their legal systems they lose the possibility of local experimentation,[155] and they are deprived of sufficient internal debate regarding the suitability of the policy choices behind the copyright norms.[156]

Numerous commentators see the practice of bundling of IP law issues with trade issues as problematic; IP-specific agreements would presumably enable IP issues to be negotiated without distractions from cross-sectoral trade-offs and deals. The 'commodification' of IP law is antithetical to the promotion of sound copyright policies, and while trade concessions can be achieved through the linking of IP interests to other interests, countries may also lose important IP interests in trade negotiations when they exchange trade benefits for IP law concessions.[157] It would be naïve to expect that copyright law negotiations could be isolated from countries' other interests, but the impact on copyright law is significantly greater when countries bargain their many other interests in the same venue and in the same rounds of negotiations as they do their IP interests.

In addition to opportunities for countries to impose their standards on other countries, international IP law negotiations (and other international negotiations) provide opportunities for certain actors to pursue their own – purely domestic – goals. Some stakeholders use countries' negotiations to manipulate their own legislatures into changing domestic legislation that the stakeholders had unsuccessfully attempted to change through actions at the national level.[158] International negotiations (certainly the daily aspects) are largely controlled by countries' executive branches, making the negotiations an alternative route for lobbyists to bypass resistance in national legislatures. In addition to a treaty's potential for reshaping national laws, a treaty

Property Law in the 21st Century: Integrating Incentives, Trade, Development, Culture, and Human Rights (New York, 2018), 62–88, at 83.

153. Kur, 'From Minimum Standards to Maximum Rules', in Ullrich et al. (eds.), *TRIPS Plus 20: From Trade Rules to Market Principles* (Heidelberg, 2018), 133–62, at 136. On the exportation of IP laws from the United States, the European Union, and the EFTA countries, *see* Kennedy, *supra* note 2, 99.
154. Ericsson, 'The Commodification of Internet Intermediary Safe Harbors: Avoiding Premature Harmonization Around a Suboptimal Standard', in Ullrich et al. (eds.), *TRIPS Plus 20: From Trade Rules to Market Principles* (Heidelberg, 2018), 245–77, at 246.
155. Yu, 'Thinking about the Trans-Pacific Partnership (and a Mega-Regional Agreement on Life Support)', 20(2) *SMU Science and Technology Law Review* (2017), 97 at 114.
156. Ricketson and Ginsburg, *supra* note 1, 174, para. 4.55.
157. Dinwoodie and Dreyfuss, *supra* note 148, 148. On the 'trade in IP', *see also* Taubman, 'Thematic Review: Negotiating "Trade-Related Aspects" of Intellectual Property Rights', in Watal and Taubman (eds.), *The Making of the TRIPS Agreement: Personal Insights from the Uruguay Round Negotiations* (Geneva, 2015), 15–52, at 20. On developing countries accepting TRIPS 'for political and not economic reasons', *see also* Straus, 'TRIPs, TRIPs-plus oder TRIPs-minus – Zur Zukunft des internationalen Schutzes des Geistigen Eigentums', in Ohly et al. (eds.), *Perspektiven des Geistigen Eigentums und Wettbewerbsrechts* (Munich, 2005), 197–212, at 197–99.
158. Reichman, *supra* note 152, 84.

may limit a country's flexibility in its future lawmaking and international negotiations; international treaties, once concluded, are unlikely to be renegotiated for many years or decades, and treaties cement their rules into national laws.

Notwithstanding the strong criticism of TRIPS-plus developments, some positive recognition may be in order for certain aspects of TRIPS-plus developments. In the absence of new agreements on many multilateral issues in IP law, bilateral and plurilateral agreements have offered opportunities to update TRIPS and other IP treaties in line with the latest technological advancements.[159] As mentioned above, the copyright law provisions in TRIPS did not address issues pertaining to the internet, and the WCT and WPPT only dealt with basic internet issues.[160] Bilateral and plurilateral agreements can upgrade copyright laws and make a major contribution to harmonisation in the absence of a multilateral consensus on solutions to the challenges of the internet. The existing FTAs might not have fulfilled all of the parties' expectations, but countries have used bilateral and plurilateral agreements to clarify provisions in existing treaties and to make some provisions more specific.[161]

Even the much-criticised fragmentation of the IP law landscape has supporters; fragmentation creates a pluralistic environment in which countries can experiment with international norms on a smaller-than-multilateral scale. Nor does fragmentation prevent countries from internal experimentation; although the experimentation must fall within agreed-upon norms, countries may still engage in 'regulatory competition' to some extent.[162] Of course the value of experimentation is diminished if it is relegated merely to a determination of how the copyright law provisions of some select developed countries function in other countries.

Finally, Kennedy suggests that some of the value of bilateral and plurilateral agreements emanates from the fact that the agreements minimise the risks of conflicts among countries over IP law and policy. Kennedy argues that the agreements help prevent disputes in the WTO over TRIPS violations; he believes that 'FTAs have delivered results through negotiation that could not have been obtained through TRIPS dispute settlement.'[163]

2. *Other Structural Features*

Critical narratives of TRIPS-plus developments tend to present developing countries as casualties of FTAs and passive recipients of international IP treaty-making, but this characterisation might not be accurate.[164] Developing countries have mastered the tactics of treaty negotiation and have taken advantage of their strengths; Dinwoodie and Dreyfuss noted that these countries have 'moved intellectual property discussions

159. Yu, *supra* note 155, 111–12.
160. *See supra* C.I.
161. Roffe, 'Preferential Trade Agreements and the Protection of Genetic Resources and Associated Traditional Knowledge', in Robinson, Roffe and Abdel-Latif, *Protecting Traditional Knowledge: The WIPO Intergovernmental Committee on Intellectual Property and Genetic Resources, Traditional Knowledge and Folklore* (London, 2017), 303–16, at 303.
162. Dinwoodie and Dreyfuss, *supra* note 148, 146.
163. Kennedy, *supra* note 2, 99.
164. For commentary that puts into perspective the gains of developing countries from TRIPS in patent law, *see* Straus, *supra* note 157, 200–05.

to specialized international organizations that share their interest in preserving flexibilities and state autonomy.'[165]

Certainly, in the past two decades WIPO has grown more receptive to the opinions of developing countries; in 2007 it adopted the WIPO Development Agenda and in 2008 it created the Committee on Development and Intellectual Property.[166] The WIPO Intergovernmental Committee on Intellectual Property and Genetic Resources, Traditional Knowledge and Folklore, established in 2000, has been an important venue for the promotion of developing countries' interests. Commentators have pointed out that even some newer FTAs have begun to evidence developed countries' awareness of and even receptiveness to the concerns raised by developing countries.[167] For example, issues relating to the protection of genetic resources and traditional knowledge, while not being included in the final main texts of FTAs, have been mentioned in special annexes to some US-initiated FTAs.

Developing countries have become more assertive in pursuing their objectives; no longer is the advancement of IP policies a one-way street. Developing countries have sought to have their interests included in the WIPO agenda;[168] they have pressed for advances in the protection of traditional crafts and indigenous art, and they also turn to traditional IP rights for protection of their domestic interests.[169] The proposal by Senegal and Congo concerning resale right is an example of developing country reliance on copyright law to protect local artists from exploitation in the markets of the developed countries.[170] Chile and a number of Latin American countries supported an international definition of limitations and exceptions,[171] and developing countries were among the strong supporters of the Marrakesh Treaty.[172]

165. Dinwoodie and Dreyfuss, *supra* note 148, 152.
166. Committee on Development and Intellectual Property, WIPO, https://www.wipo.int/policy/en/cdip/ (last visited 7 March 2020).
167. Roffe, *supra* note 161, 303.
168. On the interests of Indian copyright owners *see* T. Reddy, 'TRIPS and TRIPS-Plus Development in India', in Gervais (ed.), *Intellectual Property, Trade and Development* (Oxford, 2014), 214–38, at 237.
169. *See*, e.g., Geographical Indications Act No. 8 of 2013 (Uganda).
170. Proposal from Senegal and Congo to Include the Resale Right (Droit de Suite) in the Agenda of Future Work by the Standing Committee on Copyright and Related Rights of the World Intellectual Property Organization, SCCR, SCCR/31/5, 4 December 2015.
171. Proposal by Chile on the Subject 'Exceptions and Limitations to Copyright and Related Rights', SCCR, SCCR/12/3, 2 November 2004, available at https://www.wipo.int/edocs/mdocs/copyright/en/sccr_12/sccr_12_3.pdf (last visited 4 March 2020). The proposal was supported by Argentina, Paraguay, Uruguay, Brazil, Costa Rica, and the Dominican Republic. *See also* Proposal by Chile on the Analysis of Exceptions and Limitations, SCCR, SCCR/13/5, 22 November 2005; Proposal by Brazil, Chile, Nicaragua and Uruguay for Work Related to Exceptions and Limitations, SCCR, SCCR/16/2, 17 July 2008; Proposal on Limitations and Exceptions for Libraries and Archives, Document Presented by Brazil, Ecuador and Uruguay, SCCR, SCCR/23/5, 22 November 2011; Proposal Concerning Limitations and Exceptions for Libraries and Archives and Limitations and Exceptions for Educational and Research Institutions and for Persons with Other Disabilities, Document Presented by Argentina, SCCR, SCCR/33/4, 1 November 2016.
172. On the involvement of the Latin American countries in SCCR, *see* Correa, 'TRIPS and TRIPS-Plus Protection and Impacts in Latin America', in Gervais (ed.), *Intellectual Property, Trade and Development* (Oxford, 2014),141–79, at 162.

The emergence of new stakeholders in copyright law over the past three decades is also an important development in the copyright landscape. The expansion of protectable subject matter to databases and computer programs and the affirmation of that expansion by international law have raised the consequences of copyright law, including international copyright law, for stakeholders whose previous interests in copyright law might have been marginal. The expansion has caused scientific research and software development to be directly affected by copyright law, and the stakeholders in these fields have significant interests in shaping the course of copyright law both nationally and internationally. As a result the public interests that are vested in copyright are no longer associated solely with free speech, access to information, and access to education;[173] copyright law now affects and influences matters such as the development of and access to medicines and mobile electronic technologies.[174]

Among the new stakeholders that have emerged and have influenced copyright law debates in the past three decades are large internet intermediaries - large ISPs. Large corporate stakeholders are not new to the copyright realm, but large ISPs are different from other large corporate stakeholders. While other stakeholders typically fall into either the category of copyright owners or the category of copyright users, ISPs' interests are mixed; sometimes their interests align with those of copyright owners, but other times they align with the interests of users.[175] Additionally, ISPs' business enables them to mobilise their user base to support ISP goals. This amalgamation of interests and voices is both powerful and problematic; for example, the public's interest in the EU's proposed EU Directive on Copyright in the Digital Single Market[176] - an interest that should be welcome - seemed to fade away as soon as changes to the proposal satisfied major ISPs.

User interests have received more attention since TRIPS was adopted; various organisations and platforms have provided a voice for users' perspectives or have organised the public to take actions to promote users' interests. This broad organisational and platform spectrum ranges from well-established interest-based organisations such as the National Federation of the Blind of the United States, which supported the negotiations and the United States' ratification of the Marrakesh Treaty,[177] to the Electronic Frontier Foundation, which has lobbied in legislative contexts that have included the discussions of the EU Directive on Copyright in the

173. Reichman, 'Intellectual Property in the Twenty-First Century: Will the Developing Countries Lead or Follow?', in Cimoli et al., *Intellectual Property Rights: Legal and Economic Challenges for Development* (Oxford/New York, 2014), 111-81, at 127.
174. Reichman et al., 'Intellectual Property and Alternatives: Strategies for Green Innovation', in Cimoli et al., *Intellectual Property Rights: Legal and Economic Challenges for Development* (Oxford/New York, 2014), 356-91, at 370.
175. The allegiances are still more complicated because some entities that were traditionally owners of copyright also invest in ISP businesses.
176. Directive (EU) 2019/790 of the European Parliament and of the Council of 17 April 2019 on copyright and related rights in the Digital Single Market and amending Directives 96/9/EC and 2001/29/EC.
177. *See*, e.g., Statement of the National Federation of the Blind before the Committee on Foreign Relations, United States Senate, 18 April 2018, available at https://www.foreign.senate.gov/imo/media/doc/041818_LaBarre_Testimony.pdf (last visited 3 March 2020).

Digital Single Market,[178] and the Pirate Party (first established in Sweden in 2006 but also later in other countries), which had, at least in its beginnings, copyright law-related issues as the key point of its political platform. The readiness of users to react to and organise around copyright law topics has been apparent in the public's reactions to the proposals for PIPA, SOPA, ACTA, and the EU Directive on Copyright in the Digital Single Market.[179]

Mounting criticism of imbalanced approaches to copyright law and policy also resulted in academic and policy-centred initiatives that presented demands to national and international legislators. In 2004, in support of a proposal for the WIPO development agenda that was submitted by Brazil and Argentina, representatives of non-governmental organisations, academics, scientists, and others signed the Geneva Declaration on the Future of the World Intellectual Property Organization; the Declaration called on WIPO to impose 'a moratorium on new treaties and harmonization of standards that expand and strengthen monopolies and further restrict access to knowledge.'[180] In 2011, the Global Congress on Intellectual Property and the Public Interest, convened at the American University Washington College of Law, produced The Washington Declaration on Intellectual Property and the Public Interest, which formulated the concerns of its signatories regarding the 'unprecedented expansion of the concentrated legal authority exercised by intellectual property rights holders'[181] and called for IP rights to reflect the interests of a broad spectrum of stakeholders in pursuit of interests such as maintaining a robust public domain, strengthening limitations and exceptions, and 'supporting cultural creativity.'[182] The Declaration also called for the control and prevention of 'enforcement excesses' and the implementation of specific steps in line with the 2001 Doha and 2007 WIPO Development Agendas.[183]

Finally, private ordering has influenced the copyright law landscape in the past three decades. While contractual and guild arrangements and the arrangements of the collecting societies had long been a part of the copyright landscape, new types of private ordering emerged in the last 30 years. The open source movement, which called for the accessibility of computer source code, produced in 1989 a general public licence (GNU GPL) – a unilateral instrument under which a copyright owner could distribute copies of its work to the public while imposing selected limitations on the utilisation of the work.[184] Creative Commons followed the GNU GPL model

178. Directive (EU) 2019/790 of the European Parliament and of the Council of 17 April 2019 on copyright and related rights in the Digital Single Market and amending Directives 96/9/EC and 2001/29/EC.
179. Preventing Real Online Threats to Economic Creativity and Theft of Intellectual Property Act of 2011 ('PIPA'), S. 968, 12 May 2011; the Stop Online Piracy Act ('SOPA'), H.R. 3261, 26 October 2011.
180. Geneva Declaration on the Future of the World Intellectual Property Organization, available at https://www.opensocietyfoundations.org/uploads/32d73d81-1463-498b-9b75-cfddc6126db3/wipo_declaration_0.pdf (last visited 6 March 2020).
181. The Washington Declaration on Intellectual Property and the Public Interest, Preamble, available at http://infojustice.org/wp-content/uploads/2011/09/Washington-Declaration.pdf (last visited 6 March 2020).
182. *Ibid.*
183. *Ibid.*
184. Transcript of Richard Stallman at the 2nd International GPLv3 Conference, 21 April 2006, https://fsfe.org/campaigns/gplv3/fisl-rms-transcript.en.html (last visited 7 August 2019).

and in 2002 released its own licensing suite, giving copyright owners a menu of licences with different licensing conditions that an owner might wish to impose.[185] Both the GNU GPL and the Creative Commons licences have attracted and been used by many copyright owners, including governmental and institutional copyright owners,[186] and have evolved, with their latest versions being released in 2007 and 2013, respectively.[187] In some countries courts and legislatures have recognised the licences as valid instruments with legal effects.[188]

Another form of private ordering that has affected the daily functioning of copyright law are ISP practices and terms of use that regulate aspects of users' activities, including the creation and use of the users' own copyrighted works and the users' exploitation of the copyrighted works of others. ISP operations are guided and regulated by industry practices and national laws, such as privacy laws, personal data protection rules, and copyright laws, particularly the immunity and safe harbour rules that mitigate ISP liability for copyright infringements. ISPs have implemented the laws, some of which have extraterritorial effects, both nationally and globally because the ISPs, at least initially, created no or very few localised rules. As a result, some national rules, including the notice and takedown rules of section 512 of the US Copyright Act, have been exported from their countries of origin to other countries.

II. Substantive Issues

The diverse landscape presented in the previous two sections forms the backdrop for current developments in copyright law and is likely to shape the future of copyright law. Many critics have voiced displeasure with new treaties that continuously raise IP protections, but this development is at least in part implied in copyright law by

185. 'Creative Commons is a global nonprofit organization that enables sharing and reuse of creativity and knowledge through the provision of free legal tools.' What Is Creative Commons and What Do They Do?, Creative Commons, https://creativecommons.org/faq/#what-is-creative-commons-and-what-do-you-do (last visited 15 August 2019).
186. *See*, e.g., Commission Decision of 22 February 2019 adopting Creative Commons as an open licence under the European Commission's reuse policy, European Commission, C(2019) 1655 final, 22 February 2019; Copyright Policy, the White House, https://www.whitehouse.gov/copyright/ (last visited 15 March 2020); Creative Commons License CCDR, Government of Canada, CCDR, Vol. 45(1), 3 January 2019, available at https://www.canada.ca/en/public-health/services/reports-publications/canada-communicable-disease-report-ccdr/monthly-issue/2019-45/issue-1-january-3-2019/article-7-creative-commons-license-ccdr.html (last visited 15 March 2020); Creative Commons (CC) Licensed Publications, WIPO, https://www.wipo.int/publications/en/creative_commons.jsp?id=104 (last visited 15 March 2020).
187. Lee, FSF 'Releases the GNU General Public License', Version 3, Free Software Foundation, 29 June 2007, https://www.fsf.org/news/gplv3_launched (last visited 7 August 2019).
188. In 2004 a German court ruled that the GNU GPL was a valid legal instrument under German law. LG München I, 21 O 6123/04, 19 May 2004. Axel Metzger quoted on Slashdot, https://yro.slashdot.org/story/04/07/23/1558219/german-court-says-gpl-is-valid (last visited 6 August 2019). The US Court of Appeals for the Federal Circuit affirmed the validity of the GNU GPL under US law in 2008. *Jacobsen v. Katzer*, 535 F.3d 1373 (2008). In some countries legislative changes helped clarify the legal status of public licences. Autorký zákon, §46(5) and (6), introduced by zákon č. 216/2006 Sb., kterým se mění zákon č. 121/2000 Sb., o právu autorském, o právech souvisejících s právem autorským a o změně některých zákonů (autorský zákon) (Czech Republic).

Berne, which allows countries to enter into agreements among themselves as long as the agreements provide rights more extensive than the rights in Berne or 'contain other provisions not contrary to [Berne].'[189] A change to Berne would be necessary to remove this limitation for future copyright law treaties, which change seems unlikely at this point.

In light of the Berne status quo, commentators have proposed means through which future treaties could prevent the further strengthening of IP rights protection. Some commentators have advocated maximum standards in future treaties, or ceilings of protection, rather than the floors of protection contained in the current treaties;[190] other commentators have proposed constraints on the adoption of TRIPS-plus provisions in new bilateral and regional trade agreements.[191] Some authors have called for the express inclusion of countervailing rights in treaties, including 'user rights.'[192]

Several commentators have argued that countries – particularly developing countries – are insufficiently using the available opportunities for limitations and exceptions in existing treaties, including the limitations and exceptions under the three-step test in copyright law. These commentators have emphasised the need for countries to explore and implement these flexibilities in the existing IP treaties.[193] Frankel has suggested that stronger IP norms should invigorate a country's 'incentive for domestic calibration' of IP rights, including, in copyright law, the exploitation of opportunities for limitations and exceptions.[194]

Given the limitations that Berne has placed on future agreements and the state of the copyright law landscape, two paths for the future of copyright law seem probable: the first path is the continuation of the route chartered by the Marrakesh Treaty – the delineation of limitations and exceptions within the scope of the three-step test. The SCCR has been exploring the limitations and exceptions for libraries and archives, and for educational and research institutions, and has also been looking at limitations and exceptions for persons with disabilities other than the disabilities covered by the Marrakesh Treaty.[195]

As the discussions in the European Union have shown with respect to the proposal for the EU Directive on Copyright in the Digital Single Market, and particularly with respect to its provisions on limitations and exceptions for text and

189. Berne Convention, Article 20.
190. Dreyfuss, 'TRIPS – Round II: Should Users Strike Back', 71 *University of Chicago Law Review* (2004), 21 at 27; Kur, *supra* note 153, 146–57; Ruse-Khan, *supra* note 150, 181.
191. Maskus & Reichman, 'The Globalization of Private Knowledge Goods and the Privatization of Global Public Goods', in Maskus and Reichman (eds.), *International Public Goods and Transfer of Technology under a Globalized Intellectual Property Regime* (Cambridge/New York, 2005), 36 ff.; Frankel, 'The Fusion of Intellectual Property and Trade', in Dreyfuss and Ng (eds.), *Framing Intellectual Property Law in the 21st Century: Integrating Incentives, Trade, Development, Culture, and Human Rights* (New York, 2018), 89–114, at 108.
192. Dinwoodie and Dreyfuss, *supra* note 148, 199; Dreyfuss, *supra* note 190.
193. Yu, 'The International Enclosure Movement', 82 *Indiana Law Journal* (2007), 827 at 828 and 832; Dinwoodie and Dreyfuss, *supra* note 148, 5; Land, 'Rebalancing TRIPS', 33 *Michigan Journal of International Law* (2012), 433 at 435.
194. Frankel, *supra* note 191, 103.
195. Ncube, Reid and Oriakhogba, 'Beyond the Marrakesh VIP Treaty: Typology of Copyright Access-Enabling Provisions for Persons with Disabilities', *J. World Intell. Prop.* (2020), 1 at 14.

data mining,[196] the friction point will be the intersection of socially desirable goals and commercial interests; while countries might be amenable to adopting new limitations and exceptions for socially desirable goals, copyright owners will push against limitations and exceptions that could result in the unauthorised commercial exploitation of copyrighted works.

The second path that the future of copyright law might follow would be the path of opportunities for copyright to support cultural, social, and economic development in developing countries and least-developed countries. While specifically tailored limitations and exceptions might be instrumental in promoting this development, an expansion of certain rights under copyright might also contribute to the development. The proposal by Senegal and Congo that WIPO consider resale rights is one example of how developing countries may promote the expansion of copyright protection to advance their development goals.[197]

Considering the two possible future paths that copyright law might follow, SCCR discussions regarding the rights of broadcasters might seem to be a detour. However, the rights of broadcasting organisations have been the subject of SCCR discussions for some time and continue, to some extent, the debates that started with the negotiations of TRIPS Article 14(3); broadcasters' rights are similar to the rights to audiovisual performances that found their way into the Beijing Treaty. The SCCR might be able to complete its discussions of broadcasters' rights, and a treaty on the rights might result from the negotiations.

The focus of future copyright law initiatives should be on the many issues that arise in the internet environment; these issues are no longer aberrations, they are the norm. Among the issues that negotiators and legislators should consider are complex jurisdictional and choice-of-law issues that transcend copyright law and IP law but are acutely relevant in copyright cases. The internet raises questions that affect protectability, ownership, the scope of rights, the scope of limitations and exceptions to the rights, and the enforcement of copyright. Questions about the meaning of 'publication' on the internet,[198] about exhaustion of copyright of digital files distributed on the internet,[199] about the uses of geoblocking to limit access to copyrighted works on the internet,[200] and about the liability of ISPs are only a few of the many internet-related questions that should be answered.

The attention of policy makers and international negotiators should also turn to issues of transaction costs, which are particularly pressing in a transnational context; the context is ever-present because of the exploitation of works on the internet. In the SCCR, the European Union and its Member States raised the issues of orphan

196. Directive (EU) 2019/790 of the European Parliament and of the Council of 17 April 2019 on copyright and related rights in the Digital Single Market and amending Directives 96/9/EC and 2001/29/EC, Articles 3 and 4.

197. For the proposal by Senegal and Congo *see supra* note 170.

198. *See* the questions posed by the US Copyright Office in Notification of Inquiry, U.S. Copyright Office, Library of Congress, Federal Register, Vol. 84, No. 233, 4 December 2019, pp. 66328–34.

199. E.g., *Capitol Records, LLC v. ReDigi Inc.*, 910 F.3d 649 (2d Cir. 2018).

200. E.g., *Triple Up Ltd. v. Youku Tudou Inc.*, 235 F. Supp. 3d 15 (D.D.C. 2017); *Spanski Enterprises, Inc. v. Telewizja Polska*, S.A., 883 F.3d 904 (D.C.Cir. 2018); *Plixer Intl., Inc. v. Scrutinizer GmbH*, 905 F.3d 1, 5 (1st Cir. 2018); *Carsey-Werner Co., LLC v. BBC*, No. CV 17-8041 PA (ASx), 2018 U.S. Dist. LEXIS 33862, at *11-21 (C.D. Cal. Feb. 23, 2018).

works and collective management, both of which the European Union addressed in its legislation in 2012 and 2014, respectively.[201] Copyright transaction costs were among the motivations for the Music Modernization Act, which the US Congress adopted in 2018 to improve music licensing for streaming media services.[202]

Collective management of rights and collective licensing in the transnational context are likely to raise competition law/antitrust concerns. Greater collaboration among countries in competition/antitrust law should also be fueled by the rise of new superpowers – not only the large multinational corporations but perhaps more importantly large ISPs (whether or not multinational) that harness powerful technologies to shape public opinion. Any collaboration in competition law should intersect with IP law, including copyright law; any competition law treaty making is likely to affect copyright law.[203] More than 20 years ago, Samuelson expressed the hope that 'the TRIPs Council [would] be more attentive to competition policy issues arising in intellectual property matters than WIPO has historically been.'[204] The competition law/copyright law interface has yet to see greater attention at the international level.

E. CONCLUSION

The past 30 years of copyright law have been turbulent and exciting, and the copyright law negotiations that have occurred at the international, regional, and national levels offer valuable lessons. Reasons for hope exist for the future of copyright law: A broad range of stakeholders can voice their interests in and concerns about the course of copyright law. Countries learned the downsides of overt secretiveness and excessive clubbiness in negotiations, and the lessons led to improvements in transparency about copyright law policy making. Formal meetings of all of WIPO's assemblies and committees, including the SCCR, are now webcast live to the public and recordings

201. *See* Justifications for Topics Proposed as Future Work by the European Community and Its Member States at the SCCR of 10–12 March 2008, WIPO, SCCR/17/4, 3 November 2008; Directive 2012/28/EU of the European Parliament and of the Council of 25 October 2012 on certain permitted uses of orphan works; Directive 2014/26/EU of the European Parliament and of the Council of 26 February 2014 on collective management of copyright and related rights and multi-territorial licensing of rights in musical works for online use in the internal market.
202. The Orrin G. Hatch–Bob Goodlatte Music Modernization Act, or Music Modernization Act or MMA, H.R. 1551, Pub.L. 115–264.
203. For examples of the intersection of competition law and copyright, *see*, e.g., *Radio Telefis Eireann (RTE) v. Commission of the European Communities*, ECJ, C-241/91 P and C-242/91 P, 6 April 1995; Commission Decision on Cross-Border Access to Pay-TV Paramount Commitments, 2016 Case AT.40023 1; Case T-873/16, *Groupe Canal+ SA v. European Commission*, 2018 EUR-Lex CELEX LEXIS 904 (Dec. 12, 2018), on appeal C-132/19 P; European Commission Press Release IP/19/1590, Antitrust: Commission Accepts Commitments by Disney, NBCUniversal, Sony Pictures, Warner Bros. and Sky on Cross-Border Pay-TV Services (Mar. 7, 2019); Antitrust Consent Decree Review – ASCAP and BMI 2019, U.S. Department of Justice, https://www.justice.gov/atr/antitrust-consent-decree-review-ascap-and-bmi-2019 (last visited 15 March 2020).
204. Samuelson, 'Challenges for the World Intellectual Property Organisation and The Trade-Related Aspects of Intellectual Property Rights Council in Regulating Intellectual Property Rights in the Information Age', 21 *European Intellectual Property Review* (1999), 578 at 587.

of the proceedings are publicly available on WIPO's website.[205] Developing countries now have a firm voice in international copyright law negotiations, and the selection of Mr. Daren Tang as the WIPO Director General suggests that WIPO might continue to reflect the interests of developing countries – Mr. Tang is a former SCCR chair, is from a developing country (Singapore), and has experienced personally the negotiations of the IP chapter of an FTA with the United States.[206] Because copyright law is at the intersection of fundamental and other important rights and many interests, any new copyright laws and copyright treaties will involve matters of great sensitivity to many stakeholders. Now all these interests can be put on the table.

205. Webcasting and Speech-to-Text Transcripts, WIPO, https://www.wipo.int/webcasting/en/ (last visited 7 March 2020).
206. Circular No. 3937, WIPO, 6 November 2019, available at https://www.wipo.int/export/sites/www/about-wipo/en/elections2020/circular3937.pdf (last visited 7 March 2020).

CHAPTER 4
TRIPS and Trade Marks

Guy Tritton

A. INTRODUCTION

In twenty-first century life, the power of brands - trade marks - is everywhere. Humans prefer to buy the known to the unknown. Many English speakers will be aware of the saying 'better the devil you know than the devil you don't'. It means we like to deal with someone whom we know or buy something we are familiar with than those we do not know or we are not familiar with. It is here that brands play a powerful role. The ability of pharmaceutical companies to charge much higher prices for branded pharmaceuticals which have exactly the same active ingredients as generic pharmaceuticals is a good example. They provide reassurance in a world of almost infinite choice.

Indeed, in a scientific study, it was found that subjects much preferred drinking Coca-Cola when they drank it from a branded cup than when they drank it not knowing whether or not it was Coca-Cola. In that study, brain scans showed that much more activity in the pleasure centres of the brain for subjects when they knew that they were drinking Coca-Cola.[1]

Given this, it is not surprising that brands are worth staggering sums. Thus, in 2020, the Apple brand was valued at $182 billion.[2] It is difficult to think of any other form of intellectual property which comes close to that. Not even a landmark patent is likely to come close to that.

A good reason is that unlike other forms of intellectual property, brands are protected by perpetual monopolies. They can last forever. Provided the trade mark owner carries on paying renewal fees in countries where the trade mark is registered, its monopoly rights will last forever. The nearest any other right gets to

1. McClure, Li, Tomlin, Cypert, Montague, 'Neural Correlates of Behavioural Preference for Culturally Familiar Drinks', 42 *Neuron* (2004), 379–87.
2. 'The World's Most Valuable Brands', *Forbes*, 2020.

that is copyright which, in many countries, now lasts for 70 years after the death of the author.

In the words of an English judge when asked whether or not the shape of a chocolate bar could be protected:

'The attraction of a trademark registration is that provided it is used and the fees are paid, it gives a perpetual monopoly. The problem is the same as the attraction but from the other perspective. Unless the registration of trademarks is kept firmly in its proper sphere, it is capable of creating perpetual unjustified monopolies in areas it should not.'[3]

Many will say that there is nothing wrong with that. Trade marks do not protect market places. They can never give rise to a dominant position in a relevant market. Others are free to develop and promote new brands. But when people say that, they are often thinking of traditional trade marks – that is word marks and logos. But nowadays, in many countries, one can register a trade mark for almost anything – shapes of products, smells, tastes, colours, sounds, everyday slogans, etc. Thus, in the European Union, there is no longer a requirement that a trade mark be capable of being graphically represented.[4]

It is right to acknowledge that there are some checks against registering the same.[5] Moreover, courts are loath to give monopolies in products where the copyright and design right have expired. Thus, in 2019, in a long running war, the General Court of the European Union held that a trade mark for the well-known Rubik's Cube toy, which had been granted in 1999, was invalid.[6] But as here, such requires judicial intervention. In the marketplace, it meant that the owner of the Rubik's Cube had had a registered trade mark for 20 years with all the deterrent effect that this had on the marketplace.

When the WTO Agreement on Trade Related Intellectual Property matters (TRIPS) was signed in Marrakesh in 1994, concerns about trade mark law giving unjustified and very wide protection to undertakings did not exist. Rather, the opposite. The concern was about a failure of many countries to give effective protection to intellectual property, including trade marks. The push for an intellectual property agreement in the GATT talks that gave birth to TRIPS was the belief of first world countries that unauthorised use of 'Western' intellectual property by the developing world represented substantial losses for the holders of such rights.[7] Indeed, it was said that US companies were losing tens of billions of dollars due to counterfeiting and piracy[8] and the US Trade Act had since 1988 given the US the power to impose sanctions on countries whose intellectual property regime was inadequate.[9] There was no counter-lobbying to ensure that as well as a 'floor', i.e., minimum trade

3. *Société des Produits Nestlé SA v. Cadbury UK Ltd* [2012] EWHC 2637 (Ch), Birss J.
4. Art. 4, Regulation 2017/1001 (EUTMR).
5. Art. 7.1(e) bans the registration of signs which consist exclusively of trade marks whose shape or other characteristic results from the nature of the goods themselves, are necessary to obtain a technical result or which gives substantial value to the goods.
6. T-601/17 *Rubik's Brand Ltd v. EUIPO* ECLI:EU:T:2019:765.
7. Daniel Gervais, *The TRIPS Agreement: Drafting History and Analysis* (4th edn., Sweet & Maxwell, 2012), ¶1.12.
8. Counterfeiting is the phrase used for acts of intentional trade mark infringement.
9. Gervais, *supra* note 7.

mark protection, there was also a ceiling to prevent misuse of trade mark law by trade mark owners.

In 1988, very little progress had been made in the TRIPS negotiations. Developing and developed countries had very different agendas. In 1989, when it was discussed at the mid-term negotiations in Montreal, little had been done other than to set topics for discussion.

However, this dramatically changed when the European Community (as it was then called) tabled a proposal which many see as the spark which lit the fuse that led to the adoption of TRIPS.[10] This was boldly entitled 'Draft Agreement on Trade-Related Aspects of Intellectual Property'. It was full and detailed. It included (inter alia) detailed provisions relating to trade marks including on what a trade mark could be, that trade mark rights could be acquired by registration or use, the rights conferred by trade mark protection, exceptions to those rights (e.g. fair use of descriptive terms), grounds for revocation (e.g. lack of genuine use in a five-year period) and that the use of a trade mark should not be unjustifiably encumbered by special requirements.

The reader of this draft proposal[11] will recognise much of the wording is very similar to EU trade mark law. Indeed, in some cases, the wording is almost identical. Thus, the proposal was that trade mark protection be denied to marks which are 'devoid of any distinctive character' and that the owner of a registered trade mark had exclusive rights in preventing third parties from 'using in the course of trade identical or similar signs for goods or services which are identical or similar to those in respect of which the trademark is protected, where such use would result in a likelihood of confusion'.

This is no coincidence. In the late 1980s, the European Community had embarked upon a significant programme of harmonising IP rights in the European Community. Leaving aside semi-conductor topographies, trade marks were the first that the European Commission decided to harmonise. Differences between trade mark law of Member States was seen as a real obstacle to free movement of goods in the EU.

In 1988, the first Trade Marks Directive was adopted.[12] The genesis for this was a paper published in 1976 which was a thorough overview of the need for trade marks and the need for a single EC law on trade marks.[13] The Commission's proposal to the GATT talks had the advantage of being a proposal that was intended to harmonise the laws of Member States that had widely differing trade mark laws – a good starting point for WTO talks on harmonising provisions of IP law of WTO Member States.

The European Commission's proposal aligned closely with the final text of TRIPS. Thus, Article 16 TRIPS (rights of trade mark owners to prevent confusion) adopts the Commission's proposal almost *verbatim*, which in turn is almost identical

10. MTN.GNG/NG11/W/68 29th March 1990, Gervais, *supra* note 7, ¶1.19.
11. It can be accessed at http://www.tripsagreement.net/documents/GATTdocs/Draft_Agreement_on_Trade_Related_Aspects_of_IP_Rights_E_E.pdf (accessed 5 September 2020).
12. 89/104/EC.
13. Richard Davis, Thomas St Quintin, Guy Tritton, *Tritton on Intellectual Property in Europe* (5th edn., Sweet & Maxwell, 2018). *See* 'Memorandum on the creation of an EEC trade mark' SEC (76) 2462 July 1976.

to that of the rights conferred by a trade mark in the first Trade Marks Directive.[14] It can thus be fairly said that EU trade mark law led to and became the trade mark provisions of TRIPS.

B. OTHER TREATIES RELATING TO TRADE MARKS

Whilst TRIPS is without doubt, the most important international treaty on the substantive law of trade marks, other treaties should not be overlooked. Indeed, TRIPS requires WTO Members to adopt the trade mark provisions of the Paris Convention.[15] The Paris Convention had a different goal to TRIPS. Whereas TRIPS was, as discussed above, aimed at providing a minimum level of protection for intellectual property rights (IPRs), the main goal of the Paris Convention was to ensure that nationals of any country of the Paris Union were treated no less favourably by other countries of the Paris Union than their own nationals. As it says on the WIPO website, it was the first major step taken to help creators ensure that their intellectual works were protected in other countries.[16]

This is reflected in the trade mark provisions of the Paris Convention. In the original 1883 version, the main provision (Article 6.1) was mainly concerned with ensuring that trade marks filed in one Paris Union country were accepted for filing and protection in other countries of the Paris Union. The only express ground for refusal of a trade mark was where such would be contrary to morality or public order. This was clearly deficient and over time, amendments were made to the Paris Convention. Thus, by the amending Washington Act 1911, more detailed grounds were set out for refusal of an application for a trade mark, including where a trade mark was devoid of any distinctive character and trade marks which were, in essence, descriptive.[17] The Washington Act also added that marks may be refused registration where they infringe rights acquired by third parties in the countries where protection was claimed. The 1925 Hague Act added Article 6 *bis,* namely the right to refuse registration of a mark well-known in the country of registration as the mark of a national of another country and the refusal of protection of state emblems and heraldic symbols (Article 6*ter*). The 1958 Lisbon Act added to Article 6*bis* the obligation to prohibit the use of well-known marks.

The incremental changes to the Paris Convention reflect the changing concerns over the years of governments as to protection of intellectual property. As a result, the provisions are somewhat of a smörgåsbord. Moreover, the Paris Convention never truly escapes its origins which was not to harmonise the laws of, inter alia, trade marks, but to provide for national treatment for foreigners as if they were nationals of the Contracting State. But it is fair to say that by the latest amending act, the Stockholm Act 1967, the Paris Convention did provide for some measure of harmonisation of trade mark law in Union countries, but in a rather disorderly manner.

14. And indeed, these 'likelihood of confusion' provisions have not changed materially in later versions of the Trade Marks Directives.
15. The Paris Convention for the Protection of Intellectual Property, 1883, Art. 2.1 TRIPS.
16. https://www.wipo.int/treaties/en/ip/paris/ (accessed 6th September 2020).
17. In the Washington Act, this was Art. 6.2 but is now Art. 6*quinquies*(B).

Perhaps the most significant harmonising measure of substantive trade mark law of the Paris Union is Article *6quinquies*(B) which says:

> 'Trade marks covered by this Article may be neither denied registration nor invalidated except in the following cases:
>
> (i) when they are of such a nature as to infringe rights acquired by third parties in the country where protection is claimed;
> (ii) when they are devoid of any distinctive character, or consist exclusively of signs or indications which may serve, in trade, to designate the kind, quality, quantity, intended purpose, value, place of origin, of the goods, or the time of production, or have become customary in the current language or in the bona fide and established practices of the trade of the country where protection is claimed;
> (iii) when they are contrary to morality or public order and, in particular, of such a nature as to deceive the public. It is understood that a mark may not be considered contrary to public order for the sole reason that it does not conform to a provision of the legislation on marks, except if such provision itself relates to public order.'

These provisions are, however, subject to the application of Article 10*bis*.[18]

These provisions are well-known to trade mark lawyers throughout the world. Thus, in the European Union, the wording is reflected in both the EU Trademark Regulation and the Trade Marks Directive. It is perhaps worth noting that Article *6quinquies* does not allow for a provision against, for example, the registration of trade marks which would monopolise a technical function or arise from the nature of the goods themselves. Indeed, such a provision would be contrary to Article *6quinquies(B)*. The list there is plainly exhaustive ('may neither be denied registration nor invalidated except in the following cases').

Yet, many countries have grounds that prevent registration of such marks. Thus, Article 4.1(e) of the EU Trade Marks Directive prohibits the registration of signs which consist exclusively of:

(i) The shape, or another characteristic, which results from the nature of the goods themselves
(ii) The shape, or another characteristic, of goods which is necessary to obtain a technical result
(iii) The shape, or another characteristic, which gives substantial value to the goods.

This is an absolute ground of refusal that cannot be overcome by, for example, acquired distinctive character. The policy for this ground is fairly obvious – once one understands that trade marks can be more than words and logos. Thus, a monopoly that lasts forever in a shape that has a technical effect is plainly contrary to public

18. Art. 10*bis* requires Member States to protect nationals of a WTO Member State from unfair competition. It is not obvious how this could be said in any way to provide further grounds for refusal of an application for a trade mark.

interest. The United States also prohibits the registration of any sign that 'comprises any matter that, as a whole, is functional'.[19]

It is here that the problem lies with the Paris Convention. Its last update was in 1978. The Internet had yet to come into being. In 1978, trade marks were words and logos. The idea that the shape of a product, a smell or a taste could be a trade mark was most likely never even thought about. It is telling that the term 'trade mark' in the Paris Convention is never defined. No doubt this is because in 1883 it was considered by the draftsmen of the Paris Convention that there was no need to define what a trade mark was. Trade, industry and the public fully knew what a trade mark is. Why define the obvious. One has little doubt that in 1883, all would have wholly rejected any idea that a slogan such as 'JUST DO IT' was a trade mark or that the shape of a product could be a trade mark.

By the late 1980s, the Paris Convention was beginning to show its age. There are only so many times one can alter a convention whose origins lie in the nineteenth century and whose main goal in that century was to provide for reciprocal protection.

Other international conventions in the field of trade marks are procedural and are not aimed at harmonising substantive law of trade marks. Thus, the 1994 Trademark Law Treaty, the Madrid Protocol and Madrid Agreement all aim at making applications for trade marks in a number of countries a streamlined procedure.[20] The Madrid System allows for an international application whereby the applicant can designate the countries for which it seeks protection.

C. TRADE MARK PROVISION OF TRIPS

By the late 1980s, the consumer lived in a world of mass advertising, billion dollar brands and brand images. The concept of what could be a trade mark had expanded beyond words and logos. As discussed above, there was no international treaty as to what could be a trade mark. Thus, there was a need for a more thorough and comprehensive approach to the law of trade marks.

Moreover, economic power in developing countries meant that first world countries such as the USA were not only seeing such countries as trading rivals but also as valuable consumer markets for US brands. The problem was that, as said above, protection for, inter alia, registered trade marks was ineffectual and ineffective.

Thus, it is fair to say that TRIPS was an important 'first' at a multilateral level for intellectual property, including trade marks.[21] As will be known to readers, TRIPS sets out a minimum level of protection. It is thus not an exhaustive harmonising measure like an EU directive. WTO Member States are free to provide protection to trade mark owners beyond that.[22] Some have sought to argue that the wording that Members may

19. 15 U.S.C. §1052. A feature is functional as a matter of law if it is 'essential to the use or purpose of the article or if it affects the cost or quality of the article.' *TrafFix Devices, Inc. v. Mktg. Displays, Inc.*, 532 U.S. 23, 33, 58 USPQ2d 1001, 1006 (2001); *Qualitex Co. v. Jacobson Prods. Co.*, 514 U.S. 159, 165, 34 USPQ2d 1161, 1163–64 (1995); *Inwood Labs., Inc. v. Ives Labs., Inc.*, 456 U.S. 844, 850, n.10, 214 USPQ 1, 4, n.10 (1982).
20. The most notable exception to this is that Art. 16 of the Trademark Law Treaty allows applicants to apply for service marks.
21. Gervais, *supra* note 7, ¶2.223.
22. Art. 1.1.

provide 'more extensive protection ... provided such does not contravene [TRIPS]' means that there are limits to that, for example a kind of 'ceiling'.[23]

However, the fact is that, when it comes to the trade mark provisions of TRIPS, there is a stark contrast between the pro-trade mark owner provisions and the pro-user (defendant) provisions. Thus, Article 16 TRIPS states that the owner of a registered trade mark *shall* have the exclusive right to prevent third parties from using an identical or similar mark for identical or similar goods where a likelihood of confusion would arise. But in contrast, Article 17 (exceptions) merely says that Members *may* provide limited exceptions to the rights conferred by a trade mark *such as fair use of descriptive terms*. Indeed, not only is this provision optional but itself has a mandatory clawback ('provided that such exceptions take account of the legitimate interests of the owner of the trade mark and of third parties'). Thus, it envisages that there may *fair use* of a descriptive term which could be prevented by a trade mark owner.

In many ways, herein lies the problem with TRIPS. Because it arose out of intensive lobbying by US and EU industries, it is one-sided.[24] No man or woman attended GATT to lobby on behalf of the consumer, the common man, the owner of an SME, and indeed the main players were interested in protecting the rights of trade mark owners. There were no *amici curiae* briefs on behalf of the general public. The negotiations for TRIPS, being under the umbrella of the WTO, were first and foremost trade talks – protecting the rights of trade mark owners from loss of profits from counterfeiting. If someone had said, I would like to know that I can use the historical titles of books without fear of being sued for trade mark infringement at the talks and I speak on behalf of all writers and publishers, then maybe the limitations would have been much more comprehensive and mandatory. That did not happen and many big undertakings have profited unfairly from the same.[25]

Indeed, it could well be said that the fact that Members are not *obliged* to provide a defence of fair use of descriptive terms is striking because there can of course be no objection to the same. Put another way, Article 17 TRIPS says that there are some cases where *fair use of a descriptive term* may not be permitted – that is where it fails to take account of legitimate interests of the owner of the trade mark. But when can the interests of a legitimate owner prevail over *fair* use. The words 'fair' and 'fairness' has many means but one of them is 'even-handedness' and implicit in it is a balancing of the respective interests of parties. But it would be a very exceptional case for someone not to be allowed to use a sign *fairly* in a descriptive way. One can hardly do better than an English judge from 1910 who said 'Wealthy traders are habitually eager to enclose part of the great common of the English language and to exclude the general public of the present day.'[26]

But let us turn to the specific provisions of TRIPS that relate to trade marks.

23. Gervais, *supra* note 7, ¶2.24.
24. E.g. *see* A. Koury *Menescal* 'Those Behind the TRIPS Agreement: The Influence of the ICC and the AIPPI on International Intellectual Property Decisions', 2 *IPQ* (2005), 155–82.
25. Thus, Disney Enterprises Inc own a European Union Trademark 005618251 for 'ALICE IN WONDERLAND' for inter books – the well-known title of Lewis Carroll's book published in 1865!
26. Cozens-Hardy MR in *Joseph Crossfield & Sons Limited* [1910] 1 Ch 13 (Court of Appeal, England and Wales).

I. What Signs Are Protectable?

Article 15.1 TRIPS requires Members to provide for the registration of any signs that are 'capable of distinguishing the goods or services of one undertaking from those of other undertakings'. Article 15 says that these could be words, personal names, letters, numerals, figurative elements or combinations of colours. It also says that Members may make registrability dependent on distinctiveness acquired through use.[27]

This definition is very similar to the European Commission's proposal discussed above - in particular, the need that a sign be capable of distinguishing goods or services of one undertaking. It draws on the whole theory of trade marks that they allow the consumer to choose the goods or services that they want of one undertaking over another and thereby ensure the twin goals of effective competition and avoiding consumers being misled. This longstanding theory was cited in a number of significant cases in the 1970s by the ECJ when seeking to strike a balance between the rights of trade mark owners and the goal of the (then) European Community to achieve a single, borderless single market. In *Hoffmann La-Roche v. Centrafarm*,[28] the ECJ said that the 'essential function' of a trade mark was to guarantee the identity of the origin of a trade marked product to enable the consumer to distinguish that product from another without the possibility of any confusion. Plainly, if a sign is used which does not allow a consumer to distinguish the goods of one undertaking from another, then it cannot guarantee the identity of the goods of one undertaking from another. Thus, this definition logically follows from the essential function of a trade mark.

Article 15.2 of TRIPS says that Members may deny registration of a trade mark on other grounds provided that they 'do not derogate from the provisions of the Paris Convention'. As discussed above, Article 6*quinquies*.B Paris Convention sets out the grounds on which 'trade marks' may be denied registration. They are exhaustive.

Thus, as discussed, the EU and US provisions on refusing registration of marks whose shape or other characteristics are there to achieve a technical or functional result, regardless of whether they are distinctive or not, would appear to be contrary to TRIPS as they are not allowed under Article 15.1 and also not a ground set out in the Paris Convention. But other countries also have such prohibitions.

In the *Appellate Body Report on s.211 of the Omnibus Appropriations Act*,[29] the Appellate Body of WTO had to consider whether Article 15 TRIPS prohibited US legislation which was intended to prevent those who had an interest in trade marks related to certain businesses or assets confiscated by the Cuban government from registering the same without the original owner's consent. The Appellate Body held that this was not a breach of Article 15 because s.211 was not *inconsistent* with the grounds mentioned in Article 15. In short, Article 15 TRIPS was not concerned with ownership of marks.[30]

This decision undoubtedly seems right. Article 15 is concerned with the criteria that should apply when a national intellectual property office or court is considering whether or not to allow a sign to be registered. It was plainly not intended to deal

27. A trade mark can be inherently distinctive or acquire through use distinctive character.
28. C-102/77 [1978] ECR 1139.
29. WT/ DS176/AB of 2 January 2002.
30. Appellate Body Decision. *See* Davies et al., *supra* note 13, ¶3-024.

with the permissibility of state sanctions or punitive measures by one country against another. This is a classic example of a *lex specialis* not being interpreted as a *lex generalis* governing wholly different areas of government policy that the draftsmen and negotiators never had in mind when agreeing an international agreement. Put another way, when more than one norm applies, (here trade mark law and sanctions by one country against another country for property confiscated by the latter), the interpreter should construe all the rules of treaties 'with a sense of coherence and meaningfully ... in a way that allows, as far as possible, to view norms pertaining to different regimes as a single set of compatible obligations'[31]

But yet, this decision can give no comfort to the EU, US or indeed other countries that have grounds for refusing applications for trade marks that are not mentioned in Article *6quinquies* Paris Convention. Clearly, these provisions are trade mark provisions. They lie firmly within the realm of trade mark law. They are plainly inconsistent with the exhaustive grounds set out in the Paris Convention.

Article 15.3 allows Member States to make registrability of trade marks depend on use, but not the filing of an application. In 1994, there was a clear split between countries that afforded precedence to the undertaking first to use a mark and those who were first to file. In broad terms, common law countries like the US, Canada and the UK favoured first-to-use whereas other European countries favoured first-to-file. This does not mean that undertakings in common law countries had no need to file for registered trade marks. Registered trade marks are much easier to enforce than relying upon other causes of action, such as unfair competition or passing off. But if there was a clash of rights between two registered trade marks, in countries like the UK and the US, the first-to-use prevailed even it was the second-to-file.

In the US, consistent with Article 16.3 TRIPS, the law does not require an undertaking to have used the mark prior to filing. There must however be a bona fide intention to use the mark. Moreover, when it comes to infringement proceedings, if the defendant has used its mark prior to the filing date of a registered mark, it will generally prevail. In the EU, while fundamentally a first-to-file system, there is some protection for earlier users and if they own unregistered 'earlier rights' in a trade mark such that they can prevent (by way of injunction) the owner of a registered trade mark from using its mark, then this is not only a ground of invalidity but also a defence.[32]

In the author's experience, trade mark lawyers are very polarised about first-to-file vs. first-to-use. This tends to reflect their cultural traditions. But undoubtedly a large problem in many countries is the huge increase in trade mark filings and in particular, cyber squatters who have no interest in using a trade mark, applying for a wide range of trade marks that are used by others merely to extort monies for transferring the trade marks. Whilst these filings can be objected to on the grounds

31. Vito Todeschini, 'The ICCPR in Armed Conflict: An Appraisal of the Human Rights Committee's Engagement with International Humanitarian Law', 35(3) *Nordic Journal of Human Rights* (2019), 203. Here Todeschini was looking at the relationship between a treaty on civil and political rights and international humanitarian law but his observation could apply to any two fields.
32. E.g. under Trade Marks Directive, Art. 5.4(a) (ground of invalidity) and Art. 14.3 (defence). The latter defence only applies if use is limited to a 'particular locality'. In both cases, the user must have an 'earlier right'. Mere use is not enough. As discussed below, the exclusive rights granted under Art. 16.1 TRIPS are without prejudice to 'existing prior rights'.

of bad faith in most countries, a failure to give some protection to those who are first-to-use allows such practices to flourish.

But leaving aside cyber squatters, another major problem is the practice nowadays of applicants filing for a very wide range of goods and services in many classes regardless of whether there is any intent to use the mark for some of them. Thus, in the EU, there is no requirement that an applicant should have used or even have a bona fide intention to use the mark applied for the goods or services for which registration is sought. In a recent CJEU case, *Sky v. SkyKick,*[33] on reference from the UK where applicants for a UK mark must state on trade mark applications that they have a bona fide intention to use the mark for the goods or services for which registration is sought, the CJEU had to consider whether applications for very wide range of specifications where for many of the goods or services, the applicant had, at the time of filing, no intention to use the mark or indeed there was any likelihood that such would happen, were made in bad faith precisely because there is no other form of control against this. The judgment of the CJEU went only so far as to say that applications which have the intention of undermining third parties or are for purposes other than those falling within the functions of a trade mark constitute bad faith but only for the goods or services where there was no intention to use the mark. This finding provides little reassurance and is unlikely to deter in any way the filing for very wide specifications. The outcome is that there is a very large number of registered trade marks which cover goods and services where the undertaking has not used them for many years.

It is of course right to acknowledge that supporters of a first-to-file system say that the necessary check against the above abuses is that a registered trade mark is liable to be revoked for lack of genuine use if it has not been used for a defined period (e.g. in the EU, it is five years). This is often said to be 'use it or lose it'. Whilst this indeed does provide some balance, it requires someone to bring revocation proceedings. Moreover, it is five years from the date of registration and not the date of filing and also merely revokes the trade mark with effect from the end of the five-year period rather than *ab initio*. Furthermore, it fails to take account of the common practice of 'evergreening' whereby applicants re-apply for the same mark and specification of goods or services to avoid the problem of revocation. This practice, whilst largely condemned, is not expressly dealt with in many trade mark laws. It is normally dealt with as being made in bad faith (but that is difficult to prove) or somehow as an abuse of the trade mark system.[34] But it is not difficult to overcome such objections, such as by a trade mark owner saying that its business and trade priorities had changed, etc.

33. C-371/18 *Sky plc v. Skykick UK Limited* ECLI:EU:C:2020:45.
34. R-1849/2017-2 *Kreativni Dogadaji d.o.o. v. Hasbro, Inc.* ('Such conduct, which improperly and fraudulently extends the five-year grace period, is manifestly intended to circumvent the obligation to prove use of earlier marks and must be considered as an intention to distort and imbalance the European Union trade mark system as established by the EU legislators. Therefore the application of the contested EUTM, in so far as it included goods and services already covered by earlier registrations, ... was made in bad faith'.) Appeal dismissed, T-663/19 *Hasbro Inc v. EUIPO* ECLI:EU:T:2021:11.

II. Rights Conferred by a Registered Trade Mark

Article 16.1 TRIPS confers exclusive rights on the owner of a registered trade mark to prevent the use by third parties of identical or similar trade marks for identical or similar goods where such use would give rise to a likelihood of confusion. The exclusive right may not prejudice existing prior rights. Article 16.2 makes it clear that Article 6*bis* Paris Convention well-known marks extends to service marks. Article 6*bis* prevents the use of a trade mark which is a 'reproduction, an imitation or a translation, liable to create confusion' of a well-known trade mark. Article 16.3 extends that protection against any trade mark used for goods or services which would 'indicate a connection' between those goods or services and that of the Article 6*bis* mark, provided that the interests of the owner of the registered trade mark are likely to be damaged by use.

Here, the European Commission did not get its way. It sought protection for registered marks which have a reputation from signs, without due cause, taking unfair advantage of or which are detrimental to the distinctive character or repute of the trade mark. This provision appears almost *verbatim* in the current EU Trademark Regulation and Trade Marks Directive. The protection is limited to Article 6*bis* marks. Interestingly, the Brussels draft of Article 16.3 included the phrase 'unfairly indicate a connection'. But that was removed because many participants considered it difficult to interpret. However, to act as a counterweight, an additional requirement that 'interests of the trade mark owner are likely to be damaged by such use' was substituted. It is not clear whether it was intended by this to remove any cause of action based on a sign of a third party taking unfair advantage of the reputation of a registered trade mark. This is because this is more concerned with the *benefit* that arises to the user of a sign when that benefits from the transfer of the image of a registered mark with a reputation. Thus as said by the CJEU in *L'Oréal v. Bellure,* unfair advantage happens when where 'that party sought by that use to ride on the coat-tails of the mark with a reputation in order to benefit from the power of attraction, the reputation and the prestige of that mark and to exploit, without paying any financial compensation, the marketing effort expended by the proprietor of the mark in order to create and maintain the mark's image'.[35] It is not obvious that this damages the interests of the owner of the registered trade mark. But it would do so if the use would damage the brand image of the trade mark through inappropriate use.[36] It may also damage the licensing interests of the trade mark owner – as *ex hypothesi,* if the sign benefits from the reputation of the trade mark, there is a licensing opportunity for the owner.

A 'hot potato' topic is whether Article 16 confers merely a negative right to *prevent* others from using a registered trade mark or whether it confers a positive right to the trade mark owner the right to *use* the trade mark. This was discussed by the WTO Panel in *Australia – Tobacco Plain Packaging.*[37] This case concerned whether or not Australian law that restricted the advertising of cigarettes including a

35. C-487/07 *L'Oréal v. Bellure* ECLI:EU:c:2009:378, ¶50.
36. What is often called 'tarnishment'.
37. WT/DS435/R, WT/DS441.R, WT/DS458/R and WT/DS467/R Australia – Certain Measures concerning Trademarks, Geographical Indications and other plain packaging requirements applicable to tobacco products and packaging, 28 June 2018.

requirement that they be marketed in plain boxes with minimum branding and a ban on tobacco logo marks was contrary to Article 16 TRIPS. If the right was merely a negative right, then there could be no infringement of Article 16. However, if the right granted by Article 16 was a positive right, then plainly there was a good argument that such laws, even though for the good of public health, were contrary to Article 16.

The argument of certain governments was not that Article 16.1 conferred a 'positive' right to use the registered trade mark as they saw fit. The argument was more subtle. It was that Article 16.1 obliged Member States to refrain from 'regulatory conduct that undermines or eliminates the distinctiveness of registered trademarks'.[38] In particular, they argued that a ban on the use of non-word marks (i.e., logos) would reduce the distinctiveness of logos and graphical sign marks as consumers would no longer associate the trade marks with the products for which they are registered.

The Panel cited an earlier decision (*EC – Trademarks and Geographical Indications (Australia)* that Article 16.1 TRIPS only provides for a negative right to prevent third parties from using a sign in certain circumstances.[39] The Panel concluded that Article 16.1 did not establish a positive right for a trade mark owner to use its registered trade mark. Rather, it merely provided for a negative right to exclude others.[40] It also concluded that Article 16.1 did not confer a right to 'protect against reduction of distinctiveness of a trademark, or even a right to protect against lesser awareness of a trademark among consumers'.[41] The Panel also held that Article 16 does not require Member States to provide a minimum opportunity to use a registered trade mark.[42]

Given the fact that many countries have introduced plain packaging tobacco legislation to reduce the allure and attractiveness of cigarettes for plainly good public health reasons, it is perhaps not that surprising that the Panel dismissed the arguments that such laws were contrary to TRIPS. There plainly would have been an outcry and it would have been a very brave and indeed foolhardy panel which went against public sentiment.

In the author's view, the Panel was undoubtedly right. Thus, a trade mark registration does not justify its use on illegal goods or to infringe the rights of others. Moreover, one does need a registered trade mark to use a brand. In other words, if a registered trade mark were to confer a positive right to use a mark, it might mean that one cannot use a mark if one does not have a registered trade mark. As said by Professor Cornish:

> 'The fact that intellectual property gives a right to control the activities of others has a number of implications, often inadequately understood. The right owner does not need the right in order to exploit a market for its goods or services: a patent is not a pre-condition to exploiting one's own invention. By way of corollary, the right gives no liberty to ignore the rights of other individuals …

38. Panel Report, ¶7.1971.
39. Panel Report, EC – Trademarks and Geographical Indications (Australia), para. 7.611 fn 564. Cited at 7.1978, *Australia/Plain Packaging.*
40. ¶7.1978.
41. ¶7.2002.
42. ¶7.2030.

> or to override public liabilities: a trademark registration does not justify its use to advertise illegal goods.'[43]

It should also be said that an attack based on Article 20 TRIPS, which is discussed below, was also rejected by the Panel. The Panel held that the ban on logo marks and the restriction of use of word marks to certain forms amounted to 'special requirements' that 'encumbered' the use of a trade mark but was justifiable.

Article 17 TRIPS states that 'Member States may provide limited exceptions to the rights conferred by a trademark, such as fair use of descriptive terms, provided that such exceptions take account of the legitimate interests of the owner of the trademark and of third parties'. This provision has been discussed above as being very pro-trade mark owner and symptomatic of TRIPS being a pro-trade mark owner treaty. In *European Communities – Protection of Trademarks and Geographical Indications for Agricultural Products and Foodstuffs*,[44] the Panel held that 'legitimate interests' meant something other than full enjoyment of the legal rights conferred by a registered trade mark under Article 16.1 TRIPS. Here, the issue was whether the EC regulation for protection of geographical indications provided sufficient protection for pre-existing trade marks that are similar or identical to geographical indications (GIs). The Panel concluded that Article 16.1 obliged Members to make available to trade mark owners a right against certain uses, *including* use as a GI. However, the Panel concluded, on the basis of the evidence, that the EC regulation was justified under Article 17.

Article 18 TRIPS requires that a registered trade mark may be renewed indefinitely. Article 19 states that a registration may be cancelled if it has not been used for a period of at least three years unless there are valid reasons for non-use. Article 19.2 also says use, when subject to the control of the owner, should be recognised as use of the trade mark for the purpose of maintaining the registration. Article 19.1 follows Article 5C(1) Paris Convention which allows for cancellation after a reasonable period of non-use.

III. Use of a Trade Mark Should not Be Unjustifiably Encumbered

Article 20 TRIPS states that the use of a trade mark in the course of trade shall not be unjustifiably encumbered by special requirements. It gives examples, such as use with another trade mark, use in a special form or use in a manner detrimental to its capability to distinguish the goods or services of one undertaking from another. The rather old-fashioned word 'encumber' means to hinder, hamper or burden. As said above, in the *Australia/Plain Packaging* case, the Panel found that a ban on the use of tobacco logo marks and a restriction on the way that tobacco word marks are presented were indeed 'special requirements' that fell within Article 20 but just were justifiable on the grounds of public health. The Panel said that 'unjustifiably' in Article 20 allowed WTO Members to 'pursue legitimate societal interests'. The Panel said that:

43. William Cornish, *Intellectual Property* (8th edn., Sweet & Maxwell, 2013) cited by the English Court of Appeal in *R v. British American Tobacco* [2016] EWCA Civ 1182, ¶54. This case also concerned the lawfulness of plain tobacco packaging legislation. Leave to appeal to the Supreme Court was refused.
44. WT/DS174/R, 15 March 2005.

> 'Overall, therefore, as we understand it, Article 20 reflects the balance intended by the drafters of the TRIPS Agreement between the existence of a legitimate interest of trade mark owners in using their trade marks in the marketplace, and the right of WTO Members to adopt measures for the protection of certain societal interests that may adversely affect such use.'[45]

Article 20 TRIPS was also considered in *Indonesian Autos.*[46] Indonesia adopted import tariffs on cars ('the National Car Programme') which were proportional to the amount of foreign content of the cars. At its core, it was good old-fashioned trade protectionism and nothing to do with TRIPS. Complaints were made by the European Communities and Japan. However, somewhat as an afterthought, the United States put forward an argument that non-Indonesian car companies were encumbered from using their trade marks in Indonesia by being put at a competitive disadvantage because they did not benefit from the National Car Programme. Unsurprisingly, the Panel gave short shrift to this argument. It said that 'considerable caution' needs to be used in respect of 'de facto'-based arguments of this sort and that it would not be reasonable to construe TRIPS as preventing the granting of tariffs, subsidy or other measures of support on the grounds that it made the maintenance or use of trade marks more difficult so as to amount to a breach.[47]

Again, as discussed with the *Appellate Body Report on s.211 of the Omnibus Appropriations Act* decision, this shows that the obligations under TRIPS are not absolute. Measures taken by countries that overtly have nothing to do with intellectual property, such as protectionist measures or trade sanctions which have a *de facto* effect on, for example, the use of a trade mark, are unlikely to fall within TRIPS. Moreover, it hearkens back to the concept that a registered trade mark is not a positive right. As said by Professor Cornish in the above quote, a trade mark does not give the right to advertise illegal goods. If cigarettes had been banned on public health grounds, it would have been a brave company that argued that this deprived it of the right to use its tobacco brands. Yet, if this is a non-argument, then neither can legislation that restricts the use of a tobacco brand be objectionable.

This must be right. The goal of TRIPS was to require WTO Member States to provide for a minimum level of protection for IPRs. Its goal was plainly not to legislate in the field of public health or import tariffs and national subsidies. It would clearly be wrong to allow TRIPS to 'overreach' into other fields of law and override those fields of law.

IV. Exhaustion of Rights

As with other forms of intellectual property, TRIPS did not seek to address the highly delicate issue of exhaustion of trade marks.[48] This issue was simply too political. Some countries supported national exhaustion and others supported international

45. ¶7.2429.
46. *Indonesia – Certain measures Affecting the Automobile Industry* (WT/DS54/R, WT/DS55/R, WT/DS59R and WT/DS64/R).
47. ¶14.273, ¶14.278.
48. Art. 6.

exhaustion. The compromise reached was simply to exclude it from TRIPS.[49] The European Union has taken advantage of this by taking a 'Fortress Europe' approach whereby any goods bearing a registered trade mark may not be imported or marketed in the European Economic Area without the consent of the trade mark owner[50] even if they were placed on the market outside the EEA by the trade mark owner or with his consent.[51]

The European Community had introduced an EEA-wide exhaustion of rights principle prior to TRIPS. It was introduced into the first Trade Marks Directive[52] in the late 1980s. As the *travaux préparatoires* show, the European Commission's intention initially was to provide for international exhaustion of rights. However, the Economic and Social Committee took the view that an approach based solely on principles of trade mark law would lead to undesirable consequences (from international trade) and changed it to an EC-wide exhaustion of rights principle.[53] Thus, the decision to introduce it was political and economic and not based on principles of trade mark law.

There is a balancing act here. International exhaustion allows for effective worldwide *intra-brand* competition. The consumer benefits as local rights holders are not in a position to control prices. However, this can lead to an unhealthy 'race to the bottom' whereby prices drop so much that undertakings are unable to recover their costs and carry out effective research and development. Pharmaceutical companies have a need to adopt differential pricing models dependent on market forces and the ability of nationals to pay. What someone can afford to pay for pharmaceuticals in the Central African Republic is plainly very different to what someone can afford to pay in Switzerland. Companies have the option of either placing pharmaceuticals on the market in the former at a low price or not put them on the market there at all. If they do the former, then international exhaustion of rights will mean that prices in developed, first world countries would drop so much that any trade under the brand anywhere in the world becomes unsustainable.[54] Indeed, pharmaceutical companies may choose to use profits made from first world countries to subsidise prices in third world countries. As said, aggressive international exhaustion doctrines may ultimately impose greater costs than benefits and there may be gains to research and development if prices for goods are regulated in the relevant markets.[55]

The arguments against international exhaustion of doctrine have more force for patents rather than trade marks. Patents last only for 20 years and are granted inter alia to allow for recovery of research and development costs. The same arguments might be thought not to apply to trade marks. But trade marks protect innovation without meeting the rigid standards of patent law. Moreover, there is another issue and that is a trade mark acts to many as a guarantee of quality. If different quality standards are used for the same brand in different countries, then confusion may

49. Gervais, *supra* note 7, ¶2.99.
50. And indeed this was a political decision – *see* Davies et al., *supra* note 13, ¶3.614.
51. Art. 15 EUTMR, Art. 15 Directive 2015/2436.
52. Dir. 89/104.
53. *See* Davies et al., *supra* note 13, ¶3.613. *See also* C. Stothers, *Parallel Trade in Europe* (Hart Publishing, Oxford, 2007).
54. Although it is not clear that in fact there is economic evidence to support this argument.
55. Sarnoff, 'The Patent Systems and Climate Change', 16 *Virginia Journal of Law and Technology* (2001), 301, 359.

arise. Thus, in a UK case, prior to the Trade Marks Directive, a well-known brand of toothpaste was different in composition in Brazil to that in the UK. Consumer confusion would have happened if parallel imports had been allowed into the UK and so the English court prevented this.[56]

D. TRIPS AND THE FUTURE

The Paris Convention was already showing its age by the time that TRIPS was adopted in Marrakesh in 1994, and the world has moved on very quickly since then. The internet and the digital world was just coming into being, social media did not exist and no one had truly anticipated that with the new definition of what could be a trade mark, undertakings would start to seek trade mark protection for products for which patent or design protection had expired or never existed. Furthermore, globalisation has happened in a way that in 1994 was never foreseen. We truly live in one small world.

As said above, TRIPS came into being as the result of intensive lobbying by first world countries, mainly the United States, who perceived the need for effective enforcement of IPRs. It was not intended to strike a balance between competing industries. There was no *amicus curiae* brief on behalf of the public and small and medium-sized undertakings at the TRIPS talks.

Because TRIPS sets out minimum levels of protection, legislation that seeks to restrict or reduce the rights of trade mark owners (whether to acquire trade mark rights or to enforce them) may be contrary to TRIPs. This has already been discussed where a country has absolute grounds for refusal to register functional or aesthetic marks.

TRIPS has undoubtedly played a very important role in ensuring that IPRs are respected. Moreover, its dispute resolution mechanism has no parallel in other international IPR treaties. This gives it teeth and thus ensures that it is properly policed.

However, concerns have now swung the other way. IPRs are seen to be excessive, too invasive, reaching their tentacles into everyday life and having a claustrophobic effect. In the field of trade marks, the expansion in EU law of the functions of a trade mark from a guarantee of trade origin (essential function) to include a right to protect the brand image (communication function), a right to protect the investment made in a trade mark (investment function) and a right to advertise a trade mark without being unduly restricted means that trade marks are becoming more and more powerful.[57]

Thus, this has now been held by the CJEU to include the right to prevent the removal of a trade mark (de-branding). In *Mitsubishi*,[58] a Belgian company imported Mitsubishi forklift trucks into the EU, modified them and removed the Mitsubishi mark before placing them on the market. The ECJ held that such de-branding was an infringement. This was even though the de-branding happened in a customs warehouse and as such not in free circulation within the EU. The ECJ said

56. *Colgate-Palmolive v. Markwell Finance* [1989] RPC 497, Court of Appeal.
57. Generally, *see* Davies et al., *supra* note 13, ¶3-069 to ¶3-116.
58. C-129/17 *Mitsubishi v. Duma Forklifts BV* ECLI:EU:C:2018:594.

> 'by infringing the trademark proprietor's right to control the first placing of goods bearing that mark on the market in the EEA and by adversely affecting the functions of the mark, the removal of the signs identical to the mark and affixing of new signs on the goods by a third party, without the consent of the proprietor, with a view to importing into or placing those goods on the market in the EEA and with the aim of circumventing the proprietor's right to prohibit the importation of those goods bearing its mark, is contrary to the objective of ensuring undistorted competition.'

The reasoning is Kafkaesque. It effectively amounts to an argument that the defendant, by de-branding, circumvented the trade mark owner's right to prevent their importation into the EU and accordingly, by denying a cause of action, there exists a cause of action! Equally, as can be seen in the excerpt, the ECJ said that this is contrary to the objective of ensuring undistorted competition. But it is difficult to see how competition is affected adversely in any way by de-branding. As discussed above, a trade mark does not confer a positive right to use a mark but merely a negative right to prevent others from using it.

Indeed, there was a good reason for de-branding as the essential function of a trade mark acts as a guarantee against interference with a product prior to it being placed on a market.[59] Thus, as the defendant was modifying Mitsubishi forklift trucks prior to them being placed on the market, *retention* of the trade mark would have infringed this right. We have moved a long way from trade mark law being about preventing third parties from using an identical or similar mark in a manner that gives rise to a likelihood of confusion.

In the author's view, there is a clear need for a new TRIPS-style international agreement that provides for a balance between the rights of trade mark owners and other public interests including the right of freedom of expression, the need for competition in products where patent and design protection have expired, technological and design innovation not to be unduly hampered or restricted, the right to impart information, and so on. In short, there is a need for a user's charter which sets out clearly the rights of users, traders, writers, innovators and others to use or refer to a trade mark. If this is not done, there is a danger of IPRs being treated with derision and disrespect by the public. How many times have we read stories in the newspaper of misuse of IPRs. A good example is the well-known fast food company Kentucky Fried Chicken threatening the owners of a small English pub in north England for using the phrase 'Family Feast' for its traditional Christmas Day menu.[60] KFC owned a registration for the same. Whilst KFC climbed down after adverse press coverage, it is worrisome that such threats were even made and indeed that it was able to obtain a registered trade mark for 'Family Feast'. For every one climbdown by trade mark owners, there are a thousand climbdowns by other recipients of these threatening letters.

Indeed, there is probably a need for a general defence, like the 'fair dealing' defence in US copyright law, of 'fair use' of a trade mark. Whilst many say that this

59. C-102/77 *Hoffmann La-Roche* [1978] E.C.R. 1139, ¶7. Thus, consumers would be misled if they bought a new BMW car if a dealer had modified the engine.
60. *See* reference to this example in H. Laddie, 'The Insatiable Appetite for Intellectual Property Rights', 68(1) *Current Legal Problems* (2008).

is too general and too uncertain in its scope, there are many similar defences in international treaties. Thus, in the Berne Convention, Member States may provide for a defence to infringement of copyright where (i) it is a special case (ii) reproduction of the work does not conflict with a normal exploitation of the work and (iii) does not unreasonably prejudice the legitimate interests of the author.[61] This is known as the Berne three-step test. There is no reason why trade mark law should not have a similar defence such as use of a trade mark is permitted where (i) the use of the trade mark does not conflict with the ability of the owner to market effectively its goods and services under the registered trade mark (ii) the use does not unreasonably prejudice the legitimate interests of the trade mark owner. The impetus for this is unlikely to come from the WTO. People talk about a TRIPS + agreement but perhaps we should be talking about a Paris Convention Mark 2.

61. Art. 9(2) Berne Convention for the Protection of Literary and Artistic Works.

CHAPTER 5
TRIPS and Geographical Indications

Natale Rampazzo

A. PRE-TRIPS HISTORY OF PROTECTION OF GEOGRAPHICAL INDICATIONS

As for other intellectual property rights (IPRs) geographical indications (GIs)[1] also give a monopoly (on the use of a sign upon a product) against other competitors. In this respect, the protection given to them has to be justified as it enables encroachment on the liberty of trade. The reason for this can be tracked down in its history.[2] Indeed, the roots of GI laws date back to mediaeval times when, on the one hand, the payment of taxes and, on the other, the prevention of fraud affecting the quality of products constituted the main concern of public authorities.[3]

1. These include: *appellations/designations of origin* (implying a stronger link with the place of origin, that is, the quality and characteristics of a product must generally result exclusively or essentially from its geographical origin as they are produced, processed and prepared in a specific geographical area, using the know-how of local producers and ingredients from the region concerned), and *protected geographical indications* (PGIs) that identify products whose quality or reputation is linked to the place or region where they are produced, processed or prepared, and at least one stage in the production process must be carried out in that area, while the raw materials used in production may come from another region.

   This should also take into account the fact that GIs are a neutral concept that may apply to goods in general (even for some services), that are both food/alcoholic beverages and handicrafts. As the international and macro-regional regulation does not cover the latter, which are protected as GIs only in a few countries, we will make use of this notion mostly for drink and foodstuff.
2. *See* the short introduction by V. Mantrov, *EU Law on Indications of Geographical Origin. Theory and Practice* (Berlin-Heidelberg, 2014), 30–41.
3. In England, a promulgation was issued by Henry V (in 1419) against the adulteration of wine, requiring that wine from a geographical area should bear the label thereof and should not be mixed with other wine, in: H.T. Riley (ed.), *Memorials of London and London Life in the 13th, 14th and 15th Centuries* (London, 1868), 670. Further details in P.B. Hutt and P.B. Hutt II, 'A History of Government Regulation of Adulteration and Misbranding of Food', 39 *Food Drug Cosm. L.J.* (1984), 16.

I. Tracing the Origin of Designations of Origin

In this context, for example, wine was the first kind of agricultural product involved in a number of regulations:[4] Bordeaux wine producers (as of 1776[5]) benefitted from a number of privileges[6] to trade wine to the most remunerative (northern) markets, which was also the aim of the establishment of the Real Junta de Cosecheros (Royal Board of Winegrowers) in Spain in 1787, with reference to Rioja wines.[7] On 10 September 1756, the Companhia General da Agricultura das Vinhas do Alto Douro (also called Douro Wine Company), was founded to guarantee the quality of Portuguese wine (vinho do Porto) and fair pricing to the end consumer and to ensure whether the destination of the product was for export or for internal consumption. This purportedly[8] was the 'first' legal demarcation of a geographical area exclusively devoted to the production of a wine.[9] Indeed, already under the reign of the Grand Duke Cosimo III de Medici in Tuscany, legislation existed to protect the wine trade.[10] Between 29 September 1704 (introduction of the legislative framework concerning wine sales and the places in which it could be purchased) and 1716 he introduced regulations concerning the sale of Chianti, Carmignano, Val d'Arno di sopra and

4. *See* M. Da Passano, A. Mattone, F. Mele and P. F. Simbula (eds.), *La vite e il vino nella storia e nel diritto (secoli XI-XIX)* I-II (Rome, 2000); G. Meloni and J. Swinnen, 'Trade and terroir. The political economy of the world's first geographical indications', 81 *Food Policy* (2018), 1–20.
5. Edit du Roi, par le quell S.M. permet de faire circuler librement les vins dans toute l'étendue du royaume, de les emmagasiner, de les vendre en tous lieux, et en tous temps, et de les exporter en toute saison, par tous les ports, nonobstant tous priviléges particuliers et locaux à ce contraires, que S.M. supprime: Donné à Versailles, au mois d'Avril 1776, in A.-R.-J. Turgot, *Oeuvres VIII* (Paris, 1809) 406–36.
6. Among these should be mentioned at least the 'privilège de la descente' and the 'privilège de la barrique'. The first prevented producers of non-Bordeaux wines from accessing the Bordeaux wine market until 11 November of each year, enabling them to start selling only from this date. That caused more difficulties for them in approaching the markets abroad (England and the Netherlands above all) because of the lower temperature and the possible icing of the 'wine roads'. The 'privilège de la barrique' meant that only Bordeaux wines were entitled to use barrels of superior wood and of specified dimensions, which gave them a financial advantage as the freight charge applied per unit. In a controversial provision dated 1764, the barrique had to be branded by the producer, creating a link with the product under a 'trade mark' rule. *See* Richard, *De la protection des appellations d'origine en matière vinicole: les vins de Bordeaux* (th. Bordeaux, 1918), 187 ff.; W. van Caenegem, *Registered Geographical Indications Between Intellectual Property and Rural Policy* Part II (Bond University, 2003), 2 ff. For an interesting economic analysis based on history and aimed at assessing the variation in prices with the introduction of GIs, *see* C. Haeck, G. Meloni and J. Swinnen, 'The Value of Terroir: A Historical Analysis of the Bordeaux and Champagne Geographical Indications', 41 *Applied Economic Perspectives and Policy* (2019), 598–619.
7. On the recent developments of the Spanish approach *see* P.A. González and E. Parga Dans, 'The "terroirist" social movement: The reawakening of wine culture in Spain', 61 *Journal of Rural Studies* (2018), 184–96.
8. T. Unwin, *Wine and the Vine: An Historical Geography of Viticulture and the Wine Trade* (London, 1991, repr. 1996), 276. More recently, A. Cardoso and F.R. Silva, *Porto do Vinho* (Porto, 2007).
9. Meloni and Swinnen, *supra* note 4, at 3 et seq.
10. A.M. Pult Quaglia, 'La legislazione sul vino nella Toscana moderna', in Da Passano et al., *supra* note 4, at 209 et seq.; more recently, Z. Ciuffoletti, 'Cosimo III e la denominazione dei vini di qualità nel contesto europeo', in *ibid.* (ed.), *Terre uve vini. La denominazione dei vini di qualità nella Toscana medicea e il contesto europeo* (Firenze, 2016), 13–42.

Pomino, which were similar to the current forms of protection. By these means,[11] he established a company, a 'Congregazione', with the task of monitoring and controlling the sale of wine abroad in order to prevent fraud and deceit. This authority was to be informed of the quantity of wine produced, because in the general economic crisis of the manufacturing sector a lot of people tried to use viniculture to earn money from the increasing demand and price. In doing so, they aimed at selling the highest quantity possible even by adding water or other ingredients to the wine. This, however, had to be avoided to allow Chianti and other wines to successfully compete in international commerce. The second decree ('Sopra la Dichiarazione dé Confini delle quattro Regioni Chianti, Pomino, Carmignano, e Val d'Arno di Sopra') of 24 September 1716 protected the quality of wines to be exported through a strict demarcation of the production area, which can be considered the first regulation of this kind.[12]

At the end of eighteenth century, the phylloxera (a microscopic insect attacking the roots and leaves of grapevines) pest struck throughout Europe, and the combined reduction of the wine produced (along with the worsening of the economic conditions of the sector) and the bad faith generated by some producers putting wine on the market with a false indication of origin pushed for an international intervention in favour of transparency in trade.

II. The First International Conventions

The scene was set for a worldwide rule taking into account the preservation of the territorial value expressed by products benefitting from an indication of source or appellation of origin. Protection was under the Paris Convention for the Protection of Industrial Property (as revised in Lisbon in 1958, first signed on 20 March 1883, currently with 177 contracting parties) in Article 10, which prohibited the direct or indirect use of a false indication of the source of goods or the identity of the producer, manufacturer or merchant.[13] The provision did not explain the meaning of the relevant terms, nor did it design a common framework for protection, which was thus limited to an *ex-post* intervention (seizure on importation, seizure replaced by prohibition of importation, or seizure inside the country). An additional measure aimed at enhancing the level of protection was implemented after a series of revision conferences held in Brussels, Washington, The Hague and finally in Lisbon with the introduction and improvement of Article 10*bis*, which established that countries of the Union were bound to provide effective protection against unfair competition.[14] Unfair competition meant any act of competition contrary to honest practices in industrial or commercial matters, defined as in particular: acts directed 'to create confusion by any means whatever with the establishment, the goods, or the industrial or commercial activities, of a competitor; false allegations in the course of trade

11. Namely 'Bando sopra il commercio del vino del dì 18 luglio 1716', in *Legislazione toscana raccolta e illustrata dal dottore Lorenzo Cantini XXII* (Florence, 1806), 203 et seq.
12. Meloni and Swinnen, *supra* note 4, at 7 et seq.
13. D.S. Gangjee, *Relocating the Law of Geographical Indications* (Cambridge, 2012), 23 et seq.
14. *See* the deep analysis of Chr. Riffel, *The Protection against Unfair Competition in the WTO TRIPS Agreement* (Leiden-Boston, 2016), 17–106.

of such a nature as to discredit the establishment, the goods, or the industrial or commercial activities, of a competitor'; and finally indications or allegations the use of which in the course of trade were liable to mislead the public as to the nature, the manufacturing process, the characteristics, the suitability for purpose, or the quantity of the goods. Confusing, discrediting and misleading activities were thus prohibited in general and found to apply also to interference in the market of products originating in particular environments and territories. The object of such activities had indeed to be the 'goods', even with respect to their nature, manufacturing process, and characteristics (para. 3, point 3). These features were to protect in particular against the marketing of goods carrying labels or other elements suggesting a different (usually more renown) origin. The origin is not mentioned as such, but if we do not take this notion to be static we could argue that, from a dynamic perspective, origin can be seen in the nature (including the mere harvesting of vegetables or catching of fish) or manufacture (that is processed products), which contribute to give the special characteristics (in terms of quality) of the relevant goods.[15]

At any rate, there was criticism about the efficacy of article 10 and that is why an attempt at a (hypothetically) more efficient regulation was made some years later through the Madrid Agreement for the Repression of False and Deceptive Indications of Source on Goods (opened for signature on 14 April 1891, last revised in 1958[16] and consolidated in 1967 currently with 36 contracting parties).[17] It provided the same protection at the border (seizure of goods infringing the trade rules) as the Paris Convention in all the cases where a country or a place therein was directly or indirectly (falsely) indicated as being the country or place of origin (Article 1, para. 1). Its Article 3*bis* requires Member States to 'prohibit the use, in connection with the sale or display or offering for sale of any goods, of all *indications* in the nature of publicity *capable of deceiving the public* as to the source of the goods, and appearing on signs, advertisements, invoices, wine lists, business letters or papers, or any other commercial communication' (emphasis added). This more comprehensive and precise regulation deals with the detailed circumstances (market-oriented action, and exhibition on a visible communication support) of the prohibited conduct (the use of a deceiving indication of source) and introduces, unlike the Paris Convention and the Lisbon Agreement, a differentiation between types of goods (wine and 'no wine') which is the direct antecedent of the TRIPS regulation on GIs. In fact, the relevance of wine in the range of the goods is stressed by reference to 'wine lists' in Article 3*bis* and above all by the exception laid down in the judicial clause of Article 4 according to which national courts are in charge of decisions on the exclusion of an appellation from the scope of the Agreement due to its (acquired) generic character, while 'regional appellations concerning the source of products of the vine being,

---

15. For further general comments *see* L. Donzel, *Commentaire de la Convention Internationale signée à Paris le 20 mars 1883* (Paris, 1891), 264–340 and preparation materials for the subsequent Madrid Agreement, at 353–454; G.H.C. Bodenhausen, *Guide to the application of the Paris Convention for the protection of industrial property* (Geneva, 1968), 138–46.
16. Actes de la Conference de Lisbonne (6–31 octobre 1958) (Genève 1963) 1002 et seq. https://www.wipo.int/export/sites/www/treaties/en/documents/prep-docs/1958_oct_Lisbon-fr.pdf.
17. *See* Gangjee, *supra* note 13, at 65 et seq.; Chr. Heath, 'Geographical Indications: International, Bilateral and Regional Agreements', in Chr. Heath and A. Kamperman Sanders (eds.), *New Frontiers of Intellectual Property Law* (Oxford, Portland, 2005), 98–100.

however, excluded from the reservation specified by this Article'. The genericisation is therefore not supposed to affect vine products. The *caveat* paved the path to the privileged status of wine in TRIPS. Like the Paris Convention, no definition of 'indications of source' was given.

In the same year as the Versailles Peace Treaty,[18] France adopted the first 'national' law introducing protection for designations of origin: 'Loi du 6 mai 1919 relative à la protection des appellations d'origine', further implemented by the 'Décret-loi du 30 juillet 1935 relatif à la défense du marché des vins et régime économique de l'alcool',[19] which brought the notion of 'appellation of origin' to international attention. A small number of countries[20] ratified the International Convention on the Use of Designations of Origin and Names for Cheeses signed at Stresa on 1 June 1951. This had a reach limited to some products but introduced the concept of binary protection depending on the registration: an A Register for appellations of origin to be protected against genericisation and a B Register for products enjoying a lower standard of protection.

As a result of this trend, the Lisbon Agreement for the Protection of Appellations of Origin and their International Registration, negotiated under the chairmanship of Tullio Ascarelli[21] (31 October 1958,[22] with 30 contracting parties), represented another attempt to provide effective and enforceable protection at international level, in addition to the precedent instruments (Paris and Madrid, see Article 4).[23] The scope of protection was indeed extended beyond the false or deceptive use of indications according to a *property rule* (requiring neither proof of reputation of the sign nor fraudulent use by third parties) which thereby complemented the *liability rule* of the former systems based on the remedies against unfair competition. The Agreement

18. The Treaty obliged Germany, Austria and Bulgaria to protect goods produced or manufactured by the Allied and Associated Powers against unfair competition in commercial transactions and to prohibit and repress by any means 'the importation, exportation, manufacture, distribution, sale or offering for sale in its territory of all goods bearing upon themselves or their usual get-up or wrappings any marks, names, devices, or description whatsoever which are calculated to convey directly or indirectly a false indication of the origin, type, nature, or special characteristics of such goods' (Article 274). A special rule (Article 275) was dedicated to wines and spirits produced in any Allied or Associated State: laws or official decisions defining or regulating the right to any regional appellation in respect of these goods or the conditions of use thereof were to be abided by.
19. Some years later, in Italy the protection of the so called 'vini tipici' (traditional wines) was afforded by Royal Decree of 7 March 1924, no. 497. On the historical background of the French regulations *see* Gangjee, *supra* note 13, at 77 et seq.; G. Teil, 'Protecting Appellations of Origin: One Hundred Years of Efforts and Debates', in W. van Caenegem and J. Cleary (eds.), *The Importance of Place: Geographical Indications as a Tool for Local and Regional Development* (Cham, 2017), 147–71.
20. Belgium, Denmark, France, Italy, Norway, the Netherlands, Austria, Sweden and Switzerland.
21. Author, inter alia, of the monograph: *Teoria della concorrenza e dei beni immateriali. Istituzioni di diritto industriale*, 3rd edition (Milano, 1960).
22. Actes de la Conférence de Lisbonne (6–31 octobre 1958) (Genève 1963) 813 et seq. ('Projet d'Arrangement') https://www.wipo.int/edocs/pubdocs/fr/wipo_pub_lisbonne_1958.pdf.
23. On its genesis, *see* D. Gervais, 'Reinventing Lisbon: the case for a protocol to the Lisbon agreement (geographical indications)', 11 *Chicago J. Int. Law* (2010), 67–126; Gangjee, *supra* note 13, at 127 et seq.; A.G. Micara, 'The Geneva Act of the Lisbon Agreement for the Protection of Appellations of Origin and Their International Registration: An Assessment of a Controversial Agreement', IIC (2016), 673–96, at 675 et seq.

notably defines the term 'appellation of origin' (higher value but narrower than a GI) as 'the geographical denomination of a country, region, or locality, which serves to designate a product originating therein, the quality or characteristics of which are due exclusively or essentially to the geographical environment, including natural and human factors'. Among the natural factors are, for example, the composition of the soil, its latitude and exposure to sunlight, while the human factors could be identified as the consolidated production traditions meant in the sense of a particularly specialised expertise applied by manufacturers. Both constitute the pillars of the concept of *terroir,*[24] which can be translated as the trigger of qualities and characteristics of a product coming from a complex of environmental conditions not present in other places and from peculiar processing techniques not applicable in a different context.[25] Protection shall thus be ensured against any usurpation or imitation, even if the true origin of the product is indicated or if the appellation is used in translated form or accompanied by terms such as 'kind', 'type', 'make', 'imitation', or the like (Article 3).[26] A system of international registration for appellations of origin was established (Article 5): once protected in the country of origin, the holders of the right to use the appellation of origin (natural person or legal entity, public or private) might request their government to file a corresponding application. The registration takes place at the request of the 'country of origin', in the name of the interested parties, while the International Bureau is in charge of notifying the competent offices of the other contracting parties of any new international registration. This ensures protection in other countries (unless they signal their refusal and withstand the opposition: paras. 3 to 5) without any necessity for renewal (Article 7) for as long as it is protected in the country of origin. This prevents, at the same time, the appellation from becoming generic (Article 6). The strength of the protection system can be measured by looking at Article 5, para. 6 according to which prior use of the appellation by third parties in a given country should be terminated within two years. In answers to a questionnaire circulated in 2010 to the contracting parties, the issue of the lack of clarity of this paragraph arose with regard to the coexistence of trade marks and GIs.[27]

The lack of clarity could be a reason why the Agreement received little strategic interest on the part of some States with a low rate of quality food and wine production. Along with this observation, the changes in the laws of most Member States required by these dispositions and the already finalised process of genericisation in many countries have been difficult to overcome, although the WIPO Working groups tried to adapt some rules in order to find greater international consensus.[28]

---

24. *See*, among others, E. Barham, 'Translating terroir: the global challenge of French AOC labelling', 19 *Journal of Rural Studies* (2003), 127–38; and H.V.J. Moir, 'Geographic Indications: heritage or terroir?', Paper presented at the 10th Annual Conference of the EPIP Association (Glasgow' 2–3 September 2015).
25. The judicial definition is taken from Appeal Court Milan 1 April 2000, in *Rivista di diritto industriale* (2001/II), 113 et seq.
26. The disposition is the direct antecedent of Article 23, para. 1, TRIPS.
27. *See* on the interpretation problems: Heath, *supra* note 17, at 110–19, with interesting comparative remarks on practical cases (e.g. Israel Supreme Court (1990 and 1992) on Budweiser), and Chr. Heath and D. Marie-Vivien, 'Geographical Indications and the Principles of Trade Mark Law – A Distinctly European Perspective', 46 IIC (2015), 819–42.
28. *See* e.g. Heath, *supra* note 17, at 103–08; and the number of draft revisions formulated by different Committees and Working Groups at WIPO: on the Modification of the Regulations

Bilateral agreements flourished during the 1960s among countries not Members of the Lisbon Agreement (which came into force in France in 1966, and in Italy in 1968) as they did not require fundamental changes to existing national law: worth mentioning are the German-French Agreement of 8 March 1960 concerning the protection of French indications of source and the analogous German-Italian Agreement of 23 July 1963 concerning the protection of Italian indications of source. In both of these, the approach was a combination of trade mark law and the system of unfair competition, characterised by means of lists of products annexed to the relevant agreement, through which the indications could be protected (even those that had become generic) for products coming from the country of origin and protected as such in that country. The disadvantages were their limited reach, the time-consuming debate on the content of the lists and the suitability of bilateral agreements for parties with homogeneous economic interests.[29]

A first (supranational) systematic intervention, as an instrument in the framework of the Common Agricultural Policy, was taken in Europe with the Council Regulation (EEC) No. 2081/92 of 14 July 1992 on the protection of geographical indications and designations of origin for agricultural products and foodstuffs[30] with full legal coverage for two different classes of protected indications of source. Under this regulation, the protected designation of origin (PDO) is the name of a region, a specific place, or in exceptional cases a country used to describe an agricultural product or foodstuff originating in that region, specific place or country, and the quality or characteristics of which are *essentially or exclusively* due to the particular geographical environment with its inherent natural and human factors, and the production, processing and preparation of which take place in the defined geographical area (Article 2, para. 2, lit. a). A close link with the area of production/processing is therefore required.

On the other hand, a protected geographical indication (PGI) is the name of a region, a specific place or, in exceptional cases, a country used to describe an agricultural product or foodstuff originating in that region, specific place or country, and which possesses a specific quality, reputation or other characteristics attributable to that geographical origin and the production *and/or* processing *and/or* preparation of which take place in the defined geographical area. The clear difference between a PDO and a PGI is for the latter the sufficiency of one stage of the manufacture being connected to the geographical environment, although an element among quality, reputation or other characteristics must still originate in the relevant area.

---

under the Lisbon Agreement 2000/2001 (LI/GT/1-2); on the development of the Lisbon system (from 2009: LI/WG/DEV/X, taking into account the results of a survey held in 2010; from 2018: LI/WG/DEV-SYS/1), after the unsuccessful attempt to change the Agreement itself: Diplomatic Conference for the Adoption of a New Act of the Lisbon Agreement 2015; after the adoption of Geneva Act: for the Preparation of Common Regulations from June 2016 onwards (LI/WG/PCR/X).

29. *See* A. Chr. Streber, *Die internationalen Abkommen der Bundesrepublik Deutschland zum Schutz geographischer Herkunftsangaben* (Cologne, 1994); S. Strauch and K. Arend, 'Geographical Indications', in P.-T. Stoll, J. Busche and K. Arend (eds.), *WTO-Trade-Related Aspects of Intellectual Property Rights* (Leiden-Boston, 2009), 372 et seq.
30. F.-K. Beier and R. Knaak, 'Der Schutz der geographischen Herkunftsangaben in der Europäischen Gemeinschaft – Die neueste Entwicklung', *GRUR Int.* (1993), 602–10; Heath, *supra* note 17, at 126 et seq.

It is worth stressing the presence of two approaches in Europe prior to the adoption of the mentioned Regulation aiming to protect quality products coming from reserved environments. In southern Europe, this involved establishing a 'specification' with precise requirements of the production and of the product, subject to regular control from a supervising authority; after that it was possible to receive authorisation (normally from the competent Ministry) which granted due protection. There was also the expectation of a general awareness of the intrinsic value of the product and the relationship between the designation and the geographical area. In northern Europe, competition law was driving the system by protecting consumers from misleading activities, thereby providing indirect protection to the origin and quality of products.

Under the EU scheme, the registration procedure provided in the aforesaid Regulation followed these steps: a group[31] (or subject to certain conditions, a natural or legal person) files an application for registration to the Member State in which the area is located on the basis of a specification (on which see below); the competent national office, after a positive consideration, forwards the application to the European Commission. Once the Commission ascertains its eligibility, it publishes the relevant specification in the Official Journal if it considers that the geographical name qualifies for protection; objections may be presented within six months from the publication (Article 7); if no valid objections are received, the Commission formally enters the name in the *ad hoc* Register (Article 6). According to Article 13, registered names have to be protected against (a) any direct or indirect commercial use of the name registered in respect of products not covered by the registration, in case of comparability of the goods or exploitation of the reputation of the protected name; (b) any misuse, imitation or evocation, even if the true origin of the product is indicated or if the protected name is translated or accompanied by an expression such as 'style', 'type', 'method', 'as produced in', 'imitation' or similar; (c) any other false or misleading indication as to the provenance, origin, nature or essential qualities of the product, on the inner or outer packaging, advertising material or documents relating to the product concerned, or the packing of the product in a container liable to convey a false impression as to its origin; (d) any other practice liable to mislead the public as to the true origin of the product. This disposition is a broad synthesis of the regulation given under the international arrangements as it recalls, inter alia, the interdiction of false, deceptive or evocative use of the name referred to.

The core of the system is the presence of a set of rules for production/processing which constitutes a protocol aimed at recognising and including only qualifying products: the specification, with which an agricultural product or foodstuff must comply in order to be eligible to use a protected PDO or PGI. Its basic content consists the following items: the name of the agricultural product or foodstuff, including the designation of origin or the GI; a description of the agricultural product or foodstuff including the raw materials, if appropriate, and its principal physical, chemical, microbiological and/or organoleptic characteristics; a definition of the geographical area and the evidence of origin; a description of the method of obtaining the agricultural product or foodstuff and, if appropriate, the authentic and unvarying local methods;

31. Which basically means any association, irrespective of its legal form or composition, of producers and/or processors working with the same agricultural product or foodstuff (Article 5.1).

and specific labelling details relating to the indication PDO or PGI. Producers not meeting these specification requirements cannot make use of the protection granted.

Two other important points dealt with by this Regulation were the treatment of genericisation (before and after registration) and, crucially, the relationship with the trade marks.

Article 3 states that generic names may not be registered; as such the name of an agricultural product or a foodstuff, which – although related to the relevant area of origin – has become the common name of that product/foodstuff has to be considered. But how can this be assessed? Beyond the national and EU laws, the existing situation in the State of origin (including the areas of consumption therein) and in the other Member States should be taken into account.[32] The factors enabling the genericisation of a geographical name are of two kinds, respectively, from outside and inside the designated area: 1) producers begin to use (without permission) a geographical term to describe a product, because of its reputation, and 2) migrants from the region of origin take with them production techniques and terminology when they go elsewhere. In the absence of an adequate reaction on the part of the original producers, the link between the name and the region becomes loose, because the name can be used – even in good faith – to describe a product with certain characteristics (e.g. Cheddar cheese and Dijon mustard). On the other hand, protected names may not become generic (Article 13.3).[33]

The main rules concerning the relationship with trade marks (Article 14) are the refusal of an application for registration (or the declaration of invalidity) of a trade mark corresponding to a prior PDO or PGI and relating to the same type of product, and, conversely, a trade mark registered in good faith before the date of lodging of an application for a PDO or PGI may continue to be used even after the registration of the latter. The long-time renown of a trade mark is also a ground for rejecting such an application in order to avoid misleading the consumer as to the true identity of the product.

III. TRIPS Agreement

In the framework of the GATT negotiations that started in the mid-1980s, this regulation represented the unitary position of the European Economic Communities concerning the protection of GIs and made clear the differences between the so called

32. According to the judgement in *Parmesan* (CJEU 26 February 2008, Commission/Germany, C-132/05, point 36), in reference to the arguments of the Commission: 'a geographical designation could, over time and through use, become a generic name in the sense that consumers cease to regard it as an indication of the geographical origin of the product, and come to regard it only as an indication of a certain type of product. That shift in meaning occurred for instance in the case of the designations "Camembert" and "Brie"'. *See also* CJEU 25 October 2005, Germany et al./Commission et al., joined cases C-465/02 and C-466/02, 'Feta', with comments by D.S. Gangjee, 'Say Cheese! A Sharper Image of Generic Use Through the Lens of Feta', 5 EIPR (2007), 172 et seq.
33. D.S. Gangjee, 'Genericide: the death of a Geographical Indication?', in *ibid.* (ed.), *Research Handbook on Intellectual Property and Geographical Indications* (Cheltenham, 2016), 508–48.

'New World' and 'Old World' approaches.[34] In a negotiation document, the representative of the delegation of the European Communities introducing the proposal of his delegation emphasised 'the major trade distortions and impediments that were arising in his view because of widespread misleading use of geographical indications, in particular the misuse of names of geographical areas located on European territory which represented products specific to the natural and/or human environment in which they were elaborated'.[35] In his view, the extent of the international consensus on the level of protection to be accorded to GIs including appellations of origin was not satisfactory. While the Paris Convention had a relatively large membership, its provisions were far from representative of the minimum necessary to address trade problems in this area. The Madrid and the Lisbon Agreements received moderate support for the Community's desire to benefit from its own comparative advantage, which lay particularly in the accumulation of know-how, experience and in its specific conditions of soil and climate, and to protect them against unfair exploitation of the results of the work, investment and goodwill by third parties. The representative of Australia observed that the differences between his country and the Community on this matter lay essentially in names that had become truly generic. The representative of the United States said that his country's proposal dealt with the issue of GIs under the heading of trade marks, as in the US, the fundamental principle of protection in this area was the avoidance of consumer confusion and deceit through the prevention of misleading use of designations of origin.[36] These were the starting positions of the main actors in the relevant negotiations.

The Agreement on Trade Related Aspects of Intellectual Property Rights (TRIPS) entered into force on 1 January 1995[37] with a set of provisions concerning GIs (Articles 22–24).[38] It was the outcome of massive diplomatic activity carried out by the European negotiators aiming to establish, at least, a common ground of principles and a minimum standard of protection. The explanation for the different attitudes is again to be found in history: colonies and developing countries could not rely on valuable products provided with indications of origin and therefore applied weak protection regimes; while the EU, on the basis of its tradition and property schemes, argued for strong protection against the dilution of distinctive signs to protect its own benefits accumulated over centuries of improving expertise and use of the geographical 'assets' (e.g., soil, climate). On the other hand, there was a need for grandfathering relating to those indications that had become generic. By way of example, the US did not want to discontinue the use of the terms Chablis or

34. J.M. Cortés Martín, 'The WTO TRIPS Agreement. The Battle between the Old and the New World over the Protection of Geographical Indications', 7 *The Journal of World Intellectual Property* (2004), 287–326.
35. MTN.GNG/NG11/W/14 of 12 September 1989, p. 25.
36. *Ibid.*, p. 27.
37. R. Knaak, 'The protection of geographical indications according to the TRIPs Agreement', in F.-K. Beier and G. Schricker (eds.), *From GATT to TRIPs: the Agreement on Trade-Related Aspects of Intellectual Property Rights* (Weinheim, 1996), 117 et seq.; Gangjee, *supra* note 13, at 185 et seq.
38. The scientifically imbalanced attention to the whole family of IPRs is confirmed by the introductory chapter by W. Cornish and K. Liddell, 'The Origins and Structure of the TRIPS Agreement', in H. Ullrich, et al. (eds.), *TRIPS plus 20: From Trade Rules to Market Principles* (Berlin-Heidelberg, 2016), 3–51, where only five lines are devoted to GIs.

Champagne, while the EU envisaged the invalidity of any trade mark incorporating a GI. Finally,[39] the Parties were able to reach an agreement on minimum standards, national treatment and the most-favoured-nation clauses and on the inclusion of a clause about future international negotiations concerning the extension of the strong protection regime of wines to other agricultural products and foodstuffs.

Article 22 provides a comprehensive (legally binding) definition of GIs, similar to that given in the Lisbon Agreement but with a wider scope: 'indications[40] which identify a good [not a service[41]] as originating in the territory of a Member State, or a region or locality in that territory, where a given quality, reputation[42] or other characteristic of the good is essentially attributable to its geographical origin'. The first point is that this definition is not limited to appellations of origin as in the Lisbon Agreement. The second point concerns the reputation of the product which can derive from its geographical origin independently of quality and other characteristics. The third point is the lack of reference to natural and human factors, deleted in the final draft because its inclusion could possibly limit protection to agricultural products and exclude handicrafts. Article 22.2 contains another important development, namely the obligation for Member States to implement measures to protect GIs in their legal order. The legal means should be able to prevent the designation or presentation of a good to suggest that the good in question 'originates in a geographical area other than the true place of origin', provided that the manner misleads the public as to the geographical origin. This is a synthesis between the country-of-origin principle and the instruments of competition law: the indication of false origin as if it were the true one must be coupled with the deceiving effect driving the consumer to the alleged quality product. Beyond this target, the rule also prohibits any use which constitutes an act of unfair competition within the meaning of Article 10*bis* of the Paris Convention. The misleading effect as to the true place of origin should complement the use of the indication in the trade mark in order to enable the intervention of a Member State (voluntarily or on request) aimed at refusing (the application) or invalidating (the registration) of a trade mark containing or consisting of a PGI (para. 3).

Article 23 provides additional[43] protection for GIs of wines and spirits against their use for wines and spirits 'not originating' in the indicated place, even when the true origin of the goods is given or the GI is used in translation or accompanied by expressions such as 'kind', 'type', 'style', 'imitation' or the like. It is remarkable that protection is also granted without the presence of misleading use or an act of unfair competition. The value of a use that is not misleading and of the equitable treatment of producers can be found as criteria for action in Article 23.3, where discretion is

39. The last two drafts date back to 1990 and 1991: *see* MTN.TNC/W/35/Rev.1, 3 December 1990, Annex I and MTN.TNC/W/FA, 20 December 1991, Annex III:
40. This goes beyond the explicit geographical denomination required by the Lisbon Agreement, and includes flags, packaging, colour and so on. *See* A. Taubman, *A Handbook on the WTO TRIPS Agreement* (Cambridge, 2012), 78 et seq.
41. Art. 24.6 TRIPS.
42. On the 'five compelling reasons' to deem reputation as the basis for the link between product and place, *see* D.S. Gangjee, 'From Geography to History: Geographical Indications and the Reputational Link', in I. Calboli and W.L. Ng-Loy (eds.), *Geographical Indications at the Crossroads of Trade, Development, and Culture. Focus on Asia-Pacific* (Cambridge, 2017), 36–60, at 40 et seq.
43. The second paragraph substantially repeats the provision of Art. 22.3.

left to Member States in order to choose the practical conditions of coexistence, through suitable differentiation, of homonymous GIs (e.g. Rioja from Spain and from Argentina). Article 23.4 instead prepares the field for negotiations to be undertaken in the Council for TRIPS concerning the establishment of a multilateral system of notification and registration of GIs for wines, which will be assessed in part III.

But it is Article 24 that contains the juiciest regulation that is able to (try to) harmonise the different concepts underlying the approach to GI protection, which will be analysed in looking at their practical functioning in part II on trade agreements.

Remarkable exceptions are paragraphs 4 to 6, which have concessions to the 'New World': the first allows the use of a particular GI of another Member State identifying wines or spirits in connection with goods or services of any of its nationals or residents who have used that GI in a continuous manner with regard to the same or related goods or services in the territory of that Member State either for at least ten years preceding 15 April 1994 or in good faith preceding that date. Paragraph 5 focuses on the safeguard of the previous application or registration in good faith of trade marks against the nationally implemented measures 'on the basis that such a trade mark is identical with, or similar to, a geographical indication', while paragraph 6 points out that no Member State will be obliged to give protection to a GI with respect to goods or services (or products of the vine) for which the relevant indication is identical to the term customary used in common language as the common name for such goods or services (or grape variety) in the territory of that Member State.

IV. US and Australia Challenge EEC Regulation

On this legal basis the US and Australia in 2003 objected to Regulation EEC 2081/92 (Dispute Settlement 174 and 290).[44]

On 1 June 1999, the US had requested consultations with the European Communities (EC) contending discriminatory practice against foreign nationals and foreign products with respect to GI protection, and failure to protect foreign trade marks similar or identical to a GI. The US argued this situation to be inconsistent with the EC's obligations under the TRIPS Agreement. On 4 April 2003, the US supplemented the request by asserting that the EC Regulation limited both the GIs that the EC would be protecting and the access of nationals of other Member States to the GI procedures and protections provided under the Regulation.

On 17 April 2003, Australia also requested consultations with the EC, maintaining – consistent with the US approach – that the EC measure 1) did not immediately and unconditionally provide the nationals and/or products of all WTO Member States with any advantage, favour, privilege of immunity granted to the nationals and/or products of any other WTO Member State, 2) did not confer on the nationals and/or products of each WTO Member State treatment no less favourable than that reserved to its own nationals and/or products of national origin, 3) lowered the legal protection for trade marks. Furthermore, in not providing legal means to prevent

44. On the topic *see* M. Kennedy, *WTO Dispute Settlement and the TRIPs Agreement. Applying Intellectual Property Standards in a Trade Law Framework* (Cambridge, 2016), 150 et seq., 262 et seq.

misleading use of a GI or acts of unfair competition, the Regulation seemed to be more trade-restrictive than necessary to fulfil a legitimate objective.

The request for a panel was made on 18 August 2003 and the Report was circulated on 15 March 2005 with its subsequent adoption on 20 April 2005. The main findings can be summarised as follows: in order to register third-country GIs in the European Communities, third countries were required to adopt a GI protection system equivalent to that in the European Communities and provide reciprocal protection to products from the European Communities, with the same application and objection procedures, and inspection structures. The EC Regulation was perceived to allow protection of GIs of foreign countries only under the condition that these countries aligned their own rules and procedures with those of the EC (reciprocity). That was considered detrimental to the equal treatment of the other WTO Member States, thereby violating Article 3.1 TRIPS (national treatment principle: 'no less favourable').

Finally, as to the relationship between GIs and prior trade marks, the Panel observed that Article 16.1 obliges Member States to make available to trade mark owners a right against certain uses, including use as a GI; Article 24.5 creates an exception to GI rights rather than trade mark rights and Article 24.3 only grandfathers individual GIs, not systems of GI protection. Therefore, the Panel initially concluded that the EC Regulation was inconsistent with Article 16.1 as it limited the availability of trade mark rights but ultimately found that this was justified under Article 17 (which permits Member States to provide exceptions for trade mark rights).

The EC had eleven months and two weeks, up to 3 April 2006, to implement the recommendations and rulings of the Dispute Settlement Body. The new Council Regulation (EC) 510/2006 of 20 March 2006 on the protection of geographical indications and designations of origin for agricultural products and foodstuffs) was adopted and published on 31 March 2006, entering into force in the same date. Nevertheless, Australia and the United States disagreed that the EC had fully implemented the required changes and invited the EC to consider a revision of the same Regulation.[45]

V. New Regulations and Old Disputes

EC Regulation 510/2006[46] more clearly defines EU systems for the recognition and registration of third-country GIs, allowing individuals and groups to apply for registration of a third-country GI in the European Union without the participation of the third-country government, and provides greater protection for pre-existing trade marks. These changes are clearly progress in terms of market integration but raise a number of issues. For example, Article 11.2 states that 'in respect of geographical indications or designations of origin relating to a geographical area in a third country, verification of compliance with the specifications, before placing the product on the market, shall be ensured by one or more public authorities designated by the

45. E.g. the US contend that the new regulation may expand exceptions to trade mark rights by recognising rights only for trade marks acquired before 1 January 1996, in case of conflict with an application to register a new GI.

46. *See* C. León Ramírez, *Der Schutz von geographischen Angaben und Ursprungsbezeichnungen für Agrarerzeugnisse und Lebensmittel nach der Verordnung (EG) Nr. 510/2006* (Baden-Baden, 2007); M. Gragnani, 'The Law of Geographical Indications in the EU', 7 *J. Int. Prop. Law and Practice* (2012), 271–82.

third country and/or one or more product certification bodies'. These 'shall comply with, and from 1 May 2010 be accredited in accordance with European standard EN 45011 or ISO/IEC Guide 65'. Some third-country applicants (especially in developing countries) may have difficulty finding qualified certification bodies to perform this function at a reasonable cost to producers.[47]

The panel decision and new EU regulation brought about significant progress in the WTO negotiations because they embraced mutual recognition of GI registration systems among countries rather than requiring equivalency; furthermore, it showed that the WTO process is compatible with EU efforts to differentiate and label quality in agricultural products and foodstuffs.

Some years later, a new (series of) complaint(s) were brought by many Parties against Australia's tobacco plain packaging legislation (TPP, in force as of 1 December 2012), especially by Ukraine, Honduras, the Dominican Republic, Cuba and Indonesia.[48]

The TPP legislation prohibits logos, brand imagery, colours and promotional text other than brand and product names in a standard colour, position, font style and size appearing on tobacco packaging. The TPP forms part of a comprehensive range of tobacco control measures to reduce the rate of smoking and improve the health of Australians. The complainants contended the legislative act would have violated, inter alia, Article 22.2.b) TRIPS as an act of unfair competition (section 7.3.7 of the Panel report). In deciding this issue, the Panel framed a number of questions, including: is it possible that the promulgation of laws and regulations could constitute an act of unfair competition? In this regard, it was observed that, according to the jurisprudence concerning Article 10*bis* of the Paris Convention 1967, 'competition' and 'acts of competition' are understood in light of 'industrial or commercial matters'. They refer only to the activities that competitors undertake to further their business objectives and gain advantage over their competitors. Promulgation of legislation or other rules that regulate the market environment cannot constitute an 'act of unfair competition', since it is not related to industrial or commercial matters[49] (section 7.3.6 of the Panel report). It was questioned also whether a prohibition concerning the placement of GIs on the packaging of tobacco products could result in unfair competition. With no evidence brought by the complainants showing how TPP measures reduced a competitor's ability to distinguish its product from others, the argument was rejected. Nevertheless, the complainants also argued that the omission of GIs on tobacco packaging may also lead to confusion among consumers looking

47. Currently (as of 1 April 2021) there are 187 registered PDOs/PGIs for food, 28 for wine and spirits, and overall 44 in the application/publication process from non-EU countries (source: EU database eambrosia).
48. The official number of the dispute settlement and the date of the request for consultations are respectively WT/DS434 (13 March 2012, suspended for a mutually agreed solution); WT/DS435 (4 April 2012, appeal pending, report adopted on 29 June 2020); WT/DS441 (18 July 2012, appeal pending, report adopted on 29 June 2020) WT/DS458 (3 May 2013) and WT/DS467 (20 September 2013). On the decision *see* Chr. Geiger and L. Desaunettes-Barbero, 'The Revitalisation of the Object and Purpose of the TRIPS Agreement: The Plain Packaging Decision and the Awakening of the TRIPS Flexibility Clauses', in J. Griffiths and T. Mylly (eds.), *Constitutional Hedges of Intellectual Property* (Oxford, 2020).
49. Para. 7.2858 of the Panel report.

for a particular kind of tobacco.[50] While the Panel acknowledged that omissions may lead to confusion in certain cases, it noted that in the present case, there would be none, because, first, there is no deception or false representation as to the origin of tobacco in certain products, and secondly, the TPP measures were well publicised, ensuring that consumers would be aware of the plain packaging requirements and would not be confused thereby.

The second GI issue concerned the detriment to pre-existing rights in GIs according to Article 24.3 (section 7.3.8 of the Panel report).[51] The Panel found that the obligation in Article 24.3 applies to a measure that implements any of the provisions of Section 3 of Part II of the TRIPS Agreement. Accordingly, its application is not limited to measures that implement the obligation to provide the legal means for interested parties to prevent the use of a GI within the meaning of Article 22.2. Another key finding was that the phrase 'the protection of geographical indications that existed in that Member immediately prior to the date of entry into force of the WTO Agreement' means the state of protection of GIs immediately prior to 1 January 1995 in terms of the individual GIs which were protected at that point in time in a particular Member State (in other words: the mentioned text does not refer to the legal framework or system of protection of a Member State, as the complainants argued). The complainants therefore failed to establish how the TPP measures diminished the rights that they had in their GIs under Australian law (including general consumer protection measures addressing misleading representations or the common law tort of passing off) prior to the coming into force of the TRIPS Agreement.[52]

In 2012, a comprehensive EU Regulation[53] was adopted that further advanced harmonisation of the definitions and modified some procedural formalities and technicalities in view of the wider legal space provided by the quality schemes instead of the narrower concepts of PDO/PGI.[54] For the (still) separate PDOs, PGIs

50. For example, the Dominican Republic contended that the inability to use and develop the 'Cigarro Dominicano' GI in the Australian market made it impossible for consumers to link that sign with the reputation for high-quality cigars that the Dominican Republic was known for around the world (para. 7.2818 of the Panel report). On this point, Australia explained that the measures permitted the use of GIs on the packaging of tobacco products, if such indications were: (i) part of the brand or variant name of the product; or (ii) the country of origin of the product. Thus, Australia maintained that TPP measures did not have the effect of banning the display of GIs on tobacco packaging and products (para. 7.2833 of the Panel report).

51. In implementing this section, a Member State shall not diminish the protection of GIs that existed in that Member State immediately prior to the date of entry into force of the WTO Agreement.

52. WTO; Dispute Settlement Reports 2018 IX (Cambridge 2020) 4797–5246.

53. Regulation (EU) No. 1151/2012 of the European Parliament and of the Council of 21 November 2012 on quality schemes for agricultural products and foodstuffs, OJ L 343 of 14 December 2012; on its content *see*, inter alia, the descriptive monograph by P. Markou, *Der Schutz geographischer Herkunftsangaben nach nationalem Recht neben der Verordnung (EU) Nr. 1151/2012* (Diss. Berlin, Baden-Baden, 2019).

54. *See* the deep analysis and comparison with the former rules G.E. Evans, 'The simplification and codification of European legislation for the protection of geographical indications', in Chr. Geiger (ed.), *Constructing European Intellectual Property. Achievements and New Perspectives* (Elgar, 2013), 177–212, where she deals – against the background of the TRIPS system – with missed opportunities to extend product coverage (to handicrafts), to define the geographical area of production, to properly address the use of generic names and to clarify the interactions between GIs and trade marks.

and traditional terms in the wine sector there is now Regulation (EU) No. 1308/2013 of 17 December 2013 of the European Parliament and of the Council establishing a common organisation of the markets in agricultural products and repealing Council Regulations (EEC) No. 922/72, (EEC) No. 234/79, (EC) No. 1037/2001 and (EC) No. 1234/2007[55] (Articles 92–116) and, for spirits, Regulation (EU) No. 2019/787 of 17 April 2019 of the European Parliament and of the Council on the definition, description, presentation and labelling of spirit drinks, the use of the names of spirit drinks in the presentation and labelling of other foodstuffs, the protection of geographical indications for spirit drinks, the use of ethyl alcohol and distillates of agricultural origin in alcoholic beverages, and repealing Regulation (EC) No 110/2008[56] (Articles 21–42).

Turning back to the backbone of the international regulations established by the pre-TRIPS Agreements of Paris, Madrid and Lisbon, however, these did not seek to provide prescriptive protection for GIs, but contributed to highlight particular needs, gaps, and challenges in cross-border trade at the level of competition law, with special regard to preventing consumer deception as to the origin of a product. Although the Lisbon Agreement was aimed at the establishment of a registration system, it was not particularly successful in this respect. Still, it can be deemed as the direct antecedent of the TRIPS Agreement. But the notion of appellation of origin is narrower: it can be no more than the geographical name of a country, region, or locality, have no reputational factor, and be used for designation purposes, similar to primarily geographically descriptive marks, as it merely describes the geographical origin of the goods.[57]

VI. Lisbon Goes to Geneva

In order to complement the Lisbon System, the Working Group on the Development of the Lisbon System has since 2009 been engaged in a review of the Lisbon Agreement with the idea of extending its scope, attracting more Member States and enhancing the benefits for all Parties.[58] The Group negotiated and developed the text that was submitted to the Diplomatic Conference, composed of the 28 Member States of the Lisbon Union, Special delegations (OAPI and EU), Observer delegations (the other 89 WIPO including the US and Australia, and non-WIPO UN Members States) and Observers (24 organisations, without voting rights[59]). During the Preparatory Committee, the US and many other WIPO Member States unsuccessfully proposed amending the draft rules of procedure so as to allow non-Lisbon Member States to

55. OJ L 347 of 20 December 2013. On the economic impact *see* G. Meloni et al., 'Wine Regulations', 41 *Applied Economic Perspectives and Policy* (2019), 620–49, at 639 et seq.
56. OJ L 130 of 17 May 2019.
57. R.L. Okediji, 'The International Intellectual Property Roots of Geographical Indications', 82 *Chi. Kent L. Rev.* (2007), 1329–65, at 1341 et seq.
58. D.J. Gervais and M.Slider, 'The Geneva Act of the Lisbon Agreement: Controversial Negotiations and Controversial Results', in van Caenegem and Cleary, *supra* note 19, 15–46, at 17 et seq.; Micara, *supra* note 23, at 681 et seq.
59. *See* details in WIPO, Records of the Diplomatic Conference for the Adoption of a New Act of the Lisbon Agreement for the Protection of Appellations of Origin and their International Registration -Geneva 2015 (Geneva 2019).

vote, so that all participants would have full and equal participation in the light of an inclusive norm-setting.[60] The text was finally adopted on 20 May 2015. After that, the US proposed (again, without success) that the WIPO General Assembly consider it as not being administered by WIPO.

Notwithstanding these political hurdles, the Geneva Act achieved some important targets: it allowed greater flexibility to the international register for GIs, enabling not only national authorities but also natural persons or legal entities to file an application (Article 5.2); for the sake of legal certainty, it introduced a prescription on invalidation of the international registration, granting a transparent application procedure to rights holders (Article 19)

The most important outcome was the widening of the scope of application: the Act also applies to GIs, and the definition[61] was modelled upon the TRIPS wording. There is no need for a product to possess a specific quality or characteristic connected with the area of origin (the reputation is sufficient) and no reference to natural and human factors is made. Also, cross-border applications for a geographical area located in two or more States are admitted (as would be the case for Tokaj, an area located in Hungary and Slovakia). Instead, the definition of appellations of origin stressed the link with the area and mentioned the reputation as an effect of the quality of the products (to be protected against imitation: Article 11) and thus as a mandatory and additional requirement for registration. On this point, the US affirmed that the 'insistence that the mere existence of natural factors had some inherent value, without any objective proof of that value, made the appellation of origin definition problematic' and that 'reputation [a critical common element to AO and GI] was a measurement of whether [the] human intervention had value and whether an intellectual property right had to reward it as an incentive to creative quality products and to protect consumer's expectations'.[62] The difficulty in recognising the fundamental contribution of human factors with regard to appellations of origin was that while wine is necessarily connected with *terroir*, food and handicrafts are more related to manufacturing skills, and humans can migrate. The high level of protection pursued through the Geneva Act (Article 10)[63] was challenged by US,[64] which was in favour

60. *Ibid.*, 275 et seq. That was the result of the position taken by P. Hamamoto, US Ambassador and Permanent Representative, United Nations, Opening Statement to the Preparatory Committee of the Diplomatic Conference for the Adoption of a Revised Lisbon Agreement on Appellations of Origin and Geographical Indications at WIPO (30 October 2014), https://geneva.usmission.gov/2014/11/03/u-s-opening-statement-for-the-adoption-of-a-revised-lisbon-agreement. On that: D. Dudding, 'The Lisbon Agreement: Why the United States Should Stop Fighting the Geneva Act', 18 *Vand. J. Ent. & Tech.* (2016), 167–91, at 186 et seq.
61. Art. 2.1.ii. 'Any indication protected in the Contracting Party of origin consisting of or containing the name of a geographical area, or another indication known as referring to such area, which identifies a good as originating in that geographical area, where a given quality, reputation or other characteristic of the good is essentially attributable to its geographical origin.'
62. LI/WG/DEV/9/8 (report of the WG on the development of the Lisbon System, 9th session 23–27 June 2014), p. 10.
63. D. Gervais, 'A Look at the Geneva Act of the Lisbon Agreement: A Missed Opportunity?', in Calboli and Ng-Loy, *supra* note 42, 122–44, at 127 et seq.; *ibid.*, 'The Lisbon agreement's misunderstood potential', 1 *WIPO J.* (2009), 87–104.
64. LI/WG/DEV/8/7 (report of the WG on the development of the Lisbon System, 8th session 2–6 December 2013), pp. 5 and 25.

of a lower standard to reach a compromise among different legal systems closer to the set of TRIPS rules: the proposed provision would indeed go far beyond the likelihood of confusion or deception inherent in systems based on trade mark law and without a reasonable link to local consumer perception. On the other hand, in contrast to the Lisbon regime allowing priority of GIs over trade marks at the national level, the Geneva Act provided the introduction of a clear priority principle, by which prejudice concerning 'a prior trade mark applied for or registered in good faith, or acquired through use in good faith, in a Contracting Party' (Article 13) was excluded.

As to genericisation, according to Article 12 registered appellations of origin and registered GIs, due to their basically permanent nature, cannot be considered to have become generic in a Contracting Party.[65] As a result, protection is conferred without any requirement of use or enforcement against a user in good faith; the paradox – which is developed as a hypothesis within a typical trade mark law case – drove the US to request a requirement of use or to insert the possibility of acquiescence.[66] It has been pointed out that, due to the crucial significance of the relationship between indications becoming generic and trade marks, and the possible economic loss of exporters from Europe, the ambiguous coexistence of GIs with earlier trade marks and the missed opportunity of introducing acquiescence are regrettable.[67]

After the accession of EU on 26 November 2019, the Geneva Act entered into force on 26 February 2020.

B. TRIPS-PLUS (OR MINUS)

Intellectual property rights have increasingly become the subject matter of trade agreements in order to increase the level of protection starting from a common minimum standard set up internationally by TRIPS. Since 1995, almost 200 new trade agreements have been signed, the majority of which include a section on IPRs. Thus, regulation is about to become progressively more fragmented as these agreements can go beyond the TRIPS standards[68] (or even must go, otherwise the bilateral agreements would be no use[69]) and inconsistencies could arise in their functioning also in the light of the most-favoured-nation clause established by Article 4.d of TRIPS.[70]

With reference to GIs, the EU evaluates as TRIPS-Plus provisions those aiming: to promote deep integration, establishing a list of EU names to be protected directly

65. Gervais and Slider, *supra* note 58, 27 et seq.; Gervais, *supra* note 63, at 131 et seq.
66. LI/WG/DEV/9/8 *supra* note 62, at 25 et seq. and 36.
67. In these terms Micara, *supra* note 23, at 691.
68. Art. 24.1: 'Members agree to enter into negotiations aimed at increasing the protection of individual geographical indications under Article 23'.
69. A.F. Ribeiro de Almeida, 'The TRIPS Agreement, the Bilateral Agreements Concerning Geographical Indications and the Philosophy of the WTO', 27 EIPR (2005), 150–53, at 152. 'TRIPS-minus' provisions on GIs can be found in US FTA with Singapore: L.T. Thu Hà and D. Marie-Vivien, 'Notification and Registration System for Geographical Indications', in E. Siew-Kuan NG and G.W. Austin, *International Intellectual Property and the ASEAN Way Pathways to Interoperability* (Cambridge, 2017), 165–89, at 187.
70. *See* R, Kampf, 'TRIPS and FTAs: A World of Preferential or Detrimental Relations?', in Chr. Heath and A. Kamperman Sanders (eds.), *Intellectual Property and Free Trade Agreements* (Oxford-Portland, 2007), 87–125, at 92 et seq.; and Chr. Heath, 'The Most-Favoured Nation Treatment and Intellectual Property Rights', *ibid.*, 127–54.

and indefinitely in the third country; to obtain the extension of GI protection provided by Article 23 to products other than wines and spirits; to allow coexistence with prior trade marks registered in good faith;[71] to phase out prior uses of EU names; to ensure a right of use; to acquire the widest administrative protection possible (preventing the access to justice); and to create a cooperative mechanism.[72] The utopia of the EU needs to be adapted to smaller achievements in that it is not always possible to get protection for all EU GIs but only for a limited list.

Bilateral and multilateral agreements protecting GIs usually consist of the mutual recognition between two or more States for the protection of their domestic GIs in the contracting States,[73] and beyond that: expanded definitions of GIs, wider scope, simplification of formalities, transparency regulations, and relationship with trade marks.

The tendency to apply a one-size-fits-all pattern[74] is certainly not the exclusive domain of the EU in its trade agreements. The US also tries to export its view of how trade mark law should prevail over GIs.

I. TPP

On the one hand, the Trans-Pacific-Partnership (TPP),[75] signed on 4 February 2016,[76] whose Member States were inter alia Australia, Canada, Chile, Japan, New Zealand, Peru, Singapore and USA, takes a trade mark-centric approach. The Agreement gives a detailed example of United States' GI trade policy and the text is used in other trade negotiation forums as well. The definition of GIs is identical to that of TRIPS and draws a line connecting GIs and trade marks. Article 18.19 reads as follows: 'each Party shall also provide that signs that may serve as geographical indications are capable of protection under its trade mark system'. Articles 18.30–36 provide a set of specific rules on GIs concerning their recognition and protection through a trade mark or *sui generis* system or other legal means. In particular, each Party shall ensure that petitions or applications are processed clearly and transparently with sufficient information for the general public 'without imposition of overly burdensome formalities', and are published for opposition and cancellation if a GI is likely to cause confusion with a trade mark that is the subject of a pre-existing good faith pending application or registration in the territory of the Party or is a customary term

71. A prior trade mark should not preclude later registration and protection of a GI, which cannot be *ipso iure* a ground for invalidation or cancellation of the prior trade mark.
72. *See* in general T. Engelhardt, 'Geographical indications under recent EU Trade Agreements', 46 IIC (2015), 781–818; M. Huysmans, 'Exporting protection: EU trade agreements, geographical indications, and gastronationalism', in *Review of International Political Economy* (doi: 10.1080/09692290.2020.1844272, publ. 24 November 2020)
73. For an overview of bilateral agreements before TRIPS *see* Heath, *supra* note 17, at 121–25.
74. *See* critically D.J. Gervais, 'IP Calibration', in D.J. Gervais (ed.), *Intellectual Property, Trade and Development* (Oxford, 2014), 86–116.
75. *See*, in relation with CAFTA and CETA, Th. Cottier, D. Jost and M. Schupp, 'Setting the scene: the prospects of TRIPS-Plus protection in future mega-regionals', in F.M. Abbott, Th. Cottier and F. Gurry (eds.), *International Intellectual Property in an Integrated World Economy* (New York, 2019), 490 et seq.
76. After the withdrawal of the US on 23 January 2017, the Agreement entered into force under the name of TPP-11 on 30 December 2018.

in common language as the common name for the relevant good in the territory of the Party.[77] The relevant judiciary in the Party using a *sui generis* system should act accordingly, that is, they should be able to provide proceedings based on these grounds (Article 18.32.4). In two places in the discussed section there is a clause against the prohibition of cancellation or cessation of a GI (Articles 18.32.3 and 18.36.3) in order to avoid permanent GIs (also in the absence of substantive requirements) that could constitute barriers to trade. The agreement also includes guidelines for determining whether a term is customary in the common language of a Party, namely that it is fundamental how consumers understand the term in the territory of that Party. This perception of the public can be established by taking into account to what extent the term is used to refer to the type of goods in question (as indicated for example by dictionaries, newspapers and relevant websites); and whether the goods referenced by the term are marketed and used in trade in the territory of that Party (Article 18.33). This fortifies the position of the US and weakens that of European products bearing a geographical origin; the real problem will arise when Parties to this kind of agreement implement another parallel agreement with EU, from which conflicting obligations and inconsistent approaches can arise.[78]

Not least for this reason, the comparison between agreements signed by the same State with both the US and EU is of relevance.

II. EU Agreements and Disagreements

At present, the EU has the largest trading network in the world in place, with 41 trade agreements[79] covering 72 countries.[80]

Types of EU trade agreements include: 'first generation' agreements, negotiated before 2006, that focus on tariff elimination (e.g. with Norway, Switzerland, Mexico and Chile); 'second generation' agreements, that extend to new areas, including intellectual property rights, services and sustainable development (e.g. with South Korea, Colombia, Peru and Ecuador, Central America and Canada); Deep and Comprehensive

77. The Consortium for Common Food Names, a Washington, DC, based international initiative to preserve the right to use common food names, supports GIs associated with specialised foods from regions throughout the world, but opposes any attempt to monopolise common (generic) names that have become part of the public domain. It seeks to foster the adoption of an appropriate model for protecting both legitimate GIs and generic food names. Finally (in March 2020), it called on the EC to draw up a non-exhaustive list of generic names for which exclusive usage cannot be claimed, whose absence has been a source of confusion negatively impacting the position of international partners.
78. On the point *see* Th. Cottier, 'Intellectual Property and Mega-Regional Trade Agreements. Progress and Opportunities Missed', in S. Griller et al., *Mega-Regional Trade Agreements: CETA, TTIP, and TiSA: New Orientations for EU External Economic Relations* (Oxford, 2017), 151–74.
79. *See* the analysis of B. O'Connor and L. Richardson, 'The legal protection of Geographical Indications in the EU's Bilateral Trade Agreements: moving beyond TRIPS', 6(4) *Rivista di Diritto Alimentare* (2012), 1–29; and of M. Handler and B. Mercurio, 'Intellectual Property', in S. Lester et al., *Bilateral and Regional Trade Agreements: Volume 1: Commentary and Analysis* (Cambridge, 2015), 325–58, at 334–42.
80. https://trade.ec.europa.eu/doclib/press/index.cfm?id=2071. Data on the economic relevance of this diplomatic action can be seen in Copenhagen Economics, *Impacts of EU Trade Agreements on the Agricultural Sector* (European Union, 2016).

Free Trade Areas (DCFTA) that create stronger economic links between the EU and its neighbours (e.g. with Ukraine, Georgia and Moldova); Economic Partnership Agreements (EPA) focusing on development needs of African, Caribbean and Pacific regions; Association Agreements as frameworks for future cooperation.[81]

In order to facilitate trade in wine and to provide a framework for continued negotiations in the wine sector, the EU signed 'first generation' trade agreements - which in some cases ruled on the relevant sector in the annexes - with Australia (wine, 1994,[82] 2009[83]), Mexico (spirits, 1997[84]); Switzerland (wine and spirits, 1999–2002[85]); South Africa (wine and spirits, 1999–2002[86]), Romania, Bulgaria and Hungary (wine, 2001[87]); Macedonia (wine, 2001[88]); Chile (wine and spirits, 2002[89]); Canada (wine and spirits, 2004[90]); and the US (wine, 2006[91]). Some words on the US trade agreement before moving on. Key topics were the mutual recognition of each other's existing wine-making practices and a procedure for determining future practices; a limit on the use of certain 'semi-generic' terms in the US market (including Burgundy, Chablis, Champagne, Chianti, Claret, Haut, Sauterne, Hock, Madeira, Malaga, Marsala, Moselle, Port, Retsina, Rhine, Sauterne, Sherry, and Tokay); the allowance of US wine producers to use certain (previously prohibited) expressions on wine labels exported to the EU (including chateau, classic, clos, cream, crusted/ crusting, fine, late bottled vintage, noble, ruby, superior, sur lie, tawny, and vintage:

81. *See* on the enforcement and implementation of IP provisions Th. Jaeger, 'IP Enforcement Provisions in EU Economic Partnership Agreements', in J. Drexl et al. (eds.), *EU Bilateral Trade Agreements and Intellectual Property: For Better or Worse?* (Berlin-Heidelberg, 2014), 189–205; and J. Drexl, 'Intellectual Property and Implementation of Recent Bilateral Trade Agreements in the EU', *ibid.*, 265–91.
82. OJ L 86 of 31 March 1994, pp. 1 et seq., as amended by Commission Decision of 1 July 2003 (OJ L 336 of 23 December 2003, p. 99 et seq.)
83. OJ L 28 of 30 January 2009, pp. 1 et seq. The new agreement, replacing the former one, safeguards the EU's wine labelling regime, gives full protection to EU geographical indications, including for wines intended for export to third countries, and includes a clear Australian commitment to protect EU traditional expressions. Could it be the premise of a more comprehensive FTA? *See* the opinions in A. Elijah et al. (eds.), *Australia, the European Union and the New Trade Agenda* (Canberra, 2017). Negotiations were indeed launched on 18 June 2018.
84. In the Framework of an Economic Partnership, Political Coordination and Cooperation Agreement, Council Decision of 27 May 1997, OJ L 152 of 11 June 1997 (spirits): protection was granted to 'Tequila', 'Mezcal', 'Sotol' and 'Charanda' against around 200 European terms.
85. OJ L 114 of 30 April 2002, pp. 132 et seq.
86. Signed on 11 October 1999 in Pretoria, the Trade, Development and Cooperation Agreement entered provisionally in force on 1 January 2000 and fully on 1 May 2004. The Agreement is supplemented by three additional agreements: the Science and Technology Agreement, and the Wine and Spirits Agreements, the last two respectively in OJ L 28 of 30 January 2002, pp. 3 et seq. and 112 et seq.
87. OJ L 94 of 4 April 2001, pp. 1 et seq.
88. OJ L 342 of 27 December 2001, pp. 6 et seq.
89. OJ L 352 of 30 December 2002, pp. 3 et seq. (particularly Annex V concerning the trade on wine and Annex VI on spirits of the Association Agreement), as amended by Commission Decision of 21 November 2008 (OJ L 37 of 6 February 2009, pp. 8 et seq.).
90. OJ L 35 of 6 February 2004, pp. 1 et seq.
91. The interlocutory step in OJ L 301 of 18 November 2005, p. 14 et seq. prior to the Council Decision of 20 December 2005 on the conclusion of the Agreement between the European Community and the United States of America on trade in wine; OJ L87 of 24 March 2006, pp. 1 et seq.

all these were traditional expressions); and simplified certification requirements and a labelling protocol.

All of the agreements mentioned build on the protection granted by TRIPS to GIs for wine, but provide (in almost all cases) added protection in relation to trade marks, grape varietals, generic names and 'traditional expressions', which are typical terms used to refer to the method of production, quality, colour or type of wine and are not protected as such by TRIPS, thus suffering a high probability of becoming generic or being neglected.

The pattern of those agreements follows certain guidelines varying little from the first of this kind (Australia 1994) to that with Chile (2002) or Canada (2004). A central role is played by the mutual protection of wine names based on lists (Article 5.1 Chile; Article 6.1 Australia; Articles 10.1, 11.1, 14.1, 15.1 Canada), granted on condition that the GI is protected in the home country; traditional expressions or complementary quality (Article 9 Chile) shall be reserved exclusively for products originating in the Party to which they apply (Article 8 Chile; Article 6 Australia); registration of a trade mark for wine which is identical with, or similar to, or contains a GI protected under Article 5 shall be refused. Except for Canada, the other Parties agreed on the fact that GIs of country A must not be used in country B other than under the conditions laid down in the laws and regulations of country A, which is a coercive overprotection in respect of the TRIPS standards, whose *ratio* was rather to harmonise regulations of the parties in order to facilitate protection. The Mexico and Switzerland Agreements contain express waivers of the exceptions established in Articles 24.4–7 of TRIPS. According to this 'imperialistic' approach, the other parties have to protect terms that may have become generic product designations, and to cancel the registration of trade marks identical with or similar to protected GIs, even if such rights were acquired before TRIPS entered into force in that country (so called 'claw-back' clauses).[92]

Both parties must agree in advance on a list of mutually protected GIs. Accordingly, subsequent opposition by private parties may not be raised, and the number of PGIs may only be broadened by mutual consent and a subsequent amendment.

III. CETA

The last-mentioned way of protecting GIs is exemplified by the Canada-European Union (EU) Comprehensive Economic and Trade Agreement (CETA),[93] a landmark trade agreement that upholds and promotes the values Canada shares with the EU, signed on 30 October 2016 and entered provisionally into force on 21 September 2017. It should be noted that Canada is also a Member State of the North American

92. For example, under the Australia Wine Agreement 2009, local wine producers will no longer be able to use names such as Burgundy, Chablis, Champagne (Art. 15. Transitional Agreements), but also the traditional expressions mentioned in the 14-page long Annex III.
93. An overview of TPP and CETA in the international post-TRIPS scenario can be found in Th. Cottier et al., 'The Prospects of TRIPS-Plus Protection in Future Mega-Regionals', in Th. Rensmann (ed.), *Mega-Regional Trade Agreements* (Springer, 2017), 191–216, at 203 et seq.; Engelhardt, *supra* note 72, at 813 et seq.

Free Trade Agreement (NAFTA) which offers the opportunity to analyse the clash between two protection systems.[94]

Canada has basically confirmed its obligations already accepted under TRIPS, even the definition of GI, but the term 'good' was substituted with 'agricultural product or foodstuff' substantively changing (and limiting) the scope of protection which applies furthermore only to GIs identifying products falling within one of the product classes listed in the agreement (Article 20.17 and Annex 20-C). The obligation for Parties to provide legal means to prevent the misleading use, the use equivalent to unfair competition and the use of a GI not originating in the place of origin or not produced in accordance with its regulations meets the requirements of TRIPS standards (Article 20.19.2).[95] The following sub-paragraph 3 provides protection even where the true origin of the product is indicated or the GI is used in translation or accompanied by expressions such as 'kind', 'type', 'style', 'imitation' or the like (taken verbatim from Article 23.1 TRIPS). However, there are some exceptions. For example, the use of the GI names Asiago, Feta, Fontina, Gorgonzola and Munster need not be discontinued if these terms are accompanied by the abovementioned expressions in combination with a legible and visible indication of the true geographical origin of the product (Article 20.21.1). There are periods of (at least) five or ten years (according to the product class) preceding the date of 18 October 2013, which is instead effective – but only after a transitional grace period of five years from the entry into force of the Article 20.21 – for users of GIs for less than five or ten years, respectively (Articles 20.21.3 and 4).

If a trade mark has been applied for or registered in good faith, or if rights to a trade mark have been acquired through use in good faith, by a Party before the applicable date set out in paragraph 6 (the date of coming into force of the Sub-section C or of adding the new GI in the Annex 20-A), implementation measures adopted by that Party shall not prejudice the eligibility for or the validity of the registration of the trade mark, or the right to use the trade mark, on the basis that the trade mark is identical with, or similar to, a GI (coexistence clause, Article 20.21.5).

By conceiving the negotiation strategy as a means to protect a limited number of (the most economically relevant) individual GIs, but not the *sui generis* system itself, the EU undermines the idea that GIs are a form of IP independent of all other forms of IP rights and equivalent to trade marks.[96] With a strong emphasis on the status

94. *See also* on the Transatlantic Trade and Investment Partnership between EU and US (stopped in 2018 but currently under revival) the observations of B. O'Connor, 'The Legal Protection of GIs in TTIP: Is there an Alternative to the CETA Outcome', in F. Arfini et al. (eds.), *Intellectual Property Rights for Geographical Indications: What is at Stake in the TTIP?* (Cambridge, 2016), 19–35.
95. *See* G. Miribung, 'Inquadramento delle indicazioni geografiche tra TRIPS e CETA: qualche osservazione', 13 *Rivista di Diritto Alimentare* (2019), 23–38.
96. A missed opportunity, if not a failure: B. O'Connor, 'Geographical Indications in CETA, the Comprehensive Economic and Trade Agreement between Canada and the EU', 9 *Rivista di Diritto Alimentare* (2015), 61–67, at 65, or even a discrimination, O'Connor and Richardson, *supra* note 79, at 17: 'In theory and in law all GIs should receive the same protection. The EU does not discriminate among trademarks or other forms of intellectual property. Why discriminate for GIs?.' In practice, the decision (not only on the inclusion of GIs in FTAs, but even) on the qualification as GI is political and the real economic value of such a protection (starting from Europe) is overestimated for the majority of registered products. That's why in the negotiations

quo (Article 20.22.2), it is prohibited to add an EU GI to the relevant Annex of the Agreement 'if it is a name that on the date of the signing of this Agreement is listed in the relevant Register of the European Union with a status of "Registered", in respect of a Member State of the European Union'. A provision putting GIs below the protection standards is Article 20.22.3, which prevents adding new GIs if they are identical to a registered trade mark or a trade mark used in good faith (with an application duly filed) in respect of the same or similar products, or to the customary name of a plant variety or an animal breed existing in the other Party; or with the term customary in common language as the common name for such product. The amendment of Canada's Trade-Mark Act in order to protect the GIs of food products, which was introduced as a result of CETA, established a procedure for its direct application by EU rights-holders for the protection of GIs. The new 'open system' delivered its first result in 2018 with the protection of the name 'Prosciutto di Carpegna'.

Overall, CETA is a complex attempt to compromise between the extremes of the GI debate: the assumed necessity of a *sui generis* GI system and the adequacy of trade mark law, far from the hoped-for co-existence between two different and independent forms of intellectual property. The halfway solution consists of the calibration of legal instruments in order to meet local needs, which is the opposite of globalisation.

IV. KORUS v. KOREU

At this stage it appears appropriate to scrutinise the different approaches in the field by way of comparison of the agreements stipulated by the US and the EU with the same countries, although the examination will concern two agreements of the 'new generation' which *ratione temporis* should be addressed later. The US–Korea Free Trade Agreement (KORUS), signed on 30 June 2007, entered into force on 15 March 2012.[97] In Article 18.2 ('Trademarks including geographical indications') it provides a rule on the internal relationship between trade marks and GIs conceived as a sub-set of trade marks. Accepting the TRIPS GI definition, paragraph 2 states that each Party shall provide that trade marks shall include certification marks and GIs be eligible for protection as trade marks. This means there is a legal osmosis between the systems in which GIs are likened to certification marks. Trade marks should be protected against the use of the term customary in common language as the common name for a good or service (Article 18.2.3), while the likelihood of confusion is the basis for protecting registered trade marks against identical or similar signs for identical or similar goods or services covered by said trade mark. In this regard, a presumption is stipulated: identical signs for identical goods presume confusion. This partly reflects the US protection system, namely the principle of territoriality implying that identical signs for the same product can coexist as long as they are used in different geographical areas; the principle of speciality allowing the coexistence of similar signs

it would be excessive to take into account GIs with a very small market limited to the area of production.

97. Slightly revised on 24 September 2018 and in force since 1 January 2019. *See*, in general, W.H. Cooper et al., 'The Proposed US-South Korea Free Trade Agreement (Korus FTA): Provisions and Implications', Federal Publications. Paper 813 (2001).

when used for different goods where there is no likelihood of confusion between the signs; the 'first in time, first in right' rule (or priority principle) attributing an exclusive right to the first one to register or use the sign. That is clearly described in Article 18.2.15 ('Grounds for refusal or cancellation of a GI'): the GI applied for can generate confusion (i) with a pending trade mark application or registration in good faith, (ii) with trade mark rights which have been acquired through use in good faith and (iii) with a well-known trade mark that predates the protection or recognition of the GI in the same territory. Refusal, cancellation of the registration and prohibition of the use of a GI identical or similar to a well-known trade mark, for related goods or services, will follow if the use causes confusion, mistake, deceit or association. Interestingly, discretion (no obligation) is given to the Parties as to the means to apply for protection of GIs, through a system of protection of trade marks or otherwise, which should enable acceptance and processing of the requests with a minimum of formalities, provision of information and publicity of the procedures, and establishment of a transparent opposition procedure.

The EU–South Korea Free Trade Agreement (FTA) (KOREU), which provisionally entered into force on 1 July 2011,[98] is an example of the new generation of FTAs launched by the EU in 2007 and which go further than previous agreements in lifting trade barriers.[99]

GIs are dealt with in a special subsection (Articles 10.18–26). Regarding the method of protection, Article 10.18.6 sets out elements necessary for the registration and control of GIs, as follows: a register listing GIs protected in their respective territories; an administrative process verifying the nature of GIs according to the TRIPS definition; control provisions applying to production (that is the specification); the reservation of use of a registered name to any operator marketing the agricultural product or foodstuff conforming to the corresponding specification (see also Article 10.20); and an objection procedure that allows the legitimate interests of prior users of names to be taken into account.

Annex 10-B contains a list of GIs subject to mutual recognition (e.g. 63 Korean food products against only 60 from EU). The scope of protection (Article 10.21) is taken from Article 22.2 and 22.3 TRIPS.[100] The same article also provides for the co-existence of a GI with a prior trade mark using the broad wording of Article 24.5

---

98. Council Decision of 16 September 2010 in OJ L 127 of 14 May 2011, p. 1 et seq. *See* Engelhardt, *supra* note 72, at 797 et seq.

99. *See* Y.-D. Kang, 'Korea-EU FTA: Breaking New Ground', in Elijah et al., *supra* note 83, at 19–34, and Sun Hee Park, 'Taking Cultural Goods Seriously: Geographical Indications and the Renegotiation Strategies for the Korea-EU FTA', 11(2) *Global Policy* (2020), 23–30.

100. Registered GIs are protected against (a) the use of any means in the designation or presentation of a good that indicates or suggests that the good in question originates in a geographical area other than the true place of origin in a manner which misleads the public as to the geographical origin of the good; (b) the use of a geographical indication identifying a good for a like good not originating in the place indicated by the geographical indication in question, even where the true origin of the good is indicated or the geographical indication is used in translation or transcription or accompanied by expressions such as 'kind', 'type', 'style', 'imitation' or the like; and (c) any other use which constitutes an act of unfair competition within the meaning of Art. 10 bis of the Paris Convention.

TRIPS.[101] Article 10.23 limits the grounds for refusal or invalidation of a trade mark corresponding to a protected GI to the fact that the pertinent application was filed after the date of application for protection or recognition of the GI in the territory concerned. It requires Korea to amend its national legislation, as Article 7.1.(xiv) of the Korean Trade Mark Act of 28 November 1949, mentions, as being among the unregistrable trade marks, trade marks consisting of GIs or including such indications with regard to the origin of wines or spirits of a Member State of the World Trade Organization, and which are used in connection with wines, spirits, or other similar goods. According to the FTA, this Korean provision must be expanded in order to also cover trade marks filed for 'like goods'. There is no specific provision on the treatment of generic or common names. Finally, Article 10.24 provides for the addition of GIs to the relevant Annexes. A Working Group (Article 10.25) is in charge of managing additions of GIs to its annexes, as well as their removal.[102]

The risk of discrimination between GIs inside the domestic legal order so as to comply with international obligations can be hardly avoided if a country stipulates two different treaties with the US and the EU: 'the first to conclude a trade deal with an Asian country determines the space remaining for concluding a different deal on GIs with the other'.[103]

V. EU and US towards Singapore

The EU-Singapore trade and investment protection agreements were signed on 19 October 2018. The European Parliament gave its consent to the agreements on 13 February 2019.[104] EU Member States endorsed the trade agreement on 8 November 2019, and it entered into force on 21 November 2019.[105] Unlike South Korea, Singapore uses a trade mark system to protect GIs, but in the FTA agreed to establish a *sui generis* system of protection pursuant to Article 10.17, despite being quite hostile to the EU GI approach. The agreement requires a domestic register; an administrative process verifying the nature of GIs according to the TRIPS definition; an objection procedure allowing third parties to assert their interests; and legal means that permit the rectification and cancellation of entries in the domestic register based on the

101. Art. 10.21 reads in part: 'The protection of a geographical indication under this Article is without prejudice to the continued use of a trademark which has been applied for, registered or established by use, if that possibility is provided for by the legislation concerned, in the territory of a Party before the date of the application for protection or recognition of the geographical indication, provided that no grounds for the trademark's invalidity or revocation exist in the legislation of the Party concerned.' The affirmative provision that 'In such cases, the use of the protected designation of origin or protected geographical indication shall be permitted as well as use of the relevant trademarks' contained in the EU's Regulation 1151/2012 Art. 14(2) is not included.
102. In the last meeting of the Working Group on GIs (6 November 2019), it was decided to add 46 EU GI names to the list which will be finalised in the due course of procedure.
103. B. O' Connor, G. de Bosio, 'The Global Struggle Between Europe and United States Over Geographical Indications in South Korea and in the TPP Economies', in van Caenegem and Cleary, *supra* note 19, 47–79.
104. S.H.S. Leong, 'European Union-Singapore Free Trade Agreement: A New Chapter for Geographical Indications in Singapore', in Calboli and Ng-Loy, *supra* note 42, 235–56.
105. OJ L 294 of 14 November 2019, 3 et seq.

legitimate interests of third parties and the right holders of the registered GIs in question.

The scope of the agreement concerning GIs includes wines, spirits, agricultural products and foodstuff (Article 10.16) and in a more sophisticated manner than the one provided in Article 22.2 and 22.3 TRIPS reproduces an agreed list of products (196 EU GIs including wine and spirits). Article 10.21 deals with the relationship with trade marks. It provides the standard provision that a trade mark identical to a listed GI should be refused if registration is sought after the date of application for GI registration.[106] On the question of prior trade marks, the parties 'agreed to disagree'. Apart from the case of a contrast between a reputed or well-known trade mark and a GI which misleads consumers as to the true identity of the product (Article 10.21.4), paragraph 2 reads: 'the Parties acknowledge that the existence of a prior conflicting trademark in a Party would not *completely* preclude the registration of a subsequent geographical indication for like goods in that Party'. However, a footnote to this sentence makes clear that, 'in the case of Singapore, a GI which conflicts with a prior existing trademark is capable of being registered *with the consent* of the prior existing trademark rights holder'. Instead, in the case of the EU, such consent is not a prerequisite for the registration of a GI which conflicts with a prior existing trade mark.

In addition, the identity or similarity of a trade mark to a GI is not a reason to refuse registration, or use of the mark, provided that the application, the registration, or the acquisition of the rights through use took place in good faith before the date of application for protection of the GI in the territory concerned or before this protection was granted in the country of origin (Article 10.21.3). Nothing can be done against a continuous use of a GI for agricultural products or foodstuff (so, differently from wine and spirits), if that use was preceding 1 January 2004 for at least ten years or in good faith. A GI cannot be protected as such where this is a customary term in common language for the same goods and services in the territory of the Party.

As a result of this agreement, the Geographical Indications Act, already adopted in 2014 by the Singapore Parliament, entered into force on 1 April 2019 and aims at: establishing a Registry of Geographical Indications; enhancing the protection of GIs in Singapore; and providing improved border enforcement measures for GIs. It will not override any rights that interested parties already have under the existing regime. These rights will co-exist with those under the new regime.

The US–Singapore FTA, the first with an Asian nation, was launched on 16 November 2000 and concluded on 15 January 2003. The provisions contained therein stress, for example, that each Party provides that the owner of a registered trade mark shall have the exclusive right to prevent all third parties *not having the owner's consent* from using in the course of trade identical or similar signs, including GIs, for goods or services that are related to those in respect of which the trade mark is registered, where such use would result in a likelihood of confusion (Article 16.2.2). The wording is similar to that already used in the later EU–Singapore Agreement, yet paradoxically more restrictive. The coexistence of a trade mark with an identical or similar GI is indeed allowed with the consent of the owner on condition that

106. D. Elms, 'Understanding the EU-Singapore Free Trade Agreement', in Elijah et al., *supra* note 83, at 35–54.

such use would not lead to confusion. This is an additional requirement making the coexistence easier. Article 16.2.6 finally states that the use or effectiveness of a trade mark cannot be impaired by the use of a term customary in common language as the common name for a product (including size, placement or style of use), highlighting the centrality of trade marks as such in the legal discourse. As we can see, the complex hybridised systems are imposed via top-down models rather than generated locally on a fit-for-purpose basis. The opposite approach would only lead to unilateral attempts to harmonise the prevailing view of the stronger trading partner with the legal mechanisms of the other. The protection of well-known signs can be deemed as the only common basis.[107]

VI. Old and New Generation

Among the 'new generation' agreements containing an IP (in particular GI) section, the following deserve mention.[108]

1. *The Andean Community*

The FTA[109] with the Andean community[110] regulates GIs in Articles 207–214. The definition is the synthesis of the Lisbon system, coupling the PDO and PGI (Article 207.a: 'exclusively or essentially attributable')[111] and covers lists of GIs in Appendix 1 of Annex XIII to the Agreement (Article 207.c). The recognition is extended to GIs other than food and wine (Article 207.d; Appendix 2).[112] As long as GIs are protected

107. S. Frankel, 'Geographical Indications and Mega-Regional Trade Agreements and Negotiations', in Calboli and Ng-Loy, *supra* note 42, 147–67, at 167.
108. *See* the general analysis of D. Vivas-Eugui, Chr. Spennemann, 'The Treatment of Geographical Indications in Recent WTO Discussions and in Regional and Bilateral Agreements', in M.P. Pugatch (ed.), *The Intellectual Property Debate* (Cheltenham 2006) 305–44, almost corresponding to *ibid.*, 'The Evolving Regime for Geographical Indications in WTO and in Free Trade Agreements (1996–2015)', in C.M. Correa, A.A. Yusuf (ed.), *Intellectual Property and International Trade: The Trips Agreement* (3rd edn., Kluwer 2016), in which, despite the title, the authors do not even take into account the new EU legislation on GIs of 2012; B. Mercurio, 'TRIPS-plus provisions in FTAs: Recent Trends', in L. Bartels and F. Ortino (eds.), *Regional Trade Agreements and the WTO Legal System* (Oxford, 2006) 215–37; Kampf, *supra* note 70, at 115 et seq.; S. Nadde-Phlix, in J. Drexl et al. (eds.), *EU Bilateral Trade Agreements and Intellectual Property: For Better or Worse?* (Berlin-Heidelberg 2014) 133–58, at 142 et seq.
109. Decision 2012/735/EU, in OJ L 354 of 21 December 2012, 3 et seq., to which Ecuador acceded (Decision UE 2016/2369, in OJ 356 of 24 December 2016, 3 et seq.). Since 1 March 2013, provisionally applied with Peru, since 1 August 2013 with Colombia and since 1 January 2017 with Ecuador.
110. *See* the observations on the draft made by P. Covarrubia, 'The EU and Colombia/Peru Free Trade Agreement on GIs: adjusting Colombian and Peruvian national laws?', 6 JIPLP (2011), 330–38; Engelhardt, *supra* note 72, at 803 et seq.
111. It is thus difficult to understand the concern of O'Connor and Richardson, *supra* note 79, at 14 regarding the fact that 'according to the GI definition provided for in the agreement, these products do not fall within the scope of the FTA, which only provides for Andean DOs and European PDOs', which is not true.
112. On the point *see* P. Covarrubia, 'Geographical Indications of Traditional Handicrafts: A Cultural Element in a Predominantly Economic Activity', 50 IIC (2019), 441–66.

in the country of origin, they cannot be considered the common or generic designation of the product that they identify (Article 207.h). The scope of protection, which the Parties abide by, is established by Article 210: it should include any commercial use of GIs for identical or like products not compliant with the product specification or in so far such use exploits the reputation of GI (lit. a), any non-authorised use of GI for food creating confusion even when accompanied by indications such as style, type, etc. (lit. b), any misuse, imitation or evocation of GI for wine or spirits (lit. c), any other false or misleading indication of origin, nature or essential qualities of the product on packaging or advertising material, any other practice liable to mislead the consumer as to the true origin of the product. The priority rule is confirmed in Article 211, where a trade mark cannot be registered or remain valid if the application for it was submitted after the date of application of a GI for identical or like products in the territory of the interested country. The obligation to protect GIs does not go so far as to also require privileged treatment for reputed trade marks (Article 211.2), unless liable to mislead consumers as to the true identity of the product. A Sub-committee on Intellectual Property is in charge of managing demands for addition of new GIs (Articles 209 and 257).

2. *CARIFORUM*

The EU-CARIFORUM EPA of 1 January 2014 obligates 15 Caribbean countries to establish a system of GI protection.[113] The most significant requirements are as follows. The registration system must be reserved for 'goods originating in the geographical area concerned and that are produced in accordance with the relevant product specifications' (Article 145.B.2), that is, according to a technical administrative process considerably stronger than TRIPS standards or in the United States. The agreement calls for high level of protection of GIs by prohibiting their use on goods not originating in the geographical area, even if the usage would not confuse consumers as to the true origin (Article 145.B.3). The other dispositions reproduce the TRIPS clauses but are not limited to wines and spirits. If a GI application is made prior to a similar trade mark application, the latter must be denied if the former is ultimately approved by applying the priority principle. Lastly, this EPA seems to offer a broader scope of protection for GIs than that provided by the EU-Andean FTA.

3. *Central America*

The EU and the Central American region concluded a new Association Agreement, signed on 29 June 2012, whose trade provisions have been provisionally applied with Honduras, Nicaragua and Panama since 1 August 2013, with Costa Rica and El Salvador since 1 October 2013, and with Guatemala since 1 December 2013.[114] GIs are regulated in Articles 242-250. The general definition of GI is taken from TRIPS (Article 242), and the rights and obligations established in Part II, Section 3 of TRIPS were explicitly confirmed. Article 244 obliges the Parties to modify their legislation

113. OJ L 289 of 30 October 2008, p. 3 et seq.
114. OJ L 346 of 15 December 2012, 3 et seq. *See* Engelhardt, *supra* note 72, at 809 et seq.

in order to provide a register of protected GIs in their territory, an administrative process verifying the nature of GIs according to the TRIPS definition, the presence of a binding product specification, control mechanisms, and a right to use to legitimate operators. The Association Council may decide on the addition of new GIs (Article 247) or the inclusion in Annex XVIII (PGI) of all names from Annex XVII ('List of names to be applied for protection as GI in the Territory of the Parties') that have achieved a successful outcome after the prescribed examination procedure (Article 245). Protection is conferred by, for example, the prohibition of any use misleading the public as to the geographical origin of goods, any evocative use or practice resulting in an act of unfair competition, resilience to genericisation as long as the name stands for protection in the country of origin, enforceability of a continued and similar use in good faith of a GI of the other Party before the date of entry into force of the Agreement (Article 246). The above-mentioned rules concerning the order of priority between a trade mark and a GI and the rejection of (possibly misleading) protection of the latter towards a reputed or well-known trade mark are provided by Article 248. Also interesting is the exclusion of access to dispute settlement with regard to decisions about the protection of a GI (Article 250), aiming to put the issue before the domestic judicial instances.[115]

4. *Moldova*

The Association Agreement between the European Union and the Republic of Moldova was signed in June 2014 and has been in full effect since 1 July 2016.[116] The regulation in Articles 296–306 follows the structure and the contents of EU-Central America Association Agreement as to the definition of GIs (again the TRIPS rules: Article 296.3), to the established GIs and the addition of new GIs (Articles 297–298), to the scope of protection (Article 299), to the right of use (Article 300). The main peculiarities of the Agreement are: Article 302 provides Moldova with a transitional period of five years to put in place all complementary actions necessary to stop any unlawful use of protected GIs; in Article 299.2 there is an issue concerning wholly or partially homonymous GIs (which are not always present in such Agreements) – the solution is aligned with Article 23 TRIPS but goes beyond it, as the protection shall be granted after verifying the use in good faith, with due regard for local and traditional usage and the actual risk of confusion and the registration of a misleading name should be refused even if the name 'is accurate as far as the actual territory, region or place of origin of the product in question is concerned'. Furthermore, in the relationship with trade marks, the 'divergent' disposition containing forced coexistence appears in Article 303.5: the Parties shall protect GIs also where a prior trade mark exists, that is, even if it was applied for, registered or established by use before the date of submission of the application for protection of the GI, provided

115. A Study (European Implementation Assessment) of the European Parliamentary Research Service of July 2018 pointed out that the implementation of the rules regarding GIs should improve in reference to the real benefits for the EU partners: https://www.europarl.europa.eu/RegData/etudes/STUD/2018/621834/EPRS_STU(2018)621834_EN.pdf, p. 90, 92.

116. OJ L 260 of 30 August 2014, p. 4 et seq.

that no grounds for the trade mark's invalidity or revocation exist in the legislation of the Parties.

5. *Georgia*

The EU and Georgia signed an Association Agreement on 27 June 2014 that entered into force on 1 July 2016.[117] The Agreement introduces a preferential trade regime - the Deep and Comprehensive Free Trade Area (DCFTA), which increases market access between the EU and Georgia based on having better-matched regulations. The DCFTA has been provisionally applied since 1 September 2014. It partially reproduces (Articles 169–179) the regulation of the EU–Moldova Association Agreement. Aside from formal differences, there is only a supplementary article concerning the protection of transcription of GIs involving characters of the Georgian alphabet and the curious omission of paragraph 5 in Article 172 (= Article 299 Moldova[118]), which protected the right of any person to use, in the course of trade, that person's name or the name of that person's predecessor in business, except where that name is used in such a manner as to mislead consumers.

6. *Ukraine*

The EU and Ukraine have provisionally applied their DCFTA since 1 January 2016. This Agreement means that both sides will mutually open their markets for goods and services based on predictable and enforceable trade rules. This is part of the broader Association Agreement whose provisions on policy and cooperation have been provisionally applied since November 2014.[119] GIs are regulated according to the well-known pattern in Articles 201–211, with a special provision on temporary measures (Article 208). Until stocks of products run out, it is permitted to sell goods produced and labelled which do not comply with the requirements of the Agreement. A list of GIs is provided for which the granted protection under the Agreement shall not preclude use in order to designate and present certain comparable products originating in the Ukraine for a transitional period of ten[120] (or seven[121]) years from the entry into force. This is a very relevant exception, aimed at diminishing and progressively extinguishing the parallel market of (some) evocative trade names.

The same exception is provided in the EPA signed on 10 June 2016 with the South African Development Community comprising Botswana, Lesotho, Mozambique, Namibia, South Africa and Eswatini (formerly Swaziland).[122] The agreement became the first regional EPA in Africa to be fully operational after Mozambique started

117. OJ L 261 of 30 August 2014, p. 4 et seq. *See* Engelhardt, *supra* note 72, at 811 et seq.
118. *See also* Art. 204.5 Ukraine.
119. OJ L 161 of 29 May 2014, p. 3 et seq.
120. Champagne, Cognac, Madeira, Porto, Grappa, Armagnac, Marsala, Malaga, Tokaj.
121. Parmigiano Reggiano, Roquefort, Feta.
122. OJ L 250 of 16 September 2016, 3 et seq. Angola has an option to join the agreement in the future. The other six Member States of the Southern African Development Community region – the Democratic Republic of the Congo, Madagascar, Malawi, Mauritius, Zambia and Zimbabwe – are negotiating Economic Partnership Agreements with the EU as part of other regional groups, namely Central Africa or Eastern and Southern Africa.

applying the EPA in February 2018. In fact, in Protocol 3 to the Agreement, Article 18, the transitional measures allow the marketing of goods which, at the date of entry into force, have been produced, described and presented in accordance with the internal laws and regulations of the Parties and their bilateral obligations to each other, but in a manner prohibited by this Protocol, namely for three years by wholesalers or producers and until the exhaustion of stocks by retailers. The peculiarity of the regulation is that it incorporates in a distinct chapter the agreement on wine and spirits trade in force with the Republic of South Africa since 2002 and the special concession to South Africa in view of the development of its GIs to present up to 30 names with priority for protection in the EU (Article 7.6).

7. *Japan*

On 1 June 2015, the Act on the Protection of the Names of Specific Agricultural, Forestry and Fishery Products and Foodstuffs Act (the 'GI Act') not covering alcoholic beverages (which are covered by the Liquor Act) entered into force, providing *sui generis* protection. The Register currently lists 79 entries, with only Prosciutto di Parma as an overseas product.[123] Prior to this legislation, protection for GIs was based on a 'regionally based collective trade mark', under which there were 566 products registered by 2014. The new legislation would appear to be something of an improvement on the prospects of the EU and Japan agreeing on a common approach to GIs. The EU and Japan concluded an Economic Partnership Agreement, which entered into force on 1 February 2019[124] (Articles 14.22–30) and lists 72 foods plus 145 alcoholic beverages as EU GIs, and 48 foods plus eight beverages as Japan GIs, and follows the fundamental rules of TRIPS protection integrated with the open list system (Article 14.24 and Part 1–2, Section A-B, of the Annex 14-B; Article 14.30 for the addition of new GIs), with the substantial core of the clauses seen above. The common-name rule and the conflict of a GI with the name of a plant variety or an animal breed resulting in the likelihood of misleading the consumer are grounds to be taken into account in an opposition procedure and examination (Article 14.25.4). A particular regime is established, regardless of the product specification and for a period of seven years from the date of entry into force of the Agreement, with respect to the possibility that the operations of grating, slicing and packaging, including cutting into portions and inner packaging, of the GI product can be carried out within the territory of Japan, provided that such product is destined for the Japanese market and not for the purpose of re-exportation (Article 14.25.5). As to the relation with trade marks, listed GIs prevail over a successive application of a trade mark whose use is likely to mislead as to the quality (not the origin) of the good (Article 14.27.1); a similar disposition to Article 10.21.2 of EU–Singapore FTA reads as follows: 'the Parties acknowledge that the existence of a prior conflicting trade mark in a Party would not completely preclude the protection under this Agreement of a subsequent

123. S. Van Uytsel, 'When Geographical Indications Meet Intangible Cultural Heritage: The New Japanese Act on Geographical Indications', in Calboli and Ng-Loy, *supra* note 42, 508–29.
124. OJ L 330 of 27 December 2018, 3 et seq. An analysis of the (potential) economic impact is provided by the EC DG for Trade (June 2018): https://trade.ec.europa.eu/doclib/docs/2018/july/tradoc_157115.pdf.

geographical indication for like goods in that Party' (Article 14.27.4), in other words: the existence of the 'first-in-time, first-in-right principle' is known, but it is assumed that the competent authorities may require certain conditions for the protection of a GI which conflicts with a prior trade mark, as in the case of the homonymous signs. Good faith (in the application, registration of a trade mark or acquisition of relevant rights through use) and priority cannot be questioned as to the eligibility or the validity of a trade mark on the sole ground that it is identical or similar to the listed GI (Article 14.27.5). Among the exceptions (Article 14.29), there is a period of seven years (for agricultural products) or five years (for alcoholic beverages, including beer) in order to phase out the prior use of particular listed GIs of the other Party, with a clear and visible indication of the true geographical origin and conditions of differentiation to enable avoiding misleading consumers.

A brief observation should be made about certain clarifications in the footnotes of Annex 14-B (List of GIs); in particular it should be pointed out that protection of the individual component 'grana' of the multi-component GI 'Grana Padano' is not sought,[125] but the protection of the GI 'Nürnberger Bratwürste/Nürnberger Rostbratwürste' is sought in respect of the compound GI name and not in respect of individual terms, that is as a whole, as for Mortadella Bologna, Pecorino Romano, and Pecorino Toscano. The underlying idea is the genericisation of the term, which will be explained in the comments to recent jurisprudence in Europe *infra* section C.IV. Finally, the right of any person to use or to register in Japan a trade mark containing or consisting of the term 'parmesan' in respect of hard cheeses, is allowed unless the use would mislead the public as to the geographical origin of the good.[126]

VII. Agreements for the Future: Vietnam, Mexico, New Zealand, China

Trade and investment negotiations with Vietnam were launched in 2012 and completed in December 2015. Following the Court of Justice of the EU Opinion 2/15, and similar to the EU–Singapore agreements, the result of negotiations with Vietnam was adjusted to create an FTA and an Investment Protection Agreement. The trade and investment agreements were signed on 30 June 2019 and the European Parliament gave its consent to both agreements on 12 February 2020. The FTA can be officially concluded by the Council and can enter into force once the Vietnamese National Assembly on the one side, and all EU Member States on the other side have ratified it.[127] The FTA in Articles 12.23 to 12.33 provides rules according to the usual scheme (scope of protection, list of GIs, amendment to the list, system of registration, right of use of GIs, relationship to trade marks, enforcement, general rules, cooperation and transparency). Of some relevance are the exceptions concerning the protection of the indications Asiago, Fontina, Gorgonzola, Feta in general, and of Champagne for a transitional period of ten years, with respect to commercial use in good faith (only for cheeses, prior to 1 January 2017). The same limited name protection as

125. Like Emmental de Savoie, Brie de Meaux, Camembert de Normandie, Mozzarella di bufala campana, Provolone Valpadana, Edam Holland, Gouda Holland, West Country farmhouse Cheddar cheese (in relation to cheddar).

126. Which could not be so 'hard' to find.

127. As of February 2021, only six EU Member States have ratified it.

the mentioned above in Annex 14-B of the EU–Japan EPA is granted in Annex 12-A to some products (mostly cheeses).

In the case of the EU–Mexico FTA (EU–MX), incorporating the existing agreement on the mutual recognition and protection for spirit drinks done at Brussels on 27 May 1997, as amended, both countries have provided a legal framework that prevents misleading or unfair use or misuse of the EU or Mexican listed GIs (subsection 4, Article X.29-43). A fundamental point of the negotiation was to preserve the protection of a selection of 340 products of interest with an appellation of origin from the European Union. A document with this list – Annex II Part A – was published in the Mexican Official Gazette on 10 August 2017 to receive observations and objections to the list of EU appellations of origin to be exported to Mexico. The final document of the Treaty includes the outcome of these observations as annotations to the text. In turn, a list of 20 Mexican food appellations of origin – Annex II Part B – was included and given the same treatment. An additional list of 19 names of interest to Mexico, which identify a product originating and protected in Mexico – Annex III – was also included. This list of products was agreed to be taken in consideration provided that the scope of protection of the EU–MX is enlarged. The peculiarities of the Draft TFA are the following: a name protected under this Agreement may be used by any operator marketing a product which conforms to the corresponding specification (X.36.1) – it is not clear whether the conformity of the product to the specification is enough to make use of the registered name on the market, the mention of 'any operator' could even suggest a producer;[128] furthermore, paragraph 3 emphasises that indications and other signs referring to GIs may only be used in relation to the product protected or registered in the respective territories and produced in conformity with the corresponding specification, which seems to be contradictory when compared to paragraph 1. As a limited exception to the rights conferred by a trade mark, a prior trade mark 'in certain circumstances' (which have to be assessed on a case by case basis) may not entitle its owner to prevent a registered GI from being granted protection or used in that Party; conversely, protection of the registered GI shall not limit the rights conferred by that trade mark in any other way, including a possibility to request further renewals or variations of a distinctive sign provided that the variation does not constitute an act of unfair competition (Article X.37.1). A properly enlightening sketch on the genericisation of trade names[129] is contained in Article X.40.1-3 ('Exceptions'), taken mostly from the TPP text: indeed, as in the EU regulation, PGIs shall not become generic in the territories of the Parties, but, before enjoying such a protection, the provisions do not apply to a GI or an individual name contained in a multi-component GI which is identical with the term customary in common language as the common name for such goods or services in the territory of that Party, nor shall prejudice the right of 'any person' to use that term in association with that product in the territory of that Party. Again, at the limits of the logic,[130] the protection of the GI 'Toscana/Toscano' shall not prejudice the right

128. *See* the observations of Engelhardt, *supra* note 72, at 789 et seq.
129. *See* the analysis of genericised terms in some FTAs by A. Moerland, 'Descriptive Terms in International Trade', in Chr. Heath, A. Kamperman Sanders and A. Moerland (eds.), *Intellectual Property Rights as Obstacles to Legitimate Trade?* (Kluwer 2018) 77–105, at 97 et seq.
130. I partly disagree with B. O'Connor, 'The European Union and the United States: Conflicting Agendas on Geographical Indications – What's Happening in Asia?', 9 *Global Trade and Customs*

of any person to use, or to register in Mexico a trade mark containing this term, its translation or transliteration, provided that it does not mislead the public as to the geographical origin of the goods or infringe the GI as protected in other way (Annex II-A). For example (of the plenty to be considered), how can it be possible that the use of the word Yucatán does not recall the Mexican origin of certain goods? On the other hand, how can it be that 'Tabasco' (the name of a Mexican province) has been registered and widely used for a sauce of (exclusively) US origin?

In the ongoing negotiations with New Zealand (since June 2018), the provisory draft (GIs are in subsection 4 of the IP rules, Article X.30-38) tabled by the EU is based on the already analysed patterns. It should be observed that in New Zealand, a Geographical Indications (Wine and Spirits) Registration Act was adopted on 21 November 2006 and came into force in 2017, providing a regime (with the Regulations approved on 26 June 2017) for registering New Zealand place names as GIs both for wine or spirits. It also allows for foreign GIs to be registered.[131]

On 6 November 2019, the EU and China concluded negotiations on a bilateral agreement on cooperation on and protection of GIs. The provisional text is a consolidation of the structure and content of previous FTAs, in the part concerning GIs and following the list system (100 EU GIs against 100 China GIs) which would merit a separate analysis. This landmark agreement is expected to result in reciprocal trade benefits and demand for high-quality products on both sides. It came into effect on 1 January 2021.

VIII. Trade Re-marks

From the above, we can conclude that the external trade agenda of the EU pushes for enhanced protection of GIs not only at home, but also abroad as an essential element for promoting the export of GIs to third countries where these terms are often considered generic. GIs create value for local communities through products that are deeply rooted in tradition, culture and geography so that, in order to cope with misuse and counterfeiting, which limits access to certain markets and undermines consumer loyalty, the EU has concluded several trade and economic partnership agreements supporting the intrinsic value of GIs beyond the standards established by TRIPS.[132] These agreements follow a pattern with some changes from partner to

Journal (2014) 66–69, where he notes that for the majority of EU GIs multi-component terms containing a direct reference to a geographical place, their component parts may be used on their own without undermining the EU GI. Some of the value is built just on the integrity of designation: what about protecting only Padano, or Romano, or Toscano, as the most significant part of the geographical name? And just to be clear, Parmigiano is a pure geographical term (that is: 'coming from Parma').

131. *See* on the introduction of GI system J. Overton, W.E. Murray, 'GI Blues: Geographical Indications and Wine in New Zealand', in van Caenegem and Cleary, *supra* note 19, 197–220.

132. *See* European Commission, 2019 Report on Implementation of EU Free Trade Agreements (Luxembourg 2019), and the accompanying Commission Staff Working Document Individual reports and info sheets on implementation of EU Free Trade Agreements: https://eur-lex.europa.eu/legal-content/EN/TXT/?qid=1571409827886&uri=CELEX:52019SC0370. *See also* A. Matthews, 'What outcome to expect on Geographical Indications in the TTIP free trade agreement negotiations with the United States?', paper for 145th EAAE Seminar, Parma 2015, p. 14 et seq.

partner, but all of them carry an annex with a list of names to be protected as GIs in the territory of the Parties.

The interpretation of these agreements, particularly by 'new world' countries, conveys the opposite impression of a 'manipulative' EU tending to persuade others to impose trade barriers on US exports through (over)protection of EU GIs. In doing so, the EU could distort market competition.[133] Consideration must be paid also to this viewpoint if we strive to reach a global legal solution of this political and economic clash.

A Realpolitik approach, that is putting all efforts into granting protection just to the most economically valuable GIs, could endanger the better enforcement of GI names in general. Would it make more sense to take a tougher international stance against producers using flags, symbols or other marks that mislead consumers into thinking that the origin of, for example, American parmesan is Italian when this is not the case? Perhaps more effort could be put on the use of official labels ('original', 'authentic'),[134] not least because avoiding confusing and misleading indications in trade is not only an international obligation under the Paris Convention, but also a far less contested concept than the proprietary protection of names that may very well be in the public domain.

Anyway, the growing new generation of trade agreements is rapidly changing the scope and content of international obligations on IP as stipulated under TRIPS. In the GI sections contained in US and EU FTAs, while levels of awareness and protection are increasing, legal standards are divergent and common features are rare.

During negotiations, both the EU and the US have tried to assert their own legal ideas with the minimum adaptation possible. While the EU regards and promotes GIs as a distinctive category of intellectual property, the US do not.

This difference in approach may be observed with respect to the other exceptions under Article 24 TRIPS in general. The EU agreements explicitly or implicitly remove or restrict TRIPS exceptions such as those referring to continued and similar prior or good faith use of GIs or to the free use of generic terms.[135] In addition, the lists of protected names are rather short in US agreements, but of considerable length in EU agreements.

A comparison of EU and US FTAs demonstrates the recent shift in international IP policymaking from a multilateral (WTO or WIPO) forum to a regional and bilateral level. The lack of consistent approach and the constant search for the best outcome in each isolated negotiation cannot contribute to a truly systemic assertion of GI

133. *See* the numerous protest letters from Senate leadership to e.g. Ambassador Froman, USTR, 22 April 2016; a letter from several Members of Congress to USTR and USDA, 9 May 2014.

134. Matthews, *supra* note 132, at 19. As a matter of fact: 'Would a product labelled as "Wisconsin feta" really cause confusion in the minds of consumers as to the source of the product (this is the solution that was adopted for some EU cheese GIs in CETA for the production of these cheeses in Canada)?'.

135. On this point *see* the remarks by Moerland, *supra* note 129, at 94 et seq. on the principles developed by CJEU in the judgments Bayerisches Bier (C-343/07, point 101 et seq.) and Parmesan (C-132/05, point 53 et seq.).

protection.[136] The more that is done in many smaller areas, the less will be achieved on the international stage.

A new colonialism is at the door and developing countries have to accept new legal masters (in form of trade mark, *sui generis* or competition law) able to trigger local potential based on tradition and culture and to let them play a role in the global markets. In the conflict between global and local, the equilibrium between local economic development and global protection system could be the answer.

C. *SPES ULTIMA DEA*

As can be perceived from the above, a lot of issues are waiting for a solution, which could never come. One could thus be waiting for Godot.

Starting from the TRIPS environment and by way of the mandate given under the Doha Ministerial Declaration,[137] the two open issues are the creation of a multilateral register for wines and spirits, and the extension of a higher level of protection, provided by Article 23, beyond wines and spirits.[138]

I. Register of Wines

With regard to the establishment of a system of notification and registration,[139] the negotiations started in February 1997 and are still ongoing.[140] To date, three sets of proposals have been submitted, representing the different positions of WTO Member States.

---

136. Remarks in B.A. Melo Araujo, 'The EU's Deep Trade Agenda: Stumbling Block or Stepping Stone Towards Multilateral Liberalisation?', in *European Yearbook of International Economic Law* (2014) 263–84.
137. WT/MIN(01)/DEC/1 of 20 November 2001: 'With a view to completing the work started in the Council for Trade-Related Aspects of Intellectual Property Rights (Council for TRIPS) on the implementation of Article 23.4, we agree to negotiate the establishment of a multilateral system of notification and registration of geographical indications for wines and spirits by the Fifth Session of the Ministerial Conference. We note that issues related to the extension of the protection of geographical indications provided for in Article 23 to products other than wines and spirits will be addressed in the Council for TRIPS pursuant to paragraph 12 of this declaration' (point 18).
138. On this topic *see* Gangjee, *supra* note 13, at 265 et seq.; F. Frantz, 'Twenty Years of TRIPS, Twenty Years of Debate: The Extension of High Level Protection of Geographical Indications - Arguments, State of Negotiations and Prospects', 21 *Ann. Survey of Int'l & Comp. L.* (2016), 93–117; M. Handler, 'Rethinking GI Extension', in Gangjee, *supra* note 33 at 146–82.
139. *See* Strauch and Arend, *supra* note 29, at 414 et seq.; Taubman, *supra* note 40, at 200–05.
140. The extension to spirits was suggested during the Meeting of the Council for TRIPS on 6 November 1996 (IP/C/8, point 34): 'the Council will initiate in 1997 preliminary work on issues relevant to the negotiations specified in Article 23.4 of the TRIPS Agreement concerning the establishment of a multilateral system of notification and registration of geographical indications for wines. Issues relevant to a notification and registration system for spirits will be part of this preliminary work'. *See* the story of the post-TRIPS works in J.M. Cortés Martín, 'International Protection of Geographical Indications: the WTO multilateral register negotiations', in Gangjee, *supra* note 33 at 183–201.

The negotiations took place on the basis of two main proposals – the European Communities' proposal submitted in 1998[141] and a joint proposal from Japan and the United States submitted in 1999.[142] Separately, Hungary, supporting and developing the EC approach, submitted a modification proposal concerning the opposition/challenge procedure in the register.[143] In 2003, an alternative proposal was submitted by Hong Kong (China).[144]

One common feature (although not completely uncontroversial) of all the proposals is the fact that the participation in the registration is voluntary.

The EC 'maximalist' approach[145] envisages multilateral registration as a three-step process: first, WTO Member States would notify the Secretariat of all GIs that identify goods as originating in their territory, which would be published; afterwards, there would be a period of 18 months to examine the notifications and ask for clarifications; if necessary, there could be the possibility of challenging the registration of a notified GI (normally based on substantiated arguments; the disagreement could then be solved through bilateral negotiations or by arbitration, in the Hungarian alternative); in case of a successful settlement, if any, the notified GIs would be registered in the multilateral register receiving protection by all WTO Member States.

The second 'minimalist' proposal[146] suggests setting up a voluntary system whereby GIs would be notified and registered (without an opposition procedure) in a database that would be mandatory only for WTO Member States choosing to participate in the system.

The third proposal consists of a compromise between the two main drafts aiming at speeding up the process of establishment of the system. Registration, involving only a formal examination, should be accepted by participating Member States' domestic courts, tribunals or administrative bodies as prima facie evidence of ownership, of complying with the definition of GIs under Article 22.1 TRIPS and of protection in the country of origin. All in all, a good-faith-based system.

In recognition of the difficulties in reaching a common view, a '3-4-5' process was started,[147] that is,

141. Communication of 28 July 1998 (IP/C/W/107), reviewed on 22 June 2000, 14 June 2005 (TN/IP/W/11); and 19 July 2008 (TN/C/W/52).
142. Communication of 11 March 1999 (IP/C/W/133), reviewed on 26 July 1999 with the supporting addition of Canada and Chile. The Proposal evolved in the Communication of 23 October 2002 (TN/IP/W/5) with the addition of other WTO Member States and finally in the Draft TN/IP/W/10, last reviewed on 31 March 2011.
143. Communication of 3 May 2001 (IP/C/W/255). *See* a very useful comparison of the main elements of the proposals in the Communications from EC of 31 May 2001 (IP/C/W/259) and from US of 9 April 2002 (TN/IP/W/1).
144. Annex A of the Communication of 23 April 2003 (TN/IP/W/8).
145. Sponsored also by 108 WTO Member States: Albania, Brazil, China, Colombia, Croatia, Ecuador, Georgia, Iceland, India, Indonesia, the Kyrgyz Republic, Liechtenstein, Moldova, the Former Yugoslav Republic of Macedonia, Pakistan, Peru, Sri Lanka, Switzerland, Thailand, Turkey, the Africa, Caribbean and Pacific Group and the African Group.
146. Supported also by Argentina, Australia, Costa Rica, Dominican Republic, Ecuador, El Salvador, Guatemala, Honduras, Israel, Japan, Korea, Mexico, New Zealand, Nicaragua, Paraguay, the Separate Customs Territory of Taiwan, Penghu, Kinmen and Matsu, South Africa.
147. Ambassador Darlington Mwape of Zambia, Chairman of the Council for TRIPS, Report of 25 November 2009 (TN/IP/19).

- 3 issues: legal effects or consequences of registration, and participation in the register; notification and registration of terms in the register; fees, costs, administrative and other burdens, in particular for developing countries and least developed countries, and special and differential treatment;
- 4 questions: 'What legal obligations would be acceptable for the register to facilitate the protection of GIs for wines and spirits, as mandated by Article 23.4 of the TRIPS Agreement?', 'When making decisions regarding the registration and protection of trade marks and GIs, what significance and weight should national authorities give to the information on the register?', 'Are there any options regarding participation, other than voluntary and mandatory participation? If so, what criteria could be envisaged?', 'What form could special and differential treatment take with regard to the Register?';
- 5 principles for future work: the register's purpose is to facilitate protection for wines and spirits, not to increase protection; the register should be useful and meaningful to participating members in some way; the territorial nature of intellectual property rights should be preserved (i.e., countries' right to determine how to protect intellectual property within their own territories); the register should not be too burdensome financially and administratively; developing countries should be given special treatment that is precise, effective and operational.

A drafting group of negotiators produced a comprehensive text, containing around 208 different versions due to persistent divergent positions, presented to a formal TRIPS Council negotiation meeting on 3 March 2011.[148]

The last word on the attempt to establish this system of notification and registration can be left to Ambassador Dacio Castillo (Honduras):[149]

> 'In light of the above, it is my assessment that the situation has not improved since my predecessors' report in April 2014. It seems that in the preparations for the 10th Ministerial Conference substantive work on the GI Register does not currently represent a priority for Members. Delegations' willingness to engage substantively in the TRIPS Special Session remains at a low point and significant efforts on the part of all delegations would be necessary to overcome the persistent disagreements on the mandate and the substance of these negotiations'.

The solution could be revisited in a further implementation of a revived Lisbon system.[150]

148. Annexes 1–2 (JOB/IP/3/Rev.1) to the Report by Ambassador Darlington Mwape of Zambia, Chairman of the Council for TRIPS of 21 April 2011 (TN/IP/21).
149. Chairman of the Council for TRIPS, Report of 3 December 2015 (TN/IP/23), point 8.
150. At least this is the wish of D. Gervais, 'Current Issues in International Intellectual Property Norm-Making', in J. Drexl, H. Grosse Ruse-Khan, S. Nadde-Phlix (eds.), *EU Bilateral Trade Agreements and Intellectual Property: For Better or Worse?* (Springer, 2014), 3–17, at 7, who seems doubtful about the effective ability of the WTO to manage a register, which could become only 'a repository of notifications and no more'.

II. Extension of Protection

The second big issue in the wake of TRIPS is the extension of the high level of protection granted to wine and spirits to other products (Article 23.1).[151] Article 24.1 requires Member States to enter into negotiations aimed at increasing the protection of individual GIs under Article 23 and that the provisions of paragraphs 4 through 8 (that is the grandfather clause of continued use; *bona fide* acquired trade marks; continued use of generic terms; incontestability of trade marks and the use of names) shall not be used by a Member State to refuse negotiations or to conclude bilateral or multilateral agreements.

According to the Doha Ministerial Declaration,[152] the extension of protection represents an implementation issue, to which the 'utmost importance' should be attached. Some WTO Member States construed Article 24.1 as a reference to 'individual geographical indications under Article 23' limited to wines and spirits and thus as a mandate to negotiate the possible abolition of the current exemption under Article 24.4. The opposite view argues that Article 24.1 applies to all products and the reference to Article 23 relates only to a means of additional protection to be provided.[153]

The main argument for an extension of protection lies in the inconsistency of protection levels without any economic, systemic or legal justification. In fact, the risk of confusion between products originating in a specific region and having a special quality due to that origin on the one hand, and products using the same denomination but not having the qualities derived from that specific region on the other, is pertinent and jeopardises any product, regardless of its characteristics. The protection currently provided under Article 22 TRIPS appears inadequate. It does not prevent products whose names are ineligible for a GI from free-riding on the reputation of genuine GIs: this harms legitimate producers and the marketing of their products actually originating from the place indicated by the GI. There is also a strong legal point related to a requirement of 'low' protection: the test of the misleading effect on the public - which is tailored to suit unfair competition or consumer protection regulations, but not intellectual property protection - could result in different interpretations and decisions. Furthermore, legitimate users will have to undergo costly procedures to demonstrate that consumers are confused as to the origin of goods when suing against misleading GIs.[154] The correctness test of Article 23.1 (whether the GI is used on a product not originating in the place referred

151. In this regard, *see* the very useful the publication of WTO, General Council, Trade Negotiations Committee, Secretariat, Compilation of issues raised and views expressed on the topic of 18 May 2005 (WT/GC/W/546 - TN/C/W/25).
152. WT/MIN(01)/DEC/1 of 20 November 2001, points 12 and 18.
153. In this sense, Communication from Bulgaria, the Czech Republic, Egypt, Iceland, India, Kenya, Liechtenstein, Pakistan, Slovenia, Sri Lanka, Switzerland and Turkey of 2 October 2000 (IP/C/W/204/Rev.1).
154. *See* e.g. the Decision of the Court of Appeal 28 January 2014 - Case No. A3/2013/0936 ([2014] EWCA Civ 5) - *Fage UK Ltd. v. Chobani UK Ltd.*: 'Neither the phrase "Greek yoghurt" nor any Greek translation of it has a reputation in Greece; because in Greece is it designated by the Greek language equivalent of "strained yoghurt". ... what is called "Greek yoghurt" in the UK is called "strained yoghurt" in Greece. So, the name "Greek yoghurt" is incapable of registration under the regulation'.

to by said GI) would be objective and both administrative and judicial decisions would be uniform and harmonious. Providing certainty on the market about the origin and the quality of the goods concerned allows enhanced protection of the consumer through a higher rate of transparency and choice awareness. The intended extension would be able to grant a level playing field and equal opportunities for all WTO Member States beyond those producing wines and spirits.[155] In practice, modifications concerning Article 23 TRIPS simply seek to extend their scope to GIs for all products: the obligation to provide the legal means to interested parties to prevent certain types of imitations (Article 23.1), as well as the obligation to refuse or invalidate trade marks including GIs (Article 23.2) are extended to any situation in which the trade mark or the imitation concerns a product of the same kind as the one protected by the GI. In addition, the provision on homonyms (Article 23.3) would also apply to GIs on all products.[156]

Opponents of this extension argue that it would drive protection in the wrong direction and constitute a further divergence from the balance found in Article 22 between the interests of consumers, producers and the general public. The extension of overprotection provided in Article 23 (far from necessary) could create an additional dichotomy between the benefits that WTO Member States with many GIs receive and the costs borne by Member States with few GIs. The differential treatment was not based on economic or any other form of logic, but was rather the result of historical negotiations and specific circumstances that were particular to the wine sector. After all, why should governments grant monopoly rights in perpetuity based on an accident of history and geography?[157] In the same vein, it was argued that since a number of Member States had received many immigrants bringing their cultural traditions, including names and terms, it would be culturally problematic for Member States, predominantly those from which these people had migrated, to try to claim back terms that had been used for decades without being contested. Under such culinary traditions, for immigrants in their new and adopted country, these terms were simply generic descriptions of food products and food preparation. Immigrants' customs were acquired rights which Member States could not wipe out in the course of negotiations.

Another concern is that many GIs have become generic and no longer reflect the geographical origin, but a general set of characteristics of the product, whose relabelling, as desired by the proponents, could make consumers unable to recognise them (as no truly generic term would be available). The extension would mean extending monopoly rights in certain geographical terms for the benefit of certain producers, an outright anti-competitive measure. As an alternative, the US promotes GI protection through certification or collective marks within the ambit of trade mark law. Lastly, in a cost-benefits analysis, trade benefits through the extension seem to be outweighed by the extra financial and administrative burden to all WTO Member

155. *See* the Joint Statement by the 'GI-Friends Group' of 13 July 2004 (TN/C/4).
156. Communication from the EC of 14 June 2005 (WT/GC/W/547; TN/C/W/26; TN/IP/W/11) referring to the Communication from Bulgaria, Cuba, Cyprus, The Czech Republic, EC, Georgia, Hungary, Iceland, India, Kenya, Liechtenstein, Malta, Mauritius, Pakistan, Romania, The Slovak Republic, Slovenia, Sri Lanka, Switzerland, Thailand and Turkey of 24 June 2002 (IP/C/W/353).
157. WT/GC/W/546 - TN/C/W/25 cit. point 12.

States, especially developing countries, for the establishment of a registration system, enforcement, marketing, etc.

No consensus is in sight, and the solution is 'the solutions', that is: different fragmented bilateral or multilateral agreements outside of the WTO (more feasible and adaptable) in order to achieve growing world-wide protection, slowly and in a non-homogeneous manner, with some regulation asymmetries.

So it is clear that the effective evolution of the GI protection system cannot be seen from a WTO observatory, or even from an institutional observatory. The WIPO environment, with the launch of the flexible Geneva Act, could work better, but the horizon is uncertain and subject to change. The international arena turns back to what it is in reality: an anarchic system made of personal confrontations on the stage of cultural values and economic numbers. One-to-one meetings with the possibility of accession is the future of regional IP agreements with a focus on GIs. The addition of handicrafts in this scenario is not an option, but a must if the target is to generate smoother (*sui generis*) protection, and only by doing so can more international actors with an artisanal history be recruited.

III. Future Developments in the EU: Legislation

Again on the extension issue, this time in the EU, the possibility of extending GI protection to non-agricultural products[158] was identified in a Communication of the European Commission of 24 May 2011, observing that Member States offer different legal systems (for instance, through competition or consumer protection law, or through collective or certification marks) and only one third of them have developed specific legislation considering GIs as a specific form of intellectual property. This fragmentation of the legal framework (a real patchwork) to grant protection for GIs with regard to non-agricultural products may negatively affect the functioning of the internal market concerning traditional products, such as Carrara Marble (what typically should be a PDO[159]). Besides, protection for GIs with regard to non-agricultural products is also an important issue in bilateral and multilateral trade negotiations with third countries. The Commission therefore announced the launch of a feasibility

158. On the topic *see* A. Zappalaglio et al., 'Sui Generis Geographical Indications for the Protection of Non-Agricultural Products in the EU: Can the Quality Schemes Fulfil the Task?', 51 IIC (2020), 31–69.

159. Having said that, I fully agree with the doubts voiced by A. Profeta, R. Balling, W. Schoene, A. Wirsig, 'The Protection of Origins for Agricultural Products in Europe: Status Quo, Problems and Policy Recommendations for the Green Book', 12 *The Journal of World Intellectual Property* (2009) 622–48, at 632–33, on the regime of PDO and PGI: the 'lack of consistency [concerning specificity or quality of the products] in the differentiation, on the one hand, and the similarity of the two protection categories in requirements and the scope of their protection, on the other, is inefficient and should be aborted'. Having a twofold protection scheme at global level (TRIPS with GI and Lisbon, and EU, with DO and GI) it should be convenient to follow only one option and the TRIPS standard could be the easiest to achieve with some slight changes. Supporting the opposite view is D. Marie-Vivien, 'Do Geographical Indications for Handicrafts Deserve a Special Regime? Insights from Worldwide Law and Practice', in van Caenegem and Cleary (eds.), *supra* note 19, 221–52, at 249.

study on the issue of GIs with regard to non-agricultural and non-food products,[160] encompassing all areas of law in this context and aiming to assess stakeholders' needs and the potential economic impact of protection.[161]

Actually, EU interest in this topic was shown some years earlier with the publication (in November 2009) of a commissioned study on the protection of GIs for products other than wines, spirits, agricultural products or foodstuffs carried out by InSight, OriGIn and Agridea. Other initiatives followed: a public Green Paper[162] consultation on a possible extension of GI protection of the EU to non-agricultural products ran from July to October 2014; the public consultation was followed by a conference in January 2015.[163] The 136 responses collected originating from 18 Member States led the European Parliament to adopt a resolution[164] on 6 October 2015 in which Parliament 'calls on the Commission to propose without delay a legislative proposal ... in order to fully exploit the positive economic effects of protecting the distinctiveness and quality of such products, provide consumers with reliable information on their place and method of production, and preserve the know-how and jobs relating to them' (points 3 and 7). It is something that goes beyond the fleeting whim of EU pride and could help to trigger a new driving economy at an international level, confirmed by the latest study carried out on behalf of the Commission on the economic aspects of GI protection at EU level for non-agricultural products, published on 20 February 2020. This evaluates the effectiveness of specific GIs protection in limiting the availability of non-authentic products, assessing the value of this specific protection to consumers, and to producers of authentic geographically rooted products. The premium price of a GI product is 2.23 times the price of a comparable non-GI product (2.75 times for wine, 1.55 for food). The estimated sales value of EU GIs was EUR 62 billion in 2017 (5.7% of the entire food and drink sector), while the estimated export value was EUR 15 billion (15% of the relevant sector).[165]

I am pretty confident that at least in a couple of years, the EU will extend GI protection to appealing non-agricultural products, thereby becoming a 'trojan horse' at international level also for the agricultural GIs, if not on cultural then on economic grounds. Another recent study seeks to quantify the costs arising from the lack of

160. That is: InSight, REDD, OriGIn, Study on Geographical Indications Protection for Non-Agricultural Products in the Internal Market (2013), currently not available under ec.europa.eu/DocsRoom/documents/14897.
161. A Single Market for Intellectual Property Rights Boosting creativity and innovation to provide economic growth, high quality jobs and first class products and services in Europe (24 May 2011) - COM(2011) 287 final.
162. Making the most out of Europe's traditional know-how: a possible extension of geographical indication protection of the European Union to non-agricultural products (15 July 2014) - COM(2014) 469 final.
163. Geographical indication protection for non-agricultural products - What do we learn from the public consultation?. The results are here: https://ec.europa.eu/growth/content/conference-geographical-indication-protection-non-agricultural-products---do-we-learn_en.
164. 2015/2053(INI), in OJ C 349 of 17 October 2017.
165. The last comprehensive study commissioned by the European Commission (Tender No. AGRI-2011-EVAL-04) dates back to 2012: AND-International, Value of production of agricultural products and foodstuffs, wines, aromatised wines and spirits protected by a geographical indication (GI) - Final report. *See* recently FAO, EBRD, Strengthening sustainable food systems through geographical indications. An analysis of economic impacts (Roma 2018) 11 et seq.

EU legislation in this field and to analyse the foregone benefits for citizens, business and Member States. The report estimates that introducing EU-wide GI protection for non-agricultural products would have an overall positive effect on trade, employment and rural development.[166] Finally, on 4 November 2019 the European Commission launched a public consultation on GIs targeting the general public and stakeholders such as producers, processors, national authorities and researchers with the aim of gathering feedback on the understanding and perception of the EU quality schemes. Much ado about nothing?

IV. Developments in EU: Case Law

A brief look at EU court cases (the 'living law' as it is used to be referred to) should complete the picture. Of particular interest are the CJEU judgments on Queso Manchego[167] (evocation) and Aceto Balsamico di Modena[168] (genericisation).

The Spanish case involves the *Consejo Regulador* representing the PDO Queso Manchego and a cheese producer marketing its products associated under graphical elements evoking the La Mancha (the region in Spain that was home to Don Quixote) such as the Rosinante horse and windmills. The CJEU was called upon to clarify the concept of evocation (Article 13.1 of Regulation 1151/2012[169]) and in particular whether conceptual graphical elements of a label (instead of phonetic or graphical resemblance to the PDO/PGI) can, under certain circumstances, represent an evocation of PDO/PGI for consumers. The Court stated that the concept of 'evocation' covers a situation where the term used to designate a product incorporates part

166. C. Navarra, E. Thirion, *Geographical indications for non-agricultural products. Cost of Non-Europe Report* (EPRS, November 2019). *See* on the timeline of the implementation the measures contained in the IP EU Action Plan: Communication from the Commission to the European Parliament, the Council, the European Economic and Social Committee and the Committee of the Regions, COM(2020) 760 – Making the most of the EU's innovative potential – An intellectual property action plan to support the EU's recovery and resilience (25 November 2020): https://eur-lex.europa.eu/legal-content/EN/ALL/?uri=CELEX:52020DC0760.
167. Judgment of 2 May 2019, *Fundación Consejo Regulador de la Denominación de Origen Protegida Queso Manchego*, C-614/17, EU:C:2019:344. *See* recently also the judgment of 17 December 2020, *Syndicat interprofessionnel de défense du fromage Morbier*, C-490/19, EU:C:2020:1043, concerning the question if the reproduction of the shape or appearance of a product which has a protected name could be deemed as a practice liable to mislead the consumer as to the true origin of the product: the relevant disposition – Article 13(1)(d) of Regulation No 510/2006 and Article 13(1)(d) of Regulation No 1151/2012 – should be interpreted as meaning that they do not prohibit solely the use by a third party of a registered name and that it's necessary to assess whether such reproduction may mislead the European consumer, who is reasonably well informed and reasonably observant and circumspect, taking into account all the relevant factors in the case (point 41 and operative part).
168. Judgment of 4 December 2019, *Consorzio Tutela Aceto Balsamico di Modena*, C-432/18, EU:C:2019:1045.
169. 'Registered names shall be protected against: ... b) any misuse, imitation or evocation, even if the true origin of the product is indicated or if the protected name is translated or accompanied by an expression such as "style", "type", "method", "as produced in", "imitation" or similar; c) any other false or misleading indication as to the provenance, origin, nature or essential qualities of the product, on the inner or outer packaging, advertising material or documents relating to the product concerned, and the packing of the product in a container liable to convey a false impression as to its origin; ...'

of a registered name, so that when the consumer is confronted with the name of the product, the image triggered in his mind is that of the product whose name is protected.[170] It cannot be excluded, in principle, that figurative signs (like the horse or the windmills) may 'trigger directly in the consumer's mind the image of products whose name is registered on account of their "conceptual proximity" to such a name', bearing in mind that the reasonably well informed, observant and circumspect average consumer's perception, which is the assessment criterion for the presence of evocation, 'must be understood as covering European consumers, including consumers of the Member State in which the product giving rise to evocation of the protected name is made or with which that name is geographically associated and in which the product is mainly consumed'.[171]

In the Aceto Balsamico case, a request was made in the context of proceedings between Consorzio Tutela Aceto Balsamico di Modena and Balema GmbH concerning the use by the latter of the term 'balsamico' on the labels of vinegar-based products which did not meet the specifications set for that PGI. Taking into account the objections of Germany and Greece to the registration of this PGI, which pointed out the generic nature not of the compound proposed for registration, but only of some elements of it, namely the words 'aceto', 'balsamico' and 'aceto balsamico', or to translations thereof.[172] The Court, leveraging on this recital, confirmed that non-geographical terms of the PGI at issue, namely 'aceto' and 'balsamico', and their use in combination and in translation could not benefit from the protection of the PGI. In particular, the term 'balsamico' is the Italian translation of the adjective 'balsamic' which has no geographical connotation and which, in the case of vinegar, is commonly used to refer to a vinegar with a bitter-sweet flavour (points 33–34). By stating the connection only with a geographical name (in this case, Modena), the Court made an interpretation which is potentially in conflict with what is mandated by some EU trade agreements, where, for example, the name of the wine 'Toscano' is not protected as such. The lack of uniformity creates a confusing legal mosaic which cries out for ultimate global simplification. It is somewhat ironic that the result arrived at by the CJEU, namely that 'aceto balsamico' was not protected as a GI as such and its use could thus not be enjoined regardless of the true origin of the goods, falls short of the protection mandated by Article 10*bis*(2)(iii) Paris Convention where consumers are nonetheless misled. Misconception by consumers was ultimately denied based on domestic unfair competition law,[173] although one

170. Judgment of 4 March 1999, *Consorzio per la tutela del formaggio Gorgonzola*, C-87/97, EU:C:1999:115, point 2.
171. Points 19, 22, 50 of the judgement in the case C-614/17. It confirms substantially the content of Judgment of 7 June 2018, Scotch Whisky Association, C-44/17, EU:C:2018:415 (Glen Buchenbach): 'in the absence of (i) any phonetic and/or visual similarity between the disputed designation and the protected geographical indication and (ii) any partial incorporation of that indication in that designation, must take account of the conceptual proximity, if any, between the designation and the indication', point 56.
172. Commission Regulation (EC) No 583/2009 of 3 July 2009 entering a name in the register of protected designations of origin and protected geographical indications [Aceto Balsamico di Modena (PGI)], recital 10.
173. OLG Karlsruhe, 10 March 2021, GRUR-Prax 2021, 227 – *Deutscher Balsamico*.

could have very well arrived at the opposite conclusion, as the first instance court actually did in this case.[174]

In the end, the peculiarity of GIs is also their own main threat: the link to a specific area may result in the perception that GIs are not worthy of protection in other places.

174. LG Mannheim 15 September 2015, 2O 187/14.

CHAPTER 6
TRIPS, TRIPS Plus and the Patent Bargain

Christopher Heath

> 'Monopolies are the exception not the rule ... They need to be justified. As long ago as 1615 in this country it was said that the effect of an unjustified monopoly was "to take away free trade, which is the birthright of every subject".'[1]

A. INTRODUCTION

The field of patents was arguably the most contested one in the WTO/TRIPS negotiations.[2] This was for a significant part due to the different interests involved, yet also due to the complicated nature of the patent system in itself.

In economic terms, patents confer a right to exclude over a technical invention the use of which would otherwise be non-rival and non-exhaustive. Being non-rival and non-exhaustive is a common feature of all intellectual property rights. This contrasts to (exhaustive, rival and scarce) real property rights whose existence (backed up by proper enforcement regimes) improves the allocation of resources. Land, for example, is arguably used to a better value if available only to one person, as there is an incentive to maintain and produce which is absent if it were common property (unless we are all idealists who maintain common property for non-monetary motives).[3] The allocation of property rights (and the corresponding rights to use and exclude) helps to improve the use of scarce resources. The same is not true for

1. The late Sir Hugh Laddie, quoted in an obituary: W. Cornish and D. Alexander, 'Sir Hugh Laddie - An Appreciation', 40 IIC 2 (2009).
2. D. Gervais, *The TRIPS Agreement, A Drafting History* (2nd edn., Sweet & Maxwell, 2003), 220, writes that 'Patent provisions were a "victory" for the U.S., since they resolved "long standing trade irritants for US patent interests"', yet in the same vein 'limiting the ability of developing countries to access technology'.
3. It is of course debatable whether commonly worked land in the form of kolkhozes or kibbutzim are preferable and even more efficient than the huge estates of pre-revolutionary Russia, Eastern Prussia, modern-day Brazil, etc.

non-rival goods such as knowledge, and property rights over non-rival goods have the opposite effect in that they artificially make scarce what is inexhaustibly available. This is important to bear in mind when trying to liken intellectual property rights to real property rights.[4]

The right to exclude is thus not conferred in order to protect the owner from uninhibited use (as would be the case for tangible property), but in order to confer a certain incentive by introducing artificial scarcity. In the case of patents, such incentive is conferred in order for the inventor to make the invention public and enhance the state of the art.[5] Patents in this regard are little different from other state incentives such as subsidies or tax regimes that are also meant to encourage – or discourage – a certain behaviour. Yet unlike tax regimes, patents also trespass upon the commons and thereby not only distort – as would also tax regimes – but produce negative effects in that the commons are diminished by excluding others from using the patented technology (even those who have independently come up with the same invention, but filed their patent later or not at all). In other words, the question is not whether a patent system produces negative side effects (it does), but whether the positive effects outweigh the negative ones in a situation where the patent monopoly has indeed produced its welfare gains by enhancing the technical state of the art by making the invention available both to the person skilled in the art (by way of disclosure) and to the public at large (by the commercial marketing or use of products or processes).

Whether the patent system in macroeconomic terms is more beneficial than harmful is unclear,[6] just as how a patent system should look in order to confer maximum benefits to domestic economy.[7] There are simply too many parameters that could be adjusted in one way or another.[8] There is significant evidence, however,

4. Which is not only a doctrinal question, as terminology also influences perception. If we were unreflectedly likening intellectual to real property, it is only one step to 'the pervasive rhetorical use of the language of "theft" in intellectual property discourse ... [and the] manipulative power of the language of theft to affect rational decision-making about the socially optimal balance between intellectual property rights and ordinary freedoms ... The language of theft, in short, reduces a difficult policy debate...to a crude and simplistic drama.' P. Loughlan, 'Intellectual Property and the Language of Theft', EIPR [2007], 401, 405.
5. The use as a trade secret would not confer the same benefits: it would not protect the inventor against those who independently come up with the same invention, against the good faith acquirer of such know how, or simply against the lawful or unlawful disclosure.
6. 'That states having a patent law underwent a rapid technical progress does not imply that their progress would have been slower without patent laws. No empirical evidence available to us and no argument brought forward to date can support or contradict the view that the patent system decisively promoted technological progress and economic productivity': F. Machlup, *An Economic Review of the Patent System* (Senate Committee of the Judiciary, Washington 1958), 80. On the other hand, antitrust law suggests that at least 'without small monopolies, no enterprise system can be established.': W. Fikentscher, *Wirtschaftsrecht*, vol. 1 (Munich 1983), 41.
7. In other words, stronger protection is not always better: According to R. Falvey, N. Foster and D. Greenaway, 'Intellectual Property Rights and Economic Growth', Internationalisation of Economic Policy Research Paper No. 2004/12 (2004) http://ssrn.com/abstract=715982, at 2.]: 'the overall effects of stronger IPRs on technology acquisition and aggregate growth are in general ambiguous.'
8. To give some examples: a system where patents are not substantially examined (e.g. Italy) has the advantage that there is no need to employ many specialised technical experts who could otherwise make inventions, and allows patents to be registered more quickly, but has the disadvantage

that the ideal level of IP protection for any given country depends on the capacity of a country to make use of the benefits normally associated with patents: the capacity to innovate by access to knowledge.[9]

Finally, one should be aware that the kind of incentive used for the protection of technical inventions is useful in the context of a free-market, capitalist economy[10] where there is a market for a given invention, or where such market could be developed. It is less useful where there is no free market economy, or where there is a societal need, but no corresponding market.[11] In the latter case, other reward systems such as a public tender to come up with a solution for a given problem (e.g.

---

that legal certainty is compromised and that too many false positives are registered. Even for an examination system, one could provide for an immediate publication of the application so as to alert competitors. This has the disadvantage that an applicant can no longer protect the invention as a trade secret should it turn out that the invention is not patentable. Or one could opt for publication only upon grant, which is more beneficial to the patentee and less to the general public. One could provide for pre-registration (China, India) or post-registration opposition systems (most countries nowadays) that enhance legal certainty, but may prolong the procedure before the patent office (that has to provide corresponding personnel for such tasks). One needs to determine the patentable subject matter and optimum duration of a patent, and whether calculation should be made from the application date (nowadays the standard) or the date of grant (previously the US and Canada), and one may discourage maintenance of the patent by increasing annuities (common in most countries). One needs to determine the scope of the patent (should equivalents be covered or not?) and its exceptions.

9. This is the unanimous conclusion of the following studies: UNCTAD, *United Nations Conference on Trade and Development. Trade and Development Report 2004, UNCTAD/TDR/2004* (UNCTAD, Geneva, 2004), 96; Fink and Primo Braga, 'How Stronger Protection of Intellectual Property Rights Affects International Trade Flows', in Fink and Maskus, *Intellectual Property and Development* (2004), 21. A study by Thompson and Rushing showed that IPRs were unlikely to generate positive effects below a certain minimum threshold of economic development. Thompson and Rushing had set that level at USD 3,400 (in 1980 dollars) (M.A Thompson and F.W. Rushing, 'An Empirical Analysis of the Impact of Patent Protection on Economic Growth', 21 *J. of Econ. Dev.* (1996), 61–79) or more than USD 8,300 in 2005 dollars. An interesting 2004 study by Falvey, Foster and Greenaway (*supra* note 7), which used a different regression model, demonstrated the non-linearity of the relationship between IPRs and economic growth and identified 'threshold effects'. Essentially, the level of the positive effect of IPRs depends on whether a developing country is capable of imitating and innovating. Otherwise, IPRs may merely reinforce the market power of exporters. According to the World Bank, 'Global Economic Prospects: Trade Regionalism and Development 2005' (World Bank Publications), 111: 'The general conclusion is that countries have to develop an IPR strategy appropriate to their level of development, and then analyse carefully which, if any, IPR provisions ought to be contained in trade treaties or RTAs'. C. Juma and L. Yee-Cheong in their report *Innovation: Applying Knowledge in Development; Task Force on Science, Technology and Innovation; Millenium Project* (2005), 112–14 propose a three-tiered system of IPR and enforcement to take into account different development levels, a suggestion already voiced by the CIPR report: CIPR, *Integrating Intellectual Property Rights and Development Policy* (London 2002).

10. 'The idea of an exclusive right over inventions only developed on the basis of a capitalist economy and together with it, both being at the same time result and factor of early capitalism. Just as capitalism, [the idea of exclusive rights] found the soil for its development in the economic and philosophical atmosphere of puritanical England.': H. Isay, *Die Funktion der Patente im Wirtschaftskampf* [The Function of Patents in Competition] (Berlin 1927), 7.

11. Pharmaceutical companies when faced with the choice of where to invest their resources for research will rather develop medicines to cure illnesses such as Alzheimer's or Parkinson's (typical illnesses in developed countries with affluent consumers) than malaria (typical illnesses in tropical countries with consumers who cannot afford to pay high prices for medicines).

a medicament for a certain illness) and a purchase of the invention by government seem preferable.

This chapter proceeds with a detailed explanation of the historical foundations of domestic patent law (B.), subsequently the *international patent system* as established by the Paris Convention 1883 until the 1990s (C.), the issue of patents in the context of WTO/TRIPS (D.), and finally some thoughts on the future (E.).

B. TRADITIONAL PRINCIPLES OF PATENT LAW

The beginnings of today's patent system date back almost 400 years. Its main principles are reflected in the *patent bargain,* that is, the balance of interests between inventor/patentee and the general public. This balance is the bedrock of modern-day patent law and was already expressed in the English Statute of Monopolies 1623.

I. On the Patent Bargain

1. Basic Principles

A recent decision rendered by the UK Supreme Court summarised the principles of the patent bargain as follows:[12]

> [17] 'Elementary as it is, it is worth reminding oneself at the outset of the juridical basis on which patents are granted, sometimes called the "patent bargain". The inventor obtains a monopoly in return for disclosing the invention and dedicating it to the public for use after the monopoly has expired. The point was succinctly made by Lord Mansfield in Liardet v Johnson (1778), quoted in Hulme, "On the History of Patent Law", (1902) 18 LQR 280, 285:
>
> > "The condition of giving encouragement is this: that you must specify upon record your invention in such a way as shall teach an artist, when your term is out, to make it – and to make it as well by your directions: for then at the end of the term, the public shall have benefit of it. The inventor has the benefit during the term, and the public have the benefit after ..."
>
> The principle remains the foundation of modern patent law, and is recognised in the case law of both the United Kingdom and the European Patent Office. In EXXON/Fuel Oils (**T 409/91**) [1994] OJ EPO 653, at paras 3.3 and 3.4, the EPO Technical Board of Appeal observed that it was
>
> > "the general legal principle that the extent of the patent monopoly, as defined by the claims should correspond to the technical contribution to the article in order for it to be supported, or justified. ... This means that the definitions in the claims should essentially correspond to the scope of the invention as disclosed in the description. ... Although the requirements of articles 83 and 84 are directed to different parts of the patent application, since article 83 relates to the disclosure of the invention, whilst article 84 deals with the definition of the invention by the claims, the underlying purpose

12. United Kingdom Supreme Court of 14 November 2018 (*Warner-Lambert Company LLC (Appellant) v. Generics (UK) Ltd t/a Mylan and another*).

> of the requirement of support by the description, insofar as its substantive aspect is concerned, and of the requirement of sufficient disclosure is the same, namely to ensure that the patent monopoly should be justified by the actual technical contribution to the art."
>
> The principal conditions of validity, novelty, inventive step, industrial application and sufficiency are all, in one way or another, directed to satisfying the principle thus expressed.'

2. *Learned Hand and the Timely Filing of an Invention*

In the context of United States law, it has been discussed whether over and above the above-mentioned principles, a timely filing of the invention is another precondition for the enjoyment of patent protection, in other words part of the patent bargain. This was so held by judge Learned Hand in the case *Metallizing Engineering Co. v. Kenyon Bearing & Auto Parts Co.*[13]

According to this decision:

> 'it is a condition upon an inventor's right to a patent that he shall not exploit his discovery competitively after it is ready for patenting; he must content himself with either secrecy, or legal monopoly. It is true that for the limited period of two years he was allowed to do so, possibly in order to give him time to prepare an application; and even that has been recently cut down by half. But if he goes beyond that period of probation, he forfeits his right regardless of how little the public may have learned about the invention; just as he can forfeit it by too long concealment, even without exploiting the invention at all.... It is indeed true that an inventor may continue for more than a year to practice his invention for his private purposes or his own enjoyment and later patent it. But that is, properly considered, not an exception to the doctrine, for he is not then making use of his secret to gain a competitive advantage over others; he does not thereby extend the period of his monopoly. Besides, as we have seen, even that privilege has its limits, for he may conceal it so long that he will lose his right to a patent even though he does not use it at all. With that question we have not however any concern here.'

The theory is thus that the inventor cannot have it both ways: first protect the invention as a trade secret and subsequently patent it. This might be sustainable in the context of a system that awards the patent to the first inventor who reduced the invention to practice rather than the first inventor who filed a patent (see below for this distinction), because in the former case, any inventor who files for a patent could be defeated by the inventor already using the invention. Yet in the latter case (the first to file scenario), an inventor using the invention as a trade secret only may be left high and dry (or merely with a right of continuous use ('prior user right')) when someone else files for a patent. So the first-to-file system already provides for a sufficient incentive to file the patent. In addition, it is incorrect to assume that using an invention as a trade secret is equal to a monopolistic use: it is not, because in the absence of a disclosure, no monopoly can be granted, independent

13. 153 F.2d 516 (2nd Cir. 1946).

developers can freely use the invention and the only protection available against the misappropriation of a trade secret is under the rules of tort or unfair competition.[14] Therefore, the requirement to file a patent for an invention without using it prior to filing is not part of the patent bargain.

II. Monopolies and Free Trade

1. *The Statute of Monopolies*

The major principles underlying the patent bargain were already contained in the English Statute of Monopolies, an Act of Parliament that in 1623 abolished all monopolies but those related to 'any manner of new manufacture'.[15] The history of this statute[16] makes it clear that the main thrust was targeted at abolishing monopolies that were considered a burden to society per se. Only monopolies that, first, took away nothing from the public, and, second, contributed to the well-being of society, should be granted henceforth.

The relevant passage reads as follows:

> '[I.] All Monopolies, and Grants, &c. thereof, or of Dispensations, and Penalties, declared void. ... [This] shall not extend to any tres [letters] Patents and Graunt of Privilege for the tearme [term] of fowerteene yeares or under, hereafter to be made of the sole working or makinge of any manner of new Manufactures within this Realme, to the true and first Inventor and Inventors of such Manufactures, which others at the tyme of makinge such tres Patents and Graunts shall not use, soe as alsoe they be not contrary to the Lawe nor mischievous to the State, by raisinge prices of Commodities at home, or hurt of Trade, or generallie inconvenient; the said fourteene yeares to be [accomplished] from the date of the first tres Patents or Grant of such priviledge hereafter to be made, but that the same shall be of such force as they should be if this Act had never byn made, and of none other.'[17]

2. *Monopolies as Exceptions to Free Trade*

The Statute of Monopolies was an act of legislation to abolish all monopolies but patents. Patents are thus the exception to what would otherwise be called free trade.

14. A. Kamperman Sanders, 'The "action servi corrupti" from the Roman Empire to a Globalised Economy', in Heath and Kamperman Sanders, *Employees, Trade Secrets and Restrictive Covenants* (Kluwer Law, 2013), 1,6. And it would be incorrect to confer the same protection on trade secrets as on patents, because trade secrets do not enhance the publicly known state of the art.
15. In fact, other monopolies (in the case at issue one for playing cards) were already held void in a 1602 decision – *Darcy v. Allin* (1602) 11 Co. Rep. 846: 'Where any man by his own charge and industry or by his own wit or invention doth bring any new trade into the Realm, or any new engine tending to the furtherance of a new trade that never was used before and that for the good of the Realm, that in such case the King may grant to him a Monopoly Patent for some reasonable time until the subjects may learn the same in consideration of the good that he doth bring by his invention to the Commonwealth; otherwise not.'
16. In Landmark Cases and their Legacy
17. UK Statute of Monopolies 1623 c. 3 (Regnal. 21_Ja_1).

That patents are an exception is sometimes forgotten, namely when it comes to the interpretation of the inherent or explicitly mentioned exceptions to patents and patent law. While it is often argued that exceptions should be given a narrow reading,[18] this point of view seems to assume that patent law in general represents a rule, which it does not: patent law itself is the exception and the rights conferred should already be given a narrow reading, or, more precisely, a reading that is consistent with what is necessary under the patent bargain (*singularia non sunt extendenda praeter necessitatem*), an interpretation that should equally apply to exceptions to the exception.

The position that patents are justified *obstacles to trade* is also taken by Article XX GATT 1947 and of Articles 28, 30 EC-Treaty (now Articles 34, 36 Treaty on the Functioning of the European Union, TFEU), further explained in Part C.

3. *Patents and Monopolies*

Patents are technical monopolies and as such subject to the rules of patent law. A technical monopoly is not automatically a market monopoly,[19] yet where it becomes one, it is subject to the rules of antitrust (competition) law just as any other market monopoly. Typical examples are market dominating positions based on standard essential patents[20] or restraints of trade by the pooling of patents by competitors.[21] Whether a patent as such gives a superior bargaining position towards potential licensees, and whether the latter should thus be protected against certain abusive contractual clauses, is subject to debate.[22]

---

18. A formula often found in decisions of the CJEU, as has been analytically examined by M. Herberger, *Ausnahmen sind eng auszulegen – Die Ansichten beim Gerichtshof der Europäischen Union* (Cologne, 2016). The author qualifies the statement about narrow interpretation and argues that the CJEU in fact interprets exceptions not narrowly, but rather not beyond their purpose and necessity ('singularia non sunt extendenda praeter necessitate'). No such argument in favour or a narrow interpretation is however made by Ladas, *Patents, Trademarks and Related Rights* (Cambridge Mass. 1975), 309.
19. In the past, the US Supreme Court held that it was (*International Salt Co. v. United States*, 332 U. S. 392), but this is no longer good law (*Illinois Tool Works Inc. v. Independent Ink, Inc.*, 547 U.S. 28 (2006), and indeed there are enough patents that have no market at all.
20. K. C. Liu, 'The Taiwanese "Philips" CD-R Cases: Abuses of a Monopolistic Position, Cartel and Compulsory Licensing', in C. Heath and A. Kamperman Sanders, *Landslide Intellectual Property Cases and Their Legacy* (Kluwer Law, 2011), 83.
21. For Japan, *see* the Guidelines for the Use of Intellectual Property Rights under the Anti-Monopoly Act of 28 September 2007 and the preceding decision of the Japanese Fair Trade Commission of 20 June 1997 – *Pachinko Patent Pool* (*In re Sanyo K.K. et al.*), published in 44 Kōsei Torihiki Iinkai Shinketsushū 238; for the EU, *see* the Guidelines on the application of Article 101 of the Treaty on the Functioning of the European Union to technology transfer agreements of 21 March 2014, OJ C 89 28.3.2014, 3; for the US, *see* the US Guidelines for Intellectual Property 2007, Chapter 3: Antitrust Analysis Of Portfolio Cross-Licensing Agreements And Patent Pools.
22. Licensing agreements are now mostly regarded as pro-competitive and problematic only when there is a mutual restraint of trade between the licensee and the licensor, or where the licensor has a dominant marketing position: e.g. for Japan: Guidelines for the Use of Intellectual Property under the Antimonopoly Act of 2007, revised 2016; for the EU: Commission Regulation (EU) No 316/2014 of 21 March 2014 on the application of Article 101(3) of the Treaty on the Functioning of the European Union to categories of technology transfer agreements, and in the US the Antitrust Guidelines for the Licensing of Intellectual Property 1995.

Even as technical monopolies, patents are a burden to society because they exclude third parties from working in the protected area and divert inventive activity to non-protected areas. It is thus for good reason that their maintenance is taxed, see below.

III. The Patent Bargain – A Feature Analysis

As many of the principles expressed in the Statute of Monopolies form the basis of modern-day patent law, it is helpful to pause for a moment for a more detailed analysis of this text.

1. *Terminology*

'Letters' refer to the written document granting such right of monopoly 'to all to whom these presents shall come', in other words, to all concerned, i.e., the general public. The document thereby serves the purpose of publicity. 'Patent', from the Latin for 'open', refers to the fact that the invention over which a patent is granted shall be laid open to the general public so that it may become part of the state of the art. The English patent trolls were kept in the Tower of London.

2. *First and True Inventor*

Apart from England, the first patent laws of the US (10 April 1790) and Japan (*Sembai tokkyo jōrei* of 18 April 1885) also granted rights to the first inventor (foreign or domestic), while the French Patent Acts of 17 January and 25 May 1791 granted rights not only to the first inventor, but also to the first to introduce foreign technology into France (yet switched to the first to file system in 1807). The first German Patent Act of 25 May 1877 granted rights to the first (entitled) applicant. Whether to grant a patent to the first inventor to file, or the first to reduce the invention to practice, is a matter of policy.[23] For reasons of legal certainty and in order to encourage the publication of the invention, the first-to-file principle may appear preferable.[24] After

23. For a historical and political discussion, *see*: T. Nicolai, 'First-to-File v. First to Invent', 3 IIC (1972), 103.
24. It is a similar consideration of policy whether or not the inventor has to be a natural person. Not unlike the discussion in copyright law (droit d'auteur or rights of printers), one can view the primary focus of patent law in granting inventors their due, as expressed in the ideas behind the first French Patent Act ('S'il existe pour homme une véritable propriété, c'est sa pensée; celle-lá, du moins, paraît hors d'atteinte; elle est personnelle, elle est indépendante, elle est antérieure à toutes les transactions…' as in the preparatory report of de Boufflers, who in 1790 was asked by the French Assembly to prepare a draft for a patent law), or the US American Constitution of 1787 (Art. 1 Sec. 8) according to which 'The Congress shall have power ... to promote the progress of science and useful arts, by securing for limited times to authors and inventors the exclusive right to their respective writings and discoveries.'. Alternatively, one can view the patent system as primarily a tool for promoting innovation, in which case it would be immaterial whether the inventor is a natural person or not (for the discussion on machines as inventors, *see*: K. Bengi and C. Heath, 'Patents and Artificial Intelligence Inventions', in Heath, Kamperman Sanders and Moerland, *Intellectual Property and the Fourth Industrial Revolution* (Kluwer Law, 2020), 127.

the US switched to the first-to-file system in 2013,[25] a certain harmonisation has been reached on this point.

3. *Duration and Costs*

a) *Duration*

> 'It would have been desirable, if it were possible to devise appropriate means of determination to grant patents for a term commensurate with the importance of the invention from the point of view of technological or economic advance and also on the basis of the factor whether an invention may be put into practice immediately or whether many years of development are needed before it can be economically exploited ... Generally there has been unwillingness to change the term of patents ... in the fear that this would disturb of upset the equitable compromise already established by law.'[26]

This quotation indicates that although it would be desirable to determine the patent term individually for each invention or each technical field, this is not feasible[27] and for this reason, a general term has been set for all types of inventions. The 14 years stipulated in the Statute of Monopolies amounted to twice the duration of an apprenticeship. The term could be extended for another seven years. The first US law also provided a term of protection of 14 years, yet soon settled on 17 years from the date of grant (apparently a compromise between 14 years and 21 years, the two periods set in the original British Statute of Monopolies[28]). French law granted a term of 5, 10 or 15 years, Germany 15 years from grant. France was one of the first countries to set the term to 20 years from the date of application, while in the US and Canada, the term of 17 years was traditionally calculated from the date of grant.

---

25. By virtue of the Leahy-Smith American Invents Act of 16 September 2011.
26. Ladas, *supra* note 18, 386. Classical economic studies on the optimal duration of patents are W. Nordhaus, *Invention, Growth and Welfare, A Theoretical Treatment of Technological Change* (Cambridge Mass., 1969) and F. Scherer, 'Nordhaus Theory on Optimal Patent Life – A geometric Reinterpretation', 62 *The American Economic Review* (1972), 422–27. According to Scherer (427):

    'A "best of both worlds" policy recognizing these relationships would tailor the life of each patent to the economic characteristics of its underlying invention. This might be achieved through a flexible system of compulsory licensing, under which the patent recipient bears the burden of showing why his patent should not expire or be licensed at modest royalties to all applicants three or five years after its issue. This burden would be sustained if the patentee demonstrated that his invention fell into one or more of the categories in which longer protection is needed to satisfy the Lebensraum condition [i.e. the condition that the patent system provides a sufficient incentive for an investor to innovate] – e.g., because the market is small relative to the costs of research, or because the cost savings achieved were modest in relation to research costs.'
27. Note however that in the past, some countries provided for the possibility of an extension in cases the patent could not be exploited, something that is now covered by domestic patent extension schemes (termed 'additional protection certificates' in Europe, *see also* below), or in cases the invention showed particular inventive merit.
28. L. Amdur, *Patent Fundamentals* (New York, 1956), 53.

Article 4*bis* (5) Paris Convention would not permit a calculation from the (foreign) priority date, however.

The advantage of calculating from the application date is that the patent has a maximum duration known from the beginning and does not depend on the length of the application procedure. The advantage of calculating from the date of grant is that only a granted patent allows the patentee to effectively enforce the monopolistic effects.[29] The pitfalls of a calculation as from the date of grant can be observed for Kilby's famous semiconductor patent owned by TI and applied for in 1960 in Japan. At the time of filing, the law provided for a calculation of the 15-year patent term as from the date of (examined) publication, which in this case was 1986(!).[30] This not only made infringement litigation highly complicated, but also required Japanese industry to pay royalties for a technology that in other countries had long fallen in the public domain. And while it is true that delays in the patent grant due to a backlog at national patent offices should not disadvantage an applicant, it is equally true that in many cases, the applicant prefers to leave the application at the examination stage in order to create uncertainty. According to Zeebroeck, 'this pendency period is not only a result of the speed of processing of the patent office but also the result of a rational decision by firms to maintain or withdraw them at any point in time.'[31] Already a patent application could thus be a burden to society in that a competitor's research efforts might be driven elsewhere.

An international harmonisation both with respect to the starting point (application date rather than date of grant) and with respect to duration (now 20 years from the filing date) has only been achieved by the TRIPS Agreement, while further extensions have now been mandated by free trade agreements. See also below D. in the context of TRIPS.

b) Annuities

In practical terms, the duration of patents is closely linked to the requirement to pay annuities (renewal fees). In most countries, a patentee has to pay an annual fee to maintain the patent. Fees tend to increase the longer the patent is maintained. Under the European Patent Convention, renewal fees need to be paid from the third year onwards, starting with EUR 470, and rising up to the tenth and further years

29. Despite Art. 67 EPC which appears to equate the effects of a published application with those of a granted patent, most countries only allow the patentee to claim for a reasonable remuneration for the time of application, but not for injunctive relief. Italy does, however, while France allows the patentee to request a saisie contrefaçon already after publication: C. Heath (ed.), Patent Enforcement Worldwide, Hart 2015, 25
30. Case history, decision and comment are provided in C. Heath and A. Furuta, *Japanese Patent Law, Cases and Comments* (Kluwer Law, 2019), 537.
31. N. van Zeebroeck, 'From patent renewals to applications survival: do portfolio management strategies play a role in patent length?', *Researchgate*, January 2009, 15. He continues in that 'there is room for applicants to manipulate the system in such a way as to artificially maintain their patents pending and delay the decision of the office (particularly if it is expected to be negative). This article shows that applicants do have an influence on the duration of their non granted applications, which is sufficient reason for investigating their available instruments, such as divisional filings, in more details.' This finding may also speak against patent extension schemes based on pendency time of an application, *see infra* E IV 2.

(EUR 1,575). Renewal fees discourage the maintenance of patents and as such are a 'nuisance tax' for burdening society with monopolies. The longer they last, the more the state of the art advances and the more burdensome they become. Both levying such a tax and raising its amount over the years is therefore justified and even desirable. It would be an interesting topic of further research to gather data as to the average time national patents are upheld (in other words, up to which point in time annuities are paid), and whether there are differences between different fields of technology.[32]

c) *Costs*

Costs have always been a decisive factor in regulating demand. This is no different for patents, in particular in the absence of any competition: an inventor who wants to take out a patent in country A where patent fees are high cannot instead apply in country B where fees are low because this would not confer protection in country A. The alternative is thus, either to turn to other instruments of protection (e.g. utility models where these are available), or refrain from patenting and rely on the first-mover advantage or the protection of the invention as a trade secret. A number of studies have examined the correlation between patent fees and the number of filings and come to the conclusion 'that fees ... can be considered as an effective policy leverage by policy makers.'[33] That patent fees are not necessarily (or at all) related to the administrative costs[34] was already observed more than 150 years ago:

> 'Thomas said to me, when we parted, "'John, if the laws of this country were as honest as they ought to be, you would have come to London – registered an exact description and drawing of your invention – paid half-a-crown or so for doing of it – and therein and thereby have got your Patent."'

But:

> '...The Queen's bill was to be took to the Signet Office in Somerset House, Strand – where the stamp shop is. The Clerk of the Signet made "a Signet bill for the Lord Keeper of the Privy Seal." I paid him four pound, seven. The Clerk of the Lord Keeper of the Privy Seal made "a Privy-Seal bill for the Lord Chancellor." I paid him, four pound, two. The Privy-Seal bill was handed over to the Clerk

32. One may question whether it is correct to levy annuities already during the phase of examination before the patent is granted, i.e. before the patentee actually enjoys a right to exclude. Yet already at the application stage, they create uncertainty and may influence the behaviour of other market participants in changing their marketing and innovating strategies. As such, they are already a burden when compared to a free market.
33. G. de Rassenfosse and B. van Pottelsberghe, 'On the Price Elasticity of Demand for Patents', 74 *Oxford Bulletin of Economics and Statistics* (2012), 58, 73. 'About 20% of the growth of patent applications at the EPO in the mid-1990s can be attributed to the fee policy adopted over this period. Part of the solution to the current backlog crisis would therefore be to adopt a more stringent fee policy.'
34. 'Generally speaking, a fee structure should be devised so as to strike the right balance between the private incentives to invest in research and the social cost implied by monopolistic rents': G. de Rassenfosse, 'The role of fees in patent systems', 27(4) *Journal of Economic Surveys* (2013), 696, 714.

> of the Patents, who engrossed the aforesaid. I paid him five pound, seventeen, and eight; at the same time, I paid Stamp-duty for the Patent, in one lump, thirty pound. I next paid for "boxes for the Patent," nine and sixpence. Note. Thomas Joy would have made the same at a profit for eighteen-pence. I next paid "fees to the Deputy, the Lord Chancellor's Purse-bearer," two pound, two. I next paid "fees to the Clerk of the Hanaper," seven pound, thirteen. I next paid "fees to the Deputy Clerk of the Hanaper," ten shillings. I next paid, to the Lord Chancellor again, one pound, eleven, and six. Last of all, I paid "fees to the Deputy Sealer, and Deputy Chaff-wax," ten shillings and sixpence. I had lodged at Thomas Joy's over six weeks, and the unopposed Patent for my invention, for England only, had cost me ninety-six pound, seven, and eightpence. If I had taken it out for the United Kingdom, it would have cost me more than three hundred pound.'[35]

And while higher patent fees act as a deterrent to patent filings in general, empirical studies suggest that 'higher patent fees reduce applications for low-quality patents disproportionately.'[36]

Further questions remain. It is clear that patent fees should not act as a deterrent to innovation, just as it is clear that applications for low-quality patents are undesirable. Balancing these interests should be the task of the legislature in the same vein as deciding the amount of taxes. Yet it should be appreciated in the first place that patent fees are more than a levy to cover costs. For this reason alone, it might be preferable not to require patent offices to be self-financing, or not to advocate that patent offices should keep their fees. After all, no such suggestion has ever been made for tax offices or other public services that collect money.

4. *Exclusivity*

As is the case with monopolies in general, patents confer a right to exclude all others from using ('sole working or manufacturing') the patented technology. Exclusivity has been discussed in a number of aspects:

a) Exclusivity within the technical scope (or 'extent' according to Article 69 EPC) of the invention;
b) Exclusivity with respect to the rights conferred; connection between the forms of use;
c) Obligations and limits with respect to exclusivity (also annuities), non-commercial use, experimental use.

a) *Exclusivity within the Technical Scope of the Invention*

The **technical scope of a patent** determines the exclusive territory of the patent in relation to its technical contents. Competitors who work in similar field of technology

35. Charles Dickens, 'A Poor Man's Tale of a Patent', II(30) *Household Words* (1850). The expenses paid were equivalent to EUR 15,000.
36. G. de Rassenfosse and A. Jaffe, 'Are Patent Fees Effective at Weeding out Low-Quality Patents?', Working Paper 20785 National Bureau of Economic Research at: http://www.nber.org/papers/w20785.

need legal certainty about the forbidden area within which the patentee is allowed to exclude others. Over the centuries, it has become customary to define the exclusive territory by **patent claims.**[37] The claims are determined by the applicant. The patent offices (in examination) and the courts (in revocation proceedings) evaluate whether the scope is justified in light of the requirements of patentability.[38]

(1) The function of claims. The interpretation of patents as technical monopolies always had to accommodate two interests: first, to justify the grant by making sure that the requirements of patentability were met, and second, to allow third parties to clearly determine the area of exclusivity. The first interest was primarily taken into account by the granting authorities, the second by the courts. In the **UK**, it only became common to draft a specification and claims after the Patents Act 1852; it became mandatory with the Patents Act 1883.[39] In the **US**, claims became mandatory with the Patent Act 1836 (§ 5). Only then could the question arise as to what the function of claims is, what to do in the event of discrepancies between claim and description, and how to make sure that the patent is interpreted in the same way by the granting and enforcing authorities. According to the English House of Lords in a decision of 1938, 'if the claims have a plain meaning in themselves, then advantage cannot be taken of the language used in the body of the Specification to make them mean something different.'[40] Quite a different path was taken in **Germany** where the Patent Office determined patentability based on the wording of the claims, while the infringement courts based their assessment on the general inventive concept.[41] The current approach to claim interpretation in post-grant proceedings for all **EPC Member States** is based on Article 69 EPC according to which the extent of protection shall be determined by the claims, and the description and drawings shall be used to

37. While it is now standard practice in all countries that a patent must contain claims, the way such claims are drafted may differ from jurisdiction to jurisdiction. Under the practice of the EPC, claims should be drafted in a two part from, the first part describing prior art, the second part ('characterised in that....') the part that confers the contribution over prior art.
38. In practical terms, it is a highly important issue in this regard to what extent and how often a patent applicant or patentee may be allowed to amend the patent claims during examination and after grant. This has a formal component (at which points in time can amendments be made?), and a substantive one (which amendments are deemed allowable). In the context of the EPC (Art. 94(3), Rule 137 (3) EPC), amendments during examination cannot be refused by the examining division where a deficiency is pointed out for the first time (EPO T 937/09 of 20 July 2012). After grant, the patent can be reduced in scope either centrally (in opposition/ appeal, or under Art. 105a EPC) or before national courts (Art. 138 (3) EPC), yet the amended version must never go beyond the scope of the original application (Art. 123(2) EPC) or the patent as granted (Art. 123(3) EPC). The latter two requirements can also be found in e.g. Japan secs. 17 - 17*quinquies* Patent Act, while in the US, a post-grant broadening of the patent is deemed allowable under certain circumstances, 35 USC secs. 251, 252. *See also* below for the requirement that a patent should take away nothing from the public.
39. H. Laddie, 'Kirin Amgen - The End of Equivalents in England?', 40 IIC (2009), 3, 11; S. Strobel, 'The Emergence and Development of the Patent Specification in England', in J. Straus (ed.), *Aktuelle Herausforderungen des geistigen Eigentums - Festgabe für F.K. Beier* [Actual Challenges of Intellectual Property - Commemorative Publication for F.K. Beier] (Cologne, 1996), 185.
40. English House of Lords, *Electric and Musical Industries Ltd. v. Lissen Ltd.*, 56 R.P.C. 23 (1938).
41. E. Reimer, Äquivalenz, 'Erfindungsgegenstand, allgemeiner Erfindungsgedanke in Theorie und Praxis [Equivalents, object of invention, general concept of invention in theory and practice]', GRUR (1956), 387. This different approach is aggravated by the principle of separation of nullity/ infringement procedures-

interpret them. According to established jurisprudence, the description can be used as a patent's dictionary and thereby give terms a different meaning than they would ordinarily have.[42] However, if a term in the claim imparts a clear technical meaning, the description cannot be used to interpret the claim in a different manner: after all, a dictionary is only consulted if the meaning of a word is not clear.[43] In the **US**, the main sources for claim interpretation are the claims themselves, the description and the prosecution history.[44]

(2) For reasons of legal certainty, it is generally undesirable to interpret the technical scope of the patent beyond the wording of the claims. For reasons of doing justice to the inventor's contribution to the state of the art, it may exceptionally be desirable to do so.[45] Courts have developed the so-called doctrine of equivalents in order to determine criteria when such an interpretation beyond the claim wording is deemed justified.[46]

(3) Finally, the claims are necessary in order to determine the type of invention that is meant to be protected. One can distinguish between product/apparatus claims,

42. EP T 2221/10 of 4 February 2014.
43. EP T 1018/02 of 9 December 2003, reasons 3.8, '... the description cannot be used to give a different meaning to a claim feature which in itself imparts a clear, credible technical teaching to the skilled reader. This also applies if the feature has not been initially disclosed in the form appearing in the claim. Otherwise, third parties could not rely on what a claim actually states (cf. Article 69(1) EPC: The terms of the claims determine the extent of protection whereas the description is only used to interpret the claims) and Article 123(2) EPC would become meaningless in respect of amendments to the claims'. Cited with approval in EP T 1127/16 of 21 February 2021, as otherwise, 'an applicant (patent proprietor) could then arguably dispense with providing a clear and unambiguous formulation of claim features, e.g. during the grant proceedings, in order to be able to fall back on a more description-based interpretation at will during a subsequent opposition proceedings.' The same applies in Japan under Sec. 70 (2) Patent Act and Japanese Supreme Court, 8 March 1991 – Ra-lipase, English translation in C. Heath and A. Furuta, *Japanese Patent Law, Cases and Comments* (Kluwer, 2019), 369; and 'Germany: German Federal Supreme Court', 7 September 2004, GRUR 2004, 1023 – Bodenseitige Vereinzelungsvorrichtung. This line of thinking is not contradicted by decisions that take the description into account when determining equivalents, as these necessarily refer to subject matter not explicitly stated in the claims, *see infra*.
44. US Supreme Court, *Markman v. Westview Instruments*, 517 U.S. 370 (1996), and US CAFC, *Markman v. Westview Instruments*, 52 F.3d 929.
45. In the European context, this inherent tension is reflected in the Protocol on the Interpretation of Art. 69 according to which this provision 'should not be interpreted as meaning that the extent of the protection conferred by a European patent is to be understood as that defined by the strict, literal meaning of the wording used in the claims, the description and drawings being employed only for the purpose of resolving an ambiguity found in the claims. Nor should it be taken to mean that the claims serve only as a guideline and that the actual protection conferred may extend to what, from a consideration of the description and drawings by a person skilled in the art, the patent proprietor has contemplated. On the contrary, it is to be interpreted as defining a position between these extremes which combines a fair protection for the patent proprietor with a reasonable degree of legal certainty for third parties.'
46. Leading cases in national jurisdictions: for the US, US Supreme Court, *Warner Jenkinson v. Hilton Davis*, 117 S. Ct. 1040 (1997); for Japan, Japanese Supreme Court, 24 February 1998, 30 IIC 443 (1999) – *Ball Spline Bearing* III; for Germany, German Supreme Court, 29 April 1986, 18 IIC 795 (1987) – *Formstein*; for the UK, English Supreme Court, *Actavis UK Ltd. and anor v. Eli Lilly and Co.*, [2017] UKSC 48.

process claims, product-by-process claims, or use claims (e.g. Rule 43(2) EPC).[47] Their scope of protection is different:

- Product/apparatus claims confer protection regardless of the way the product has been made or is meant to be used. In view of the inventor's contribution to the state of the art, this is justified for apparatus claims where the use is self-explanatory in light of the constructive details of the apparatus or machine: the inventive merit of a steam engine that would justify a patent can be appreciated without being aware of all its uses. Rather, specific uses for a machine normally require constructive adaptations that could again be patentable as a different apparatus. Further specifications of an apparatus might lead to dependent patents, the use of which may require consent of the owner of the basic patent (example: where a patent relates to the wheel, further specifications such as a wheel made from a specific material may be patentable, but require use of the basic patent). This relatively straightforward concept faces difficulties when applied to chemical or pharmaceutical compositions where the inventive merit relates either to the way they are obtained (product patent, as below), or their specific use: a pharmaceutical composition confers little to the state of the art unless it is known against which illness it provides a remedy.[48] In the past, many countries excluded pharmaceutical product patents either for reasons of public policy (affordable access to pharmaceuticals) or for the doctrinal consideration that a pharmaceutical product patent[49] covering all its possible

47. EP G 2/88 of 11 December 1989: 'There are basically two different types of claims, namely a claim to a physical entity (e.g. product, apparatus) and a claim to a physical activity (e.g. method, process, use). These two basic types of claim are sometimes referred to as the two possible "categories" of claim. In this decision, however, the word category is used to refer generally to the various different possible classifications of claim. Within the above two basic types of claim various sub-classes are possible (e.g. a compound, a composition, a machine; or a manufacturing method, a process of producing a compound, a method of testing, etc.). Furthermore, claims including both features relating to physical activities and features relating to physical entities are also possible. There are no rigid lines of demarcation between the various possible forms of claim.'
48. Which is inconsistent with the broad scope of protection now conferred to chemical compounds: 'Indications related to the technical or therapeutic use of a claimed substance do not form part of the object of a product patent. Therefore, they do not need to be disclosed in the original application ... the above claim over the object of a chemical product invention as a result leads an unfettered right of exclusivity of the patentee in relation to the commercial use of the claimed chemical substance': German Supreme Court, 14 March 1972, English translation in 3 IIC (1972), 386 – *Imidazolines*. In similar fashion for the US: *Parke-Davis v. H.K. Mulford* 189 F 95 (SDNY 1911). The requirement of industrial applicability (below) requires that some form of industrial use is indicated, however. It is disputed whether a substance occurring in nature can be patented either if it can be distinguished from the one occurring in nature, e.g. due the degree of purity, or because in nature it does not exist in isolated form. A recent US Supreme Court decision held that naturally occurring DNA that was isolated could not be patentable: *Ass'n for Molecular Pathology v. Myriad Genetics, Inc*, 133 S. Ct. 2107 (2013): 'a naturally occurring DNA segment is a product of nature and not patent eligible merely because it has been isolated.' It is unclear whether this decision should also read for other chemical compounds, and how it can be reconciled with *Parke-Davis*.
49. Pharmaceutical product patents can take many forms, however: a patent for the active ingredient would give protection for all kinds of uses, dosages and compositions (in liquid form, as capsules,

uses would confer on the inventor more than the actual contribution to society. This is not least evidenced by the fact that both inventions for a further medical (or even non-medical) use are recognised, as are 'selection inventions' [50] that protect a substance with a specific effect in a narrowly defined value within an already known (or even patented) range. Absolute product protection for chemical and pharmaceutical substances thus goes beyond the inventive contribution to society in that it protects the substance regardless of the process of manufacture[51] and the manner of use.[52] The discussion is not completely theoretical in that when analysing the TRIPS obligations, these can hardly be interpreted in a manner that would give an inventor more than would be justified by his contribution to society.

- Process patents can be granted over a new manner of manufacture.[53] Process patents are generally considered 'weaker' in their scope of protection than product patents as they give no protection over the product as such. However, where the product to be produced is already known, only new ways of production or use (see below) may be patented. As mentioned above, in the past many countries excluded chemical substances from patent protection, thereby only allowing their manufacture to be protected. The weakness of such protection became obvious in Germany when competitors particularly in Switzerland started to manufacture the compounds in Switzerland and subsequently imported them to Germany. As the manufacture had taken place abroad, and no product protection was available, there was little that could be done. In 1891, the German Patent Act was amended to extend process protection to the 'products directly obtained from such process'. This extension to the protection of process patents in 1958 was codified in the Paris Convention (Article 5*quater*) and the TRIPS Agreement (Article 28.1 (b)). The TRIPS Agreement in Article 34 requires Member States to introduce as a rule of evidence the presumption that a product identical to

etc.). A narrower scope of protection is conferred on reformulations of known molecules (salts, esters, etc.), as the product is more specific. But also here, all forms of uses and dosages are covered.

50. E.g. EP T 198/84, OJ EPO 1985, 209; English High Court, *I.G. Farbenindustrie's Patent*, (1930) 47 RPC 239 (Ch.D.)
51. Interesting to note that the first German Patent Act of 1877 did not grant product patents 'for all substances chemically made' because such protection would hinder the development of different or better processes for their manufacture: Berichte der Deutschen Chemischen Gesellschaft 1877, 508.
52. Criticism in this regard is voiced by P. Götting, 'Kritische Bemerkungen zum absoluten Stoffschutz', GRUR (2009), 256. According to R. Kraßer, 'the argument that the inventor of a substance has made such substance available must be countered that the inventive merit of providing a substance can only be grounded in its surprising qualities...for which reason it is mandatory that such qualities are discovered': Kraßer, *Patentrecht* (5th edn., 2004), § 11 III d 6.
53. So-called 'product-by-process' patents are in fact product patents where the product is described by the process whereby it is produced. The scope of such patent is identical to a product patent with respect to prior art: EP T 863/12 of 23 September 2015, yet may be interpreted as a process-limited product for infringement purposes: English High Court, *Hospira v. Genentech* [2014] EWHC 3857.

the one obtained by a patented process has actually been produced by such patented process, at least where the product is also new.

- Use patents can be granted for a (hitherto unknown) way a product is used. As the use of apparatuses is normally known or within the reach of a person skilled in the art, such form of protection is normally limited to chemical or pharmaceutical substances. As has been pointed out above, as the only inventive contribution in relation to a chemical substance can be its way of manufacture or its manner of use, use patents are the form of protection that most closely matches the inventor's contribution to the state of the art. This however clashes with the fiction that the first discovery of a chemical substance exhausts the inventive achievement and thereby merits a product patent. In other words, where a product patent for a chemical substance allows the patentee to exclude all others from using that substance for any kind of use, known or not, there should be no room for acknowledging an inventive activity (and further patenting) for additional, hitherto unknown uses or applications (which is indeed the position of a number of countries, such as India). The EPC in this regard creates a fiction that nonetheless allows the grant of medical use patents:

  > 'By virtue of a legal fiction Article 54(4) and (5) EPC acknowledges the notional novelty of substances or compositions even when they are as such already comprised in the state of the art, provided they are claimed for a new use in a method which Article 53(c) EPC excludes as such from patent protection. In such cases, the notional novelty and following it the non-obviousness, if any, is not derived from the substance or composition as such but from the purpose the claimed substance or composition is related to, namely its intended therapeutic use ... In respect of second and further medical indications the EPC now allows use-related product claims.'[54]

  The Enlarged Board went on to acknowledge the patentability of a known pharmaceutical for a known medical use, yet in a different and hitherto unknown way of application (dosage):

  > 'The Enlarged Board comes to the conclusion that there can only be one sensible way of construing the requirement underlying the specificity of use, namely merely by contrast to the generic broad protection conferred by the first claimed medical application of a substance or composition, which is in principle not confined to a particular indication. Thus, the new use within the meaning of Art. 54(5) EPC need not be the treatment of another disease ... From the very wording of decision **G 5/83**, point 21 of the Reasons, the Enlarged Board of Appeal cannot deduce that said ruling was to be restricted to a new indication in the sense of a new disease...'

  This position is shared by some,[55] but not all[56] national jurisdictions in Europe.

54. EP G 2/08, 2010 EPO OJ 456 - Dosage Regime/Abbott Respiratory.
55. English Appeal Court in a decision of 21 May 2008; German Federal Supreme Court, 19 December 2006, - GRUR Int. 2007, 423 - *Carvedilol II*.
56. Protectability denied by: Paris District Court, 28 September 2010, 42 IIC 474 (2011) - *Dosage Regime/Finasteride*.

While the scope of patents for new uses or new dosage regimes closely matches the inventor's contribution to society,[57] their practical enforcement is highly problematic[58] because the patent's scope only relates to the particular use of a substance, while other uses are outside the patent monopoly. And as a patent may take away nothing from the public at the date of application or priority (for this principle, see below), the patentee must be allowed to enjoin third parties from using the substance but for the specific use that is patented. Should infringement thus be determined by the intention of the potential infringer, or rather by the get-up of the products as sold?[59] The UK Supreme Court was in two (if not more) minds about this:

> 'I hold, together with Lord Reed, Lord Hodge and Lord Briggs, that if Claims 1 and 3 had been valid, they would not have been infringed. We differ, however, as to the reasons. I consider, together with Lord Reed, that the intention of the alleged infringer is irrelevant and that the sole criterion of infringement is whether the product as it emerges from the manufacturing process, including any labelling or accompanying leaflet, is presented as suitable for the uses which enjoy patent protection...
>
> A person's exposure to liability for infringement of a Swiss-form patent depends on the purpose for which the patent-protected product was manufactured.
>
> Dealers in generic pregabalin going about a lawful business of supplying it for its non-patented use are entitled to conduct their trade lawfully, as no doubt most would wish to. The courts cannot properly adopt a solution that makes that impossible.
>
> In a purpose-limited process claim, the badge of purpose is the physical characteristics of the product as it emerges from the relevant process, including its formulation and dosage, packaging and labelling and the patient information leaflet which in EU (and other) countries will identify the conditions for whose treatment the product is intended. I shall call this the "outward presentation" test.
>
> "Outward presentation" is a rough paraphrase of the German "sinnfällige Herrichtung" which is the major part of the test of infringement applied to purpose-limited patent claims by the German courts.
>
> ....
>
> Following the hearing we considered whether an alternative approach would be to abandon the search for an appropriate mental element altogether. It would treat the identification of the purpose for which the product was manufactured as conclusively determined by a review of the fully manufactured product, including its packaging, labelling and enclosed patient instructions, upon the conceptual

57. If any: The UK Supreme Court in *Actavis v. ICOS*, 29 March 2019, [2019] UKSC 15, para. 68 cites with approval an earlier decision according to which 'nearly always such dosage regimes will be obvious – it is standard practice to investigate appropriate dosage regimes. Only in an unusual case such as the present (where, *see infra*, treatment for the condition with the substance had ceased to be worth investigating with any dosage regime) could specifying a dosage regime as part of the therapeutic use confer validity on an otherwise invalid claim.'
58. S. Bostyn, 'Personalised medicine, medical indication patents and patent infringement: emergency treatment required', 2 *Intellectual Property Quarterly* (2016), 151–201.
59. Patent Offices should be aware that granting use patents may not be unlike launching unguided rockets: 'Once the rockets are up, who cares where they come down? – "That's not my department", says Wernher von Braun' (Tom Lehrer, *That was the Year that Was*).

> basis that the relevant purpose was an aspect of the physical characteristics of the product emerging from the manufacturing process.'[60]

The problems encountered in enforcing use patents are similar to those encountered when relying on the provisions for contributory or indirect infringement: sailing between the Scylla of negating protection (because the products can be legitimately used) and the Charybdis of taking something away from the public (because the products can be legitimately used): damned if you do, damned if you don't. See also below for indirect infringement.

b) *Exclusivity with Respect to the Rights Conferred*

A patent is a monopoly that allows the patentee to exclude all others from commercially working the patented invention within its technical scope.[61] 'Commercially working' must be interpreted in the light of the system's purpose, which is to grant the patentee a reward for the disclosure of the invention. The reward is not any form of direct compensation, but realised by way of commercially marketing the patented products (or processes) under monopolistic conditions. In order to fulfil its part of the patent bargain, the state must thus guarantee the patentee within the patent's technical scope and duration[62] the possibility of commercial marketing under monopolistic conditions. To this end, patent law grants the patentee a number of exclusive uses: manufacture, offer for sale, keep in stock, sale, import, export, etc. However, these rights are not granted independently of each other, but for the only purpose of securing the patentee's commercial monopoly and allowing the patentee to make a one-time profit for each item sold.[63] By way of example, one can cite Section 53(1) Dutch Patent Act according to which:

> 'A patent shall give the patent holder ... the exclusive right: ... (b) to apply the patented process in or for its business, or to use, to bring into circulation or to

60. UK Supreme Court of 14 November 2018, *Warner-Lambert Company LLC (Appellant) v. Generics (UK) Ltd t/a Mylan and another.*
61. 'Others' are even those that have independently come up with the same invention, yet have not been the first to file the invention. In such case, a public prior use may lead to an invalidation (lack of novelty), while a non-public prior use may give the prior user a right to a continued use, which however is limited in scope and difficult to prove.
62. It should be noted in this regard that most domestic patent laws grant such rights of exclusive commercial use only from the day of grant rather than from the day of application. In practice, this can mean the loss of exclusivity for a number of years due to the examination procedure. This can be justified by the fact that patents are rarely granted as applied, and sometimes not granted at all. Under certain circumstances, the patentee may claim compensation for the commercial use of the patent prior to grant, however.
63. 'Every patent grants all forms of exploitation rights to the extent possible according to the type of invention: it is improper to grant a patent with the mere right of use, another with the mere right of manufacture. It is equally impossible to subsequently relegate the patent to such step ... The use and distribution of patented products, be it that the product or the manufacture is patented, is always in connection with the manufacture, it is a continuation of the latter, it is a further economic development of the patent exploitation that lies in the manufacture.' J. Kohler, *Handbuch des deutschen Patentrechts* [Handbook of German Patent Law] (Mannheim, 1900), 613.

sell on, to hire out or deliver the product derived directly from the application of that process, or otherwise to trade in that product, *or to offer it, to import it or have it in stock for any of those purposes*.' (Emphasis added)

The act of commercial use that needs to be protected is the first commercial marketing, because here the patent bargain is at its most congruent: the first commercial marketing allows the patentee to obtain a monopolistic profit and coincides with the interest of society that the patented products are made available. The consequences of this doctrine developed by Josef Kohler ('connections between the forms of use') are explained below.

Although the patent bargain does not mandate patent law to prohibit commercial acts other than the sale, it is helpful for the purposes of enforcement to also prohibit preparatory acts, and now so mandated by TRIPS Article 28(a).

c) *Exceptions, Limitations and Obligations*

There are certain limitations or exceptions intrinsic to the patent bargain which are dealt with at this stage. Politically motivated exceptions and limitations for subject matter considered 'generally inconvenient' are dealt with below.

As has been pointed out above, limitations and exceptions have by no means to be interpreted narrowly, because they limit what is already the exception to free trade. Rather, the limitations must be understood as being an integral part of the general fabric of patent law and the patent bargain.

aa) Exceptions and Limitations

(1) The above-mentioned 'connection between the forms of use' implies two inherent limitations:

First, due to the connection of the different forms of use, secondary acts of use, such as stockpiling, offering for sale and advertising, can only infringe if they relate to the preparation or exercise of an infringing sale. This is of importance where, for example, the offer for sale relates to sales abroad,[64] where an offer for sale relates to a sale after the patent will expire,[65] or where the act of stockpiling is made for products to be sold after the patent will expire.[66]

64. Found infringing by Italian Supreme Court, 3 April 2003, German translation in GRUR Int. (2004), 876 – *Omeprazole*. However, the offer for sale relates to products whose commercial marketing is not subject to the patentee's exclusive rights and therefore cannot interfere with the exclusive rights granted to the patentee.
65. Found infringing by the Dutch Supreme Court, 22 June 2012, IIC (2014) – *G-Standard*. Also here, the patentee's commercial monopoly is not affected by sales beyond the expiration of the patent to which these offers referred. The fact that potential customers are alerted to the future availability of competing products and refrain from purchasing the patentee's goods is not a counter-argument because such alert could also be made by third parties (e.g. newspapers): pointing out the availability of competing products available after patent expiry is nothing the patentee could legitimately prevent.
66. Found infringing by the WTO Panel DS 114 of 13 March 2000 – Canada/Patent Protection of Pharmaceutical Products, http://www.wto.org/english/tratop_e/dispu_e/cases_e/ds114_e.htm. This case is further discussed below in connection with the WTO cases.

Secondly, that the first commercial use of a patented product by the patentee or with his consent 'exhausts' all further transactions of this product. This 'exhaustion' doctrine is now generally recognised at least within the context of domestic trade,[67] although in certain jurisdictions based upon an implied licence for further commercial use.[68] Exhaustion in this regard always relates to a specific product and can never refer to the act of manufacture (because manufacture necessarily relates to a new product).[69]

(2) Another exception inherent in the patent system is the one for trial, experiment and research. It must be open to any third party to use the patented products or processes for the purpose of developing alternatives and in order to verify that the patented technology can be carried out by a person skilled in the art in accordance with the patent disclosure and common general knowledge.

The patent system only achieves its objective to stimulate innovation where others can use the existing state of the art (including patentable subject matter) in order to find improvements or alternatives. Whether this exception also applies to clinical trials undertaken with the purpose of obtaining governmental marketing approval has been widely debated.[70] The answer should be in the affirmative. Where clinical trials are conducted in order to ensure safety and compatibility of these products so as to guarantee public health and well-being, such clinical trials must be deemed beneficial to research and development in the patented substance and therefore to the overall objective of advancing science. They should thus qualify as 'experimental research'.[71] Many jurisdictions by now have codified this so-called 'Bolar' exception.[72]

---

67. Japanese Supreme Court, 1 July 1997, 29 IIC (1998), 331 - *BBS Car Wheels*; German Federal Supreme Court, 14 December 1999, GRUR (2000), 635 - *Karate*; US Supreme Court, *Impression Products v. Lexmark*, 30 May 2017, 581 US (2017).
68. E.g. English High Court, *Roussel Uclaf S.A. v. Hockley Int'l Ltd.*, [1996] R.P.C 441.
69. The question of when a product is newly manufactured and when only repaired is a complicated one and should be interpreted in light of the patent's contribution to prior art. The exchange of the part that gives inventive merit to the patent should be considered infringing. *See*: C. Heath, 'Intellectual Property Liability of Consumers, Facilitators and Intermediaries - The Case of Patents', in Heath and Kamperman Sanders, *Intellectual Property Liability of Consumers, Facilitators and Intermediaries* (Kluwer Law International, 2012), 195–217. For the question of exhaustion related to self-replicating goods, *see*: C. Heath, 'Patent Exhaustion Rules and Self-Replicating Technologies', in Calboli and Lee, *Research Handbook on Intellectual Property Exhaustion and Parallel Imports* (Edward Elgar, 2016), 289–307.
70. For a comparative discussion, *see*: S. Maeda and H. Akimoto, 'The Impact of Public Health Issues on Exclusive Patent Rights', 33(4) *AIPPI Journal of the Japanese Group* (English edition), (2008) 192–95; A comparative analysis was provided by: W. R. Cornish, 'Experimental Use of Patented Inventions in European Community States', 29 IIC (1998) 735; C. Heath, 'The Patent Exemption for "Experimental Use" in Clinical Trials', 22(6) *AIPPI Journal of the Japanese Group* (English edition) (1997) 267; J. Straus, 'On the Admissibility of "Biological Equivalence Test" During the Patent Term for Obtaining a Regulatory Approval for Patented Drugs by Third Parties', 23(6) *AIPPI Journal of the Japanese Group* (English edition) (1998) 211.
71. E.G. Japanese Supreme Court, 16 April 1999, 30 IIC 448 (1999] - *Clinical Trials III;* German Federal Supreme Court, 11 July 1995, GRUR 1996, 109 - *Klinische Versuche I.*
72. Named after US CAFC *Roche v. Bolar*, 221 USPQ 1937 (Fed. Cir. 1984). Codified by e.g. sec. 271(e)(1) of Title 35 U.S.C.; EU Directive 2004/27/EC, Art. 10(6).

(3) Further, there is a public interest in making sure that only those inventions are patented that enable a skilled person to put them into practice. Insufficiently disclosed inventions do not meet the inventor's side of the bargain and do not enrich the state of the art. Since patent offices in the course of examination cannot carry out experiments to make sure that an invention actually works, it falls upon third parties (normally competitors) to falsify the inventor's promise in the course of opposition or revocation proceedings. To this end, a competitor must be able to work the patented invention according to the specification in order to verify that the invention can actually be carried out.

Neither of the above cases affects the patentee's commercial monopoly, as the invention is not used for the needs the invention is meant to serve.[73]

(4) It has been stated above that the patent allows the patentee to exclude all other from *commercially* exploiting the patent. Patents, just as trade marks, form part of the 'industrial rights' as listed in the Paris Convention. For this reason, acts of private use cannot infringe, which in fact is specified in most domestic patent laws.[74]

bb) Obligations

The discussion as to whether the right to exclude all others from commercially working the patented invention comes with a corresponding obligation for the patentee to use the invention is as old as the patent system. Josef Kohler has argued that there is such an obligation:

> 'The underlying idea for this general principle is the following: while it is normally left to each person to use or not to use his rights, this is equitable if such lackadaisical behaviour of the individual does not bring significant disadvantage to the general public; but if this is the case, the individual may not withhold an important cultural asset from the public by way of non-use: the use of a right thus becomes a social duty. This applies in all cases where the owner has a monopoly, so that by non-use the whole right will be withheld from this country or the whole world: one may not exploit a monopolistic position only negatively, one may not use it to suppress others, without granting the public the fruits of such economic gains; and this is especially true for an invention with its social character and its immense impact on all circumstances of life.'[75]

73. This is different where research is not carried out on, but with the invention, e.g. where the invention is a research tool in itself. Here, traditional patent law doctrine would not arrive at any exception, because use of the research tool as an assay or such like makes use of the patented technology for purposes unrelated to the improvement of the technology as such. Whether this also unduly hampers researchers is another matter and has been discussed by e.g. J. Barton, 'Research Tool Patents', *Bulletin of the World Health Organisation* (2002), 121, 123: https://www.ncbi.nlm.nih.gov/pmc/articles/PMC2567728/pdf/11953790.pdf. Barton suggests a general exception for all types of academic type research. Also: F. Bor, 'Exemptions to Patent Infringement applied to biotechnology research tools', 28 EIPR (2006) 510; D. Booton, 'Patents for Diagnostic Tools: An Economic Analysis', IPQ (2013), 187. The latter two publications discuss the need for compulsory licences over such research tools or kits.
74. Ladas, *supra* note 18, 413.
75. Kohler, *supra* note 63, 613. Kohler wants to prevent the mere production abroad by levying high taxes on imported products (615). According to Ladas, *supra* note 18, 'the constitutional objective

In other words, in failing to exploit the patent the patentee does not fulfil his part of the bargain. In order to foster certain economic policies, sanctions against the failure to domestically exploit patents have been part of many domestic patent laws since the beginning.[76] After all, patents were granted in order to foster the growth of domestic industry, and a lack of exploitation would run counter to this purpose. For this reason, many domestic patent laws in the nineteenth century envisaged forfeiture of the patent in the case of insufficient exploitation or even importation.[77] The Paris Convention in Article 5 limited these options to the possibility of issuing so-called compulsory licences (whereby the state allows an enterprise to exploit the patent upon adequate compensation of the patentee). The TRIPS Agreement in Article 31 restricts the grant of such compulsory licences even further. In spite of the enormous amount of ink and lobbying spent on this issue,[78] the most pragmatic answer found by the courts was to deny the patentee injunctive relief in certain circumstances, namely for lack of exploitation[79] and where the patent forms part of an essential standard,[80] which, unsurprisingly, is highly contested. Denying injunctive relief is a compulsory licence by another name and serves the purpose even better because the infringer is already working the patent.

5. *'New (and Useful) Manner of Manufacture'*

This requirement also serves a number of purposes and has subsequently been broadened in several regards.

a) First, the novelty requirement serves the purpose of refusing monopolistic rights over subject matter that is already known and thereby in the public domain: a patent may take away nothing from the public. In addition to the novelty requirement, countries have developed the further requirement of inventive step (e.g. Article 56 European Patent Convention[81]) or non-obviousness (e.g. Section 103 US Patent Act[82]). This requirement serves a double purpose. First, to deny monopolies on subject matter within the ordinary grasp of the person skilled in the art (trivial modification of existing subject matter), as the subject matter could be arrived at by putting

of promotion of science and useful arts would be defeated by a patentee who deliberately decides not to use the invention himself and not to licence others'.

76. *See* the overview provided by Ladas, *supra* note 18, 415. Non-working could entail either forfeiture or the issuance of a compulsory licence.
77. Explicitly provided for in the French Patent Act of 1844, abolished only in 1968.
78. A. Koury Menescal, 'Those Behind the TRIPS Agreement: The Influence of the ICC and the AIPPI on International Intellectual Property Decisions', 2 IPQ (2005), 155–82.
79. E.g. US Supreme Court, *eBay Inc. v. MercExchange*, L.L.C., 547 U.S. 388 (2005).
80. E.g. European Court of Justice, 16 July 2015, case C-170/13, imposing certain conditions on the infringer (willing licensee) and the patentee (must have offered a licence under FRAND terms); Japanese IP High Court, decision of 16 May 2014, 46 IIC 124 (2015) – *FRAND Declaration* (denying injunctive relief in proceedings on the merit); The Hague Court of Appeal, 17 March 2020, *Sisvel v. Xiami Corp. et al.* (denying an interim injunction);
81. 'An invention shall be considered as invoking an inventive step if, having regard to the state of the art, it is not obvious to a person skilled in the art.'
82. No patent can be obtained 'if the differences between the subject matter sought to be patented and the prior art are such that the subject matter as a whole would have been obvious at the time of the invention was made to a person having ordinary skill in the art…'

together several (normally two) pieces of prior art, or, in the graphic description of a US decision, 'first picture the inventor as working in his shop with the prior-art references, which he is presumed to know, hanging on the walls around him'.[83] The second reason for the inventive step requirement is to avoid an inundation of patent offices with trivial improvements (be it for preventing others from use, or for the purposes of freedom to operate). The major challenge has been to interpret this requirement in an objective and foreseeable manner[84] and to avoid hindsight analysis: based on hindsight, most inventions may appear to be obvious. Some jurisdictions require that in order to deny inventive step (or affirm obviousness), prior art must already point to the problem addressed by the claimed invention.[85] This is not the position of the European Patent Office. The EPO applies a problem-solution[86] together with a could-would approach,[87] where the combination of prior-art documents could lead to the claimed solution if such combination would actually have been considered by the person skilled in the art. As a rule, this is not the case where either of these documents come from different or remote fields of technology, or number more than two.

As mentioned above in the context of process patents for chemical compounds, the grant of such product patents may lead to the consequence that new uses, dosage regimes or forms of application lack novelty or inventive step because they are already comprised in the basic product or could have been derived therefrom in an obvious manner.[88] For example, the new Indian Patent Act Section 3(d) (as of 2005) states the following are not inventions according to the Act:

> '*The mere discovery of a new form of a known substance which does not result in the enhancement of the known efficacy of that substance* or the mere discovery of any new property or new use for a known substance or of the mere use of a known process, machine or apparatus unless such known process results in a new product or employs at least one new reactant.
>
> Explanation: For the purposes of this clause, salts, esters, ethers, polymorphs, metabolites, pure form, particle size isomers, mixtures of isomers, complexes, combinations and other derivatives of known substance shall be considered to be the same substance, unless they differ significantly in properties with regard to efficacy.'

83. US Court of Customs Appeals, *Application of Winslow*, 365 F2d 1017 (CCPA, 1966).
84. *See* G. Szabo, 'The Problem-Solution Approach in the European Patent Office', 26 IIC (1995) 457.
85. For a while, the TSM (Teaching-Suggestion-Motivation) developed by the US CAFC was relatively rigidly applied, which was criticised in the US Supreme Court decision *KSR International v. Teleflex*, 550 US 398 (2007). Still, a pointer in the prior art is considered as one element when assessing inventive step.
86. According to EP T 1543/06 of 29 June 2007, 'the cornerstone of the assessment of inventive step by the EPO is the problem-solution approach, which is fundamentally technical in nature. Such an approach must necessarily differentiate between technical and non-technical features when applied to "mixed" or hybrid inventions.'
87. EP T 2/83 of 15 March 1984: 'In a case where the applicant had supplemented a known layered tablet by the provision of a barrier between the layers, the Board held that the proper question to be asked was not whether the skilled man could have provided the barrier but whether he would have done so in expectation of some improvement or advantage.'
88. UK Supreme Court in *Actavis v. ICOS*, 29 March 2019, [2019] UKSC 15 for dosage regimes.

A constitutional challenge of this provision was unsuccessful.[89] In fact, the provision codifies a position also taken by other jurisdictions.[90]

b) Secondly, the requirement qualifies the inventor's contribution to society as part of the patent bargain in that a monopolistic right can only be granted for a hitherto unknown *technical achievement*. From this point of view, it is also justifiable to grant rights for technical achievements that are novel but do not meet the requirements of inventive step. Many countries do so in the field of utility models, a category of industrial property recognised under the Paris Convention (Article 1(3)).[91] It is also justifiable under the aspect of contribution to society to grant so-called importation or registration patents. Patents of importation are those that a person (often not the inventor) introduces into a jurisdiction where such technology had hitherto been unknown[92] - in other words a premium for industrial espionage. Nowadays, this system survives only in the form of confirmation patents that can be applied in countries on the basis of a patent granted abroad.[93] Such a patent's duration is then dependent upon the foreign patent that served as a basis for its grant.[94] While possible under the Paris Convention, such patents run counter to the principle of

89. *See* G. Parthasarathy and H. Goddar, 'Patentability of Pharmaceutical Products in India - The Novartis Case', 40 IIC (2009) 38. The provision at least highlights the problematic practice of pharmaceutical companies to indirectly prolong patents on their substances by the subsequent filing of small variants, so-called 'ever-greening'. *See* R. Reis and C. Chamas, 'The Green Green Grass of Evergreening Patents', in Heath, Kamperman Sanders and Moerland, *Intellectual Property Rights as Obstacles to Legitimate Trade?* (Kluwer Law, 2018), 131.
90. In EP T 41/17 of 14 January 2020, the Board found the improvement of a crystalline form to a polyform was obvious and could be arrived at by routine methods of screening.
91. A comparative overview of utility model laws is provided by U. Suthersanen, 'The Economic Efficacy of Utility Model Protection', in C. Heath and A.Kamperman Sanders, *Industrial Property in the Bio-Medical Age* (Kluwer Law, 2003), 231.
92. E.g. under the French Patent Act of 1791, a person who introduced a foreign invention to France ('quiconque apportera le premier, en France, une découverte étrangère'), could obtain a patent.
93. Nowadays, revalidation patents, or patents of importation, appear an oddity in that they allow a monopoly for subject matter already in the public domain. But not so long ago, two sets of rules permitted the patent owner to request registration of a foreign patent *telle quelle*. One was the British system of registered patents, available to the owner of a British patent or an EP patent granted for the UK. The other was the system of confirmation/revalidation/importation patents particularly used in many Latin American countries well into the twentieth century, and also mentioned in the 1889 Montevideo Treaty on Patents ratified by Argentina, Bolivia, Paraguay, Uruguay and Peru. In such system, the owner of any patent abroad could request revalidation of such patent in a country that allowed this for the unexpired term of the basic patent (the patent in the country of priority filing) on condition that no local working by third parties had taken place. For Argentina, *see* G. Giay and M. B. O'Farrel, 'Revalidation Patents and Their Viability Under Argentine and International Law', 36 IIC (2005) 345.
94. Under the 1882 Brazilian Patent Act, the Brazilian (dependent) patent was revoked if the foreign patent (or any of the foreign patents?) was cancelled or forfeited for whatever reason: Brazilian Patent Law 3129 of 14 October 1882, Art. 5 § 2 no. 6 (Colleção das Leis 1882, I, 82). In fact, the 1882 law was ambiguous about the term of the Brazilian dependent patent (Art. 3 § 3), yet made clear that no substantive examination should take place in case a foreign patent was 'imported' into Brazil.

independence and territoriality (and thereby sovereignty, see below), and do not serve any meaningful purpose.[95]

c) 'Manner of manufacture' may relate to manufacturing processes or the resulting products. The differences have been explained above. As the patent system was conceived around mechanical inventions, problems related to chemical substances (including use claims) did not arise back then.

d) The US Constitution mentioned 'useful arts' and thereby introduced another requirement that should be read together with new, namely 'new *and useful*'. One may argue that the requirement of usefulness is redundant because a useless invention is either insufficiently described (see below) and for this reason not patentable, or irrelevant (because it cannot be applied to anything), and patents for such an invention would therefore not harm the public. However, as was argued above in relation to absolute product protection for new chemical compounds, there may be no incentive to search for industrial applications of a compound already patented. The European Biotech Directive (Directive 98/44 of 6 July 1998) in Article 5 (3) now specifically clarifies that discovering a genetic sequence without identifying its use is not a patentable invention because it lacks industrial application. Apart from such special cases, industrial application is rarely an issue.[96]

6. *The Patent's Scope Should Be Commensurate with the Inventor's Contribution*

This part of the patent bargain is mirrored in the modern-day requirements of sufficient disclosure and industrial application. Gone are the days under the Venetian Patent Act of 19 March 1474 where the inventor had to show to the Serenissima that his invention actually worked.[97] Nowadays, models of the invention no longer have to be carried to the Patent Office, and it is deemed sufficient that the description enables a notional skilled person to carry out the invention. Should this not be the case, then either the information function of the patent has not been complied with,[98]

95. For their history, *see* Ladas, *supra* note 18, 374–76. To give them a meaningful purpose, Ladas proposes a domestic working requirement for such patent within two years from grant. Yet, a domestic working requirement can no longer be imposed under TRIPS (Art. 27.1 – importation of products will do).
96. One example may be *perpetua mobili* (because they cannot be made), but one can well argue that such kind of apparatus (also) cannot be patented because they are insufficiently described (because they do not produce the promised result according to the description).
97. Sordelli, 'Intérêt social et progrès technique dans la "parte" vénitienne du 19 mars 1474 sur les privilèges aux inventeurs', in AIPPI (ed.), *La legge Veneziana sulle invenzioni, Scritti di diritto industriale per il suo 500 anniversario* (Milan, 1974), 251. The law specified that a patent could only be granted once 'it is reduced to perfection, so that it can be used and exercised'.
98. F.-K. Beier, 'Das Patentwesen und seine Informationsfunktion', GRUR Int. (1977), 252. The function of the patent as information is already contained in the word 'patent', from the Latin for 'open', used in phrases such as 'patently absurd'. The function of a patent as public teaching and information is, for example, specified in the French Patent Act of 1791 according to which 'Il sera libre à tout citoyen d'aller consulter, au secrétariat de son département, le catalogue des inventions nouvelles; il sera libre, de même, à tout citoyen domicilié de consulter, au dépôt général établi à cet effet, les spécifications des différentes patentes actuellement en exercise'

or the invention does not meet its promise. An example is a *perpetuum mobile*: either it has been insufficiently described and a person skilled in the art cannot make it work, or the invention is incapable of being applied.

a) Industrial Application

Although listed as an essential element of patentability, the scope of this requirement is rather limited given the broad definition of industry in Article 1(3) Paris Convention. Arguably, an invention that contravenes the laws of nature (e.g. a *perpetuum mobile*) cannot be industrially applied, just as discoveries such as a new universe or a genetic sequence without indicating any function.[99] For the requirements of utility or technical progress that are often discussed in the context of inventive step, see the discussion below under TRIPS.

b) Sufficient Disclosure

> 'Sufficiency is one of the established tools by which is measured the correspondence, or lack of it, between the protection afforded by the claim and the technical contribution to the art made by the disclosure of the invention in the patent. The other main tools are novelty, inventive step and industrial application ... The benefit afforded to the public is not merely the disclosure, but the ability to "work the invention" after the expiry of the monopoly by the use of the disclosure. Where the invention enables patentees to make a particular product, and they seek a monopoly over the making and exploitation of the product (which is what a product claim does), they must disclose enough in the teaching of the patent to enable the public also to make the product.'[100]

Sufficiency must always be determined at the relevant priority date with respect to a specific claim, be it for a product, process or use. Where the claim promises a certain result or effect, as would be the case in a use claim, failure to produce such effect renders the invention insufficiently disclosed. Where for a product or process, no novel effect can be determined, this has a bearing on the evaluation of inventive step in that instead of an improvement over prior art, only an alternative can be

(Art. 11 of the Patent Act of 15 May 1791). By the US Patent Act of 1836, a patent library was established that contained granted patents just as other prior art documents that were used for substantive examination. It was the first of its kind.

99. According to EP T 870/04 of 11 May 2005, 'For the purposes of Art. 57 EPC, the whole burden cannot be left to the reader to guess or find a way to exploit an invention in industry by carrying out work in search of some practical application geared to financial gain without any confidence that any practical application exists...A vague and speculative indication of possible objectives that might or might not be achievable by carrying out further research with the tool as described is not sufficient fur fulfilment of the requirement of industrial applicability.' To ensure compliance with Art. 5(3) of Directive 98/44 of 6 July 1998 on the legal protection of biotechnological inventions, EPO Implementing Regulation R.29(3) expressly requires that the industrial application of a sequence or partial sequence of a gene must be disclosed in the patent application.

100. UK Supreme Court, *Regeneron v. Kymab* (24 June 2020) [2020] UKSC 27.

claimed (for which, in general, it is more difficult to show that it was not obvious). This at least is the approach taken by the EPO.[101]

Difficult questions arise where the patent (and the state of the art at the priority date) allows a skilled person to make some, but not all embodiments covered by the claim, in other words where the patent does not enable a skilled person to perform the claim over the whole range.[102] According to the leading EPO case,

> 'there is absolutely no doubt that all these claims must be so construed as to relate to fuel oils containing wax crystals smaller than 1,000 nanometres. The appellant has admitted that no way of obtaining such fuel oils was disclosed or could be found in the body of relevant common general knowledge. However, in the Board's judgment, in order to fulfil the requirement of article 83 EPC, the application as filed must contain sufficient information to allow a person skilled in the art, using his common general knowledge, to carry out the invention within the whole area that is claimed.'[103]

In practical terms, where the insufficiency relates to a distinguishable part of the claim, the patentee may in opposition, appeal or in national proceedings (Article 138 (3) EPC) limit the claim accordingly in order to avoid revocation.

c) *Plausibility*[104]

Plausibility is one aspect for determining sufficiency of disclosure[105] and inventive step.[106] The concept of plausibility was developed by the EPO jurisprudence

---

101. EP T 588/93 of 21 January 1996 and T1791/08 of 11 March 2008.
102. Not to be confused with the question as to whether the description needs to show more than one way of making the invention (no, point 3.1.5 of EP T 292/85 (OJ EPO 1989, 275)), or indicate the best mode of doing so (in Europe no, in the US yes).
103. EP T 409/91 of 18 March 1993 (*Exxon/Fuel Oils*), and also T 226/85 of 17 March 1987 (*Novartis/Stable Bleaches*).
104. A. Slade, 'Plausibility as a sine qua non of patent law?', IPQ (2020), 180–203; C. Floyd, 'Plausibility, where from and where to?', GRUR (2021) 185.
105. EP T 1164/11 of 18 February 2015 regarding a medical device: 'In the absence of a plausible explanation of the claimed effect and without any test results or experimental evidence demonstrating that this effect is achievable with the claimed device, the Board must conclude that the claimed invention is not disclosed in a manner sufficiently clear for it to be carried out by the person skilled in the art, in breach of Article 83 EPC.'
106. EP T 939/92 of 12 September 1995: '1. If a claim concerns a group of chemical compounds per se, an objection of lack of support by the description pursuant to Article 84 EPC cannot properly be raised for the sole reason that the description does not contain sufficient information in order to make it credible that an alleged technical effect (which is not, however, a part of the definition of the claimed compounds) is obtained by all the compounds claimed. 2. The question as to whether or not such a technical effect is achieved by all the chemical compounds covered by such a claim may properly arise under Article 56 EPC, if this technical effect turns out to be the sole reason for the alleged inventiveness of these compounds.' EP T 950/13 of 3 February 2017 approached the issue of plausibility from the point of view of sufficient disclosure and ultimately affirmed sufficiency also in light of post-published evidence: 'the teaching that dasatinib is suitable for the treatment if CML based on its functional analogy to imatinib as BRC-ABL inhibitor is not rendered implausible, because it may not have been obvious in view of the prior art.' Even if sufficiently disclosed, a patent may fail at the hurdle of inventive step because the effect has not been made credible: T 488/16 of 1 February 2017.

predominantly in the fields of pharmaceuticals and biotechnology, in particular in the context of 'second medical use' claims in order to exclude speculative patents that were based merely on assertions as to the alleged technical effect of a claimed subject matter. The main idea behind this is that it is not the purpose of the patent system to grant a monopoly for technical speculations that cannot be realised at the time of filing. It is:

> 'the general legal principle that the extent of the patent monopoly, as defined by the claims should correspond to the technical contribution to the article in order for it to be supported, or justified. ... This means that the definitions in the claims should essentially correspond to the scope of the invention as disclosed in the description. ... Although the requirements of articles 83 and 84 are directed to different parts of the patent application, since article 83 relates to the disclosure of the invention, whilst article 84 deals with the definition of the invention by the claims, the underlying purpose of the requirement of support by the description, insofar as its substantive aspect is concerned, and of the requirement of sufficient disclosure is the same, namely to ensure that the patent monopoly should be justified by the actual technical contribution to the art.'[107]

In that regard, the definition of an invention as being a contribution to the art, i.e. as solving a technical problem and not merely putting one forward, requires that it is at least made plausible by the disclosure in the application that its teaching solves indeed the problem it purports to solve. Thus, even if supplementary post-published evidence, such as simulation or experimental data, may under the proper circumstances also be taken into consideration, it may not serve as the sole basis to establish that the application solves indeed the problem it purports to solve.[108] This is because the respective patent application must contain sufficient information to make it at least plausible that a solution to the underlying technical problem has really been found.

7. *Be not Contrary to the Lawe nor Mischievous to the State, by Raisinge Prices of Commodities at Home, or Hurt of Trade, or Generallie Inconvenient*

On the face of it, this requirement may have been useful to placate critics of the patent system, but is otherwise contradictory. The main effect of eliminating competition by way of a patent is to be able to reap monopolistic rewards, that is, to raise prices. And most, if not all, patents that are of economic importance are 'generally inconvenient' in that they exclude others from implementing the patented teaching.

According to decision T 716/08 of 19 August 2010, 'absolute proof of the achievements of an effect is not required for an effect to be "plausible"'. According to the UK Supreme Court (by majority), there should be some indication (experimental or theoretical) which would cause the skilled person to think there was a reasonable prospect that the assertion would prove to be true: *Generics (UK) (trading as Mylan) v. Warner-Lambert Company Ltd* [2018] UKSC 56.

107. EP T 409/91 EXXON/Fuel Oils [1994] OJ EPO 653, points 3.3 and 3.4.

108. EP T 1329/04 of 28 June 2005: 'The definition of an invention as being a contribution to the art, i.e. as solving a technical problem and not merely putting forward one, requires that it is at least made plausible by the disclosure in the application that its teaching solves indeed the problem it purports to solve.'

Very little has remained of the other exceptions as well. Article 4*quater* Paris Convention clarifies that it is no reason to refuse or invalidate a patent whose 'subject matter is subject to restrictions or limitations resulting from domestic law'. This is generally understood to mean that a mere sales bar under domestic law is not sufficient reason to refuse an application, or invalidate a patent, see also Article 27(2) TRIPS.

It is however possible to refuse a patent whose subject matter contravenes the *ordre public*, e.g. Article 53(a) EPC and Article 27(2) TRIPS because it is prejudicial to human health or the environment. Examples may be an invention to forge currency, or for landmines.

Given that patents are instruments of steering investment, it is somewhat surprising that patent law has not been used to a greater extent towards fostering inventive activity conducive to society.

In the pre-TRIPS era, a good many countries have excluded patents for chemical or pharmaceutical inventions, or food products,[109] either because there was no domestic industry that could benefit from patent protection, or because a rise in prices in this field was indeed deemed 'generally inconvenient'.

Still, one wonders whether States should not use the patent incentive in order to direct industrial policy in a more future-oriented manner. Just as tax laws are used to encourage or discourage certain behaviour, so could patent laws: while the European Patent Office refuses patents related to inventions that require the destruction of embryonic stem cells (Rule 28.1(c) EPC)[110] because of a contravention of *ordre public*, one wonders why patents are still granted that induce smoking or help the distribution of cigarettes. While some, but not all of such patents may fall foul of *ordre public*, all such inventions relate to a behaviour that most States want to discourage rather than encourage.[111] In this regard, one should however be clear what this exemption can achieve, and what not. First, it cannot have the consequences of prohibiting manufacture or sale, but merely to withhold an incentive. Secondly, it may lead to the fact that what is considered immoral in the absence of patent protection may be practised by the world at large rather than only by the patentee.[112] But as long as the patent system is considered as an encouragement to innovation, no such incentive should be available to what is considered socially unacceptable, however much such perception may change or prove wrong in retrospect. For example, States cannot on

109. An overview is provided by Ladas, *supra* note 18, 309–13.
110. In the context of the EPC, *see* EP G 2/06 of 25 November 2008 (*WARF/Stem Cells*). In the context of the Biotech Directive, CJEU case C-34/10 – *Brüstle*. Literature: T. Calamé, *Öffentliche Ordnung und Gute Sitten als Schranken der Patentierbarkeit gentechnologischer Erfindungen* (Basel, 2001).
111. The WHO Framework on Tobacco Control 2003 entered into force in 2005 and has 168 signatories.
112. According to M. Bartels, 'Ethical Limits For Patentability', 52 IIC (2021), 44, 46 'those potential benefits [from exclusion] come with huge costs. Besides causing legal uncertainty and contradictions within the not yet fully harmonized European patent system, exclusions carry significant risks of producing consequences which are unintended and undesirable, either at the time of the implementation of the exclusion or at some later stage.' These detriments, however, are inherent in any system of incentives.

the one hand constitutionally guarantee the well-being of animals and on the other hand incentivise innovation that leads to needless suffering.[113]

Patent incentives may further be used to encourage investment in technologies that are future-oriented, such as in the energy sector, at the expense of industries not credited with future potential. Implementing such a policy would face difficulties not only in relation to TRIPS (Articles 7 and 8 TRIPS do not appear to assist in justifying further exceptions to patentability), but also in aligning such policy with innovation cycles and foreseeability of investment. These are tasks for the legislator rather than a domestic patent office.

In a recent contribution, Justine Pila has argued for a much broader interpretation of the *ordre public* exception:

> 'There is a strong argument to be made for expanding the limited scope that currently exists for considering the moral and public policy implications of patenting individual technologies. As argued at greater length elsewhere, among the reforms needed in this regard are a new definition of "ordre public", extending beyond the protection of public security, physical integrity, and the environment [fn. omitted]; a lower burden for opponents raising an art.53(a) objection; acceptance of the relevance of a patent's economic effects when assessing the implications of granting it; and a separate, precautionary-based procedure, for assessing the moral and public policy implications of commercializing (by patenting [fn. omitted]) an emerging technology'[114]

This approach would essentially interpret *'order public'* as 'generally inconvenient', which would be in line with the function of patents to provide incentives (only) for desirable inventions, yet on a practical level would require patent offices to make decisions that should be left to domestic policy makers. That domestic policy makers in the last decades have taken a rather hands-off approach to patent legislation despite increasing frictions between patent law and the interests of society at large is lamentable, though.

8. *Must Take Away Nothing from the Public*

This is the final promise of the patent bargain. This time, it is a promise by the State to the public that in the late sixteenth century more and more vociferously rebelled against monopolies, sometimes granted for subject matter that was already in the public domain (such as playing cards) and that led to a rise in prices. Of course, many of the above parameters, most notably the novelty requirement, already made sure that subject matter in the public domain could no longer be patented. But the promise not to take anything away from the public has more to it, in terms of both doctrinal and practical matters.

113. Patentability of which was denied in EP T 1553/15 of 28 September 2020 (undue suffering of rabbits without an identifiable justification).
114. J. Pila, 'Reflections on a post-pandemic European patent system', 42 EIPR (2020) 530, 533.

a) *Novelty*

Novelty is not only required in order to provide a contribution, but also in order that the monopoly takes nothing away from the public. Something that is in the public domain, be it in applied or written form, can no longer be subject to a monopoly. It has been explained above that with respect to a meaningful contribution to society, both absolute (world-wide) and relative (domestic) novelty can qualify. Arguably, the same is true when it comes to the promise not to take anything away from the public: prior art available or known only abroad is by definition not available to the public for whose territory the patent is granted. Due to the availability of most written documents on the internet, it is however no longer feasible to limit written prior art to the domestic realm. This may be different for oral knowledge or public use.[115]

b) *Grace Period*

Not the requirement of contribution, but of taking away nothing from the public collides with the interest of the inventor to publish the invention prior to filing:

> 'William said, "John, if you make your invention public, before you get a Patent, any one may rob you of the fruits of your hard work. You are put in a cleft stick, John. Either you must drive a bargain very much against yourself, by getting a party to come forward beforehand with the great expenses of the Patent; or, you must be put about, from post to pillar, among so many parties, trying to make a better bargain for yourself, and showing your invention, that your invention will be took from you over your head." I said, "William Butcher, are you cranky? You are sometimes cranky." William said, "No, John, I tell you the truth;" which he then delivered more at length. I said to W. B. I would Patent the invention myself.'[116]

Back then under the Statute of Monopolies, it was held immaterial by whom the patented invention was made public prior to the application for a patent:

> 'If the public once becomes possessed of an invention by any means whatever, no subsequent patent can be granted for it, either to the true and first inventor himself, or to any other person, for the public cannot be deprived of the right to use the invention and a patentee of the invention could not give any consideration to the public for the grant, the public already possessing everything that he could give.'[117]

In a later case, it was held:

> 'Public use ... means a use in public, not by the public, I think there is no room for doubt that the use by the defender of his own paint was of this character.

115. Under the EPC, public prior use is relevant wherever it occurs. In 1994 the EPO granted European Patent No. 0436257 to the US Corporation W.R. Grace and USDA for a 'method for controlling fungi on plants by the aid of a hydrophobic extracted neem oil' that was subsequently revoked in opposition due to a proven prior use in India.
116. Dickens, *supra* note 35.
117. English Court of Appeal, *Patterson v. Gaslight & Coke*, 3 Appeal Cases 244 [1875].

> It is quite true that, in order to obtain letters patent, the inventor must disclose his secret to the public in return for the monopoly conferred upon him. But such a disclosure as that is not necessary to the prior use, which will anticipate and so avoid a patent.'[118]

In order to provide an amenable solution to the hardship mentioned in Dickens' story, some jurisdictions have introduced a grace period. A **grace period** refers to an exception of the absolute novelty standard in that the publication of an invention even prior to patent filing is not considered prior art for this very invention. Some countries such as the US[119] , Canada[120] and Japan[121] allow for a grace period of twelve months, while Article 55 EPC and the corresponding provisions under the domestic laws of Germany,[122] France,[123] the United Kingdom,[124] and Italy[125] grant a grace period of six months only in very limited circumstances, namely if the invention was published with the intention of harming the inventor or applicant.

While there have always been proponents of a grace period,[126] such period creates legal uncertainty and allows for strategic (defensive) publishing while maintaining the option to file for a patent.

c) *Contributory Infringement*

Another possible conflict with the above promise to take away nothing from the public arises in the provisions on indirect or **contributory infringement** as these 'prevent all third parties not having had consent from supplying or offering to supply ... a person, other than a party entitled to exploit the patented invention, with means, relating to an essential element of that invention, for putting it into effect therein, when the third party knows, or it is obvious in the circumstances, that these means are suitable and intended for putting that invention into effect.'[127] The effect of such provision is that even suppliers of non-infringing products can be made liable for infringement if these products are supplied with the intention that a patented invention be put into effect. In other words, there is no infringement in principle, but thinking makes it so. The considerations are similar to those explained above for use patents where products or processes that are in the public domain as such

118. Scottish Court of Session, *Gill v. Coutts*, [1896] RPC125.
119. Two years until 1940 under sec. 4886 of the US Patents Act 1870. Current rules under sec. 102(b) and (d) of the US Patents Act 1952.
120. Sec. 28(2)1(a) Canadian 1952 Patents Act.
121. Sec. 30 Japanese Patent Act. The provision was amended in 2018 due to obligations under the TPP and extended the previous grace period of six months to one year.
122. Sec. 3(4) German Patent Act 1981.
123. Sec. 9 French Patent Act 1968.
124. Sec. 2(4) UK Patents Act 1977.
125. Sec. 15 Italian Law on Patents for Inventions of 1939.
126. Notably Josef Kohler was critical of the fact that 'the inventor loses unaccountable wealth without deeper justification' if a law did not come to the inventor's rescue in case of such unauthorised publications: Kohler, *supra* note 63, 199. Also J. Straus, *Die Bedeutung der Neuheitsschonfrist für die außerindustrielle Forschung in den Ländern der europäischen Wirtschaftsgemeinschaft* (1986).
127. Cited from the provision of Art. 26 Community Patent Act 1975. Most European countries have adopted similar provisions.

are supplied for a specific (patented) use. In both cases, a supplier may be enjoined from doing what previously was permissible with the consequence that the patent in question does take away from the public.[128]

9. *Guaranteeing the Promise*

The system as outlined above is of considerable complexity and particularly with respect to its purported benefits – information and incentive to innovate – requires proper implementation. This aspect is further addressed in the last section of this chapter. At this stage, in all brevity the following should be mentioned:

a) Legal certainty (in most countries) has been provided by substantive examination (first under the US system 1836) which ensures that no monopoly is granted without an examination for patentability requirements. To this end, most jurisdictions provide for a pre-grant or post-grant opposition system that allows any person (not only interested persons) to raise objections. After all, any person challenging a patent by way of opposition contributes to society by clearing the register of undeserved monopolies (where the patent is revoked), by reducing monopolies to the scope of their technical contribution (where the patent is limited in scope), or by adding legal certainty (where the patent is maintained unamended).[129] Patents that are granted without meeting the requirements of patentability put in jeopardy the patent system's purpose of fostering industrial development in that competitors wishing to engage in research and development may divert such activities due to such wrongful titles. A further reason is that by opposition proceedings, legal certainty is enhanced. This is of relevance since despite differences in national grant and enforcement practice, the general picture is that patents do not normally stand a better than even chance of being upheld in administrative or judicial proceedings (see also below for the latter point). The contribution to society by raising an opposition is thus threefold:

128. Aware of this problem, there have been a number of attempts on how to limit this undesired result. US law for example holds infringing only the supply of parts that in themselves are patented: US Supreme Court, *Aro Manufacturing Inc v. Convertible Top Replacement*, 27 February 1961, 365 US 336. In Europe, there seems to be a growing consensus that only the supply of parts that embody the 'inventive merit' of an invention can be enjoined. *See* Dutch Hoge Raad 31 October 2003, BIE 2004, 285 – *Senseo*. Further discussion in C. Heath, 'Consumers, Facilitators and Intermediaries – Infringers or Innocent Bystanders? The Case of Patents', in Heath and Kamperman Sanders, *Intellectual Property Liability of Consumers, Facilitators and Intermediaries* (Kluwer Law, 2012), 195.

129. EP T 1839/18 of 10 March 2021 in connection with a 'straw man' opposition. Interestingly enough, opposition systems in most countries are directed at an objective control of the right rather than an individual legal interest to have the patent revoked. Unlike actions for nullity, no specific legal interest is required for an opponent to challenge the patent exactly because enhancing legal certainty with respect to a right that burdens the public at large is in the public interest (A. Halfmeier, *Popularklagen im Privatrecht* (Heymanns, 2006), 255, 275). The reasons why an opponent challenges the patent (commercial; ethical; strawman for another) are thus irrelevant and not to be questioned. Oppositions are handled by the Patent Office in quasi-administrative proceedings. A corollary to the possibility for anyone to challenge the patent is the limited time within which this can be done (a couple of months from grant, normally). Later challenges before the courts require a legal interest and are normally raised as a counterclaim to infringement.

(1) undeserved monopolies may be revoked or limited to their due scope;
(2) industrial development is fostered in that the direction of innovation is not led astray by wrongfully granted monopolies;
(3) legal certainty is enhanced.

It is thus in the public interest to provide a simple, cost-effective and timely remedy for reviewing the grant of a patent.

b) The function of information is safeguarded by the requirement of a patent specification which became common only in the eighteenth century,[130] and a publication of the invention after 18 months from the filing date, a compromise between the extreme positions of not publishing an application at all (so that the inventor could still retain the invention as a trade secret in case the patent was not granted), and an immediate publication of every patent application.[131]

c) In order to safeguard the patent bargain, the patent system contains two necessary, inherent limitations that need to be provided even in the absence of a specific provision, namely the necessity for competitors (or the public at large) to verify, even in a commercial context, that the patented invention works, in other words that it delivers what has been promised, and the (commercial) use of an invention to find improvements (or alternatives). These limitations have been addressed in greater detail above.

C. THE INTERNATIONAL PATENT SYSTEM

The international plane of patent law is sharply divided between IP agreements (essentially the Paris Convention and the special agreements entered into by Member States in accordance with Article 19 Paris Convention), and trade agreements starting with the WTO/TRIPS Agreement. The former were meant to determine the rules of intellectual property rights in order to foster innovation, the latter in order to foster trade.

I. The Paris Convention

1. *Overview*

The Paris Convention for the Protection of Industrial Property was last revised in 1967 and amended in 1979 with a membership of 177 states as of 24 September 2020.[132]

130. According to L. Pessers, *The Inventiveness Requirement in Patent Law* (Kluwer Law, 2016), 85, 'the specification requirement, that occasionally appeared in the seventeenth century, was customary since 1734 and gained a secured footing in *Liardet v. Johnson* (1778) Web Pat Cas 52, NP.'
131. Publication after 18 months seems to originate in a Dutch amendment to the Patent Act in 1963. Publication was decreed in connection with a system of deferred examination (B. van Bentham, 'Die Erfahrungen mit dem System der aufgeschobenen Prüfung in den Niederlanden', GRUR Int. (1966), 617). It then became an international standard under the PCT (Art. 21). In the context of the Covid Waiver debate (*see infra*), the question has occurred whether even this period is too long in order to obtain proper information for highly time-sensitive research.
132. F.K. Beier, 'One Hundred Years of International Co-operation – The Role of the Paris Convention

The Paris Convention recognised the sovereignty of States in matters of industrial policy by the freedom to set up a patent system or not,[133] the freedom to exclude certain subject matter that was 'mischievous' or inconvenient to the State,[134] the freedom to distinguish between domestic manufacture and importation,[135] the freedom to determine the establishment, duration and limits of patent rights.[136] Intrusions on a country's industrial policy were kept to a minimum: national treatment and limits to forfeiture. As the Paris Convention (like other international conventions in the field of industrial property law) has as its objective the protection of 'nationals of any country of the Union', own nationals may be excluded from the benefits the Convention confers.[137]

The Paris Convention is guided by three major principles: National Treatment, Priority and Independence of Rights. Apart from that, there are other principles that also deserve mention, including the encouragement to conclude further specific agreements between Member States, Article 19.[138] Although drafted on their behalf, very little is said about the rights of inventors. Article 4*ter* Paris Convention only requires that 'the inventor shall have the right to be mentioned as such in the patent.'

2. National Treatment

The Paris Convention in Article 2 defines industrial property as patents, utility models, industrial designs, trade marks, service marks, trade names, indications of

---

in the Past, Present and Future', 15 IIC (1984) 1. The most detailed commentary on the Paris Convention is provided by the three-volume treaties of Ladas, *supra* note 18.

133. The detailed rules on patents in the Paris Convention certainly indicate that it was expected from Member States that they have a patent system in the first place. On the other hand, listing patents as one form of industrial property in Art. 1(2) cannot be evidence that there must be a corresponding system of protection in place: many Member States do not protect utility models or appellations of origin, both of which are explicitly mentioned. At a certain time, the Netherlands and Switzerland were members to the Paris Convention, yet had no patent system.
134. Unlike the Berne Convention, the Paris Convention has no catalogue of inventions member states have to protect. In the past, particularly common were exclusions of pharmaceutical product or process patents in order to keep domestic prices of pharmaceuticals low.
135. Art. 5A(2) refers to 'failure to work', which was understood as domestically working the patent. The opposite view (it was sufficient to provide goods by way of importation) was taken by H. Isay, 'Zur Frage des Ausübungszwanges für Patente innerhalb der Union (On the Question of Use Requirement for Patents Within the Union)', GRUR (1904), 116.
136. All these issues were determined by the sovereignty of each state under the principle of independence of rights, *see infra*.
137. It is thus at a country's discretion whether the right of priority is also extended to applications that base their priority filing on an earlier domestic (rather than foreign) application. E.g. in Germany, this right was only granted in 1981 (now sec. 40 German Patent Act), while the EPC allowed this from the start, Art. 88 EPC.
138. It is under this provision that all special agreements between Member States have been concluded: the Madrid Agreement, the Madrid Protocol, the Trademark Law Treaty and the Singapore Treaty on the Law of Trademarks in the field of trade marks, the Madrid Arrangement for the Repression of False and Misleading Indications in the field of Unfair Competition, the Lisbon Agreement and the Geneva Act thereto in the field of Appellations of Origin, the Hague Agreement for the Protection of Designs, the PCT, the Budapest Treaty and the Patent Law Treaty in the field of patents. Further, a number of classification treaties: https://www.wipo.int/treaties/en/

source or appellations of origin, and the repression of unfair competition. Instead of making the acquisition of rights subject to reciprocity, the Paris Convention and all subsequent international IP treaties apply the principle of *national treatment*. National treatment, inter alia, allows nationals of countries without a corresponding domestic protection to obtain industrial property rights in other countries on the same footing as domestic nationals. Thereby, Swiss nationals could obtain patents in, say, England and France on the same conditions as nationals of these countries despite the fact that Switzerland at the time the Paris Convention was concluded had no patent law and did not give protection to inventions. Countries were also barred from charging foreigners higher application fees than their own nationals. However, foreign nationals can be requested to file their application through a domestic agent, Article 2(3). The principle of national treatment was a significant concession by countries with a high protection standard (e.g., France) to countries that offered no comparable protection. Controversies over national treatment have mostly related to indirect or de facto discrimination.[139]

3. *Right of Priority*

Equally important in practical terms was the *principle of priority* established by the Convention. As patent protection was only granted to inventions deemed novel and inventive, the procurement of patent protection in more than one country always carried the uncertainty that between the first and subsequent filings, the invention could become publicly known, or third parties could claim protection by way of an intervening application. The second problem was particularly acute in countries where not only the inventor could ask for patent protection, but everyone who had imported a new technology, as was then the case under French law.[140] The principle of priority gave protection to the inventor and facilitated the filing of patents in more than one country. The mechanism introduced was a one-year period from the first filing of an invention for subsequent filings in other countries, Article 4C (1).[141] If undertaken within one year, the subsequent filing was treated as having been filed at the first filing date in two respects: first, for examining novelty and inventive step and, secondly, for determining better rights. Article 4B. If an invention was filed in France on 1 April 2000, and subsequently in Japan on 20 March 2001, the relevant state-of-the-art to be examined for the Japanese application was the state-of-the-art as of 1 April 2000. The same was true if another person had filed the same or a similar invention in Japan on 20 December 2000. Also in this respect, the filing on 20 March 2001 was treated as if it had already been filed in Japan on 1 April 2000. The period of protection for a patent is not dependent upon the filing date of the priority filing, but the date of domestic filing, Article 4*bis* (5).

---

139. C. Heath, 'National Treatment under the Paris Convention', in Kamperman Sanders (ed.), *The Principle of National Treatment in International Economic Law* (Edward Elgar, 2014), 223–47.
140. As is highlighted by J. Vojácek, A Survey of the Principal National Patent Systems, London 1935, 137.
141. The date of filing was not to be included in the calculation, Art. 4C (2).

The right of priority is perhaps the most difficult construct in international patent law[142] and has given rise to a number of questions:

- Should the right of priority be regarded as accessory to the application, or can it be independently transferred?[143]
- Priority may be claimed by 'any person who has duly filed an application ... or his successor in title'. Would this imply that the successor in title must prove entitlement at the day of filing the subsequent application, or could such transfer also be effected later, possibly with retroactive effect?[144] In the case of multiple applicants, would a successor in title need to show succession to all original applicants?[145] Which law should apply to the transfer?[146]
- In the case where the priority filing is broadened by the subsequent filing and thus not all elements of the subsequent filing can claim priority (a case envisaged by Article 4F), could the priority filing be cited against the newly added elements ('toxic priority')?[147]

For the questions of whether all original applicants need to approve the subsequent application, and how who is an 'applicant' should be determined, decision **T 844/16** (as above) held that this should be based on an autonomous interpretation of the Paris Convention rather than on national law ('116. The Board thus finds that the "national law" that determines who "any person" is, is in this case, the Paris Convention.')

4. *The Independence of Rights*

The independence of rights for patents is stipulated in Article 4*bis* and must be 'understood in an unrestricted sense', Article 4*bis* (2). The independence of rights is a synonym for national sovereignty, and the provision clarifies that the fate of patents obtained (or refused) in one country in no way prejudices the fate of (even

142. The issue has been monographically dealt with by R. Wieczorek, *Die Unionspriorität im Patentrecht* (Cologne, 1973).
143. A. Osterrieth and O. Axster, *Die internationale Übereinkunft zum Schutze des gewerblichen Eigentums* (Berlin, 1903), 74 ('unselbständiges Zubehör der Erfindung'), According to Ladas, *supra* note 18, 462–63, 'The right of priority is not an independent right, but a defense only... it is erroneous to consider the right of priority as an independent right'. Under the EPC, it is now established practice that the right of priority can be independently transferred: EP T 62/05; also Singer, Stauder and Bremi, *Europäisches Patentübereinkommen* (7th edn., 2016), Art. 87 note 59. Yet this also implies that the transfer of the application as such is insufficient to prove that also the right of priority has been transferred: EP T 407/15 of 27 October 2020.
144. Denied in EP T 1201/14 (Transfer of right of priority) of 9 February 2017.
145. This was denied in the EP T 844/18 (CRISPR) of 16 January 2020.
146. *See* the discussion in EP T 1201/04 of 9 February 2017, point 3.1.2 of the reasons. It could be the law of the first application, the law of the subsequent application, the law chosen by the parties or the law where at least one of the parties has their residence (left open which of these to apply).
147. Denied in EP G 01/15 of 29 November 2016: 'Under the EPC, entitlement to partial priority may not be refused for a claim encompassing alternative subject-matter by virtue of one or more generic expressions or otherwise (generic "OR" claim) provided that said alternative subject matter has been disclosed for the first time, directly, or at least implicitly, unambiguously and in an enabling manner in the priority document. No other substantive conditions or limitations apply in this respect.'

the same) patent in another country, unless of course domestic legislation stipulates differently, e.g. in the case of patents of importation.[148] Article 4*bis* (5) makes a particular reference to the duration of patents obtained with the benefit of priority and prohibits the former British practice of calculating the duration of a domestic patent from the date of the (foreign) priority filing.[149]

The principle of independence has sometimes been cited in order to prohibit the parallel importation of patented products marketed abroad by the patentee or with his consent. For example, Nuno Pires de Carvalho writes in this respect: 'The fact that patent rights are exhausted in the territory of one country should have no impact whatsoever on the patent rights valid in the territory of another country, given that those rights are entirely independent.'[150] That is correct, but those in favour of international exhaustion do not argue that a domestic patent in the country of importation should be exhausted for a specific product because the right is exhausted in the country of first marketing, but because the patentee by the first marketing has obtained the one-time reward that a patent allows him to obtain for each product.[151]

In light of recent developments - patent rights being recognised as private rights under TRIPS, the level playing field in the area of patents as mandated by TRIPS, efforts to harmonise[152] substantive patent law - recognising state sovereignty is perceived an inconvenient obstacle by patent applicants. Efforts to dismantle this core principle of the Paris Convention come in two disguises:

One is the pervasive language of theft that at times is used when differences in domestic patentability requirements are denounced,[153] the second is the allegedly

148. In the nineteenth century, a number of domestic patent laws stipulated a dependence of the domestic patent on a foreign patent over the same invention, be it for the existence (when revoked abroad, the domestic patent should also be revoked (France and Brazil)) or for the duration (Spain, Brazil).

149. Ladas, *supra* note 18, 512-13.

150. N. Pires de Carvalho, *The TRIPS Regime of Patent Rights* (3rd edn., 2005), 115.

151. C. Heath, 'Parallel Imports, Exhaustion and International Trade', in Heath et al., *supra* note 89, 25-45. Also the US Supreme Court, *Impression Products v. Lexmark International*, 30 May 2017, 581 US___(2017) now takes this stance.

152. One should of course be aware that 'harmonisation' is usually a battle of standards that leads to a loss of sovereignty. Already for this reason harmonisation cannot be an end in itself: C. Heath, Harmonisation of International Patent Law? 39 IIC 210 (2008).

153. According to J. Straus and N. Klunker, 'Harmonisation of International Patent Law', 38 IIC (2007) 907, 920, 'a number of developing countries do not respect patent protection for certain categories of inventions, and instead *appropriate the inventions free of charge* at the time when they cross the border' (emphasis added). One should read this twice: 'appropriate the inventions'. 'Appropriate' seems to suggest that there is a 'natural' property right in any invention regardless of the patentability criteria, and this is rather incorrect. Property in a patent is defined by the domestic criterion of patentability and nothing else. The above phrase appears to be 'the pervasive rhetorical use of the language of "theft" in intellectual property discourse ... [and the] manipulative power of the language of theft to affect rational decision-making about the socially optimal balance between intellectual property rights and ordinary freedoms.... The language of theft, in short, reduces a difficult policy debate ... to a crude and simplistic drama': P. Loughlan, 'Intellectual Property and the Language of Theft', EIPR (2007), 401, 405.

'legitimate expectation' that a patent granted in one country should equally be granted elsewhere.[154]

The Paris Convention allows a wide margin for countries to pursue their own industrial policy, and attempts to introduce mandatory protection levels ultimately failed, see below.

II. Other International Institutions and Agreements

1. *International Organisations*

a) Convention Establishing the World Intellectual Property Organization (WIPO) of 1967 with a membership of 193 states as of 24 September 2020.

The World Intellectual Property Organization (WIPO) was established in 1967 as a successor to BIRPI, a bureau for the management of intellectual property treaties. WIPO is a suborganisation of the UN responsible for administering IP treaties that require or permit an international filing (e.g., the PCT, the Madrid Agreement/ Protocol, the Lisbon Agreement and the Hague Agreement), for promoting the development of all other IP treaties or the conclusion of new ones, and for matters of cooperation, assistance and dissemination of information on intellectual property, Article 4 WIPO Treaty. WIPO is located in Geneva and draws most of its funds from administering the PCT, thereby making the organisation financially much more independent than other UN organisations.

b) UNCTAD is a permanent intergovernmental body established by the United Nations General Assembly in 1964 (195 Member States). It has long been a forum for developing countries to voice their concern about the negative effects of intellectual property rights, namely patents, on domestic development and the necessity to provide exceptions. The 1974 report on 'The Role of the Patent System in the Transfer of Technology to Developing Countries' recommended a revision of the international patent system for 'making patent laws and practices capable of effectively complementing other instruments of policy for national development'.[155]

---

154. This becomes an argument in the context of investor-state settlement disputes where an investment that was based on legitimate expectations is lost. In the area of patents, this was argued in *Eli Lilly & Co. v. Government of Canada*, UNCITRAL, ICSID Case No. UNCT/14/2, Final Award, 16 Mar. 2017. Yet the Tribunal was not persuaded by this argument: 'Claimant has also alleged that its legitimate expectations were grounded in, or at least reinforced by, Respondent's obligations under NAFTA Chapter 17 and the form and contents requirement of the PCT. The Parties have exchanged extensive submissions on these international instruments, all of which the Tribunal has considered. However, nothing therein alters the Tribunal's analysis. For all of the reasons stated above, Claimant has failed to establish, as a matter of fact, that Respondent breached any international obligations by invalidating the Strattera and Zyprexa Patents.'
155. UNCTAD Report 1974, 140. A 1977 Draft International Code of Conduct for the Transfer of Technology to Developing Countries negotiated under the auspices of UNCTAD remained – a draft.

c) Also the UN itself has become involved in IP policy[156] by way of its studies on sustainable development. A 2018 study on economic development comes to the following conclusions:

> 'First, a review of empirical evidence has generally failed to find much effect of IP institutions, notably patents, on innovation – the raison d'être of IP. While the incentivizing effect of IP on any given innovator's R&D activities is indisputable, its effect on system-wide innovation could be counteracted by several factors. These include the adverse effects of IP institutions on innovation diffusion, follow-up innovations and competition, which could be partly attributed to the lack of clear boundaries of IP and the absence of efficient and liquid IP markets.
>
> Second, the increasingly restrictive global intellectual property rights (IPR) regime poses significant challenges to countries, especially developing ones, in accessing frontier technologies and fully participating in the Fourth Industrial Revolution, which would in all likelihood lead to greater technology and development gaps. It may also lead to failures in addressing global problems such as climate change due to the underutilization of technologies that could provide effective solutions if appropriately diffused.'[157]

d) Finally, the World Health Organisation (WHO) has increasingly become involved in the topic of access to medicines.[158] In the course of the WTO dispute settlements on tobacco legislation, studies by the WHO may very well helped the WTO panels to take a new look at Articles 7 and 8 TRIPS (see below).

2. *Treaties*

(1) The Patent Cooperation Treaty of 1970, last amended 1979 (PCT) with a total membership of 153 states as of 24 September 2020.[159]
In the absence of a world patent, the PCT facilitates the filing of patents in several countries by delaying the actual filing procedures in other countries, providing for a search report and a preliminary examination. An international search report is prepared by a number of designated national and international patent offices within eight months after the 12-month priority period and provides the applicant with a preliminary examination within an additional ten months. Thereby, patent applications only enter the domestic phase 30 months after the initial filing.

(2) The Patent Law Treaty 2000 (in force since 2005) with 42 members as of 24 September 2020.

156. United Nations, *World Economic and Social Survey 2018: Frontier Technologies for Sustainable Development, E/2018/50/Rev.1-ST/ESA/370* (United Nations, 2018), 11–17.
157. H. Chen and M. Para-Lancourt, 'The Fourth Industrial Revolution, IP and Development: The World Economic and Social Survey 2018 and Beyond', in Heath et al., *supra* note 24, 31.
158. A WHO report entitled Public Health, Innovation and Intellectual Property Rights was published in 2006: https://www.who.int/intellectualproperty/report/en/
159. A very interesting analysis of the Patent Cooperation Treaty and its possible further development is provided by M. Nolff, *TRIPs, PCT and Global Patent Procurement* (London, 2001).

The Patent Law Treaty that was signed in Geneva on 2 June 2000 streamlines certain formalities of the application procedure, does away with the requirement of representation of foreigners for the mere purpose of paying a fee, and requires reinstatement where certain deadlines were missed.

(3) The Budapest Treaty on the International Recognition of the Deposit of Micro-organisms for the Purposes of Patent Procedure 1977, last amended 1980, with a membership of 82 states as of 24 September 2020.
The Budapest Treaty facilitates the international filing of patents for micro-organisms. Since micro-organisms cannot be properly described, they have to be submitted by way of sample. This is not done at the individual patent offices, but may be done at one of the currently 33 recognised international depository authorities.

(4) The International Convention for the Protection of New Varieties of Plants (UPOV) of 1961, last amended in 1991, with a membership of 76 States as of 24 September 2020.[160]
As many domestic patent systems exclude plant varieties from the subject matter of patent protection, the UPOV Convention provides for a system of *sui generis* protection for plant varieties that are new, distinct and stable. The so-called breeders' exemption shall allow further research and development into new varieties,[161] and the so-called farmers' exemption permits a re-sowing of the protected varieties for purposes of personal consumption.[162]

III. International Trade and Harmonisation of IP Rights

It might be helpful at this stage to pause for a moment and ask the question as to how a system that started as a tolerated exception to the rules of free trade, that in the mid-nineteenth century came close to being abolished and that in some countries actually was abolished, could become such a prominent part of international trade.

One answer is that the system was shaped by the numerous conferences of the Paris Convention, be it in the preparation or the subsequent revision thereof,[163] by the discussions waged before the UN in the 1960s,[164] by the impasse to further revise the Paris Convention[165] by subsequently putting this topic on the agenda of the GATT

160. For an analysis of UPOV, *see* R. Greengrass, 'UPOV and the Protection of Plant Breeders – Past Developments, Future Perspectives', 20 IIC (1989) 622.
161. V. Prifti, *The Breeding Exception to Patent Rights: Analysis of Compliance with Article 30 of the TRIPS Agreement* (Springer, 2015).
162. V. Prifti, (2015). 'Understanding the Farmers' Privilege in "Monsanto Laws"', SSRN Electronic Journal, 10.2139/ssrn.2708600.
163. *See* the chapter 'Origin and History of the Union' in Ladas, *supra* note 18, 59–94.
164. An account of which is provided by A. Koury Menescal, 'Changing WIPO's Ways?', 8 *Journal of World Intellectual Property* 761, 764–75.
165. The last meaningful attempt to revise the Paris Convention dates back to 1981/1982. Demands by developing countries for enhanced obligations of use (revision of Art. 5A) were ultimately unsuccessful. Report by H. Kunz-Hallstein in GRUR Int. (1982), 45.

revision conferences[166] and by the ongoing efforts of international harmonisation of the patent system.[167] This perspective looks at the legislative developments that in the case of the Paris Convention were implemented by unanimity, and in the case of the UN and the GATT negotiations by majority.

Another answer is that those experts who sat at the negotiating tables or in the relevant discussion rounds did not primarily represent the public interest, but the interests of rights owners.[168] The reason for this was that expertise in the field of patent law was and continues to be available mostly amongst rights owners' associations, namely the Association for the Protection of Industrial Property Rights (AIPPI) and the International Chamber of Commerce (ICC), as is highlighted by the writings of Koury Menescal: [169]

> 'Both the ICC and AIPPI could wield influence through the contributions of their members who at the same time were part of the official government delegations:[170] ICC had representatives in the delegations of Germany, France, United States, United Kingdom and the Netherlands. And AIPPI had 63 of its members (and some supporters) within official government delegations.[171] The organization was proud of its omnipresence: "the influence of the AIPPI [together with the ICC] made itself shown by the presence and the authority of the gentlemen who lead it and who occupied many posts of command at Lisbon. These are the men who have made prevalent the doctrines and the spirit of the AIPPI [and the ICC]"[172].'

Koury Menescal (p. 179) concludes as follows:

166. A brief history is provided by Taubman, Wager and Watal, *A Handbook on the WTO TRIPS Agreement* (Cambridge, 2012), 4–8, and particularly the first phase of the Uruguay round by Beier and Schricker, *GATT or WIPO? – New Ways in the International Protection of Intellectual Property* (IIC Studies, Weinheim, 1989).
167. E.g. the 'Substantive Patent Law Treaty' negotiated under the auspices of WIPO between 2000 and 2006, yet abandoned. In the last decade, the strategy of industrialised countries has been to increase the level of protection by way of a bilateral or multilateral free trade agreement that via the most-favoured nation treatment under TRIPS then becomes a new de facto standard.
168. According to R. Jacob, 'Is IP out of Control?', *Journal of Intellectual Property Law & Practice* (2020), 98, 99, 'we need to devise better ways of changing and advancing IP law. Lobbyists will always have their place and always have. But it should not be enough for them to get what they want simply by being the ones that shout louder than anyone else... Neither the public interest nor those who could provide more objective assessments and contributions play a sufficient part...'
169. A. Koury Menescal, 'Those Behind the TRIPS Agreement: The influence of the ICC and the AIPPI on International Intellectual Property Decisions', *Intellectual Property Quarterly* (2005), 155–82. The citation can be found on p. 165.
170. In her analysis on the important roles lawyers played, e.g. as advisors on patents in large corporations, she shows that many of these lawyers were involved in chambers of commerce, and some, e.g. John T. Connor (Merck) and J. Russell Wilson (Monsanto), had been active in the US government before: , Edith L. Fisch, Matthew Foner and Albert P. Blaustein, *Lawyers in Industry* (Oceana, New York, 1956), 78, 81, 82, 132 et seq.
171. *AIPPI Annuaire* (1959), 24.
172. *AIPPI Annuaire* (1959), 89.

'Although ICC's and AIPPI's explicit influence in international policy and law decreased around the mid-1970's[173] – which does not mean that their real influence decreased[174] – these "non-governmental organizations" have strictly pursued their goal of lobbying on behalf of their members, multinational corporations inter alia.[175] Especially the ICC did this with a remarkable perception of the relevance of intellectual property for international trade: The so-called trade-related aspects of intellectual property rights from early on were consciously taken into account by the ICC, which also influenced the discussions inside AIPPI. With its extensive work in both fields, the ICC amongst its members was sowing the seeds[176] for recognizing the value of intellectual property for international trade and private business, and for pursuing an international agreement such as WTO/TRIPS.

This author believes that the battle between producers and consumers of intellectual property that characterized the process on the establishment of the WTO/TRIPS Agreement[177] was actually lost in the 1960's within the discussion

173. First, specifically in the field of intellectual property, in which the ICC and the AIPPI 'were practically the only organizations that the international bodies consulted', up to the 1970s, these organizations noticed that they were losing this prime position because of the 'large number of international associations of private law active in the same field' (*AIPPI Annuaire* (1972/I), 15). Second, the growth of multinational enterprises in the 1950s and 1960s (for literature of that time on this issue, *see* Richard W. Mansbach, Yale H. Ferguson and Donald E. Lampert, *The Web of World Politics: Nonstate Actors in the Global System* (Prentice-Hall, New Jersey, 1976), 189 et seq.), and, consequently, their direct influence as transnational actors in international economy, policy and law (e.g., Louis T. Wells, Jr., 'The Multinational Business Enterprise: What Kind of International Organization?', in Robert O. Keohane and Joseph S. Nye (eds.), *Transnational Relations and World Politics* (Harvard University Press, Cambridge, Mass., 1972), 97–114; and Johan Galtung, *The True Worlds: a Transnational Perspective* (The Free Press, New York, 1980), 312 et seq.), so that the ICC and the AIPPI were no longer alone in defending business interests in international forums. This is further elaborated in the author's forthcoming final thesis.

174. The ICC was also there to influence the WTO/TRIPS process: 'For almost half a century, ICC gave strong support to the several successive rounds of negotiations to liberalize world trade carried out under the aegis of GATT. We were particularly supportive of the ambitious Uruguay Round negotiations, which resulted in unprecedentedly wide-ranging agreements to further reduce tariff and non-tariff barriers to trade, and which initiated a process of extending multilateral rules to new trade-related policy areas of major importance to world business' (www.iccwbo.org/home/statements_rules/statements/1999/multilateral_trade_negotiations_june 1999.asp – accessed 8 March 2004 [yet no longer available]. The AIPPI was not much different. *See*, e.g. Joan Clark, *Die Rolle des GATT/TRIPS, der Weltorganisation für geistiges Eigentum (WIPO) und der AIPPI in der künftigen Entwicklung des Schutzes von geistigem Eigentum* (AIPPI, 1997), 487–93.

175. 'There is little doubt that the responsibility and influence of the international business community has greatly increased due to the activity of the ICC.' ('International Chamber of Commerce: Recent Activities', in *Journal of World Trade Law*, Vol. 2 (1968), 587).

176. P. Drahos, and R. Mayne, *Global Intellectual Property Rights: Knowledge, Access and Development* (Oxfam, Oxford, 2002), 90, mention Edmund T. Pratt Jr. as one of these seeds to grow up: he influenced the process that ended in the WTO/TRIPS Agreement, was a member of the boards of the New York Chamber of Commerce and Industry, worked at Pfizer since 1964, and was the company's Chairman from 1972 to 1992. He had a 'central role in pushing the linkage between intellectual property and trade' in the negotiations and discussions that led to the establishment of the WTO/TRIPS Agreement.

177. *Ibid.*, 14.

> following the "Brazilian Resolution". Those who defended the protection of private interests of patent holders against the public interest, in particular the ICC and the AIPPI, made all efforts to have their position prevail within the international and national intellectual property systems. They were extremely successful in this endeavour, and were succeeded by later efforts of developed countries and multinational corporations to have the WTO/TRIPS Agreement signed.
>
> This author also believes that the convergence of intellectual property and trade issues that characterizes the WTO/TRIPS Agreement, and was contested by developing countries, actually started with the Resolution 1713 of 1961,[178] instigated by the ICC. There, the ICC was defending its mission of "facilitating international trade without any restrictions",[179] and supporting a system for the protection of intellectual property that presented no constraints to international free trade.'

From a socio-political point of view, the above efforts were influential for three developments:

1. That revision conferences to the Paris Convention gradually limited the scope of domestic policy making in the patent field and that once a stalemate was reached in this forum, the discussions shifted to the arena of international trade law.
2. The above-mentioned 'Brazilian Resolution'[180] led to an intense discussion before the UN, the result of which was to cement the position of BIRPI (the predecessor of WIPO) as the only internationally competent body to deal with the international patent system, much to the dismay of many developing countries.[181] Even today, where intellectual property rights have become

178. The study by Ulf Anderfelt gives some support to this position, when he considers the international patent legislation and its effects on developing countries as, e.g., international trade restrictions; and the activities and decisions in this respect following the Brazilian resolution. *See*, U. Anderfelt. *International Patent-Legislation and Developing Countries* (Martinus Nijhoff, The Hague, 1971), 172 et seq. and p. 213 et seq.
179. ICC (ed.) *Industrial Property*, vol. 1 (1962), 38.
180. 'The Role of Patents in the Transfer of Technology to Under-Developed Countries', Resolution sponsored by Brasil and Bolivia, UN General Assembly Doc. A/C.2/L.565, 8 November 1961, in MRE, Ofícios Recebidos da Missão do Brasil junto às Nações Unidas. No. 1225 of 9 November 1961, I, Brasília, Brazil, December 1961. One of the aims of this resolution was to revise the international patent system outside the Paris Convention by 'holding an international conference with the aim of adjusting the existing patent conventions to the needs of developing countries'.
181. The amendment to entrust BIRPI with this exclusive position was proposed by Denmark. It was narrowly adopted by 21 votes in favour (most developed countries), 20 votes against (all of which were developing and socialist countries) and 25 abstentions; *see* United Nations, Official Records of the General Assembly, Sixteenth Session, Annexes, 19 September 1961-23 February 1962 and 7–28 June 1962, New York, 1963, UN GA Official Records (XVI), p. 46. As Koury Menescal writes: 'Hence, no revision of the international patent system could be effected outside the Paris Union, an institution in which developed countries had exerted their dominance for almost one hundred years and where any amendments to the Convention required unanimity. This was a considerable blow to Brazil whose foremost aim in tabling the resolution was to challenge the Paris Union by having future IP rules laid down by the UN.' (A. Koury Menescal, 'Changing WIPO's Ways? – The 2004 Development Agenda in Historical Perspective', 8 *Journal of World Intellectual Property* (November 2005), 761, 771). Koury

pervasive in many aspects of societal life, UN bodies outside WIPO have been reluctant to address intellectual protection through the lens of other societal interests, such as health, freedom of expression and protection of privacy.[182]

3. Even where intellectual property rights are regarded as trade-related, this does not necessarily determine the patentable subject matter, duration and scope of protection as long as there is an equal playing field: free trade, one could conclude from a reading of the Statute of Monopolies, is in fact best served by minimal exceptions thereto. And yet, there has been both: successful efforts to broaden intellectual property rights, and modestly successful efforts of international harmonisation.

Efforts to strengthen the international patent system were, apart from the above-mentioned institutions, also supported by academic writings until about 1990, including by F.K. Beier, who at times put conviction that a stronger patent system was good for all countries[183] without hard evidence.[184]

Efforts of harmonisation were already made in the wake of the Paris Convention. In fact, the initial idea of the Paris Convention was an international harmonisation of patent laws[185] which could not be achieved. Harmonisation in effect means a battle of standards and, where substantive requirements of patent law are concerned, is not graced with a presumption of being beneficial: if the optimum level of protection cannot be empirically determined even for one given country, harmonisation can be for better or worse, and there is evidence that a uniformly high level of protection[186] regardless of the stage of development does not benefit countries below a certain level of development (see under A. above). The matter is more equivocal where the

---

Menescal notes that the first director of WIPO, Bodenhausen, had been actively involved in the ICC and AIPPI, and the second director, Bogsch, was made a member of honour by the AIPPI in 1989 (167, 168) and concludes: 'There is conclusive evidence that the WIPO's decisions have been strongly influenced by ICC and AIPPI experts advocating patent-holder's rights at the expense of the public interest and the needs of the developing world.'

182. *United Nations, World Economic and Social Survey 2018: Frontier Technologies for Sustainable Development, E/2018/50/Rev.1-ST/ESA/370* (United Nations, 2018), 11–17, and Hoi Wai Jackie Cheng and Mariangela Parra-Lancourt, 'The World Economic and Social Survey 2018 and Beyond', in Heath et al., *supra* note 24, 29.

183. *See*, for example, F.-K. Beier, 'The Significance of the Patent System for Technical, Economic and Social Progress', 11 IIC (1980), 563–84: According to him, evidence 'give sufficient support to my basic thesis that the patent system, in its historically developed and currently practiced form, constitutes a proven, indispensable instrument for technical, economic and social progress' (579); *idem*, 'Scientific Research, Patent Protection and Innovation', 6 IIC (1975), 367–81.

184. As mentioned at the beginning of this chapter, evidence is rather equivocal and the best balance of private and public interest in this field is rather elusive and seems to depend on the capacity of a given country to innovate: R. P. Merges and R. R. Nelson, 'On the Complex Economics of Patent Scope', 90(4) *Columbia Law Review* (May 1990), 839–916; Drahos and Mayne, *supra* note 176; P. Drahos and J. Braithwaite, *Information Feudalism: Who Owns the Knowledge Economy?* (Earthscan, London, 2002).

185. A. Osterrieth and O.Axster, *Die internationale Übereinkunft zum Schutz des gewerblichen Eigentums* (Berlin, 1903), X-XI.

186. Normally, harmonisation in the IP field gravitates towards the longest periods of protection, or the broadest definition of patentable subject matter, and proponents of harmonisation understand it this way: J. Straus and N. Klunker, 'Harmonisation of International Patent Law', 38 IIC (2007) 907, 921.

harmonisation of features unrelated to the level of protection or protectable subject matter is concerned, e.g. the grace period or how to define the requirements of using priority. Harmonisation is positively desirable in the field of formalities.[187]

D. THE FRAMEWORK OF PATENT PROTECTION AS ESTABLISHED UNDER THE TRIPS AGREEMENT

I. From Incentives to Innovation to a Level Playing Field

Despite the incorporation of the Paris and Berne Convention principles by reference (TRIPS Article 2), one should be clear that the patent system as established by the TRIPS Agreement functions under different premises, as has been set out in more detail in the opening chapter of this book:

The Paris Convention and other WIPO instruments (e.g. the PCT) are meant to provide a system that stimulates *innovation* based on the rationale of the patent bargain. Consequently, very little minimum standards are imposed[188] and countries are given significant leeway for configuring the IP system in accordance with domestic needs. Thereby, countries are relatively free to pursue a domestic industrial policy. The requirement of national treatment refers to persons. A most-favoured nation treatment is particularly excluded by Article 19 that permits, even encourages, more specific agreements between some of the Member States.

The GATT Agreement 1947[189] had as its purpose the stimulation of *free trade*. Particular reference is made to Article V (freedom of transit) and Article XI (freedom of importation). In this context, industrial property rights are regarded as exceptions (Article XX d) with a certain potential for conflicts in such fields as freedom of transit, freedom of importation and enforcement. The provision of national treatment (Article V) refers to goods, not persons, and so does the requirement of most-favoured nation treatment (Article I).

WTO/TRIPS, although purportedly based on the above two pillars (stimulating innovation and free trade) regards a *level playing field as a prerequisite to free trade*. For this purpose, minimum standards as such become necessary, although their level is irrelevant in principle as long as they are equal. Equality is initially ensured by the implementation of the agreement, and subsequently by the MFN obligation that however no longer relates to goods, but to persons and thereby directly contradicts Article 19 Paris Convention: Every kind of additional IP protection granted in a future free trade agreement, be it bilateral or multilateral, must automatically be granted to persons from other countries although such countries may not be obliged to grant the advantages that led to the concession in the first place.[190]

---

187. E.g. by the Patent Law Treaty 2000 as a special agreement under Art. 19 Paris Convention: https://www.wipo.int/treaties/en/ip/plt/
188. Those that can be found in the Paris Convention are related to preventing distortions of fair (not free) trade, e.g. Art. 10*bis* or Art. 6*bis*.
189. Recognising, as an aside, the Free Territory of Trieste in Art. XXIV 3b).
190. Some free trade agreements require e.g. the extension of the protection period for patents in case of regulatory delays or long pendency of an application. In the context of the Paris Convention, such extension could be granted for nationals of certain member states only in the context of an agreement concluded within the ambit of Art. 19 Paris Convention. In the

Under TRIPS, conflicts with domestic industrial policy are inevitable, and with free trade possible.[191]

II. Principles of Patent Law as Established by the TRIPS Agreement[192]

1. *The Starting Point*

The objective set out in the preamble of TRIPS is to avoid 'distortions and impediments to international trade', and to this end protect intellectual property rights and ensure their enforcement.[193] This is complemented by Articles 7 (Objectives) and 8 (Principles), two provisions that did not feature prominently in the early interpretation of TRIPS provisions and have been given more interpretative weight only recently. The problem with a broad interpretation of these provisions is that the objectives and principles mentioned therein, namely the balance of producers and users, social and economic welfare and a balance of rights and obligations (Article 7) is limited by the Article 8 obligation that measures to achieve such end, namely to 'protect public health and nutrition, and to promote the public interest' must be 'consistent with the provisions of this Agreement', in other words, these goals can only be achieved to the extent that they are consistent with the following TRIPS provisions. Thereby, 'Art. 8 does not create any exceptions to TRIPS obligations, but it would shield measures from non-violation complaints under TRIPS.'[194] The other function of these two provisions is that exceptions or unclear terms in the agreement itself can be interpreted in light of Articles 7 and 8, as was confirmed by the Appellate Body with respect to Article 20 TRIPS and the term 'unjustifiably' when it held that:

> 'the Panel [in first instance] observed that "Article 8 offers ... useful contextual guidance for the interpretation of the term 'unjustifiably' in Article 20." The Panel also remarked that the societal interests referred to in Article 8 may provide a basis of the justification of measures under Article 20. Thus, we agree with Australia that, in any event, the reliance on the Doha Declaration was not of decisive importance for the Panel's reasoning since the Panel had

---

context of GATT, granting such extension to certain nationals only would not give rise to an Art. I complaint because the favour does not refer to a product. In the context of TRIPS, however, such favour has been granted to all foreign applicants or patentees irrespective of whether a country is a member of the specific free trade agreement in question. This becomes even more pronounced where free trade agreements mandate additional types of protection (e.g. geographical indications) that then could not be granted on a basis of reciprocity.

191. E.g. in cases where IP rights are invoked to impede the transit of goods: e.g. M. Senftleben, 'The Seizure of Transit Goods', in Heath et al., *supra* note 89, 107, and Request for Consultations by India, European Union and a Member State - Seizure of Generic Drugs in Transit (WT/DS408/1), World Trade Organization (WTO), 19 May 2010; Request for Consultations by Brazil, European Union and a Member State - Seizure of Generic Drugs in Transit (WT/DS409/1), WTO, 19 May 2010.
192. N. Pires de Carvalho, 'The Rule of Patent Law as established by the TRIPS Agreement and its role in promoting trade rather than invention', in Bagley and Okediji, *Patent Law in Global Perspective* (Oxford, 2015), 673.
193. It is an interesting question in this regard whether 'overprotection' may lead to trade barriers: Heath et al., *supra* note 89.
194. Matthew Kennedy, *WTO Dispute Settlement and the TRIPS Agreement* (Cambridge, 2016), 177.

reached its conclusions about the contextual relevance of Articles 7 and 8 of the TRIPS Agreement to the interpretation of Article 20 before it turned to the Doha Declaration. The Panel relied on the Doha Declaration simply to reconfirm its previous conclusions regarding the contextual relevance of Articles 7 and 8 of the TRIPS Agreement.'[195]

2. *Existing Subject Matter*

a) *Article 70.2 TRIPS*

The question of retroactive protection with respect to pre-TRIPS subject matter is addressed in a couple of provisions, namely in part VI ('Transitional Arrangements', Articles 65-67), and Article 70 ('Protection of Existing Subject Matter'). According to Article 65.2, a 'developing country is entitled to delay for a further four years the date of application'. As was held by the Brazilian Appeal Court (STJ), no specific declaration of a developing country was necessary to avail itself of this period, and any developing country was entitled to this transitional arrangement *ex lege.*[196] The court in a later decision distinguished this general grace period from the one in Article 65.4 (obligation to extend patent protection to subject matter hitherto not protected) that required a specific declaration to this end ('...may extend...')[197]

As to case law, **WTO DS 170**[198] concerned Canada's patent law that for patents applied pre-1989 provided for a duration of 17 years from grant (rather than 20 years from the date of filing). In some cases, this of course can amount to a protection of less than 20 years from the date of filing, namely where examination procedure takes less than three years. As Canada's law had already been amended prior to the TRIPS Agreement, the first question concerned applicability of the TRIPS rules. In this regard, Article 70.2 provides:

> 2. Except as otherwise provided for in this Agreement, this Agreement gives rise to obligations *in respect of all subject matter existing* at the date of application of this Agreement for the Member in question, and which is *protected* in that

195. WTO Appellate Body, case WT/DS/435/AB of 6 June 2020, https://docs.wto.org/dol2fe/Pages/SS/directdoc.aspx?filename=q:/WT/DS/435ABR.pdf&Open=True
196. Brazilian Federal Appeal Court (STJ), decision of 15 April 2009, English translation in 41 IIC 601 (2010), headnote 3: 'The transition period for developing countries specified in Art. 65.2 TRIPS is a right a developing country can rely on even in the absence of any declaration, be it under domestic law or before the WTO. The issue is different for the additional transition period stipulated in Art. 65.4 TRIPS.'
197. Brazilian Federal Appeal Court (STJ), Grand Chamber, decision of 28 April 2010, English translation in 41 IIC 610 (2010), headnote 2: 'It is not possible for Brazil to rely on the grace period as stipulated in Art. 65.4 TRIPS due a lack of any legislative intent to do so. However, forfeiture of this grace period in no way precludes application of the more generic grace period specified in Art. 65.2 TRIPS that is a right conceded to Brazil and that, as such, cannot be affected by any absence of Brazil's intention to avail herself thereto, as there is no obligation that might require Brazil to declare an interest to use this period as a condition for its use (*see* Decision of the Federal Appeal Court, 15 April 2009 (Extraordinary Appeal No. 960.728 - RJ 2007/0134338-8), Nancy Andrighi, rapporteur).'
198. https://www.wto.org/english/tratop_e/dispu_e/cases_e/ds170_e.htm

> Member on the said date, or which meets or comes subsequently to meet the criteria for protection under the terms of this Agreement ... (emphasis added)

While Canada had argued that Article 70.1 excluded *acts* which had occurred prior to TRIPS, the Panel held that the duration did not concern the act of grant, but rather the protection of existing subject matter. In the context of Brazil (that until 2000 provided for a protection period of 15 years from grant), the Appeal Court came to the conclusion that TRIPS did not oblige Member States to extend patents over existing subject matter, yet the issue was never raised in a dispute resolution context.[199] Intuitively, it is of course questionable what incentive, if any, is provided by the retroactive extension of the protection period, as this amounts to a burden to society without anything in return. Based on this rationale, retroactive extension of the protection period for copyrights was (unsuccessfully) challenged before the US Supreme Court.[200]

b) *Article 70.8 and 70.9 TRIPS*

The transitory provisions in Article 70.8 require that even where countries avail themselves of their status of developing countries and thus have to comply with the TRIPS provisions only five or ten years after entry into force (general entry into force on 1 January 1995, compliance as of 1 January 1996, Article 65.1 for developed countries, as of 1 January 2000 for developing countries, Article 65.2, twice extended until 2021 with a further extension under consideration) must allow at least the filing of applications for hitherto excluded subject matter in order to preserve the right of priority even if such applications are only examined once protection of the subject matter has become available.

These so-called pipeline patents stipulated in Article 70.8 were a significant concession for developing countries in the TRIPS negotiations. They are a de facto retroactive application of the agreement to certain kinds of inventions hitherto excluded from patentability by many developing countries, mainly in the field of pharmaceuticals and food. Grace periods are not foreseen in this respect. According to Article 70.8 TRIPS, countries that at the date of entry did not allow for the protection of pharmaceuticals, etc., were required to accept and examine patent applications with such subject matter in applying the first filing abroad as a priority date – in effect an extension of the 12-month priority period of the Paris Convention. When found to meet the criteria of patentability as of the priority date, (or the actual filing date, should the applicant so wish) the patent shall be granted for 'the remainder of the patent term, counted from the filing date in accordance with Art. 33 of this Agreement.' Where no priority is claimed, the applicant should of course be entitled to a patent term of 20 years from the filing date. But where priority is claimed, often from years

199. Brazilian Federal Appeal Court (STJ), Grand Chamber, decision of 28 April 2010, English translation in 41 IIC 610 (2010), headnote 4: 'In order to avoid an obligation for retroactive protection of TRIPS in a given Member State (Art. 70.1), and in accordance with the right offered under the Agreement to defer its entry into force (Art. 65), it is clear that there is no obligation to comply with the Agreement for those rights over inventions that have already been granted.'
200. US Supreme Court, *Eldred et. al. v. Ashcroft*, 15 January 2003, 537 US 186.

back, the issue is not so clear. Taking the actual filing date would disproportionately extend patent protection in developing countries. If, say, a patent enjoys a priority from 1986, and the filing in a developing country takes place in 1997, protection abroad would lapse in 2007 at the latest, while it would be 2017 if one were to take the 1997 filing date as a starting point. Some guidance can be found in the footnote to Article 33 that in such situations allows for a computation of the term 'from the filing date in the system of original grant.' The issue becomes more complicated if there is no original grant, for example because the original filing was abandoned and only a subsequent application is granted. But still, the wording seems clear enough even in these cases to take the original foreign filing as a starting point for calculating the 20-year period.[201] Thus, Article 70.8 TRIPS means an extension of the right of priority and allows disregarding of the principle of independence of rights to the extent that a foreign filing date may be taken as a starting point for calculating the 20 year term of protection, something that otherwise would not be permitted under Article 4*bis* (2) Paris Convention ('their normal duration').

In addition, Article 70.9 requires the grant of exclusive marketing rights (EMRs) for patent applications under Article 70.8 for a maximum period of five years until the patent application has been examined or marketing approval has been granted. It is a condition for such EMRs that a patent application has been filed, the patent has been granted in another Member State, and marketing approval has been obtained there, 'subsequent to the entry into force of the WTO Agreement'. Again, the wording is not entirely clear. Taken at face value, the provision would apply only to those patent applications filed abroad after the entry into force of the WTO Agreement, but this is certainly not what the provision wants to achieve. Exclusive marketing rights differ from patents in that the former do not extend to those acts of third parties that do not directly affect the monopolistic marketing of the patented product.

This mechanism as described above became the subject of two cases against India, **DS 50** and **DS 79**:[202] these cases were brought by, respectively, the US (DS 50) and the EU (DS 79) because India in the absence of patent protection for pharmaceutical products failed to provide a clear regime so as allow the filing of such corresponding patent applications within the transitional period (Article 70.8) and failed to grant exclusive marketing rights for such products up to five years from the date of obtaining marketing approval. Both were considered inconsistent with TRIPS, in particular because there was a lack of legal certainty with respect to what measures were actually available in India:

> 'In our view, India is obliged, by Article 70.8(a), to provide a legal mechanism for the filing of mailbox applications that provides a sound legal basis to preserve both the novelty of the inventions and the priority of the applications as of the relevant filing and priority dates. No more... And...we are not persuaded that India's

201. Not least due to the unclear wording, the duration of such pipeline patents was subject to a number of disputes in Brazil where the Federal Appeal Court (STJ) ultimately held that the duration should be calculated as 20 years from the first foreign filing: Brazil STJ, decision of 15 December 2009, 35 IIC 996 (2010).

202. WTO DS 50 of 19 December 1997 (Appellate Body) – 'India – Patent Protection for pharmaceutical and agricultural chemical products' https://www.wto.org/english/tratop_e/dispu_e/cases_e/ds50_e.htm.

> "administrative instructions" provide a sound legal basis to preserve novelty of inventions and priority of applications as of the relevant filing and priority dates.'[203]

III. Minimum Standards

In accordance with the above logic that only a level playing field can establish conditions for free trade, the TRIPS Agreement establishes minimum standards[204] for patent protection in a number of respects.

1. *Minimum Duration of Patents, Article 33*

For the domestic plane, see above. On the international plane, a proposal tabled by the Italian delegation at the 1958 Lisbon Conference to provide for a uniform period of protection of 18 years was not adopted, as it was considered a matter of national law.[205] The period now stipulated in Article 33 was oriented towards the maximum standard.

2. *Patentable Subject Matter*

a) Unlike previous agreements, TRIPS in Article 27 requires patent protection for all inventions and thereby prohibits exceptions from patentability as were common particularly in developing countries.

b) The patentability requirements mentioned in Article 27.1 are novelty, inventive step and industrial application, while the requirement of sufficient disclosure is mentioned in Article 29.1. These requirements have been explained above in the context of the patent bargain. There is some force to the argument that Member States may not require additional requirements of patentability, or provide further exclusions.[206]

While no WTO dispute with respect to patentability requirements has been raised, the following issues could be or have actually been discussed within the ambit of TRIPS as possible additional requirements or exclusions:

(1) Some jurisdictions require that an invention possesses 'utility'. For example, under US law, in order to be patentable inventions must be 'new and useful'. This requirement certainly touches upon sufficient disclosure in that an invention that for one reason or another cannot be reduced to practice is either insufficiently disclosed or does not meet the promise that it can be applied in industry. However, utility can also be understood as 'improvement',

---

203. WTO Dispute Settlement decision WT/DS/AB/50 India – Patents of 19 December 1997, paras. 58 and 70. https://docs.wto.org/dol2fe/Pages/SS/directdoc.aspx?filename=Q:/WT/DS/50ABR.pdf&Open=True
204. Art. 1.1 TRIPS clarifies that Members may opt for more extensive protection, which is somewhat contradictory to the purported goal of a level playing field in that it again creates different levels of protection and thereby obstacles to trade. One may argue that this is somewhat mitigated by the most-favoured nation obligation, *see infra*.
205. Ladas, *supra* note 18, 388.
206. N. Pires de Carvalho, *The TRIPS Regime of Patents and Test Data* (4th edn., 2014), 288.

for example 'a gain in simplicity or construction, efficiency of operation, reduction of accidents or pain'.[207] In this respect, it can rather be understood as a specific interpretation of inventive step.[208]

In Canada, as was extensively argued in *Eli Lilly v. Canada*,[209] utility is also a requirement of patentability. One of the two patents that were subject to a panel dispute in the context of NAFTA concerned a so-called selection patent that was challenged – and ultimately revoked – for want of utility. According to the first instance court, one rather limited clinical study was 'too small in size and too short in duration to provide anything more than interesting but inconclusive data.'[210] The matter was appealed to the Federal Court of Appeal, which basically confirmed the trial court's decision, and leave to appeal was then refused by the Supreme Court of Canada.[211] Also in the case of the other patent, the court was unconvinced that the patent fulfilled 'the promise of the '113 patent ... that olanzapine is substantially better ("marked superiority") in the clinical treatment of schizophrenia (and related conditions) than other known antipsychotics, with a better side-effects profile, and a high level of activity at low doses'.[212] Utility in this case was argued (but denied) on the basis of one human study disclosed in the patent, yet the study showed no decreased side effects.[213] It appears that the 'utility' requirement as interpreted by the Canadian courts can be likened to the requirement of 'plausibility' as interpreted by the EPO and the British courts. As explained above, this requirement partly refers to sufficiency and partly to inventive step and there is nothing to suggest that it would not be in line with the patent bargain or the TRIPS Agreement. In the wake of the *Eli Lilly* investor-State dispute settlement decision, the Canadian Supreme Court nonetheless abandoned its previous stance on the utility requirement.[214]

207. Ladas, *supra* note 18, 308.
208. '[I]t is not difficult to conceive that a person might endeavour to monopolize a known article of trade, by a patent for some immaterial alteration or addition to it, on the speculation that the public would give him credit for the patent article being superior to the old one. To prevent such deceit, this general rule is laid down, that the new manufacture or subject must be material and useful. ... A patent for [an] improvement would be good, for it is a substantive invention: yet in general the substitution of one material for another in making a manufacture is insufficient to support a patent.' R Godson, *A Practical Treatise on the Law of Patents for Inventions and of Copyright* (Saunders and Benning, London 1840) 67–69, quoted after Pessers, *The Inventiveness Requirement in Patent Law: An Exploration of its Foundations and Functioning* (Kluwer, 2016), 87–88.
209. *Eli Lilly v. the Government of Canada*, Final Award, 16 March 2017 at www.italaw.com/cases/1625.
210. *Novopharm v. Lilly, Novopharm Ltd. v. Eli Lilly and Co.*, 2010 FC 915, at para. 113.
211. *Eli Lilly and Company v. Teva Canada Limited*, 2011 FCA 220; leave to appeal refused, 34396 (8 December 2011).
212. *Eli Lilly Canada Inc. v. Novopharm Limited*, 2011 FC 1288, para. 124.
213. *Eli Lilly Canada Inc v. Novopharm Limited*, 2012 FCA 232, leave to appeal to SCC refused, 35067 (May 16, 2013). For an in-depth analysis of this case, *see* Daniel Gervais, 'Lilly v. Canada', in C. Heath and A. Kamperman Sanders, *Intellectual Property and International Dispute Resolution* (Kluwer Law, 2019), 169.
214. *AstraZeneca Canada Inc. v. Apotex Inc.*, 2017 SCC 36 (30 June 2017). Referring to the argument made by the appellant in the case that the promise of the patent doctrine violated NAFTA and

(2) Also different legislative definitions of the inventive step requirement have come under scrutiny for TRIPS compliance,[215] in particular the revised Indian Patent Act (as above)[216] that requires 'a technical advance as compared to the existing knowledge or having economic significance.' Further, the Act excludes patenting for any new property or new use for a known substance.

The requirement of 'technical advance' is not necessarily equivalent to 'inventive step' in that the former excludes non-obvious alternatives .[217] Apart from the interest of a competitor to find non-infringing alternatives, also the public might benefit from alternative solutions in that market choice is enhanced. Yet in light of the different interpretations of the inventive step requirement over the centuries,[218] it is hard to argue that equating inventive step with technical advance and thereby excluding non-obvious alternatives introduces an additional requirement of patentability.

The exclusion of new properties or new uses can be justified by the scope granted to a product patent: if such patent comprises all known uses, there is a good case to argue that nothing is left for further use patents[219] (see above). Whether this is politically desirable or not, is another matter.[220]

c) Certain exceptions may be provided for inventions contravening the *ordre public* ('obnoxious to the state', see above and below), which in the context of the EPC has

TRIPS, the court noted in footnote 1: 'This argument was advanced prior to the final arbitration award in Eli Lilly and Co. v. Canada rendered by the International Centre for Settlement of Investment Disputes under NAFTA (I.C.S.I.D. Case No. UNCT/14/2), March 16, 2017.' The court nonetheless concluded as follows: 'The Promise Doctrine in its operation is inconsistent with the purpose of s. 27(3) of the Act which calls on an inventor to "fully describe the invention and its operation or use". Thus, the Promise Doctrine undermines a key part of the scheme of the Act; it is not good law.' (*ibid.*, at para. 51).

215. A very instructive analysis in this regard is provided by R. Romandini, 'Flexibilities under TRIPS', 15 *J. Marshall Rev. Intellectual Property L.* (2016) 150.
216. Parthasarathy and Goddar, *supra* note 89.
217. Under the EPC, non-obvious alternatives are patentable, *see supra*.
218. According to Coke, *The Third Part of the Institutes* of England (1644) ch LXXXV para. 184, 'such a privilege as is consonant to law, must be substantially and essentially newly invented; but if the substance was in esse before, and a new addition thereunto, though that addition make the former more profitable, yet is it not a new manufacture in law; and so it was resolved in the exchequer chamber, Pasch, 15Eliz., in Bircot's case for a privilege concerning the preparing and melting, etc., of lead ore; for there it was said, that that was to put but a new button to an old coat; and it is much easier to add then to invent. And there it was also resolved, that if the new manufacture be substantially invented according to law, yet no old manufacture in use can be prohibited.' So no patents on putting new buttons on an old coat. Pessers, The Inventiveness Requirement in Patent Law: An Exploration of its Foundations and Functioning, Kluwer 2016, 69/70, explains this insistence on a high-level inventive step with the distrust for monopolies and the protection of labour, as particularly more efficient, labour-saving technologies were excluded.
219. It is less convincing to argue that TRIPS does not require the grant of 'use' patents: C. Correa, *Trade Related Aspects of Intellectual Property Rights* (2006), 274. This would only appear correct in the context of absolute product protection. Where patents are limited to a specific use (to the extent that only the specific use makes the product a useful contribution to the art), most product patents in certain areas such as pharmacy would amount to purpose-limited products.
220. Parthasarathy and Goddar, *supra* note 89, argue that particularly developing countries could be interested in encouraging the research in new uses of known products.

been interpreted as a balancing exercise.[221] TRIPS further acknowledges the alternative possibility of protecting plant varieties under the UPOV system (see above).

3. *Protection against 'Takings'*

Already the Paris Convention had limited circumstances under which a patent could be forfeited or a compulsory licence be issued (Article 5A). Article 31 TRIPS limits this further with a rather narrow catalogue of requirements to be fulfilled. Article 31 TRIPS must now be read together with Article 31*bis*, a provision inserted in suit of the Doha Declaration. Whether in the wake of the Covid health crisis further exceptions or limitations to the exercise of patent rights will be negotiated is anybody's guess.

4. *Freedom of Exploitation*

a) No distinction between local production and importation may be made, Article 28.1. This is a very problematic provision in view of the fact that the local production requirement has traditionally been an element of industrial policy (just as the forfeiture upon importation). The Paris Convention allowed such distinction, and some countries have maintained it (such as Brazil); a corresponding dispute settlement action was dropped for reasons unrelated to the merit of the case.[222]
b) Freedom to sell and license, Article 28.2. This may be interpreted to mean that no undue burden may be placed on licensing and selling patent rights. In the past, a good number of countries have put in place strict controls of licensing agreements (see above), yet the wording of the provision is rather vague as to what extent such controls can be exercised.
c) Just as established in the field of trade marks, patents give a right to exclude, not a right to use. For patents, there is no provision corresponding to Article 20 that would require justification for encumbrances of use.

IV. Exceptions and Limitations

1. *Limited Exceptions, Article 30*

Article 30 provides for exceptions to the rights conferred under Article 28 TRIPS and has been interpreted in the same way as other exceptions in the field of copyrights (Article 13) and trade marks (Article 17), namely by way of a three-step test. The burden of proof in these cases is especially problematic, see below.[223]

---

221. In EP T 1553/15 of 28 September 2020, the Board balanced the suffering of animals (significant) with the potential benefit to mankind (low, not least because there seemed to be many alternatives available).
222. DS 199 – Brazil: Measures affecting patent protection, raised by the US in May 2000: https://www.wto.org/english/tratop_e/dispu_e/cases_e/ds199_e.htm
223. M. Kennedy, 'The Burden of Proof and the "Three-Step Test" in Disputes under the TRIPS Agreement', 45 IIC (2014) 161.

This provision was interpreted in dispute **DS 114** – Canada: Patent Protection for Pharmaceutical Products.[224] The case concerned two features of Canada's patent law that the EU argued were not compliant with TRIPS. The first allowed the stockpiling of products still under patent protection with the aim of selling them once the patent expired:

> Patent Act, Section 55.2(2). 'It is not an infringement of a patent for any person who makes, constructs, uses or sells a patented invention in accordance with subsection (1) to make, construct or use the invention, during the applicable period provided for by the regulations, for the manufacture and storage of articles intended for sale after the date on which the term of the patent expires.'

The second feature provided that obtaining government approval for marketing a pharmaceutical was not considered an act of patent use.

The exclusive rights under Article 28.1 a) TRIPS are the following: 'making, using, offering for sale, selling, or importing for these purposes that product.'

While both cases were only argued under Article 30 (exceptions), it is even questionable whether the use of a substance for the purposes of clinical trials[225] or the stockpiling must necessarily be considered acts of infringement in the first place, see below.

In the case of clinical trials, the DS panel found this feature compliant with TRIPS.

In relation to the stockpiling provision, the Panel found this not to be compliant with Article 30 and reasoned as follows:

> '7.18...There was no dispute as to the meaning of Article 28.1 exclusive rights as they pertain to Section 55.2(2) of Canada's Patent Act. Canada acknowledged that the provisions of Section 55.2(2) permitting third parties to "make", "construct" or "use" the patented product during the term of the patent, without the patent owner's permission, would be a violation of Article 28.1 if not excused under Article 30 of the Agreement. The dispute on the claim of violation of Article 28.1 involved whether Section 55.2.(2) of the Patent Act complies with the conditions of Article 30
>
> ...
>
> 7.33 The Panel could not accept Canada's argument that the curtailment of the patent owner's legal rights is "limited" just so long as the exception preserves the exclusive right to sell to the ultimate consumer during the patent term. Implicit in the Canadian argument is a notion that the right to exclude sales to consumers during the patent term is the essential right conveyed by a patent, and that the rights to exclude "making" and "using" the patented product during the term of the patent are in some way secondary. The Panel does not find any support

224. WTO DS 114 of 13 March 2000 – 'Canada/Patent Protection of Pharmaceutical Products', http://www.wto.org/english/tratop_e/dispu_e/cases_e/ds114_e.htm.

225. Generic manufacturers in order to market the generic product have to obtain marketing approval and to this end use the substance for clinical trials. While the substance either as a generic or biosimilar necessarily falls within the ambit of the patent on the originator's drug, it is disputed whether trials with the purpose of establishing bio-equivalence can be interpreted as 'trial or research'.

> for creating such a hierarchy of patent rights within the TRIPS Agreement. If the right to exclude sales were all that really mattered, there would be no reason to add other rights to exclude "making" and "using". The fact that such rights were included in the TRIPS Agreement, as they are in most national patent laws, is strong evidence that they are considered a meaningful and independent part of the patent owner's rights.
>
> ...
>
> 7.35 In view of Canada's emphasis on preserving commercial benefits *before* the expiration of the patent, the Panel also considered whether the market advantage gained by the patent owner in the months after expiration of the patent could also be considered a purpose of the patent owner's rights to exclude "making" and "using" during the term of the patent. In both theory and practice, the Panel concluded that such additional market benefits were within the purpose of these rights. In theory, the rights of the patent owner are generally viewed as a right to prevent competitive commercial activity by others, and manufacturing for commercial sale is a quintessential competitive commercial activity, whose character is not altered by a mere delay in the commercial reward. In practical terms, it must be recognized that enforcement of the right to exclude "making" and "using" during the patent term will necessarily give all patent owners, for all products, a short period of extended market exclusivity after the patent expires. The repeated enactment of such exclusionary rights with knowledge of their universal market effects can only be understood as an affirmation of the purpose to produce those market effects.'

The decision appears problematic both on counts of procedure and substantive law.

On the side of procedure, the Panel separated the analysis of exclusive rights and the one on exceptions and found that the burden of proof for the latter lay on the defendant. This however mixed up exceptions to Members' obligations and exceptions to private rights:

> 'The ordinary WTO dispute settlement practice on burden of proof is suitable for disputes under TRIPS, but its application requires a proper interpretation of the function of each provision at issue. The GATT/WTO practice has been followed in TRIPS disputes but misconstrued in cases on exceptions to intellectual property rights, which has wrongly placed the burden of proof on respondents to demonstrate a TRIPS-consistent legal regime from the outset. What appears to be a similarity between obligations and exceptions in TRIPS and GATT masks the fundamental difference between TRIPS articles that jointly define a minimum standard and GATT articles that apply one at a time in the final determination.'[226]

In other words, a standard of protection and thus the overall scope of protection must be ascertained as a whole. It is not the defendant that needs to prove that the exception is TRIPS-compliant, but the plaintiff that needs to prove that the defendant's patent regime in a certain regard is non-compliant. A later decision took a more appropriate stance:

226. Kennedy, *supra* note 194, 147.

> 'In our view, the burden of proof in respect of a particular provision of the covered agreements cannot be understood in isolation from the overarching logic of that provision and the function which it is designed to serve. On the contrary, it is by having regard for the function and rationale of a particular provision that an adjudicator can, adequately, assess the manner in which the burden of proof should be allocated under that provision.'[227]

With respect to substantive issues, it is exactly the rationale of patent law that the Panel might have misconstrued. In accordance with the above explanations on the patent bargain, the patentee should enjoy a commercial monopoly for exploiting the patented invention during the period of protection. In the case at issue, it was clear that the stockpiling would not affect the exclusive marketing of the patent during its period of protection, but rather thereafter. The patentee would thereby be allowed to enjoy a de facto monopoly even after expiration of the patent, which is inconsistent with the patent bargain. Even if one were to construe the stockpiling rule as an exception, the Panel should have interpreted Article 30 TRIPS in light of the objectives in Articles 7 and 8, which it never did.

The decision is thereby one of the least convincing in the field of WTO/TRIPS.[228]

2. *Parallel Imports, Article 6*

Article 6 exempts regimes that relate to the parallel importation (importation outside the channels authorised by the rights owner) of protected goods from being made subject to a dispute. The importation of goods lawfully marketed abroad by the rights owner may thus be allowed (international exhaustion), or be allowed within certain customs unions (regional exhaustion) or not be allowed at all (national exhaustion). Whether all these regimes are compliant with GATT Article X (free movement of goods) is another matter that has been addressed above. It should be noted that Article 6 TRIPS does not mandate any specific regime a country takes on this issue, but rather exempts any rules in this regard from being made subject to a dispute resolution. From a doctrinal point of view, it is bizarre that an issue of fundamental importance to free trade should not be regulated (due to disagreements amongst Member States) and that international exhaustion not be made the default rule: 'It is astonishing that the WTO Agreement should still consider it compatible with fair world trade for consumers in different countries to be played off against each other'.[229]

227. WTO DT/DS 406/AB US-Clove Cigarettes of 24 April 2012, para 286.
228. C. Garrison, 'Exceptions to Patent Rights in Developing Countries', UNCTAD paper, August 2006, 42.
229. H. Ullrich, 'Technology Protection according to TRIPs', in Beier and Schricker (eds.), *From GATT to TRIPS* (Weinheim, 1996), 357, 385.

E. PATENT DEVELOPMENTS AFTER TRIPS

I. The Doha Declaration of 20 November 2001 and a Possible 'Covid Declaration' of 2021

a) The Doha Declaration (Declaration on the TRIPS Agreement and Public Health of 14 October 2001) concerns a movement within the ambit of the WTO that related to the interpretation of the TRIPS Agreement. In the Declaration, it was noted that countries had a right to define conditions of a national emergency and to issue compulsory licences in this regard. Further, that countries had a right to determine the appropriate exhaustion regime (Article 6 TRIPS). Finally, in order to allow countries without sufficient production capacities with respect to products they had issued a compulsory licence for to request the production by companies in third countries, Article 31*bis* was introduced into TRIPS in 2005 (in force since 23 January 2017) and allows for the export of patented products to countries that have declared a compulsory licence for a given patent yet have insufficient manufacturing capacity to domestically produce it. As was held in case **DS 435**, the Doha Declaration as such can also be used to interpret TRIPS:

> 'We recall that paragraph 5(a) of the Doha Declaration provides that, "[i]n applying the customary rules of interpretation of public international law, each provision of the TRIPS Agreement shall be read in the light of the object and purpose of the Agreement as expressed, in particular, in its objectives and principles." We agree with the Panel that paragraph 5(a) of the Doha Declaration reflects "the applicable rules of interpretation, which require a treaty interpreter to take account of the context and object and purpose of the treaty being interpreted". Accordingly, regardless of the legal status of the Doha Declaration, we see no error in the Panel's reliance on this general principle of treaty interpretation.
>
> 6.658. Furthermore, we note that the Panel referred to paragraph 5(a) of the Doha Declaration to confirm that "Articles 7 and 8 of the TRIPS Agreement provide important context for the interpretation of Article 20."'

b) Amidst the world-wide Covid pandemic, an initiative was launched by India and South Africa in October 2020 to agree on a 'Waiver From Certain Provisions Of The Trips Agreement For The Prevention, Containment And Treatment Of Covid-19',[230] an issue which at the time of writing is vividly discussed. The initiative was prompted by the unequal access of countries to vaccines against Covid 19, the fact that intellectual property rights over vaccines were an obstacle to the production of vaccines by anyone who so desired, and that Art. 31*bis* TRIPS (export waiver) was too cumbersome to be of use. The proponents of a waiver suggest a general license to use patents and clinical data related to the production of Covid vaccines for a period of three years.[231]

230. https://docs.wto.org/dol2fe/Pages/SS/directdoc.aspx?filename = q:/IP/C/W669.pdf&Open = True
231. South Africa Department of Trade and Industry, Presentation to the Joint DTIC and DIRCO PC on the TRIPS Waiver, 1 June 2021, https://www.tralac.org/documents/resources/covid-19/4333-presentation-to-the-joint-dtic-and-dirco-pc-on-the-trips-waiver-1-june-2021/file.html. 'TRIPS Pandora's box: a proposal made in vain?', 43 EIPR (2021) 349.

A waiver analogous to the provisions of Art. 31, 31*bis* TRIPS is no guarantee of supply. It is merely an instrument that prevents a patentee from enforcing its rights and therefore requires the existence of third parties able, willing and authorised to produce vaccines. Whether these exist is not very clear,[232] but a waiver mechanism for this or future pandemics could stimulate countries to set up domestic manufacturing capacity (see also below (5) in the context of access).

The waiver initiative has been criticised as unsuitable or counter-productive,[233] yet is interesting in that it highlights a number of shortcomings of the current IP system, not least its heavy focus on property protection and trade liberalisation while other fundamental interests such as health and environment take second place.[234] Another observation is that intellectual property rights are only part of the puzzle of how to ensure a sufficient supply of vaccines for all.[235]

(1) The need for a holistic view. One issue stressed by the proponents of a waiver is the fact that a mere focus on patent law (and the corresponding provisions on compulsory licensing) is insufficient. Rather, in order to be effective, the waiver must also encompass clinical data (Art. 39.3 TRIPS), potentially copyrighted material such as user manuals, etc., trade secrets and even trade marks (e.g. for cases where repackaging becomes necessary).[236] Of these, the initiative explicitly mentions patents and clinical data, which have become a sort of second-tier protection for pharmaceutical inventions (see chapter 7). Of the other rights involved, a waiver

---

232. D. Gervais, The TRIPS Waiver Debate, https://ipkitten.blogspot.com/2021/05/guest-post-trips-waiver-debate-why-and.html, points to the company Teva.
233. The critical responses to the proposal e.g.by the European Commission: Communication of the European Union, *Urgent Trade Policy Responses to the COVID-19 Crisis: Intellectual Property*, 4 June 2021 (IP/C/W/680), available at https://docs.wto.org/dol2fe/Pages/SS/directdoc.aspx?filename=q:/IP/C/W680.pdf&Open=True. Or the Max Planck Institute: https://www.ip.mpg.de/fileadmin/ipmpg/content/stellungnahmen/2021_05_25_Position_statement_Covid_IP_waiver.pdf may insufficiently take into account that the Waiver Initiative could simply be an expression of a broader necessity to interpret the TRIPS Agreement in a more holistic manner and to question the established view that WTO/TRIPS should be a self-contained rulebook. For a further discussion, *see also* chapter 2 of this book. Also: M. Montana, 'Covid-19 and India's and South Africa's attempt to reopen the TRIPS Pandora's box: a proposal made in vain?', 43 EIPR (2021) 349.
234. 'What is clear is that the access barriers highlighted by COVID-19...are not restricted to narrow specific contexts but are widespread. They are created by, and are a feature of, our existing IPR frameworks. More room is required for consideration of the public(s) interest(s), not just during a global health crisis, but on an ongoing basis. The "new normal" needs to advance equitable access to IPR protected subject matter for all public(s)': R. Walsh et al., 'Intellectual Property Rights and Access in Crisis', 52 IIC (2021), 379, 410.
235. One may even question whether IP issues are the most important ones in order to arrive at an optimum vaccination of the population: Contract issues and particularly the drafting of supply contracts have rightfully been mentioned as equally critical: P. Lambert, 'A slippery slope with contract no longer regal? Pandemic pressures on intellectual property freedom and the need for clarity as king', 43 EIPR (2021) 535.
236. And things do not even stop there. Patents may even relate to technologies far removed from vaccines, e.g. face masks to contain the spreading of the virus. Here, an Italian inventor came up with 3D printing technology for producing cheap masks. The inventor Mr. Fracassi stated that despite filing a patent for his 3D printed valve for such masks, he shared the CAD file for free, which was downloaded more than two million times all around the world: https://www.epo.org/news-events/events/conferences/2020/3d-printing/broadcast.html.

of trade secret protection looks difficult to enforce (although a waiver in regard of patents and clinical data may provide leverage in negotiation), and a waiver of trade mark rights in regard of repackaging, rebranding or de-branding may very well fall within the scope of TRIPS exceptions under Arts. 17, 20 as interpreted in the WTO *Australia/Plain Packaging* case.

Since Arts. 31, 31*bis* TRIPS only refer to patents, these provisions appear insufficient in the current situation. An instrument that prevents the right owner from enforcing ancillary rights such as those under Art. 39 TRIPS may thus be desirable and assist third parties with marketing capacity to obtain marketing approval themselves.

(2) The function of the patent system to provide information. There is a lamentable shortage of information in regard of which patents (or other intellectual property rights, for that matter) are actually related to the production of vaccines. One needs to bear in mind that different technologies are used (mRNA; Vector, etc.), and that the production of a vaccine may not only require the use of patents for the active ingredient, but also for products such as carriers, or for processes related to the production, etc. In this regard, one should also bear in mind that patent applications are laid open only after 18 months, so there may be relevant application that are not even known. Only once the above is clear can it be ascertained via public registers where patent applications and registrations actually exist; the situation may very well differ from country to country.

Furthermore, it is not clear whether the information contained in the relevant patents is actually sufficient to carry the invention. This may be due to an insufficient disclosure (see above), or to the fact that additional know how is necessary to carry out the best mode of the invention, or that the information relates to ancillary technology.

Whether the above speaks for or against a waiver is hard to say. It would be imperative for either the WTO, the WIPO or major national patent offices to assist in drawing up a list of relevant patents, and the national health authorities of relevant marketing authorisations and related clinical studies in order to obtain clarity as to which rights are may actually be covered by such waiver. Given the situation that production of a vaccine may require the use of a number of patents, a waiver related to all rights that have to be used to this end may assist in providing legal certainty. After all, the provisions of Arts. 31, 31*bis* TRIPS seem to envisage compulsory licences for specific rights rather than for determined purposes. A blanket waiver without specifying the rights has the advantage that also unforeseen issues could be covered (production of masks; storage of vaccines; parallel importation; user manuals etc.) that are hard to anticipate.

(3) The function of the patent system to provide incentives. One of the concerns related to conferring compulsory licences[237] is the diminished incentive for patentees to innovate. While a compulsory licence in the given case may serve the purpose of making the patented invention available (although via a third party), in the long run this may have a negative effect on innovation. In the case of Covid vaccines,

237. A very helpful comparative overview over the different types of compulsory licenses, namely those for the public interest, for food and medicine, is provided by Ladas, *supra* note 18, 430–34.

pharmaceutical companies will of course monitor closely whether in future pandemics innovative efforts will still be worth their while.[238] In this regard, two points deserve mention:

First, the involvement of governments in both the funding of research and in being the customer of the vaccines. The past months have shown not only the importance of good contract drafting in order to secure supply, but also highlighted that many of the vaccines now on the market have been developed with public funding, begging the question whether public funding should not entail certain rights over the research results or at least preferential access thereto.

Second, that the producers of the vaccine could make more profits if they had more production capacity: Profits are made not by artificial scarcity, but by sheer numbers. Even if more producers were on the market, profits would not diminish due to the sheer size of the market (everybody needs to get vaccinated). This is a reverse SEP/FRAND situation even in the presence of theoretically competing technologies because these are not mutually exclusive but interchangeable with the ultimate goal of complete market saturation in a short time. Due the limited production capacity, production of vaccines by third parties (and a corresponding licensing fee) would increase rather than diminish the profit of patentees.[239]

The first point above would speak in favour of developing national instruments to govern the rights over government funded research. The US has done with the 1980 Bayh-Dole Act, as contractual solutions have been found wanting. Such instrument may not necessarily require relinquishment of IP ownership, but rather obligations on access of the final products. According to Ellen t'Hoen, there is an 'urgent need for global collaboration, access conditions on public funding and upfront agreements on access and affordability with those engaged in the development of new medical technologies.'[240] In the case of Europe, harmonised access and ownership rules for publicly funded research look desirable also in order to avoid unequal supply amongst different countries.

The second point rather speaks in favour of a waiver offering FRAND licensing conditions, as 'the size of the market for COVID-19 vaccines and treatments is likely to be so large that companies will be able to recover vast sums even if there is a tiny return on each individual item.'[241]

(4) Exclusion and efficiency. Patent law carries the implicit assumption that exclusion is the best way of providing innovative efficiency. This is generally true where the patentee is willing and able to supply the market with the patented products. *Unwillingness* of the patentee to make the patented invention available may be considered a breach of the patent bargain (as argued by Josef Kohler, as above) and

238. E.g. the Max Planck Institute's statement, point 6: 'A waiver of IP protection would not serve the interest of the society, as it would create a disincentive for companies to pursue research in those [the one's related to the vaccines, but also in ancillary] areas.'

239. Also J. Pila argues that there is a FRAND situation in the case of essential medical technologies: J. Pila, 'Reflections on a post-pandemic European patent system', 42 EIPR (2020) 530, 533. That a low royalty rate can be compensated by market size is also acknowledged by Ladas, *supra* note 18, 433.

240. E. t'Hoen, 'Covid-19 and the comeback of compulsory licensing', *Medicines Law & Policy*, https://medicineslawandpolicy.org/2020/03/covid-19-and-the-come-back-of-compulsory-licensing/.

241. R. Walsh et al., 'Intellectual Property Rights and Access in Crisis', 52 IIC (2021), 379, 392.

lead to sanctions in the form a compulsory licence. In the Covid-19 case, companies rather appear *unable* to sufficiently supply the market. Exclusivity thereby leads to inefficiency without this being a breach of the patent bargain. Still, in a case of overwhelming public interest, also this would be a recognised situation in which compulsory licences could be granted. Seen from this angle, the requested waiver would not appear necessary, but not be harmful, either.

(5) The crucial aspect that links all the above issues is access. Access to information, to technology and to the final products. While only access to technology is a patent-related issue, the Covid 19 crisis has demonstrated that all these issues are interlinked and that a common answer must be found. It is undesirable that insufficient access to vaccines leads countries or even states or provinces to compete with each other in securing supply by export bans, interference in supply chains or else.[242] It is equally undesirable that producers of vaccines try to obscure their production or storage locations and play off countries against each other.[243] One answer to this has been a strengthening of domestic manufacturing capacities and the establishment of essential libraries. The draft US Emergency Medical Manufacturing Library Act would create 'a repository of FDA-approved plans and specs for improvised manufacturing of critical items during a crisis that could then be built by non-traditional makers in times of crisis. A publically available library of simple-to-build designs, already pre-approved through regulatory hurdles, can speed enlistment of these non-traditional manufacturers to support traditional suppliers in a time of national crisis.' [244]

A Covid Waiver in whatever form could not only provide incentives for improving domestic manufacturing capacity, but also provide leverage for improving the flow of information.

In addition, it could be an occasion for a reform of the domestic and international patent system so as to make it more conducive to the needs of society at large.

II. The WIPO Development Agenda

The WIPO Development Agenda was a joint proposal presented by Brazil and Argentina before the WIPO General Assembly in October 2004 calling for the establishment of a 'Development Agenda' for this United Nations body[245] in order to make WIPO change its ways. The Development Agenda and a corresponding 'Geneva Declaration on the Future of the World Intellectual Property Organization'[246] highlighted the following shortcomings of WIPO:

- 'The mantras that "more is better" or "that less is never good" are disingenuous and dangerous – and have greatly compromised the standing of WIPO, especially among experts in intellectual property policy'.

242. Lambert, *supra* note 235.
243. In March 2021, 24 million vaccine doses of Astra Zeneca were found in Southern Italy while the company had not made good its promises of delivery to EU countries.
244. Cited after Lambert, *supra* note 235.
245. WO/GA/31/11, 27 August 2004, in www.wipo.int/documents/en/document/govbody/wo_gb_ga/pdf/ wo_ga_31_11.pdf (accessed 11 October 2020). *See also* www.grain.org/rights/tripsplus.cfm?id = 60 (accessed 10 September 2020).
246. www.cptech.org/ip/wipo/genevadeclaration.html (accessed 14 October 2020).

- 'A "one size fits all" approach that embraces the highest levels of intellectual property protection for everyone leads to unjust and burdensome outcomes for countries that are struggling to meet the most basic needs of their citizens'.
- 'For generations WIPO has responded primarily to the narrow concerns of powerful publishers, pharmaceutical manufacturers, plant breeders and other commercial interests'.

Accordingly, WIPO should take a more balanced view taking into account the interests of developing countries, should fundamentally reform its technical assistance programmes, and

> 'for WIPO, to take appropriate measures to distinguish between user organizations representing the interests of IP right holders and NGOs representing the public interest'.[247]

Subsequently, 'the WIPO General Assembly agreed to further examine' the proposal initially presented by Brazil and Argentina in order 'to enhance the development dimension in all of WIPO's work'[248] and decided on the following:

> First: 'to convene inter-sessional intergovernmental meetings to examine the proposals originally submitted by Brazil and Argentina as well as additional proposals of member states'.
>
> Second: 'The meetings will (…) be open to WIPO accredited intergovernmental and non-governmental organizations (NGOs)'.
>
> Third: 'A report on these issues will be presented to the General Assembly in 2005 for its consideration. This decision also calls for the organization, in cooperation with other multilateral organizations, of an international seminar on intellectual property and development, open to all stakeholders, including NGOs, civil society and academia'.

Since the end of 2004, the debate on the bold proposal for a 'WIPO Development Agenda' has continued. Interesting publications have emerged,[249] but a change in the direction of WIPO has not become manifest.

---

247. Art. 71 United Nations Charter, and the Resolution 288 X (B) of the UN Economic and Social Council (ECOSOC), in which such organisations are defined as follows: 'Any international organization which is not established by inter-governmental agreement shall be considered as a non-governmental organization' (UN ECOSOC Official Records (II). Annex 8 (document E/43), p. 314). This opened the door to organisations not only of different fields – social, economic, cultural, educational, etc. – but also with very different proposals and goals on what to reach by such a consultative status. Thus, ICC and AIPPI have also been considered non-governmental organisations within the UN system, since both were granted consultative status by the UN Economic and Social Council (ECOSOC). Since 1946 the ICC has the highest level consultative status, i.e., the *general* one; the AIPPI was granted with the *special* consultative status in 1960. Brazil and Argentina wanted to limit the term 'NGO' to those organisations that actually work on behalf of public rather than private interests.
248. WIPO Press Release 387, of 5/10/2004, in www.wipo.int/edocs/prdocs/en/2004/wipo_pr_2004_397.html# (accessed 12 October 2020).
249. E.g. Netanel (ed.), *The Development Agenda* (Oxford, 2009); Andréa Koury Menescal, 'Changing WIPO's Ways?', 8 *Journal of World Intellectual Property* (2006) 761.

III. Patent Law Treaty

The Patent Law Treaty, done at Geneva on 1 June 2000, concerns a streamlining of formal patent procedures. It was originally signed by 59 States (and the EPO), and has been ratified by 42 contracting States, inter alia the US, Japan, Canada and the UK, but not yet by the EPO or Germany. Neither have China or Korea signed the Treaty.

IV. TRIPS Plus Provisions in Free Trade Agreements (FTAs)[250]

A number of bilateral and multilateral trade agreements have been concluded both by the US and the EU. Practically all these agreements also address intellectual property rights and go beyond TRIPS by limiting freedoms established by TRIPS (e.g. by limiting the lawfulness of parallel imports in the US Singapore FTA; by introducing a grace period of 12 months in the TPP/CPTPP), by extending protection periods (e.g. by increasing copyright protection to 70 years as in the EU, Japan, FTA), by introducing patent extension schemes, mandating a grace period[251] etc. Jens Hillebrand Pohl in the introductory chapter has highlighted the 'spaghettification' that has ensued from these TRIPS-plus obligations that, as was mentioned earlier, are asymmetrical in that the benefits of enhanced patent protection under Article 4 TRIPS must be made available to all applicants or patentees regardless of nationality, while the advantages (e.g. better market access) obtained in return will only be provided to one country. With an increasing number of FTAs signed between states, the overall effect may gravitate towards a general TRIPS-plus standard that then becomes the 'new normal'.

1. Data Protection in the Field of Pharmaceuticals

The issue of enhanced protection of test data is addressed in the contribution by Peter Yu (chapter 7) and not further elaborated here. While strictly speaking not an issue of patent law, it nonetheless has an equivalent effect in some cases.

2. Patent Extensions in General

Two grounds are addressed in FTAs as to why patents should be extended: either for marketing delays due to requirements of marketing approval (patent term extension or supplementary protection certificates), or for delays in the granting procedure. The former is available in many industrialised countries, be it as patent extension

250. C. Ho, *Access to Medicine in the Global Economy* (Oxford, 2011), 223–50; C. Keim, *TRIPS-plus Patentschutzklauseln in bilateralen Freihandelsabkommen der EU* (Heymanns, 2017).

251. Ho, *supra* note 250, lists the following: U.S.-Pan. Trade Promotion Agreement, U.S.-Pan, Art. 15.9(7), 28 June 2007, available at http://www.ustr.gov/trade-agreements/free-trade-agreements/panama-tpa/final-text; U.S.-Korea Free Trade Agreement, U.S.-Korea, Art. 18.8(7), 30 June 2007, available at http://www.ustr.gov/trade-agreements/free-trade-agreements/korus-ft a/final-text; United States-Morocco Free Trade Agreement, U.S.-Morocco, Art. 15.9(8), 15 June 2004, available at http://www.ustr.gov/trade-agreements/free-trade-agreements/morocco-ft a/ final-text.

schemes[252] or 'supplementary protection certificates'.[253] Patent extension schemes have given rise to numerous issues of interpretation and have not particularly brought legal certainty to the field,[254] in particular where the system does not stop at an extension but also drags issues of possible infringement by generic manufacturers into the equation ('patent linkage').[255]

Extension schemes are provided in the following FTAs: EU-Korea (Article 10.35), five years; EU-Singapore, Article 11.31, five years; EU-ANDEAN, Article 230, extension optional; EU-Vietnam IP Chapter, Article 8.3, two years. US Agreements KORUS and US-CAFTA-DR do not specify a period of extension, but require an extension both in cases of delays in the grant and in delays for marketing approval: KORUS four years from the date of application, US-CAFTA-DR five years. No period is specified that would qualify as an unreasonable delay in marketing approval.

Extension schemes for delays encountered in the examination phase are provided for example in Article 18.48 TPP, not in force.[256] They are problematic given the evidence that delays are often not the fault of the patent offices but tactical choices of the applicant, see above.

3. *Obligation to Protect New Uses*

As has been mentioned above, TRIPS does not define what should be understood as inventive step and consequently allows for an interpretation whereby new uses of known substances (in particular first, second and further medical uses) are not considered novel or inventive. The same goes for dosage regimes, etc.

A number of FTAs now require the protection of further medical uses of known substances, for example Article 20 F.1 (2) of the USMCA (not yet in force): 'Subject to paragraphs 3 and 4 and consistent with paragraph 1, each Party confirms that patents are available for inventions claimed as at least one of the following: new uses of a known product, new methods of using a known product, or new processes of using a known product.'

---

252. Introduced (in the US) under the Drug Price Competition and Patent Restauration Act 1984, 35 USC § 156; Japan secs. 67(2) etc. Patent Act introduced in 1987 (extension up to five years).
253. EU Council Regulation No. 1768/92 of 18 June 1992, now EC Regulation No. 469/2009 (extension up to five years, maximum time of exclusivity 15 years).
254. According to Robin Jacob, a 'chaotic system': Jacob, *supra* note 168, 98, 100.
255. Originally devised in the US, but now exported via free trade agreements, e.g. the US-China Economic and Trade Agreement of 15 January 2020 that led to a change in Chinese domestic law on this issue. Ho, *supra* note 250, further lists: U.S.-Singapore FTA, art. 16.8(4)(c); U.S.-Chile FTA, art. 17.10(2)(b); CAFTA, art. 15.10(3); U.S.-Australia FTA, art. 17.10(5); U.S.-Morocco FTA, art. 15.10(4).
256. Ho, *supra* note 250, lists the following: U.S.-Jordan Free Trade Agreement, U.S.-Jordan, Art. 4(23), 24 October 2000, 41 I.L.M. 63 , available at http://www.ustr.gov/trade-agreements/free-trade-agreements/jordan-ft a/final-text (extension for regulatory delay only); U.S.-Singapore FTA, Arts. 16.7(7), 18.8(4)(a) (extension for patent or regulatory delay); U.S.-Chile Free Trade Agreement, Arts. 17.9(6), 17.10(20(a)), 6 June 2003, available at http://www.ustr.gov/trade-agreements/free-tradeagreements/chile-ft a/final-text (extension for patent or regulatory delay); U.S.-Austl. FTA, Arts. 17.9(8), 17.10(4) (extension for patent or regulatory delay); U.S.-Morocco FTA, Arts. 15.9(7), 15.10(3) (extension for patent or regulatory delay).

4. *Restriction of Parallel Imports*

Article 6 TRIPS leaves the regulation of parallel imports to a Member's discretion. The Doha Declaration reinforces this. Some FTAs oblige Members to restrict the parallel importation, however. One example is the US-Singapore FTA that obliges Singapore to restrict the parallel importation of pharmaceuticals. The irony is that after the US Supreme Court decision (above), it is the US that falls foul of this obligation.

5. *Investor-State Dispute Settlement (ISDS) Mechanisms*

Giving investors a right to sue a State for alleged expropriation is a typical mechanism provided in FTAs.[257] Also issues of IP have been addressed in the context of this type of litigation, for example concerning trade marks in the case brought by Philipp Morris against Uruguay (plain packaging), and in the field of patents in the case brought by Eli Lilly against Canada (standard of enabling disclosure), see above. ISDS is a toxic form of enforcement devoid of democratic legitimacy that has contributed nothing to the development of intellectual property law, has a chilling effect on domestic policy[258] and more often than not annihilates domestic efforts in the field of health

257. An overview over this form of treaty enforcement is provided by C. Heath and A. Kamperman Sanders, 'Investor-State Dispute Settlement (ISDS) in Intellectual Property and Beyond', in Heath and Kamperman Sanders (eds.), *Intellectual Property and International Dispute Resolution* (Kluwer Law, 2019), 1–20. Claims of private investors against States enforcing laws to protect environmental or labour standards are not limited to developing countries, though. In 2009, Vattenfall sued Germany in ISDS proceedings against having to comply with environmental obligations with respect to a power plant in Hamburg. Germany settled and the additional environmental obligations were waived: https://isds.bilaterals.org/?case-study-vattenfall-v-germany-i&lang=en The pervasive nature of this kind of enforcement mechanism is enhanced by the financial resources private investors can and seem to be willing to spend. After the Achmea decision of the CJEU held the enforcement of ISDS decisions based on intra-EU agreements unlawful (C-284/16, decision of 6 March 2018), and 23 Member States in an agreement of 5 May 2020 (Agreement for the Termination of intra-EU Investment Treaties) decided to enact legislation that would no longer allow ISDS proceedings in investment agreements between EU Member States, no less than two constitutional complaints were raised in Germany by Achmea (the complaining investor in the Achmea case) because the arbitration decision was not honoured: 2 BvQ 97/20 (against German legislation implementing the agreement of 5 May 2020), dismissed as inadmissible on 5 February 2021 and 2 BvR 557/19 (alleging that the CJEU acted ultra vires when deciding the Achmea case; still pending). For the field of intellectual property rights, Suzy Frankel 'Interpreting the Overlap of International Investment and Intellectual Property Law', (2016) *Journal of International Economic Law* 1, at 5 notes: 'Investment tribunal arbitrators when making decisions (including the interpretation of the agreements at issue) are likely to focus on the function of IP as a set of property rights rather than as equally important parts of the international IP structure, which enables tailoring of those rights to reward innovation appropriately (rather than excessively) and to maintain regarding interests, such as when property rights need to be balanced with affordability and availability of medicines … [T]hat does not require and should not result in detaching the property aspects of IP from its other functions and objectives.'
258. Heath and Kamperman Sanders, *supra* note 257, and R. Cooper Dreyfuss, 'Investor-State Dispute Settlement as a constraint on Intellectual Property Lawmaking', in Anselm Kamperman Sanders and Anke Moerland (eds.), *Intellectual Property as a Complex Adaptive System* (Edward Elgar, 2021).

care, labour laws or environmental protection. A UN Report of 14 July 2015 presented by Alfred-Maurice de Zayas in this regard mentions the following:

> 'One of the most egregious ICSID arbitrations concerned the case by United States-based Occidental Petroleum against Ecuador concerning the termination of an oil production site in the Amazon, and resulting in an award of $1.76 billion to Occidental ($2.4 billion with interest), which Ecuador accused of multiple human rights violations and environmental destruction... One of the worst aspects of this case is that Ecuador was justified in terminating Occidental's permit under Ecuadorian law and the contract and still the investor–State dispute settlement tribunal penalised Ecuador'.[259]

In a volume dedicated to the lawsuits against plain packaging, Anselm Kamperman Sanders and myself found it 'appalling that private investors should be entitled to sue a state behind closed doors, before an ad hoc tribunal of three arbiters of doubtful independence and little idea of the finer points of IP, with no possibility of appeal and with potentially devastating consequences for the state in question. In other words, a state being held hostage and (if bad comes to worse) convicted by three blind men on a donkey.'[260]

F. FUTURE ISSUES

The foregoing has shown that a lot has been done to cast the current system in stone: to put intellectual property titles on the same footing as property rights, to require minimum levels of protection, to limit exceptions and to scare off the pursuit of public interest policies by ISDS enforcement structures. Yet a system on autopilot sits ill with a rapidly changing world. A system that has been conceived to provide incentives to innovation and thus address societal challenges should be calibrated to societal needs and be able to respond to demographical, technological, economic, climatic and sociological changes. The main challenge for the future is therefore to regenerate the patent system to the needs and changes of society. This can occur in various ways.

I. Rule Making

With the advent of WTO/TRIPS, domestic patent systems have become part of a different political equation. They no longer need to respond to their function of fostering domestic innovation, but of fostering domestic well-being in the context of international trade. Discontents of the patent system may thus be offset by advantages in other fields of trade. Imagine that under a hypothetical bilateral trade agreement between the EU and Britain, the UK may be obliged to grant patentees the right to prevent the importation of patented products even where marketed abroad by

259. www.citizen.org/documents/oxy-v-ecuador-memo.pdf". The report is available at: https://www.ohchr.org/EN/HRBodies/HRC/RegularSessions/Session30/_layouts/15/WopiFrame.aspx-?sourcedoc=/EN/HRBodies/HRC/RegularSessions/Session30/Documents/A_HRC_30_44_ENG.docx.
260. Heath and Kamperman Sanders, *supra* note 257, 1

the domestic patentee (national or regional exhaustion), yet in turn would obtain facilitated access of its banks to the European financial market. In order to access the overall economic impact, one should bear in mind the asymmetry that the rights conferred on the patentee would have to be granted to all patentees and not only those of EU countries, Article 4 TRIPS. As already the economic impact of limiting the regimes of international exhaustion cannot be economically verified, it is even less clear what these are, if any, under such a quid-quo-pro agreement. Rule-making of intellectual property laws in such a context therefore suffers from a significant asymmetry of representation and expertise, lack of transparency and democratic legitimacy.[261] Public interest is not sufficiently represented due to the secrecy of most negotiations and due to the fact that the interests the negotiating partners put on the table are mostly those of industrial players, defects that are often downplayed against alleged benefits.[262] This situation may not only lead to public concern and distrust,[263] but also to constitutional challenges.[264] The preferable way forward would thus seem to ensure transparency and due participation in the phase of negotiations. In addition, as a concrete follow-up to the WIPO Development Agenda, it might be worthwhile attempting to negotiate an agreement that sets maximum standards and

261. Jacob, *supra* note 168, 98–102: 'My thesis today is that we need to devise better ways of changing and advancing IP law. Lobbyists will always have their place and always have. But it should not be enough for them to get what they want simply by being the ones that shout louder than anyone else... Neither the public interest nor those who could provide more objective assessments and contributions play a sufficient part, as they would if they were appointed to a commission supported by a competent secretariat.'

262. The problem is perhaps that neither claim is entirely verifiable, yet the lack of empirical evidence that trade liberalisation has significantly increased GDP has been highlighted by Joseph Stiglitz and Andrew Charlton, *Fair Trade for All: How Trade can Promote Development* (Oxford University Press, 2005), p. 34.

With respect to the EU-Canada FTA (CETA), the following has been stated: 'Proponents of the comprehensive economic and trade agreement (CETA) emphasize its prospective economic benefits, with economic growth increasing due to rising trade volumes and investment... However, all these quantitative projections stem from the same trade model, which assumes full employment and neutral (if not constant) income distribution in all countries, excluding from the outset any of the major risks of deeper liberalization. This lack of intellectual diversity and of realism shrouding the debate around CETA's alleged economic benefits calls for an alternative assessment grounded in more realistic modeling premises. At a minimum, this shows that official studies do not offer a solid basis for an informed decision on CETA.' Pierre Kohler and Servaas Storm, 'CETA without blinders: how cutting "trade costs and more" will cause unemployment, inequality, and welfare losses', 4 *International Journal of Political Economy* (2016). Similar claims are made with respect to the alleged losses that counterfeiting causes. X. Seuba (*The Global Regime for the Enforcement of Intellectual Property Rights* (Cambridge, 2017)) writes: 'estimates concerning the scale of infringement, the value of intellectual property or the impact of intellectual property infringement have been elaborated by private stakeholders who often have a direct interest in the object of analysis [p. 67] ... [in fact] producing a reliable evaluation of the general effects of intellectual property infringement is still out of reach [p. 69]'.

263. The ACTA ratification had to be aborted due to strong reservations of the European Parliament and public resistance regarding both its contents and the way the agreement was negotiated: Duncan Matthews and Petra Zikovska, 'The Rise and Fall of the Anti-Counterfeiting Trade Agreement (ACTA)', 44 IIC (2013) 626.

264. E.g. the constitutional challenge in Germany, currently pending before the Constitutional Court (2 BvE 4/16) concerning the Canadian EU Free Trade Agreement CETA.

compulsory limits to patent protection so as to avoid an ever-increasing broadening without scientific evidence of its purported benefits: if limits to patent rights had been fought as hard as limits to the international protection of geographical indications (see chapter 5 by Natale Rampazzo in this book), the system would certainly look different.

The current Covid crisis is also a timely reminder that certainly on a national, if not international level, new rules (or rules in the first place) should be negotiated for the ownership of and access to the results of research undertaken with public funds.

II. Enforcement

In the context of both rule-making and enforcement, more effort will have to be made to balance intellectual property rights with other societal concerns. In the context of domestic legislation, this is normally ensured by a proper interpretation of the constitution.[265] However, this is more difficult where agreements are entered into that do not require or allow such a balancing exercise, and where specific tribunals decide about compliance without taking a country's other obligations, such as under UN Agreements, into account.[266] This is even more pronounced in the context of ISDS tribunals that lack any democratic legitimacy.

265. E. g. in Petition 409/09 before the High Court of Kenya (*Ochieng et al. v. Attorney General*) (2012), provisions of intellectual property law were interpreted in the light of fundamental rights such as life, health and human dignity: https://www.escr-net.org/sites/default/files/Judgment-Petition-No-409-of-2009%20Anti%20counterfeit%20case.pdf.
266. This is a complex issue, *see* chapter 2. Yet a WTO Tribunal or an investor-state dispute panel would normally not take into account obligations extraneous to the agreement in the context of which they have been established, even in cases where all parties are bound by such other obligations (e.g. the Universal Declaration of Human Rights 1948): *See* Joos Pauwellyn, 'The Interplay between the WTO Treaty and other international legal instruments and tribunals', in C.-E. Côté, V. Guèvremont, R. Ouellet (eds.), *Proceedings of the Québec City Conference on the WTO at 20*, held in September 2015 (Presses de l'Université de Laval, 2018). With such a narrow interpretative approach, the tribunal may avoid the criticism of 'judicial activism', yet not come up to the social responsibilities that all parties to the dispute have subscribed to and may not do justice to Art. 31(3) c) Vienna Convention on the Interpretation of Treaties. This is also problematic because internationally recognised rules of international public law take precedence over international agreements, Art. 53 Vienna Convention (critical as to whether fundamental rights have reached the status of ius cogens to such a degree that they may be invoked against intellectual property rights infringement: Xavier Seuba, *The Global Regime for the Enforcement of Intellectual Property Rights* (2017), 59–61 who however also advocates a precedence of human rights treaties over IP related treaties. Yet we may be at the threshold where environmental protection and sustainable development not only becomes an obligation states can be held accountable for, but a recognised rule of international law that can be invoked against companies (The Hague District Court, decision of 26 May 2021 in re Dutch Shell, https://uitspraken.rechtspraak.nl/inziendocument?id=ECLI:NL:RBDHA:2021:5339) and states (German Federal Supreme Court, decision of 24 March 2021, 1 BvR 2656/18, https://www.bundesverfassungsgericht.de/SharedDocs/Entscheidungen/DE/2021/03/rs20210324_1bvr265618.html). Prior to the Doha Declaration, the WTO Panels even paid little tribute to the object and purpose of the agreement, *see* e.g. the narrow reading of obligations in the DS case against Canada (Susy Frankel, 'The interpretation of international intellectual property instruments in national, regional and international courts and tribunals', in Geiger, Nard and Seuba, *Intellectual Property and the Judiciary* (Edward Elgar, 2018), 441, 449). A future solution

III. Patent Specific Issues

a) The above two points were of a general nature, but not only related to issues of intellectual property. Particularly for patent law, one should not be oblivious to the fact that historically there were instances where the patent system escaped abolition only by a whisker.[267] The message of these anti-patent waves should be this: a legal system that no longer serves the purpose for which it was created in the short term creates discontent and in the long term faces extinction.

The doctrinal discussion on whether intellectual property should be put on the same footing as real property obscures the fact that intellectual property rights are not an end in itself, but a means to foster certain societal needs.[268] In this context, it is as legitimate for a country to protect the health of its citizens, the environment, etc., as it is to stimulate and protect innovation by way of patents. Their creation, maintenance, protection, limitation, enforcement, revocation and lapse should not be regarded through the lens of property, but through the lens of due process, foreseeability, transparency, legitimacy of expectations and balancing of interests.

b) In particular, issues of patentability should be more closely linked to emerging societal needs and in addition will need to be evaluated due to new technologies.

The first issue concerns industrial policy and the question of whether a patent system should provide incentives for any kind of innovation, or whether in certain fields of technology, incentives should no longer be provided because society actively discourages their use. Pursuing this would mean to give more room to *ordre public* considerations in the field of patents, not unlike what has been suggested in international trade law under Article XX a) GATT. In this regard, the discussion on the Covid-19 Waiver has shown the need for a discussion on the public benefits of the patent system and greater legislative intervention. To reflect public interest in general.

The second issue concerns the challenges to patent law brought about by artificial intelligence.[269] Self-learning and self-inventing machines may require us to

---

could be to oblige the contracting parties to comply with certain environmental or labour standards, as has been advocated for the EU-Mercosur agreement that (at the time of writing) looks likely to fail because such standards have not been clearly written into the agreement. Perhaps the 2018 WTO decisions DS 435, 441, 458 and 467 on the lawfulness of Australia's tobacco legislation may mark the start of a different approach in this regard. One may equally pursue a broader interpretation of the exception to 'public morals' offered in GATT Art. XX(a), which has the advantage that one could rely on a provision within the WTO context.

267. Fritz Machlup and Edith Penrose 'The Patent Controversy in the Nineteenth Century', 10(1) *Journal of Economic History* (1950), 1–29.

268. 'Patents are rights to prohibit use of protected material (inventions). If seen as a form of property, they may benefit from fundamental or human rights to the protection of private property. This is so even in the absence of a viable market. To that extent, they are, like other property rights, rights to exclude. Yet, the denial of access to patented pharmaceuticals to patients who cannot afford them, when they, or their government, could afford those products at a generic rate (that is, without the patent rent) is sometimes seen as an affront to another human right, namely the right to health.' D. Gervais, 'Lilly v. Canada, Lessons for International Intellectual Property Law and Policy', in Christopher Heath and Anselm Kamperman Sanders, *Intellectual Property and International Dispute Resolution* (Kluwer, 2019), 169, 183.

269. For an in-depth analysis of this topic, *see* K. Bengi and C. Heath, 'Patents and AI Inventions' in Heath et al., *supra* note 24, 127–61.

re-define the 'person skilled in the art', may challenge the 'could-would approach' used for determining inventive step and will require an answer to the question of whether machines, based on the use of unforeseeable algorithms, may themselves come up with patentable inventions and qualify as inventors. Particularly the latter is a fundamental question: while the first patent systems revolved around the 'first and true inventor', modern patent systems appear to attach less importance to the person of the inventor. Under the European Patent Convention, the identity of the inventor is not verified, and an applicant who claims to be the successor in title only has to state how the title was obtained. One may thus conclude that modern patent systems attach more importance to the subject matter of an invention than to its creator.[270]

It is also questionable whether well-established doctrines such as the 'could-would approach' that is used by the European Patent Office[271] in order to determine inventive step will still be appropriate when self-learning algorithms can easily combine prior art documents of unrelated fields and suggest solutions based on such combinations. Also the person skilled in the art may have to be redefined when being assisted by self-learning algorithms, in other words the threshold for considering a solution inventive may rise.

And finally, one may wonder how the use of artificial intelligence will transform the way patent offices work and provide their services, and correspondingly, how the tasks of examiners will change.

270. It is of course legitimate to ask whether a machine inventor would require an incentive by way of a reward in order to come up with more inventions: machine inventors have no families to feed. But not unlike the case of under-age inventors whose rewards are administered by their parents, the rewards of machine-made inventions may go the owners of the machine and thereby create an incentive to improve such machines, or their algorithms. Also in this case, the incentive provided by the patent system is not lost. On the other hand, allocating inventorship to algorithms may have far-reaching implications for the rules on remunerating employed inventors and not least for this reason it may appear preferable to have the issue decided by legislation. The English High Court in *Thaler v. Comptroller of Patents* ([2020] EWHC 2412 (Pat)) refused an application for an invention conceived by a programme not least because the applicant Mr. Thaler could not demonstrate how he had obtained the invention from the inventor (as a machine cannot transfer property). Two cases in this regard are currently pending before the EPO Boards of Appeal, cases J 8/20 and J 9/20 related to applications EP 18 275 163 and EP 18 275 174.

271. EP T 2/83 of 15 March 1984: 'In a case where the applicant had supplemented a known layered tablet by the provision of a barrier between the layers, the Board held that the proper question to be asked was not whether the skilled man could have provided the barrier but whether he would have done so in expectation of some improvement or advantage.'

CHAPTER 7
TRIPS in the Field of Test Data Protection

*Peter K. Yu**

A. INTRODUCTION

On 15 April 1994, the Agreement on Trade-Related Aspects of Intellectual Property Rights (TRIPS Agreement) was adopted in Marrakesh. For the past 25 years, this Agreement has established for both developed and developing countries the international minimum standards for the protection and enforcement of intellectual property rights. One area in which such standards were deficient, if not non-existent, before the founding of the World Trade Organization (WTO) concerns the protections for undisclosed test or other data for pharmaceutical and agrochemical products. Article 39.3 of the TRIPS Agreement became the first multilateral provision in the field of test data protection.

As Jayashree Watal, a former TRIPS negotiator for India, recounted, the protection of undisclosed information 'has never been the subject of any multilateral agreement' until the adoption of the TRIPS Agreement.[1] Daniel Gervais concurred: '[The field] of what in various national laws may be called "trade secrets", "confidential information" or the like … is not regulated in multilateral conventions, apart from the general obligations in respect of unfair competition found in art.10*bis* of the Paris Convention.'[2] Carlos Correa went even further to describe the protection

* Copyright 2021 Peter K. Yu. Regents Professor of Law and Communication and Director, Center for Law and Intellectual Property, Texas A&M University. This chapter draws on research the author conducted for earlier articles in the *Florida State University Law Review*, the *Texas A&M Journal of Property Law* and the *Texas A&M Law Review Arguendo*.

1. Jayashree Watal, *Intellectual Property Rights in the WTO and Developing Countries* (Kluwer Law International, The Hague, 2001), 4.
2. Daniel Gervais, *The TRIPS Agreement: Drafting History and Analysis*, 3rd ed. (Sweet and Maxwell, London, 2008), 424.

of undisclosed test or other data as 'one of the most significant innovations brought about by the TRIPS Agreement'.[3]

This chapter takes stock of the evolution of international standards for protecting undisclosed test or other data for pharmaceutical, agrochemical and, more recently, biological products. Focusing on Article 39.3 of the TRIPS Agreement, the chapter begins by recapturing the origins and normative contents of this provision. It then identifies several unresolved issues surrounding the provision as well as the related concerns for developing countries. The chapter concludes by outlining three distinct sets of challenges that will have serious ramifications for the future development of international standards in the field of test data protection.

B. THE PAST

The TRIPS negotiations began at the Ministerial Conference of the General Agreement on Tariffs and Trade in Punta del Este, Uruguay in September 1986. As recounted in the *Resource Book on TRIPS and Development*, compiled by the United Nations Conference on Trade and Development and the International Centre on Trade and Sustainable Development:

> '[A]t the time of TRIPS negotiations there were significant differences in comparative law with regard to the scope and modalities of protection of undisclosed information of commercial value. … Differences in pre-existing comparative law were even greater with regard to test data relating to pharmaceuticals and agrochemicals. Only a few countries had developed rules on the matter before the negotiation of TRIPS. Thus, the USA introduced a regulatory data protection regime for pesticides in 1972, and in 1984 adopted regulatory exclusivity provisions for medicines. The latter provided for five years of exclusivity for new chemical entities, and three years for data filed in support of authorizations based on new clinical research relating to chemical entities which have already been approved for therapeutic use. The EU member states provided exclusivity protection for the data filed in support of marketing authorization for pharmaceuticals since 1987.'[4]

The need for protections for test or other data arises when regulatory authorities require pharmaceutical and agrochemical companies to submit these data for the marketing approval of their products. While the submitted data are confidential, proprietary and highly valuable, the authorities need them to evaluate the products' safety and efficacy. Should the pharmaceutical and agrochemical companies not submit the requested data, they will be unable to secure the needed approval to market their products. Should they comply with the request, however, their competitors may take unfair commercial advantage of their proprietary data. These companies understandably demand greater protections for the undisclosed test or other data they submit to regulatory authorities.

3. Carlos M. Correa, *Trade Related Aspects of Intellectual Property Rights: A Commentary on the TRIPS Agreement* (2nd edn., Oxford University Press, Oxford, 2020), 351.
4. UNCTAD–ICTSD Project on Intellectual Property Rights and Sustainable Development, *Resource Book on TRIPS and Development* (Cambridge University Press, Cambridge, 2005), 522.

I. The Provision

To provide protections for test or other data for pharmaceutical and agrochemical products,[5] Article 39.1 states that, '[i]n the course of ensuring effective protection against unfair competition as provided in Article 10*bis* of the Paris Convention (1967), Members shall protect ... data submitted to governments or governmental agencies in accordance with paragraph 3'. Article 39.3 further provides:

> 'Members, when requiring, as a condition of approving the marketing of pharmaceutical or of agricultural chemical products which utilize new chemical entities, the submission of undisclosed test or other data, the origination of which involves a considerable effort, shall protect such data against unfair commercial use. In addition, Members shall protect such data against disclosure, except where necessary to protect the public, or unless steps are taken to ensure that the data are protected against unfair commercial use.'

The first sentence of Article 39.3 focuses on the obligation to protect 'against unfair commercial use'. Based on the provision's ordinary meaning, this obligation will not arise unless five conditions have been met.[6] First, to warrant protection, the test or other data at issue must be undisclosed – or, more properly worded, undisclosed to the public at the time of submission.[7] Secondly, the protection is available to data for pharmaceutical or agrochemical products only. Thirdly, the products involved have to 'utilize new chemical entities' – a term that TRIPS negotiators have intentionally left undefined[8] but that has since sparked controversy in the developing world.[9] Fourthly, the test data have to be submitted 'as a condition of approving the marketing of' these products, not on a voluntary basis.[10] Finally, the origination of the protected data has to 'involve[] a considerable effort', somewhat akin to the requirement of 'a substantial investment' in Article 7(1) of the EU Database Directive.

The second sentence of Article 39.3 of the TRIPS Agreement focuses on the obligation to protect against the disclosure of submitted test or other data. This obligation resembles the one laid down in the North American Free Trade Agreement (NAFTA), which was adopted in December 1992 before the TRIPS Agreement. Article

5. As Carlos Correa defined: 'Test data is the information generated to demonstrate the efficacy and safety of new chemical entities for use as pharmaceuticals or agrochemicals. In the case of pharmaceuticals, such data include the results of pre-clinical studies (pharmacodynamic, pharmacokinetic, and toxicological tests) and of phases 1 to 3 of clinical studies.' Correa, *supra* note 3, at 359. Unlike 'test data', 'other data' as used in Article 39.3 does not have any standard definition. As Professor Correa continued, '"other" data may include ... manufacturing, conservation, and packaging methods and conditions, but only to the extent that it is *necessary* to submit them in order to obtain marketing approval'. *Ibid.* at 362.
6. Peter K. Yu, 'Data Exclusivities and the Limits to TRIPS Harmonization', 46 *Florida State University Law Review* (2019) 641, 649–50.
7. G. Lee Skillington and Eric M. Solovy, 'The Protection of Test and Other Data Required by Article 39.3 of the TRIPS Agreement', 24 *Northwestern Journal of International Law and Business* (2003) 1, 35.
8. Correa, *supra* note 3, at 363.
9. Srividhya Ragavan, 'Data Exclusivity: A Tool to Sustain Market Monopoly', 8 *Jindal Global Law Review* (2017) 241, 252–55.
10. Correa, *supra* note 3, at 361.

1711.6 of NAFTA states that 'no person other than the person that submitted them may, without the latter's permission, rely on such data in support of an application for product approval during a reasonable period of time after their submission'. If the submitted data are to be disclosed, Article 39.3 of the TRIPS Agreement requires WTO members to meet one of two conditions. First, the disclosure is permitted if it is 'necessary to protect the public'. This necessity requirement is similar to what is found in Article XX of the General Agreement on Tariffs and Trade. Secondly, WTO members may disclose the submitted data if 'steps [have been] taken to ensure that the data are protected against unfair commercial use'. These protective steps help fulfil the primary objective of the first sentence of Article 39.3.

Finally, for either the first or second sentence of Article 39.3, the TRIPS Agreement does not lay down any standard regarding the duration of protection. The lack of such standard stands in sharp contrast to the language found in NAFTA and other TRIPS-plus bilateral, regional and plurilateral agreements. Article 1711.6 of NAFTA explicitly states:

> '[A] reasonable period shall normally mean not less than five years from the date on which the Party granted approval to the person that produced the data for approval to market its product, taking account of the nature of the data and the person's efforts and expenditures in producing them.'

Although the 1990 Brussels draft of the TRIPS Agreement included a NAFTA-like standard, that standard was later removed as a compromise between developed and developing countries.[11] In addition, commentators have criticised the arbitrariness of the five-year period. As Aaron Fellmeth observed:

> 'Five years of data exclusivity may not be enough to compensate the drug developer adequately for products requiring the most complex and extensive testing (which is why most European states grant ten years of exclusivity), while five years may be excessive for the straightforward testing associated with the most profitable drugs (which means that the harm caused by the European standard is doubly egregious in those situations). A predetermined, uniform monopoly period is a very blunt policy instrument because it treats all drug marketing approval efforts alike when, in fact, they may vary significantly.'[12]

II. WTO Complaints

Since the adoption of the TRIPS Agreement, the WTO Dispute Settlement Body has handled only two Article 39.3 complaints, which related to each other and involved the same parties. On 6 May 1999, the United States filed a complaint against Argentina,[13]

---

11. UNCTAD-ICTSD Project on Intellectual Property Rights and Sustainable Development, *supra* note 4, at 525.
12. Aaron Xavier Fellmeth, 'Secrecy, Monopoly, and Access to Pharmaceuticals in International Trade Law: Protection of Marketing Approval Data under the TRIPs Agreement', 45 *Harvard International Law Journal* (2004)443, 478–79.
13. World Trade Organization, 'Argentina – Patent Protection for Pharmaceuticals and Test Data Protection for Agricultural Chemicals: Request for Consultations by the United States' (WT/DS171/1, 1999).

following the Clinton Administration's suspension of half of Argentina's trade benefits under the US Generalized System of Preferences in April 1997.[14] In addition to alleging inadequate protection of pharmaceutical products under the patent system or through exclusive marketing rights, the WTO complaint claimed that Argentina had violated the TRIPS Agreement by repealing a regulation that had provided ten years of protection for undisclosed test or other data for agrochemical products.

On 30 May 2000, slightly more than a year later, the United States filed a second complaint against Argentina alleging a lack of adequate protection of undisclosed test or other data for pharmaceutical and agrochemical products.[15] In addition to select patent provisions in Argentina, the United States challenged Argentine laws and regulations that covered such protection – namely, Law 24.766, Regulation 440/98 and other related measures. The complaint noted Argentina's 'fail[ure] to protect against unfair commercial use of undisclosed test or other data, submitted as a requirement for market approval of pharmaceutical or agricultural chemical products'.

From a standpoint of TRIPS interpretation, this complaint was highly important, as it could have resulted in the issuance of a WTO panel report – and, perhaps, even a follow-up Appellate Body report. Nevertheless, the two parties did not give the WTO Dispute Settlement Body an opportunity to weigh in on the international obligations under Article 39.3 of the TRIPS Agreement. They settled the dispute on 31 May 2002, without the complainant requesting the establishment of a WTO panel. Although the parties reached mutually agreed upon solutions on a long list of patent issues, they did not resolve their disagreements over test data protection.[16] Instead, the notification of settlement stated that both parties 'agreed that differences in interpretations shall be solved under the [Dispute Settlement Understanding] rules' and that Argentina further 'agree[d] to submit to the National Congress within one year an amendment to Argentinean law' should the WTO Dispute Settlement Body find the law inconsistent with Article 39.3 of the TRIPS Agreement. Because the United States did not take any further action, the WTO Dispute Settlement Body has yet to provide an official interpretation of Article 39.3.

C. THE PRESENT

As in other areas of intellectual property law examined in this volume, Article 39.3 of the TRIPS Agreement has been the product of difficult compromise between developed and developing countries during the TRIPS negotiations. As Professor Correa recounted:

> '[I]n [their] starting positions in the TRIPS negotiations, developing countries rejected any form of protection for know-how under the Agreement. At the other extreme, proposals were made by some industrialized countries in order to

14. Fellmeth, *supra* note 12, at 457.
15. World Trade Organization, 'Argentina – Certain Measures on the Protection of Patents and Test Data: Request for Consultations by the United States' (WT/DS196/1, 2000).
16. World Trade Organization, 'Argentina – Patent Protection for Pharmaceuticals and Test Data Protection for Agricultural Chemicals and Argentina – Certain Measures on the Protection of Patents and Test Data: Notification of Mutually Agreed Solution' (WT/DS171/3, WT/DS196/4, 2002).

> establish a minimum period of exclusive protection (five years for pharmaceuticals) for the protection of the tests and data submitted for marketing approval.'[17]

The disagreement between these two groups of countries is easy to understand. For countries with a strong pharmaceutical or agrochemical industry, greater protection of undisclosed test or other data is important because it would provide additional incentives for research and development while increasing the countries' competitive and comparative advantage.[18] For countries without such an industry, however, greater protection of undisclosed test or other data could be highly detrimental. In the case of pharmaceutical products, for instance, greater protection of undisclosed test or other data would increase healthcare costs, reduce access to medicines and delay market entry of generic drugs.[19] Such protection would not only jeopardise public health[20] – at both the domestic and global levels – but it would also raise ethical questions about unnecessary or duplicative testing.[21]

I. Data Reliance

During the TRIPS negotiations, two areas were highly contested, and they eventually paved the way for the establishment of new international standards through TRIPS-plus bilateral, regional and plurilateral agreements. The first area concerns whether regulatory authorities can rely on the originator's previously submitted test or other data when determining whether to grant marketing approval of follow-on pharmaceutical and agrochemical products.[22] Such reliance occurs when these authorities approve new products based on evidence provided by bioequivalence studies.[23] To prevent follow-on developers from free riding on the originator's submitted data, Article 1711.6 of NAFTA creates a separate obligation for prohibiting data reliance:

> 'Each Party shall provide that for data … that are submitted to the Party after the date of entry into force of this Agreement, no person other than the person that submitted them may, without the latter's permission, rely on such data in support of an application for product approval during a reasonable period of time after their submission. For this purpose, a reasonable period shall normally

17. Correa, *supra* note 3, at 360.
18. Carlos María Correa, 'Unfair Competition under the TRIPS Agreement: Protection of Data Submitted for the Registration of Pharmaceuticals', 3 *Chicago Journal of International Law* (2002) 69, 69; Skillington and Solovy, *supra* note 7, at 12–15; Peter K. Yu, 'The Political Economy of Data Protection', 84 *Chicago-Kent Law Review* (2010) 777, 784.
19. Yu, *supra* note 18, at 785.
20. Fellmeth, *supra* note 12, at 475–76; Christine D. Galbraith, 'Dying to Know: A Demand for Genuine Public Access to Clinical Trial Results Data', 78 *Mississippi Law Journal* (2009) 705, 721–35; Yu, *supra* note 18, at 786.
21. Nuno Pires de Carvalho, *The TRIPS Regime of Patent Rights*, 3rd ed. (Alphen aan den Rijn: Kluwer Law International, 2010), 605; Carlos M. Correa, 'Protecting Test Data for Pharmaceutical and Agrochemical Products under Free Trade Agreements', in Pedro Roffe, Geoff Tansey and David Vivas-Eugui (eds.), *Negotiating Health: Intellectual Property and Access to Medicines* (Earthscan, London 2006), 93; Fellmeth, *supra* note 12, at 474.
22. Correa, *supra* note 3, at 365; Gervais, *supra* note 2, at 428.
23. Joan Rovira, 'Creating and Promoting Domestic Drug Manufacturing Capacities: A Solution for Developing Countries?', in Roffe, Tansey and Vivas-Eugui (eds.), *supra* note 21, at 234.

mean not less than five years from the date on which the Party granted approval to the person that produced the data for approval to market its product, taking account of the nature of the data and the person's efforts and expenditures in producing them. Subject to this provision, there shall be no limitation on any Party to implement abbreviated approval procedures for such products on the basis of bioequivalence and bioavailability studies.'

Unlike NAFTA, the TRIPS Agreement does not include explicit language mentioning data reliance. When the TRIPS negotiators met in Brussels in December 1990, that draft contained the following bracketed language, which did not make it to the final text of the TRIPS Agreement:

> '4A PARTIES, when requiring, as a condition of approving the marketing of new pharmaceutical products ... , the submission of undisclosed test or other data, the originator of which involves a considerable effort, shall [protect such data against unfair commercial use. Unless the person submitting the information agrees, the data may not be relied upon for the approval of competing products for a reasonable time, generally no less than five years, commensurate with the efforts involved in the origination of the data, their nature, and the expenditure involved in their preparation. In addition, PARTIES shall] protect such data against disclosure, except where necessary to protect the public.'[24]

Drawing on this important piece of negotiating history, and utilising an interpretive approach endorsed by the Vienna Convention on the Law of Treaties,[25] one can fairly state that the TRIPS negotiating parties did not achieve consensus over the data reliance issue.[26] Indeed, the removal of the Brussels draft language strongly supports the view that the TRIPS Agreement does not prohibit regulatory authorities from relying on previously submitted test or other data. As Jerome Reichman emphatically declared:

> 'To ignore the clear evolution of the text in favour of quasi-exclusive rights in regulatory data, in a form that was proposed but ultimately excised from the 1994 Final Act, would in effect amount to imposing unbargained-for trade concessions beyond what was agreed in TRIPS without any legal foundation whatsoever.'[27]

---

24. UNCTAD-ICTSD Project on Intellectual Property Rights and Sustainable Development, *supra* note 4, at 525.
25. Article 32 of the Vienna Convention calls for the inclusion of 'the preparatory work of the treaty and the circumstances of its conclusion' as 'supplementary means of interpretation'.
26. For two very different accounts of the negotiations on Article 39.3 of the TRIPS Agreement, see Fellmeth, *supra* note 12, at 454-60; Skillington and Solovy, *supra* note 7, at 15-21.
27. Jerome H. Reichman, 'The International Legal Status of Undisclosed Clinical Trial Data: From Private to Public Goods?', in Roffe, Tansey and Vivas-Eugui (eds.), *supra* note 21, at 140; Public Citizen, 'Data Exclusivity in the Regional Comprehensive Economic Partnership (RCEP)' 2 <www.citizen.org/system/files/case_documents/rcep-data-exclusivity_0.pdf> accessed 20 October 2020. By contrast, Jacques Gorlin, who directed an ad hoc coalition of major US corporations that pushed for the establishment of the TRIPS Agreement, offered a diametrically opposed viewpoint: 'United States negotiators agreed to drop the non-reliance language, because they viewed the phrase as no more than "belts and suspenders", that is, the accepted definition at the time of "protection against unfair commercial use" included non-reliance for a fixed period of time for new chemical entities and the second phrase was, therefore, not needed.' Jacques

Moreover, the use of bioequivalence studies to grant marketing approvals does not always require the use or disclosure of previously submitted test or other data. As Professor Reichman continued:

> '[I]t is not the confidential data themselves that are being unfairly used, even if a first comer is compelled to submit them in order to meet health and safety requirements. It is the health and safety outcome to which the data lead that is being used (a matter of public record) ...'[28]

Although Professor Reichman made this observation in the mid-2000s, it is particularly relevant to today's emerging big data environment, which Section 4.2 will further discuss. In this new technological environment, what is highly valuable are the collected test data and their ability to provide a large and comprehensive dataset[29] - not so much the specific health and safety outcomes proven by those data. Indeed, any follow-on developers seeking to use or reuse these data in a big data environment will have to either generate the test data themselves or secure a licence to use the originators' data. Having the specific health and safety outcomes alone will not meet their needs.

As if these issues were not complicated enough, many jurisdictions still do not require the submission of test data to secure the marketing approval of pharmaceutical and agrochemical products. As Professor Correa observed, in these jurisdictions, 'in order to obtain the registration of a similar product it was sufficient to prove that it had been approved or commercialized in certain foreign countries'.[30] Because the relevant test data are not submitted 'as a condition of approving the marketing of' the regulated products, Article 39.3 does not apply.[31]

II. Data Exclusivities

The second, highly contentious area during the TRIPS negotiations, which the final text of Article 39.3 seems to have settled, relates to the requirement that WTO members introduce a data exclusivity regime. Commentators, myself included, have noted ad nauseum how data exclusivity is a TRIPS-plus demand that has gone beyond the WTO requirements.[32] Article 39.3 introduces two obligations: one 'against unfair commercial use' and the other 'against disclosure'. There is no additional obligation to provide exclusive rights in undisclosed test or other data for pharmaceutical and agrochemical products.

J. Gorlin, *An Analysis of the Pharmaceutical-Related Provisions of the WTO TRIPS (Intellectual Property) Agreement* (Intellectual Property Institute, London, 1999), 48.

28. Reichman, *supra* note 27, at 142.
29. Viktor Mayer-Schönberger and Kenneth Cukier, *Big Data: A Revolution That Will Transform How We Live, Work and Think* (Houghton Mifflin Harcourt, Boston, 2014), 19–31, 98–122.
30. Correa, *supra* note 3, at 361.
31. *Ibid.*
32. Commission on Intellectual Property Rights, *Integrating Intellectual Property Rights and Development Policy: Report of the Commission on Intellectual Property Rights* (Commission on Intellectual Property Rights, London, 2002), 50; Correa, *supra* note 3, at 374; Watal, *supra* note 1, at 199.

Thus far, developed countries and their pharmaceutical and agrochemical industries have taken the position that data exclusivity is necessary to provide effective protections for undisclosed test or other data. As Professor Correa observed:

> 'Despite the fact that Article 39.3 does not provide for the granting of exclusive rights, research-based industry and the governments of some developed countries have argued that the investment made for producing test data can only be recognized if a minimum period (eg five years for pharmaceuticals, ten years for agrochemicals) of exclusivity is granted.'[33]

Likewise, the European Commission declared:

> 'In theory, any country maintaining an *effective* system to implement obligations under [Article] 39.3, even if different from non-reliance over time, would not be in breach of its TRIPs obligations, but we are not aware of many alternatives and it is clear that what the TRIPs-negotiators had in mind was data exclusivity over a certain period of time.'[34]

Article 39.1 specifically requires WTO members to 'ensur[e] effective protection against unfair competition as provided in Article 10*bis* of the Paris Convention (1967)'. When the obligations of Article 39.1 and 39.3 are linked together – as suggested by the italicised language advanced by the European Commission – one could make an argument that the TRIPS Agreement requires WTO members to introduce a data exclusivity regime to protect undisclosed test or other data so as to ensure effective protection in this area.

Nevertheless, it is difficult to reconcile this argument with both the ordinary meaning of Article 39.3 and its negotiating history, including the highly influential 1990 Brussels draft. The claim of effective protection is greatly weakened by the TRIPS Agreement's failure to define the term 'effective'.[35] As if this ambiguity were not challenging enough, that term could also be interpreted in light of the objectives and principles set forth in Articles 7 and 8 of the TRIPS Agreement[36] and the technology transfer commitment provided in Article 66.[37] All in all, it is doubtful that the WTO requires its members to introduce a data exclusivity regime to offer effective protection under Article 39.3, unless the term 'effective' is defined from the perspective of the pharmaceutical and agrochemical industries.

Another plausible, and more convincing, argument concerns the interpretation of the term 'unfair commercial use'. The validity of this argument likely varies according to one's perspective. Some WTO members, policymakers and commentators have

33. Correa, *supra* note 3, at 359.
34. European Commission, 'Compulsory Licensing and Data Protection' 21 <www.concurrences.com/IMG/pdf/eu_-_compulsory_licensing.pdf> accessed 20 October 2020.
35. Peter K. Yu, 'From Pirates to Partners (Episode II): Protecting Intellectual Property in Post-WTO China', 55 *American University Law Review* (2006) 901, 927.
36. On the different ways to use Articles 7 and 8 to promote TRIPS flexibilities, see Peter K. Yu, 'The Objectives and Principles of the TRIPS Agreement', 46 *Houston Law Review* (2009) 979, 1018–46.
37. Paul J. Heald, 'Mowing the Playing Field: Addressing Information Distortion and Asymmetry in the TRIPS Game', 88 *Minnesota Law Review* (2003) 249, 286.

taken the position that reliance is per se unfair commercial use,[38] as such reliance allows the originator's competitors to acquire a commercial advantage. For example, the European Commission

> 'argue[d] that Article 39.3 was intended to prevent generic manufacturers from relying upon the originator's data as a 'shortcut' to marketing approval, by giving the originator exclusive use of its data for a period of time sufficient for it to recoup the costs incurred in running trial tests and producing and compiling data for submission to regulatory authorities.'[39]

Likewise, Professor Correa made the following observation regarding the United States' use of a similar argument:

> '[E]ven when neither the authority nor the competitor actually "use" the data without the originator's authorization (for instance, when the approval is given without any re-examination of the data) such unfair use might arise. In the complaint that the US made against Australia [via an investigation under Section 301 of the 1974 Trade Act], for instance, the US argued that relying on the innovator's data allowed free-riding by generic drug companies on "the innovator company's investment in developing the test data and thus puts the innovator company at a competitive disadvantage ... The US claims that Article 39 para (3) means that generic companies are not allowed to derive commercial benefit from the innovator's test data."'[40]

In the past decade, the United States has actively pushed for the inclusion of the term 'commercial advantage' in TRIPS-plus bilateral, regional and plurilateral agreements. Article 23.1 of Anti-Counterfeiting Trade Agreement (ACTA), for example, sought to increase the criminal enforcement obligation by redefining the term 'commercial scale' as used in Article 61 of the TRIPS Agreement.[41] This provision declares: 'acts carried out on a commercial scale include at least those carried out as commercial activities for direct or indirect economic or commercial advantage'. Article 18.77 of the Trans-Pacific Partnership (TPP) Agreement, which is now part of the Comprehensive and Progressive Agreement for Trans-Pacific Partnership (CPTPP), further provides:

> In respect of wilful copyright or related rights piracy, 'on a commercial scale' includes at least:
>
> (a) acts carried out for commercial advantage or financial gain; and

38. de Carvalho, *supra* note 21, at 616; European Commission, *supra* note 34, at 19; Skillington and Solovy, *supra* note 7, at 33; Antony Taubman, 'Unfair Competition and the Financing of Public-Knowledge Goods: The Problem of Test Data Protection', 3 *Journal of Intellectual Property Law and Practice* (2008) 591, 606.
39. European Commission, *supra* note 34, at 18.
40. Correa, *supra* note 3, at 368.
41. This term was particularly problematic in *China – Measures Affecting the Protection and Enforcement of Intellectual Property Rights,* when the WTO panel found that the United States failed to provide sufficient evidence to 'demonstrate what constituted "a commercial scale" in the specific situation of China's marketplace'. World Trade Organization, 'China – Measures Affecting the Protection and Enforcement of Intellectual Property Rights: Report of the Panel' (WT/DS362/R, 2009), para. 7.614.

(b) significant acts, not carried out for commercial advantage or financial gain, that have a substantial prejudicial impact on the interests of the copyright or related rights holder in relation to the marketplace.

III. Other Unresolved Issues

Apart from data reliance and data exclusivity, the various compromises between developed and developing countries during the TRIPS negotiations and the continuous disagreements between these two groups of countries have generated four unanswered questions, raising concerns among policymakers in developing countries and their supportive commentators and nongovernmental organisations. These questions have also sparked the development of new standards or clarifications at the bilateral, regional and plurilateral levels. Because many of these questions relate to pharmaceutical products and implicate public health, the illustrations below will focus on these products, although one could easily make analogies to agrochemical products.

The first question concerns whether data exclusivity protections continue even when the relevant pharmaceutical product does not receive patent protection, such as when that product is in the public domain or when the previously granted patent has been subsequently invalidated.[42] As Professor Correa observed:

> 'The issue of protection of data is especially relevant to off-patent products, since in cases where the product is patented, the patent holder can, in principle, exclude *any* competition during the lifetime of the patent. It has also been ... particularly problematic for many developing countries that had excluded patent protection for pharmaceuticals until the entry into force of the TRIPS Agreement in those countries. Because of such exclusion, in those countries there was a large pool of pharmaceutical or agrochemical products that fell outside any patent rights. Data protection systems could, if they provided exclusivity, become a partial substitute for patent protection.'[43]

For pharmaceutical products that receive patent protection, the duration of data exclusivity protection is usually shorter than the term of patent protection. In most circumstances, the protection of test or other data will expire before the end of the patent term. While the administrative delay caused by the regulatory approval process could shorten the effective marketing period of patented pharmaceutical products to about 14 years,[44] that period is still much longer than the usual five-year period of data exclusivity for these products. Should a product's patent term be extended based on the Hatch-Waxman Act of 1984, or similar provisions in TRIPS-plus bilateral, regional and plurilateral agreements, the product will enjoy a longer exclusive marketing period.

For pharmaceutical products that do not receive patent protection, however, data exclusivity law could provide substitutional protection. Although Article 39.3 of the

42. Ragavan, *supra* note 9, at 252–53.
43. Correa, *supra* note 3, at 361.
44. Kevin Outterson, 'The Vanishing Public Domain: Antibiotic Resistance, Pharmaceutical Innovation and Intellectual Property Law', 67 *University of Pittsburgh Law Review* (2005) 67, 72 fn. 24.

TRIPS Agreement conditions protection on the existence of 'new chemical entities', it does not require the relevant entities to meet the novelty standard commonly found in patent law.[45] Instead, the TRIPS Agreement provides WTO members with wide discretion to set their own standards. For instance, policymakers and commentators in developed countries have widely considered the term 'new chemical entities' to require only the lack of prior regulatory approval of the pharmaceutical products at issue.[46] The past decade has also seen the United States and other WTO members actively utilising TRIPS-plus bilateral, regional and plurilateral agreements to clarify the definition of newness. A case in point is Article 18.52 of the TPP Agreement, which states that 'a *new pharmaceutical product* means a pharmaceutical product that does not contain a chemical entity that has been previously approved in that Party'. Even though the word 'new' in Article 39.3 suggests that the TRIPS Agreement does not require protections for 'existing chemical entities that have been reformulated or sold for a new indication',[47] Article 18.50.2 of the TPP Agreement goes beyond the TRIPS requirements to provide test data protections 'for a period of at least three years with respect to new clinical information submitted as required in support of a marketing approval of a previously approved pharmaceutical product covering a new indication, new formulation or new method of administration'.

The second question pertains to the use of compulsory licences - or, in TRIPS terms, '[the] use [of a patent] without authorization of the right holder'. Article 31 of the TRIPS Agreement delineates the complex conditions under which these licences are to be issued for patented products. Article 31*bis*, which was adopted in January 2017, further extends the compulsory licensing arrangement to countries with insufficient or no drug manufacturing capacity.[48] Unlike those two provisions, however, Article 39.3 is not subject to the compulsory licensing arrangement provided in the TRIPS Agreement. Indeed, if one goes back to the composite text in the 23 July 1990 report advanced by Lars Anell, the chair of the TRIPS Negotiating Group, that text includes a distinct sentence declaring that '[t]here shall be no compulsory licensing of proprietary information'.[49] The lack of coverage for compulsory licensing arrangements has therefore sparked an interesting debate concerning whether WTO members can utilise the test or other data submitted to regulatory authorities for the purposes of granting marketing approval to pharmaceutical products that have been, or are to be, issued under compulsory licences.[50] Also debatable is

45. Correa, *supra* note 3, at 362; Ragavan, *supra* note 9, at 252–54; Skillington and Solovy, *supra* note 7, at 27; UNCTAD-ICTSD Project on Intellectual Property Rights and Sustainable Development, *supra* note 4, at 530.
46. Correa, *supra* note 3, at 363; Gervais, *supra* note 2, at 427; Skillington and Solovy, *supra* note 7, at 25–28.
47. Robert Weissman, 'Data Protection: Options for Implementation', in Roffe, Tansey and Vivas-Eugui (eds.), *supra* note 21, at 166.
48. On the development of Article 31*bis* of the TRIPS Agreement, see Peter K. Yu, 'The International Enclosure Movement', 82 *Indiana Law Journal* (2007) 827, 872–86.
49. Negotiating Group on Trade-Related Aspects of Intellectual Property Rights, Including Trade in Counterfeit Goods, 'Chairman's Report to the GNG [General Negotiating Group]: Status of Work in the Negotiating Group' (MTN.GNG/NG11/W/76, 1990), 23.
50. Correa, *supra* note 3, at 359; de Carvalho, *supra* note 21, at 649; Ellen F.M. 't Hoen, Pascale Boulet and Brook K. Baker, 'Data Exclusivity Exceptions and Compulsory Licensing to Promote Generic Medicines in the European Union: A Proposal for Greater Coherence in European

the possibility for waiving data exclusivity protection upon the issuance of such licences.[51]

The third question regards the meaning of 'undisclosed' information. Based on its ordinary meaning, the term does not include 'information that is already public (eg, because it has been published in scientific journals or by another national health authority)'.[52] Although this issue was not significantly important in the past, it will likely become more important in the future, especially with the growing push for the sharing of test or other data under open-access arrangements. For example, the European Medicines Agency adopted a new publication policy that requires the agency to proactively publish test data that have been submitted to the agency after 1 January 2015 for initial marketing authorisation.[53] The agency also publishes data that have been submitted after 1 July 2015 as part of an application for a new indication or line extension. In addition, the UN Secretary-General's High-Level Panel on Access to Medicines called on governments to

> 'require that the unidentified data on all completed and discontinued clinical trials be made publicly available in an easily searchable public register established and operated by existing mechanisms such as the [World Health Organization] Clinical Trials Registry Platform, clinical-trials.gov or in peer reviewed publications, regardless of whether their results are positive, negative, neutral or inconclusive.'[54]

During the COVID-19 pandemic, World Health Organization Director-General Tedros Ghebreyesus asked 'all countries, companies and research institutions to support open data, open science and open collaboration so that all people can enjoy the benefits of science and research'.[55]

The final question involves the interplay, and often the overlap, of the different forms of intellectual property rights for pharmaceutical products.[56] Since the mid-

---

Pharmaceutical Legislation', 10(19) *Journal of Pharmaceutical Policy and Practice* (2017) 6; Weissman, *supra* note 47, at 168–74.

51. Correa, *supra* note 21, at 94; de Carvalho, *supra* note 21, at 650–51; 't Hoen, Boulet and Baker, *supra* note 50, at 4–5; Weissman, *supra* note 47, at 168–70.
52. Correa, *supra* note 3, at 362. Professor Ragavan concurred: 'Article 39 leaves … room to determine the question of whether data undisclosed in one part of the world should be considered undisclosed in another part of the world.' Ragavan, *supra* note 9, at 251.
53. European Medicines Agency, 'European Medicines Agency Policy on Publication of Clinical Data for Medicinal Products for Human Use' (EMA/240810/2013, 2014); Daria Kim, 'Enabling Access to Clinical Trial Data: When Is Unfair Use Fair', 14 *Chicago-Kent Journal of Intellectual Property* (2015) 521.
54. UN Secretary-General's High-Level Panel on Access to Medicines, *Promoting Innovation and Access to Health Technologies* (Geneva: United Nations, 2016), 37.
55. World Health Organization, 'WHO Director-General's Opening Remarks at the Media Briefing on COVID-19 – 6 April 2020' < www.who.int/dg/speeches/detail/who-director-general-s-opening-remarks-at-the-media-briefing-on-covid-19---6-april-2020 > accessed 20 October 2020; Peter K. Yu, 'Modalities, Challenges, and Possibilities: An Introduction to the Pharmaceutical Innovation Symposium', 7 *Texas A&M Journal of Property Law* (2021) 1, 23.
56. Yaniv Heled, 'Patents vs. Statutory Exclusivities in Biological Pharmaceuticals – Do We Really Need Both?', 18 *Michigan Telecommunications and Technology Law Review* (2012) 419, 476–79; Srividhya Ragavan, 'The Drug Debate: Data Exclusivity Is the New Way to Delay Generics', 50 *Connecticut Law Review Online* (2018) 1, 4.

2000s, the United States and other developed countries have actively negotiated bilateral, regional and plurilateral agreements. Although Article 39.3 of the TRIPS Agreement offers only limited protection to undisclosed test or other data, these newly developed TRIPS-plus agreements have called for not only market or data exclusivity for test or other data for pharmaceutical and agrochemical products but also for a considerable increase in patent standards, extension of the patent term due to regulatory delay, protections for new uses (or second indications) of known chemical compounds, linkage of drug registration to patent status, and strengthened enforcement in relation to the seizure of in-transit drugs.[57] Given the increasing demands for these new protections, policymakers and commentators are understandably concerned that the simultaneous introduction or adjustment of multiple intellectual property standards would lead to overprotection.[58] Some commentators have also explored the substitutability of the different forms of intellectual property rights.[59] After all, if the protections for undisclosed test or other data have already been increased to provide additional incentives, a country may not need to simultaneously extend the patent term.[60]

D. THE FUTURE

The previous section has covered the continuous disagreements between developed and developing countries over the appropriate scope, duration and limitations of Article 39.3 of the TRIPS Agreement as well as the developed countries' aggressive use of bilateral, regional and plurilateral negotiations to ratchet up the international standards for protecting undisclosed test or other data for pharmaceutical, agrochemical and biological products. This section turns to three distinct sets of challenges that will affect the future development of international standards in the field of test data protection: (1) new subject-matter; (2) technological advances; and (3) changing geopolitics.

---

57. Yu, *supra* note 48, at 867–69. The linkage of drug registration to patent status is often discussed alongside the protection of test or other data for pharmaceutical products, due in large part to the pharmaceutical industry's concurrent demands. On this linkage, see Brook K. Baker, 'Ending Drug Registration Apartheid: Taming Data Exclusivity and Patent/Registration Linkage', 34 *American Journal of Law and Medicine* (2008) 303; Carlos M. Correa, 'Bilateralism in Intellectual Property: Defeating the WTO System for Access to Medicines', 36 *Case Western Reserve Journal of International Law* (2004) 79, 88–91.
58. Peter K. Yu, 'Data Exclusivities in the Age of Big Data, Biologics, and Plurilaterals', 6 *Texas A&M Law Review Arguendo* (2018) 22, 26.
59. Robin Feldman, *Drugs, Money, and Secret Handshakes: The Unstoppable Growth of Prescription Drug Prices* (Cambridge University Press, Cambridge, 2019), 103; Gregory Dolin, 'Exclusivity without Patents: The New Frontier of FDA Regulation for Genetic Materials', 98 *Iowa Law Review* (2013) 1399; Daniel Gervais, 'The Patent Option', 20 *North Carolina Journal of Law and Technology* (2019) 357; Heled, *supra* note 56; John R. Thomas, 'The End of "Patent Medicines"?: Thoughts on the Rise of Regulatory Exclusivities', 70 *Food and Drug Law Journal* (2015) 39.
60. Heled, *supra* note 56, at 461–64; Ragavan, *supra* note 9, at 250–51; Yu, *supra* note 48, at 895; Yu, *supra* note 18, at 784–85.

I. New Subject-Matter

The first set of challenges concerns the growing importance and popularity of biologics and personalised medicines, which have 'revolutionized the healthcare and pharmaceutical industries'.[61] Thus far, commentators have noted the challenge in obtaining sufficient protections for these products through the patent system.[62] Because biologics involve biological materials, as opposed to chemicals, their protections often need to rely on process patents rather than product patents.[63] In addition, Article 39.3 of the TRIPS Agreement does not grant protection to biologics because those products are not considered 'new chemical entities' within the meaning of the Agreement.[64] The insufficient protection provided by the TRIPS Agreement indeed explains why the European Union, Japan and the United States have eagerly pushed for specific provisions relating to biologics in bilateral, regional and plurilateral trade negotiations.

It is therefore no surprise that the protections for undisclosed test or other data for biological products have been particularly controversial toward the end of the TPP negotiations.[65] Article 18.51, the provision for biologics, calls for the establishment of a market exclusivity regime, similar to the not-so-controversial provisions for pharmaceutical and agrochemical products. Although the United States initially pushed for twelve years of protection for biologics,[66] similar to the standard found in the country, the TPP negotiating parties ended up with 'at least eight years from the date of first marketing approval'. That compromise term would last longer than the five-year market exclusivity period for chemical drugs but shorter than the ten-year period for agrochemical products. To address the strong disagreement among the TPP negotiating parties, Article 18.51 further allows each party to decide whether to offer market exclusivity for at least eight years or to offer such exclusivity for at least five years and then supplement such exclusivity with 'other measures' for the remaining years.

With the arrival of the Trump Administration, Canada, Mexico and the United States negotiated the United States–Mexico–Canada Agreement (USMCA) to replace NAFTA. The new agreement entered into effect on 1 July 2020. During the USMCA

61. Yu, *supra* note 58, at 22.
62. Heled, *supra* note 56, at 450–61; W. Nicholson Price II, 'Making Do in Making Drugs: Innovation Policy and Pharmaceutical Manufacturing', 55 *B.C. Law Review* (2014) 491, 527.
63. Price, *supra* note 62, at 527; W. Nicholson Price II and Arti K. Rai, 'Manufacturing Barriers to Biologics Competition and Innovation', 101 *Iowa Law Review* (2016) 1023, 1051; Trevor Woodage, 'Blinded by (a Lack of) Science: Limitations in Determining Therapeutic Equivalence of Follow-on Biologics and Barriers to Their Approval and Commercialization', 9 *Stanford Technology Law Review* (2012) 15.
64. Srividhya Ragavan, 'The (Re)Newed Barrier to Access to Medication: Data Exclusivity', 51 *Akron Law Review* (2017) 1163, 1185–86.
65. Frederick M. Abbott, 'The Evolution of Public Health Provisions in Preferential Trade and Investment Agreements of the United States', in Pedro Roffe and Xavier Seuba (eds.), *Current Alliances in International Intellectual Property Lawmaking: The Emergence and Impact of Mega-Regionals* (International Centre for Trade and Sustainable Development and Centre for International Intellectual Property Studies, Geneva and Strasbourg, 2017), 55; Burcu Kilic and Courtney Pine, 'Decision Time on Biologics Exclusivity: Eight Years Is No Compromise', *Intellectual Property Watch* (27 July 2015).
66. Kilic and Pine, *supra* note 65.

negotiations, the United States managed to convince its two negotiating partners to adopt the position it took in the early stages of the TPP negotiations. Instead of requiring protections for 'at least eight years from the date of first marketing approval' – as provided for in Article 18.51 of the TPP Agreement – Article 20.49 of the 2018 text of the USMCA offers protections 'for a period of at least ten years from the date of first marketing approval of that product in that Party'. That provision, however, does not retain the second TPP option that allows signatory parties to offer market exclusivity for at least five years and then supplement such exclusivity with 'other measures' for the remaining years. The provision also omits the review clause in Article 18.51.3 of the TPP Agreement, which recognises that 'international and domestic regulation of new pharmaceutical products that are or contain a biologic is in a formative stage and that market circumstances may evolve over time'.

Interestingly, despite these successful negotiations, the biologics provision in neither the TPP Agreement nor the USMCA entered into force. Following the Trump Administration's withdrawal from the former,[67] the 11 remaining parties adopted the CPTPP and suspended Article 18.51 (in addition to other controversial provisions, including the TRIPS-plus provision for undisclosed test or other data for pharmaceutical products). In December 2019, Canada, Mexico and the United States also agreed to amend the USMCA by removing Article 20.49 and other contentious provisions. Such removal responded in part to the concern US policymakers had over the agreement's high protections for biological products and their hope that an amendment would 'increase competition and enhance patient access to more affordable prescription drugs', including biological products.[68] To a large extent, the removal of these two provisions show the continuous controversies surrounding the appropriate protections for undisclosed test or other data for biological products.

II. Technological Advances

The second set of challenges relates to technological advances in the pharmaceutical sector. While legal standards have always lagged behind these advances, international treaty language has lagged behind even further. As I noted in an earlier book chapter, 'from initial negotiation to final ratification to full implementation, it takes a considerable amount of time, effort, energy and resources to complete a trade agreement. The rate at which such an agreement is developed can hardly keep pace with the rate of technological change.'[69] Likewise, Colin Picker cautioned: '[D]elay is the rule in the formation of international law. Usually, international law

67. On the United States' withdrawal from the TPP Agreement and its aftermath, see Peter K. Yu, 'Thinking about the Trans-Pacific Partnership (and a Mega-Regional Agreement on Life Support)', 20 *SMU Science and Technology Law Review* (2017) 97, 101–10.
68. Letter from Representative Jan Schakowsky et al. to Robert E. Lighthizer, US Trade Representative (11 July 2019) <https://schakowsky.house.gov/sites/schakowsky.house.gov/files/migrated/uploads/lighthizermeds.pdf> accessed 20 October 2020.
69. Peter K. Yu, 'Trade Agreement Cats and the Digital Technology Mouse', in Bryan Mercurio and Ni Kuei-Jung (eds.), *Science and Technology in International Economic Law: Balancing Competing Interests* (Routledge, Abingdon, 2014), 202.

is created over long periods, by the gradual acceptance of customary state practice or after long treaty negotiations.'[70]

Apart from the ever-increasing popularity of biological products and personalised medicines mentioned above, two new sets of technological developments have emerged. First, a fast-growing number of commentators are now exploring the use of artificial intelligence and machine learning in the pharmaceutical sector, including for research and development.[71] Advances in this area led the compilers of the Global Innovation Index to select the future of medical innovation as the theme of their 2019 report.[72] As Pratap Khedkar and Dharmendra Sahay observed in that report: 'A third of all [artificial intelligence] investments in healthcare are projected to be in drug discovery, specifically using computer simulation to find better molecules faster. Companies are also beginning to leverage [artificial intelligence] and data to reduce clinical trial costs and waste, though progress has been slower than desired.'[73] Likewise, the WHO, the World Intellectual Property Organization and the WTO acknowledged in their trilateral study on access to medical technologies and innovation: 'Artificial neural networks ... have been used in drug discovery for screening compounds in the automated design of new classes of medicines and in finding novel uses for known medicines. ... [Artificial intelligence] is already being used in the design and analysis of clinical trials.'[74]

Secondly, big data analytics have already 'transformed the fields of biotechnology and bioinformatics while ushering in major advances in drug development, clinical practices, and medical financing'.[75] As data become more valuable, it is un-

70. Colin B. Picker, 'A View from 40,000 Feet: International Law and the Invisible Hand of Technology', 23 *Cardozo Law Review* (2001) 149, 184.
71. On the use of artificial intelligence and machine learning in the health area, see Eric J. Topol, *Deep Medicine: How Artificial Intelligence Can Make Healthcare Human Again* (Basic Books, New York, 2019); Ma Huateng, 'Application of Artificial Intelligence and Big Data in China's Healthcare Services', in Soumitra Dutta, Bruno Lanvin and Sacha Wunsch-Vincent (eds.), *Global Innovation Index 2019: Creating Healthy Lives – The Future of Medical Innovation* (Cornell University, INSEAD and World Intellectual Property Organization, Ithaca, Fountainbleu and Switzerland, 2019); David W. Opderbeck, 'Artificial Intelligence in Pharmaceuticals, Biologics, and Medical Devices: Present and Future Regulatory Models', 88 *Fordham Law Review* (2019) 553; W. Nicholson Price II, 'Medical AI and Contextual Bias', 33 *Harvard Journal of Law and Technology* (2019) 65; W. Nicholson Price II and Arti K. Rai, 'Clearing Opacity through Machine Learning', 106 *Iowa Law Review* (2021) 775.
72. Dutta, Lanvin and Wunsch-Vincent (eds.), *supra* note 71.
73. Pratap Khedkar and Dharmendra Sahay, 'Trends in Healthcare and Medical Innovation', in Dutta, Lanvin and Wunsch-Vincent (eds.), *supra* note 71, at 89.
74. World Trade Organization, World Health Organization and World Intellectual Property Organization, *Promoting Access to Medical Technologies and Innovation: Intersections Between Public Health, Intellectual Property and Trade* (World Trade Organization, World Health Organization and World Intellectual Property Organization, Geneva, 2020), 89.
75. Yu, *supra* note 58, at 22. On such transformation, see Ryan Abbott, 'Big Data and Pharmacovigilance: Using Health Information Exchanges to Revolutionize Drug Safety', 99 *Iowa Law Review* (2013) 225, 227; Sam F. Halabi, 'The Drug Repurposing Ecosystem: Intellectual Property Incentives, Market Exclusivity, and the Future of New Medicines', 20 *Yale Journal of Law and Technology* (2018) 1, 32–34; Yu, *supra* note 6, at 686–88; Jamie Cattell, Sastry Chilukuri and Michael Levy, 'How Big Data Can Revolutionize Pharmaceutical R&D' < www.mckinsey.com/industries/pharmaceuticals-and-medical-products/our-insights/how-big-data-can-revolutionize-pharmaceutical-r-and-d > accessed 20 October 2020.

derstandable why those collecting or generating test or other data for pharmaceutical or agrochemical products would prefer stronger protections for such data. Because a substantial portion of the value derives from the reuse, or initially unintended use, of the data,[76] the more protection there is, the more value these data collectors or generators can extract from these data and the more lead time they will have for such extraction.

Moreover, the use of big data analytics in the pharmaceutical sector may require the provision of new incentives to motivate drug developers to upgrade their legacy technologies and to invest in new analytical tools to optimise innovation, improve clinical trial efficiency and strengthen product quality, safety and efficacy.[77] These costly investments, in turn, will generate a new cycle of demands for stronger data protection to help recoup the developers' up-front investments.[78] In responding to these demands, policymakers should exercise caution, as overprotection could fragment the data market.[79] Such fragmentation would undermine the benefits of new, innovative data analytical techniques while precipitating what Rebecca Eisenberg and Michael Heller have described as the 'tragedy of the anti-commons'.[80]

III. Changing Geopolitics

The final set of challenges relates to changing geopolitical positions in the developing world. Although commentators continue to highlight the North-South divide in international trade and intellectual property negotiations, the geopolitical landscape has become increasingly complex.[81] Indeed, the past two decades have seen large developing countries slowly accepting higher intellectual property standards in regional and

76. Mayer-Schönberger and Cukier, *supra* note 29, at 153; Mark Burdon and Mark Andrejevic, 'Big Data in the Sensor Society', in Cassidy R. Sugimoto, Hamid R. Ekbia and Michael Mattioli (eds.), *Big Data Is Not a Monolith* (MIT Press, Cambridge, MA, 2016), 69; Margaret Foster Riley, 'Big Data, HIPAA, and the Common Rule: Time for Big Change?', in I. Glenn Cohen, Holly Fernandez Lynch, Effy Vayena and Urs Gasser (eds.), *Big Data, Health Law, and Bioethics* (Cambridge University Press, Cambridge, 2018), 251.
77. W. Nicholson Price II, 'Big Data, Patents, and the Future of Medicine', 37 *Cardozo Law Review* (2016) 1401; Cattell, Chilukuri and Levy, *supra* note 75; Megan Nichols, '5 Ways Big Data Is Transforming the Pharmaceutical Industry' *Geektime* (8 May 2017) <https://perma.cc/FJF6-SYHN> accessed 31 January 2021.
78. Nichols, *supra* note 77; Yu, *supra* note 6, at 687–88.
79. Josef Drexl, 'Designing Competitive Markets for Industrial Data: Between Propertisation and Access', 8 *Journal of Intellectual Property, Information Technology and Electronic Commerce Law* (2017) 257, 260 and fn. 16; Wolfgang Kerber, 'A New (Intellectual) Property Right for Non-Personal Data? An Economic Analysis', *Gewerblicher Rechtsschutz Und Urheberrecht Internationaler Teil* [*GRUR Int*] (2016) 989, 990; Peter K. Yu, 'Data Producer's Right and the Protection of Machine-Generated Data', 93 *Tulane Law Review* (2019) 859, 889.
80. Michael Heller and Rebecca Eisenberg defined 'the tragedy of the anti-commons' as a situation in which 'multiple owners each have a right to exclude others from a scarce resource and no one has an effective privilege of use'. Michael A. Heller and Rebecca S. Eisenberg, 'Can Patents Deter Innovation? The Anticommons in Biomedical Research', 280 *Science* (1998) 698, 698.
81. Peter K. Yu, 'Intellectual Property Negotiations, the BRICS Factor and the Changing North–South Debate', in Rostam J. Neuwirth, Alexandr Svetlicinii and Denis De Castro Halis (eds.), *The BRICS-Lawyers' Guide to Global Cooperation* (Cambridge University Press, Cambridge, 2017), 148–49.

international negotiations – with the introduction of TRIPS-plus intellectual property standards in the Regional Comprehensive Economic Partnership being a leading example.[82] China's recent efforts to raise the standards for protecting undisclosed test or other data for pharmaceutical and biological products are particularly revealing.

In April 2018, the National Medical Products Administration of China released the draft Provisional Measures for the Implementation of Test Data Protection for Pharmaceutical Products. Article 5 not only provides six years of protection to data submitted for the regulatory approval of innovative drugs (*chuangxin yao*) – a TRIPS-plus standard that China accepted upon WTO accession[83] – but the provision also offers twelve years of protection to undisclosed test or other data for innovative therapeutic biologics (*chuangxin zhiliao yong shengwu zhipin*). If adopted, this 12-year standard will put China in parity with the United States. It will also be 'higher than the standard laid down in even the most aggressive TRIPS-plus bilateral, regional, and plurilateral agreements'.[84]

Outside the field of test data protection, China also recently introduced a new provision offering a limited extension of the patent term to compensate for the time lost when a pharmaceutical product undergoes regulatory review. Modelled after the Hatch-Waxman Act of 1984 in the United States, Article 42 of the 2020 Patent Law, which took effect in June 2021, grants up to five years of term extension to patents in innovative drugs.

Taken together, these legislative and regulatory changes have provided some exciting new developments in the Chinese pharmaceutical sector.[85] Although these changes target the Chinese market, they are globally significant for three reasons. First, they show that China is no longer content serving as a supplier of active pharmaceutical ingredients, even though it has already been the world's largest supplier of these ingredients and its second largest pharmaceutical market.[86] Instead, China wants to develop a research-based pharmaceutical industry and expand its share of the global market for new pharmaceutical products.[87] Secondly, although the Chinese populace remains deeply concerned about the lack of access to essential medicines, the country's current position contrasts sharply with the position taken by India – another leader of the developing world. As my colleague Srividhya Ragavan and other

82. Peter K. Yu, 'The RCEP and Trans-Pacific Intellectual Property Norms', 50 *Vanderbilt Journal of Transnational Law* (2017) 673, 737–40. The Regional Comprehensive Economic Partnership negotiations have involved Australia, China, Japan, New Zealand, South Korea, the ten members of the Association of Southeast Asian Nations (ASEAN) and, until recently, India.
83. World Trade Organization, 'Report of the Working Party on the Accession of China' (WT/ACC/CHN/49, 2001), para. 284. In addition to six years of protection, China also accepted the WTO-plus obligation of not allowing for data reliance.
84. Peter K. Yu, 'China's Innovative Turn and the Changing Pharmaceutical Landscape', 51 *University of the Pacific Law Review* (2020) 593, 607.
85. Mark Cohen, 'Draft of Data Exclusivity Rules Released by CFDA' <chinaipr.com/2018/04/26/draft-of-data-exclusivity-rules-released-by-cfda/> accessed 20 October 2020.
86. Peter K. Yu, 'Access to Medicines, BRICS Alliances, and Collective Action', 34 *American Journal of Law and Medicine* (2008) 345, 363; Issaku Harada, 'China Extends Drug Patents to 25 Years' *Nikkei Asian Review* (16 May 2018), <asia.nikkei.com/Politics/China-extends-drug-patents-to-25-years> accessed 20 October 2020.
87. Yu, *supra* note 84, at 607–08; Yu, *supra* note 6, at 694. China currently 'produces about four percent of the world's new pharmaceutical products'. Yu, *supra* note 84, at 594.

commentators have observed, India remains sceptical of the benefits provided by strong protections for undisclosed test or other data for pharmaceutical and biological products.[88] To a large extent, India's current position is not that different from the strong opposition it mounted during the TRIPS negotiations.[89] Finally, China is hoping to use its new laws and policies to attract foreign pharmaceutical manufacturers, similar to how it has enticed electronic, telecommunication and other industries to relocate research-and-development facilities to the country. Stronger protections for undisclosed test or other data for pharmaceutical and biological products will certainly make the country more appealing for conducting clinical trials.[90]

E. CONCLUSION

Twenty-five years ago, the TRIPS Agreement succeeded in setting new international minimum standards for protecting undisclosed test or other data for pharmaceutical and agrochemical products. Yet, because of the continuous disagreements between developed and developing countries, Article 39.3 is filled with compromises between these two groups of countries and has had limited impacts in the field of test data protection.[91] These disagreements continue even today, as is evident in ongoing bilateral, regional and plurilateral trade negotiations.

As new issues and technologies emerge and as geopolitical positions change, it will be interesting to see how the international standards in the field of test data protection will evolve. Will these developments lead to more convergence (similar to what we have seen between China and United States) or more divergence (as reflected in the push to suspend the TPP provisions for pharmaceutical and biological products)? Or will the new technological developments change the global pharmaceutical landscape so much that the convergence-divergence debate is no longer relevant? A quarter of a century may not be enough to provide answers to these questions, but the past two decades of developments have helped us understand why these questions are now being explored in the field of test data protection.

88. Ragavan, *supra* note 64, at 1188; Prashant Reddy T., 'The Data Exclusivity Debate in India: Time for a Rethink?', 10 *Indian Journal of Law and Technology* (2014) 8, 17–25.
89. Watal, *supra* note 1, at 19; Peter K. Yu, 'Currents and Crosscurrents in the International Intellectual Property Regime', 38 *Loyola of Los Angeles Law Review* (2004) 323, 359 and fn. 195.
90. Cohen, *supra* note 85.
91. Peter K. Yu, 'TRIPS and Its Contents', 60 *IDEA* (2020) 149, 185.

CHAPTER 8
TRIPS and Enforcement: Balance and New Challenges

Xavier Seuba

A. INTRODUCTION

Intellectual property enforcement norms enable the fulfilment of substantive rights and obligations, in a weighing and balancing process that takes place in the context of the broader legal order, in dialogue with fundamental rights, competition law and free trade principles. Since the adoption of the Agreement on Trade-Related Aspects of Intellectual Property Rights (TRIPS), intellectual property enforcement became a priority issue of the international intellectual property normative and institutional agenda. This chapter defends that proportionality, flexibility and judicial discretion are inherent in the traditional approaches of intellectual property enforcement, clearly recognised in TRIPS, and are of central relevance to respond to current challenges arising from digitisation and the stalemate of multilateralism.

Norms on enforcement have a capital importance in any legal system. From a practical point of view, they determine the effectiveness of the system, thus transforming rights and obligations of substantive content into tangible entitlements. The fulfilment of norms that create substantive rights and obligations - primary rules - largely depends on the functioning of norms on enforcement - secondary rules. The latter regulate, among other aspects, the reaction to infringement, the consequences of infringement and who is to adjudicate. Secondary rules play a systemic role, since it is in the combination of primary and secondary rules where the constitutive characteristic of the legal system lies.[1]

Norms on intellectual property enforcement are not only the gearwheels of the clockwork, but also mould and sculpt primary norms. Substantive rights and

1. *See* X. Seuba, *The Global Regime for the Enforcement of Intellectual Property Rights* (Cambridge University Press, Cambridge, 2017), 11–34.

obligations are subject to the provisions found in enforcement related sections of national statutes and international treaties, which determine the method for implementation and shape the scope of substantive protection. Aspects such as the conditions for awarding an injunction, or the methods for estimating damages awards, severely influence substantive rights, their power to exclude and economic value. In reality, the relationship between substantive entitlements and enforcement remedies is so intense that the line between the corresponding norms is often thin and can be easily blurred.

National governments have traditionally been reluctant to surrender sovereignty over the implementation of intellectual property rights.[2] This is probably the reason why intellectual property enforcement was generally ignored in multilateral treaties preceding TRIPS, notably the Paris Convention for the Protection of Industrial Property and the Berne Convention for the Protection of Literary and Artistic Works. These conventions contain little guidance as to the specific means for intellectual property enforcement.[3] The provisions enshrined therein are limited in number and scope, afford a great margin of discretion and have limited impact on enforcement.[4] Paris and Berne contain no references to general goals or principles relating to enforcement. While references to remedies exist, they are marginal.[5] Certainly the Paris and Berne conventions did not provide 'governments with the necessary guidance concerning appropriate and modern' enforcement standards.[6] Naturally, this was a policy choice.

It was only after the Uruguay Round that intellectual property enforcement became a priority issue in the international intellectual property normative agenda. Multilateral, plurilateral and bilateral treaties at the present time regulate numerous aspects of intellectual property enforcement and set up international bodies in charge of overseeing the implementation of the obligations set forth therein. Such an objective is achieved by the activation of dispute settlement mechanisms and the implementation of monitoring and reporting systems. Both diplomatic and jurisdictional means of dispute settlement coexist in international intellectual property law. The latter include judicial and arbitral settlement by international courts, quasi-judicial bodies and *ad hoc* temporary bodies. While the proliferation of dispute settlement bodies is a sign of dynamism and robustness of the system, it may also create problems of forum shopping and jurisdictional overlaps.[7]

---

2. F.M. Abbott, 'Innovation and technology transfer to address climate change: Lessons from the global debate on intellectual property and public health', ICTSD Issue Paper no. 24, 2009, 6–7.
3. D. Gervais, 'Criminal Enforcement in the US and Canada,' in C. Geiger (ed.), *Criminal Enforcement of Intellectual Property: A Handbook of Contemporary Research* (Edward Elgar, 2012), 269.
4. P. K. Yu, 'Shaping Chinese Criminal Enforcement Norms through the TRIPS Agreement', in C. Geiger (ed.), *Criminal Enforcement of Intellectual Property: A Handbook of Contemporary Research* (Edward Elgar, 2012), 287.
5. This is the case for injunctions for specific rights and situations, the seizure of imported goods, some procedural rights and references to norms on legal standing. *See* in detail, Seuba, *supra* note 1, 100–02.
6. World Intellectual Property Organization, *WIPO Intellectual Property Handbook: Policy, Law and Use* (World Intellectual Property Organization, Geneva, 2004), 214.
7. *See*, on this phenomenon and proposed options, X. Seuba, 'Jurisdictional overlaps in international intellectual property', in C. Geiger (ed.), *Research Handbook on Intellectual Property and Investment Law* (Edward Elgar, 2020), 267–86.

Most recent international normative developments in the area of enforcement have been accomplished by means of the transplantation of intellectual property norms through a range of channels. The pattern observed of partially transplanting intellectual property statutes, not taking into account the balance existing in the original norm, is worrying. In actual practice, those norms militate against the interests they allegedly intend to protect, hence not only rightsholders may one day become intellectual property infringers, but biased international norms face societal rejection. Normative proposals of such a nature reduce the diversity of elements of relevance in the weighing and balancing process for the enforcement of intellectual property rights.[8]

B. THE TRIPS AGREEMENT AS GLOBAL FRAMEWORK

I. Context, Content and Objectives of the TRIPS Agreement Part on Enforcement

Part III of TRIPS is devoted to intellectual property enforcement within national jurisdictions. Five sections make up this part, and address general obligations, civil and administrative enforcement, provisional measures, border measures and criminal enforcement. The 20 articles contained in Part III create a relatively sophisticated reference for WTO members, while leaving a considerable margin of manoeuvre to national implementation. In terms of content, TRIPS provisions on enforcement can be divided into three groups depending on their expected outcome.

First, some articles state how enforcement must be put into practice, and use an imperative terminology. An example is Article 41.1 of TRIPS, which establishes that the members of the WTO 'shall ensure that enforcement procedures as specified in this Part are available'.[9] Subsequent treaties have increased the number of imperative provisions. In other cases, TRIPS instructs members to empower courts to do something or to adopt certain decisions, but it does not prescribe a specific result. This is the most common type of provision in the Agreement.[10] Finally, TRIPS also proposes some further possibilities of for enforcement, but leaves their implementation to the discretion of the WTO members.[11]

The first section of Part III of TRIPS, on general obligations, incorporates the articles that shape the implementation of all enforcement-related articles in the Agreement. Article 41, on general obligations, is particularly important since it clarifies the goals and sets out the principles for the interpretation and implementation of the

8. X. Seuba, 'Transplantation of the Law as a Legislative Technique in the Intellectual Property Domain', VVAA, *Penser le droit de la pensée. Mélanges en l'honneur de Michel Vivant* (2020).
9. *See* TRIPS Articles 41.1-4, 42.1, 46, 49, 50.4, 50.6, 50.8, 51, 52, 54, 55, 58, 59, 61.
10. This is generally introduced under a construction stating that 'judicial authorities shall have the authority to ...'. *See* TRIPS Articles 43.1, 44.1, 45.1, 46, 47, 48.1, 50.1, 50.2, 50.3, 50.7, 53.1, 56, 59.
11. When this is the case, usual expressions are 'Members may provide that the judicial authorities shall have the authority to ...' or 'Members may authorise the judicial authorities to ...'. *See* TRIPS Articles 44.2, 45.2, 47, 48.1, 51, 50.5, 57, 60.

entire Part III. Several subsections of Article 41 have been transplanted to numerous plurilateral and bilateral agreements.[12]

The 'primary obligation'[13] of WTO members in the area of enforcement is to set up effective methods for the enforcement of intellectual property rights, as mandates in Article 41.1 of TRIPS. Whether this is an obligation of result or an obligation of means has been the subject of debate. In our view, most of the time the emphasis is rather on the tools than on specific results. In some cases, TRIPS provisions lay down clear and immediately enforceable mandates, while in other cases the possibilities for implementation are manyfold. It is important to keep in mind that TRIPS is an instrument that lays down minimum standards and commits parties to an overall satisfactory level of intellectual property enforcement.[14]

Article 41.1 of TRIPS must be read in light of the private nature of intellectual property rights and in conjunction with Article 41.5, which states that nothing in the agreement 'creates any obligation with respect to the distribution of resources as between enforcement of intellectual property rights and enforcement of law in general'.[15] The latter is commonly regarded as a concession made to developing countries,[16] which wanted to contextualise the new obligations in the broader framework of general law enforcement[17] and pre-empt demands for resources to set up specialised courts or strengthen intellectual property enforcement.[18] This provision is frequently invoked in policy-related forums, under the general understanding that it 'should temper IPR owners' expectations.'[19] In this respect, while the WTO Panel report in the *China – Intellectual Property Rights* made it clear that Article 41.5 does not establish a general permission to infringe, it also stated that 'Article 41.5 is an important provision in the overall balance of rights and obligations in Part III of the TRIPS Agreement'.[20] Fulfilling both premises – obligation to enforce while simultaneously making use of the right not to modify the distribution of resources – seems difficult to reconcile.[21]

---

12. This is interesting, because the transplanted subsections have their origin in the North American Free Trade Agreement (NAFTA). In this sense, compare Article 41 of the TRIPS Agreement with Article 1714 of the NAFTA FTA and EIA (1994).
13. F. M. Abbott, 'WTO Dispute Settlement Practice Relating to the Agreement on Trade-Related Intellectual Property Rights,' in F. Ortino and E.-U. Petersmann (eds.) *The WTO Dispute Settlement System: 1995–2003* (Kluwer Law International, 2004), 427.
14. Bronckers, Verkade and McNelis, *TRIPS Agreement: Enforcement of Intellectual Property Rights* (Office for Official Communications of the European Communities, Luxembourg, 2000), 14.
15. *See* also Article 2.2 of ACTA.
16. *See* T. P. Stewart, *The GATT Uruguay Round: A Negotiating History* (Kluwer Law International, 1993), 541; UNCTAD-ICTSD, *Resource Book on TRIPS and Development* (Cambridge University Press, Cambridge, 2005), 585.
17. *See* J. Watal, 'US–China intellectual property dispute: A comment on the interpretation of the TRIPS enforcement provisions', 13 *The Journal of World Intellectual Property*, 337.
18. *See* P. K. Yu, 'Are Developing Countries Playing a Better TRIPS Game?', 16 *UCLA Journal of International Law and Foreign Affairs* (2011), 326.
19. *See* T. Trainer, 'Intellectual Property Enforcement: A reality gap (insufficient assistance, ineffective implementation)', 8 *John Marshall Review of Intellectual Property Law*, 51.
20. *See* WTO Panel, *China – Intellectual Property Rights*, WT/DS362/R, 26 January 2009, para. 7.594.
21. *See* X. Seuba, 'Checks and Balances in the Intellectual Property Enforcement Field: Reconstructing EU Trade Agreements,' in C. Geiger (ed.), *Constructing European Intellectual Property: Achievements and New Perspectives* (Edward Elgar, 2013), 417–18.

TRIPS enforcement provisions set up 'minimum standards of due process'[22] that crystallise general principles of law,[23] such as general principles on judicial procedure widely accepted in domestic legal orders. Inherent components of the right to a fair trial mentioned in Articles 41 and 42 include the right to a reasoned decision in writing, the right to a procedure and sentence within a reasonable time limit, the right to affordable procedures, the right to be heard, the right to a review, the right to a timely and detailed written notice, the right to representation by independent legal counsel, and the right to procedures without burdensome requirements concerning mandatory personal appearances. That is, they set up a very complete charter touching upon due process standards and lay down fundamental due process principles that may have decisive effects on the adjustment of enforcement procedures to the requirements resulting from the right to a fair trial. In particular, the TRIPS Agreement sets forth the principles of equity and fairness in enforcement procedures, which apply to all parties in a dispute.[24]

The general provisions and basic principles of the TRIPS Agreement impact on Part III of the agreement. The relevance of Articles 7 and 8 of the Agreement is notable and has been explored in great depth by doctrine[25] and some WTO case law.[26] Moreover, these articles are repeatedly quoted in policy statements in multilateral fora,[27] mostly by developing countries,[28] and in some intellectual property chapters of PTAs.[29] Although some caution must be expressed concerning their practical impact, the principles and objectives enshrined in Articles 7 and 8 are relevant for enforcement-related articles. This is particularly the case for references made in Article 7 to the link between intellectual property enforcement and the promotion of technological innovation, the transfer and dissemination of technology, the mutual

22. *See* J. Reichman, P. Lange, 'Bargaining around the TRIPS Agreement: The case for ongoing public-private initiatives to facilitate worldwide intellectual property transactions', 9 *Duke Journal of Comparative and International Law*, 34,
23. M. Blakeney, 'International intellectual property jurisprudence after TRIPS', in D. Vaver, L. Bentley (eds.), *Intellectual Property in the New Millennium* (Cambridge University Press, 2004), 7.
24. *See* UNCTAD-ICTSD, *Resource Book on TRIPS and Development*, 582; J. Straus, 'Reversal of the Burden of Proof, the Principle of "Fair and Equitable Procedures" and Preliminary Injunctions under the TRIPS Agreement', 3 *Journal of World Intellectual Property* (2000), 811; C. Heath, 'Comparative Overview and the TRIPS Enforcement Provisions', in C. Heath and L. Petit (eds.), *Patent Enforcement Worldwide: A Survey of 15 Countries: Writings in Honour of Dieter Stauder* (2nd edn., Hart, Oxford, 2005), 12.
25. *See* P. K. Yu, 'The Graduated Response' 62 *Florida Law Review* (2010), 1373–430; H. Grosse Ruse-Khan, 'A Comparative Analysis of Policy Space in WTO Law,' *Max Planck Institute for Intellectual Property, Competition and Tax Law Research Paper Series* 02-02 (2008).
26. *See* for instance WTO Dispute Settlement Panel, *Canada – Patent Protection of Pharmaceutical Products*, WT/DS114/R, 17 March 2000, para. 7.26, stating that the goals and limitations stated in Articles 7 and 8.1 must be borne in mind when interpreting Article 30 of the TRIPS Agreement on exceptions.
27. *See* Recommendation 45, WIPO Development Agenda (2007), A/43/16, Annex A.
28. *See* Request for Consultations by India, *European Union and a Member State – Seizure of Generic Drugs in Transit*, WT/DS408/1, 19 May 2010, p. 3.
29. *See* Article 139.2 EU-CARIFORUM States FTA and EIA (2008); Article 195 EU-Colombia and Peru FTA and EIA (2013).

advantage of producers and users, social and economic welfare, and the balance of rights and obligations.

II. Dispute Settlement and TRIPS Agreement Enforcement Provisions

TRIPS articles on intellectual property enforcement have been litigated in several WTO disputes, either as the main intellectual property area at issue or as a subsidiary object of concern in the context of broader cases. The reports drafted by WTO panels and the – rare but existing – decisions of the Appellate Body that allude to the TRIPS enforcement provisions have had an important impact. Amendments to national laws have been adopted in the areas of civil, border and criminal enforcement in response to decisions of dispute settlement bodies and to mutually agreed solutions. Likewise, mutually agreed solutions have anticipated normative changes in regional and international fora.

Before moving to specific civil, criminal and border enforcement provisions, TRIPS Article 41 deserves specific attention as it establishes overarching obligations of relevance in all enforcement areas. This article has been invoked in several cases. This is the case of the panel report *China – Intellectual Property Rights* with reference to 'effectiveness' in the context of the TRIPS Agreement, and the understanding that the demand of effectiveness involves an obligation to make the remedies available to the parties. On a different subject, but also involving Article 41, in *EC – Trademarks and Geographical Indications* the application of Part III in a dispute concerning registration of geographical indications was raised. The panel confirmed that the obligations enshrined in Part III are applicable to all intellectual property rights covered in TRIPS by virtue of Article 1.2, including geographical indications.[30] However, the panel noted that the dispute related to the acquisition of intellectual property rights, a subject regulated in Part IV of the TRIPS Agreement.

The link established between Part III and the intellectual property rights covered by the agreement was also relevant in the *US – Section 211 Appropriations Act* dispute. In that case, the Appellate Body concluded that trade names are covered by the TRIPS Agreement.[31] While the controversy mainly revolved around substantive

30. *EC – Trademarks and Geographical Indications*, WT/DS290/R, 15 March 2005, para. 7.731.
31. Because Paris Convention, Article 8 covering trade names is explicitly incorporated into TRIPS Article 2.1. *US – Section 211 Appropriations Act*, WT/DS176/AB/R, 2 January 2002, paras 333 and 338. The scope of 'intellectual property' covered by the TRIPS Agreement goes beyond the categories enumerated in Part II. First, it must be noticed that TRIPS 'categories' do not necessarily coincide with the headings of Sections 1 through 7 of Part II, but with the categories that are the *subject* of those sections. This is the case of plant variety protection, for example, which does not have a specific section in the TRIPS Agreement but must be protected pursuant to TRIPS Article 27.3(c). Secondly, as the Appellate Body noted regarding trade names, other intellectual property types also fall within the scope of 'intellectual property' protection regulated in the TRIPS Agreement, even if they are not explicitly mentioned; TRIPS Agreement Article 2.1 references Articles 1–12 and 19 of the Paris Convention, which results in the protection of not only trade names but also utility models. Thirdly, the TRIPS Agreement does not protect all currently existing forms of intellectual property protection. This affects categories that have been developed with particular emphasis by both developing and developed nations. In the first group, mention must be made of the sui generis protection of traditional knowledge, while in the second group mention can be made of the protection of non-original databases.

aspects,[32] both the panel and the Appellate Body dealt with TRIPS Agreement Article 42, which addresses the requirements of 'fair and equitable procedures' in the context of civil enforcement. The Appellate Body found that the United States measure at issue (the Section 211 Appropriations Act) was not inconsistent with Article 42, as it gave right holders access to civil judicial procedures, as required under Article 42, which is a provision on procedural obligations.

Two recent WTO panel reports affecting Russia and Saudi Arabia have interpreted the security exception in TRIPS Article 73(b)(iii) in connection with enforcement obligations, notably Articles 42 (general obligations regarding civil enforcement) and 61 (criminal enforcement).[33] In *Saudi Arabia – Intellectual Property Rights,* the Kingdom of Saudi Arabia invoked Article 73(b)(iii) to defend measures that prevented a company headquartered in Qatar from receiving Saudi legal advice through civil enforcement procedures before Saudi courts. Saudi Arabia raised the same exception to justify its rejection to provide criminal procedures against a company located in Saudi Arabia and accused of piracy. The panel adopted the analytical framework developed by the panel in *Russia – Traffic in Transit,* and identified several factors that need to be considered: existence of war or emergency in international relations, the adoption of the measures in that moment, link between actions and the protection of essential security interests.[34] According to the panel, the existence of 'war or other emergency in international relations' must be objectively determined and is not subject to the subjective discretionary determination of the state invoking the exception.[35] On the contrary, the articulation of essential security interests would seem discretionary, although subject to good faith of GATT Article XXI(b)(iii). As is happens with the decisions quoted above, these two would also deserve separate attention. Still, what is important in the context of the present chapter is that both panels tried to achieve a reasonable equilibrium to reconcile the protection of territoriality and sovereignty while respecting international trade and intellectual property obligations.[36]

32. The panel and Appellate Body found that the TRIPS Agreement and Berne Convention regulate the properties of trademarks, but not ownership of trademarks.
33. *See, Russia – Measures Concerning Traffic in Transit,* Panel Report, WT/DS512/R, 5 April 2019. *Saudi Arabia – Measures Concerning the Protection of Intellectual Property Rights*, Panel Report, WT/DS567/R, 16 June 2020.
34. More specifically, (i) whether the existence of a 'war or other emergency in international relations' has been established in the sense of subparagraph (iii) to Article 73(b); (ii) whether the relevant actions were 'taken in time of' that war or other emergency in international relations; (iii) whether the invoking Member has articulated its relevant 'essential security interests' sufficiently to enable an assessment of whether there is any link between those actions and the protection of its essential security interests; and (iv) whether the relevant actions are so remote from, or unrelated to, the 'emergency in international relations' as to make it implausible that the invoking Member considers those actions to be necessary for the protection of its essential security interests arising out of the emergency. *Saudi Arabia – Intellectual Property Rights*, para 7.242. *See* C Glöckle, 'The Second Chapter on a National Security Exception in WTO Law: The Panel Report in Saudi Arabia – Protection of IPR', *EJIL: Talk!* 22 July 2020, available at https://www.ejiltalk.org/the-second-chapter-on-a-national-security-exception-in-wto-law-the-panel-report-in-saudi-arabia-protection-of-ipr/
35. *Russia – Traffic in Transit*, para. 7.71, 7.100.
36. The approach of the panels also reflects the intention of the drafters of Article XXI of GATT 1947. *See*, UN Economic and Social Council, 'Second Session of the Preparatory Committee of the United Nations Conference on Trade and Employment' Verbatim Report, Thirty-Third Meeting

The impact of disputes concerning the TRIPS Agreement does not depend on having a report adopted by a panel. Often, normative changes at the national level have been adopted because a mutually agreed solution has been adopted. This has been the case in the areas of civil, border and criminal enforcement.

Regarding civil enforcement, provisional measures are a case in point. In disputes initiated by the United States and targeting Argentina, Sweden and Denmark, a mutually agreed solution that required the amendment of national laws was reached. In the Argentinian case, the agreement with the United States included an amendment of the regulation concerning interim injunctions. The amended Argentinian legislation had to include the *fumus boni iuris* and *periculum in mora* principles, an evaluation of the balance of interest in the award of an interim injunction, other guarantees set forth in TRIPS Agreement Article 50, and the possibility of continuing with the alleged infringing activity if a caution was paid.[37] The Swedish and Danish cases were closely connected and resulted in the amendment of norms regarding provisional measures for the preservation of evidence. Denmark and Sweden adopted bills providing that, in case of threat of infringement, courts may order a search for infringing materials, documents or other relevant evidence. The search may be ordered *inaudita altera parte* if there is a risk that materials or documents could be removed, destroyed or altered.[38]

Something similar can be said regarding border enforcement. In 2010, Brazil and India requested consultations with the European Union and the Netherlands regarding repeated seizures on patent infringement grounds of generic drugs originating in third countries but transiting the Netherlands. In July 2011, an understanding between India and the European Union was reached. The agreement established that the mere fact that medicines transit European territory, and that there is a patent applicable in this territory, does not constitute enough grounds for the intervention of customs authorities. However, if there is a substantial likelihood of diversion of such medicines onto the European market, customs authorities may take action. Subsequently, in 2012, the European Union adopted guidelines implementing the understanding and giving examples of possible indications of risk of diversion. This very same approach was adopted in the new European regulation concerning border measures.

Disputes relating to criminal enforcement of intellectual property rights have also resulted in a mutually agreed solution linked to the amendment of national legislation. In March 1998, the United States denounced the regular broadcasting by Greek TV stations of copyrighted motion pictures and television programs without the authorisation of copyright owners. Six months later, a new law was adopted in Greece. The law ordered the imposition of criminal sanctions for copyright counterfeiting and

of Commission A, E/PC/T/A/PV/33, (24 July 1947) 20–21. *See also*, GATT, *Analytical Index: Guide to GATT Law and Practice* (1995) 600.

37. *Argentina – Patent Protection for Pharmaceuticals and Test Data Protection for Agricultural Chemicals – Argentina – Certain Measures on the Protection of Patents and Test Data, Notification of Mutually Agreed Solution*, WT/DS171/3, WT/DS196/4, IP/D/18/Add.1, IP/D/22/Add.1, 20 June 2002.

38. *Sweden – Measures Affecting the Enforcement of Intellectual Property Rights, Notification of Mutually-Agreed Solution*, WT/DS86/2 IP/D/10/Add.1, 11 December 1998; *Denmark – Measures Affecting the Enforcement of Intellectual Property Rights, Notification of Mutually-Agreed Solution*, WT/DS83/2 IP/D/9/Add.1, 13 June 2001.

the possibility of closing down TV stations that infringed intellectual property rights. In March 2001, a mutually agreed solution between Greece, the United States and Europe recognised the satisfaction of the United States with the law and measures adopted. In that agreement, Greece undertook to maintain current legislation and continue with the effective actions adopted since the new law was enacted.[39]

Among the cases that have made their way through a panel or the Appellate Body, the one exclusively dealing with enforcement is *China – Intellectual Property Rights*. The measures at issue in that case were the thresholds for criminal procedures and penalties for infringement of intellectual property, the disposal of infringing goods confiscated by customs authorities, and the denial of protection and enforcement to works not authorised for publication or distribution within China. With respect to the numerical thresholds for finding criminal liability, the panel did not validate such thresholds but underlined that TRIPS does not order the criminalisation of all copyright and trademark infringements and that the key notion in that context is one of 'commercial scale'. On a different matter, the panel also made it clear that the conditions set forth in the border measures section apply to imports but not to exports. It also noted that auctioning goods seized on importation is not contrary to TRIPS, but doing so in a way that the product can be reused merely by removing the trademark is. As to the denial of copyright protection, the panel underlined that the circulation of protected works can be prohibited, but this does not extend to not granting copyright protection to prohibited works.

C. PLURILATERALS AND BILATERALS

The move towards increased standards of intellectual property protection has continued in both bilateral and plurilateral fora since the adoption of TRIPS. While most plurilateral attempts to strengthen intellectual property enforcement standards have derailed, many bilateral agreements have been successfully concluded, a trend that endures and seems the foreseeable path, notably in light of the alleged end of multilateralism.

I. Plurilateral Attempts to Regulate Enforcement

The Anti-Counterfeiting Trade Agreement (ACTA) is the sole international treaty ever concluded with exclusive focus on intellectual property enforcement.[40] Signed in 2011, the ratification of the agreement was rejected by the European Parliament in 2012, a rebuff that meant the *de facto* end of ACTA as an international treaty. The agreement had erected the most complete international regime on intellectual property enforcement up until that moment, and the provisions set forth therein have heavily influenced intellectual property enforcement standards adopted in subsequent plurilateral and bilateral agreements.[41]

39. *Greece – Enforcement of Intellectual Property Rights for Motion Pictures and Television Programs, Notification of Mutually Agreed Solution*, WT/DS125/2 IP/D/14/Add.1, 26 March 2001.

40. Regarding ACTA, *see* in detail P. Roffe, X. Seuba (eds.), *The Anti-Counterfeiting Trade Agreement: Genesis and Aftermath* (Cambridge University Press, Cambridge, 2014).

41. The name of this international treaty is certainly misleading, since ACTA (anti-counterfeiting

From a normative point of view, ACTA had two notable characteristics. First, in relation to civil, criminal and border enforcement it incorporated the obligations set forth in TRIPS but remained silent on the many instances where TRIPS codifies the rights of alleged infringers. Secondly, ACTA strengthened the standards of protection and created new rights in areas not specifically regulated in the TRIPS Agreement, such as the digital environment. ACTA also introduced general provisions to guide interpretation, and incorporated by reference important TRIPS principles, including those set forth in TRIPS Articles 7 and 8. Numerous provisions of ACTA were drafted in permissive or ambiguous terms, which would open the door to explore the potential of TRIPS Articles 7 and 8 and their quasi-legislative function. A relative status quo for civil enforcement,[42] some advances in the area of border enforcement[43] and important concern and ambiguity for criminal enforcement[44] portray a fallen agreement.

The other plurilateral agreement regulating enforcement is the Trans-Pacific Partnership Agreement (TPP).[45] Once negotiations concluded, the TPP became the most sophisticated trade agreement enshrining intellectual property standards, including enforcement standards. Signed in February 2016, President Trump however withdrew from the TPP in January 2017. The TPP section on enforcement includes general principles and detailed articles touching upon civil, criminal and border enforcement. It also enshrines important references to enforcement of intellectual property rights in the digital domain. It largely builds upon previous agreements, in particular ACTA and the trade agreement between the United States and the Republic of Korea. Even though in some specific respects the TPP goes beyond these treaties, in some other instances it is a more balanced text and includes checks and balances frequently absent in PTAs. This is the case with the general provisions of the TPP intellectual property chapter, where a number of guarantees and basic principles missing in PTAs are enacted.

trade agreement) is not just concerned with trade or trademarks, as the reference to 'trade agreement' and 'counterfeiting' would suggest. Instead, it is the only international treaty ever adopted with exclusive focus on intellectual property enforcement.

42. While the civil enforcement provisions of ACTA restate what was already available to right holders in signatory members, the conflict between legal traditions became evident when trying to go beyond some remedies. The limits were clear with respect to the award of damages, where continental law and common law traditions clash.
43. As far as border enforcement is concerned, ACTA introduced relevant changes. It essentially expanded border enforcement obligations and ordered control of both importation and exportation. It recognised, moreover, the possibility of controlling transit, while allowing parties to exclude the control of goods protected by patents and trade secrets. The combination of such recognition and the power not to exclude patents can be read as a permission to control the transit of patented goods, even if this possibility was a matter of national and international debate during ACTA negotiations.
44. Criminal enforcement was the area attracting most concern. The articles adopted in ACTA were vague when analysed from the point of view of fair trial standards, the chief argument made by the global movement for rejecting the agreement. Such ambiguity heavily influenced the negative vote of the European Parliament.
45. The origins of the TPP are found in the P4 trading group, set up in 2005 by Chile, Brunei Darussalam, Singapore and New Zealand. In 2009 the United States joined the P4 negotiations, followed later on by a larger group of nations with a view to becoming a major trading block.

II. Bilaterals and Intellectual Property Enforcement

The number of PTAs exploded after the WTO Agreement was adopted in 1994. As of the early 2000, PTAs have become the preferred tool to foster increased protection of intellectual property whenever negotiations in other fora made no progress. PTAs have been a leading source of new normative intellectual property obligations, also in the area of enforcement. Beginning with the United States' agreements, and soon thereafter with the European Union, EFTA, South Korea and Japan agreements, the main trading powers have made intellectual property enforcement a key objective of PTAs.

The interest in enforcement comes as no surprise. The Trade Promotion Authority Act of the United States established that the purpose of the United States in the area of enforcement is 'providing strong enforcement of intellectual property rights, including through accessible, expeditious, and effective civil, administrative, and criminal enforcement mechanisms'. In a similar vein, the European Union also made it clear in 2004 and 2014 policy documents (the so-called 'strategies' for the enforcement of intellectual property rights in third countries) that intellectual property rights enforcement is a priority target of the PTAs it negotiates.[46]

Both in the case of the United States and the European Union, two central features and effects of enforcement provisions in PTAs become clear. First, the expansion of the scope of the enforcement regime of the TRIPS Agreement. New areas and new topics, not dealt with in TRIPS, are regulated in PTAs. Secondly, intellectual property enforcement provisions in PTAs clarify and broaden articles of the TRIPS Agreement considered too general or ambiguous. Generally, this means strengthening intellectual property obligations: what in the TRIPS Agreement were options, in PTAs become obligations, additional requirements to public authorities are set up, more rights for rightsholders with respect to several civil and border enforcement situations are enacted, and new situations become the object of criminal sanctions.[47]

Of course, not all PTAs that regulate intellectual property address enforcement, and not all agreements that regulate enforcement do it with the same intensity. A differentiation can be made between treaties that make a general reference to intellectual property enforcement and those that regulate this area in detail. Treaties can also be identified depending on the area or areas of intellectual property enforcement that they regulate, namely civil, criminal, border, and digital enforcement.[48] Likewise, an evolution can be observed, and more recent treaties become not only more demanding but also better pieces of legislation, thus they introduce missing safeguards. While a detailed analysis of enforcement provisions in PTAs goes beyond the scope of this chapter, subsequent paragraphs introduce the features of PTAs in the areas of digital and border enforcement, as well as regarding general obligations on enforcement.

---

46. *See* X. Seuba and E. Dan, 'The European foreign policy for intellectual property enforcement', in J. Drexl, A. K. Sanders, *The Innovation Society and Intellectual Property* (Edward Elgar, 2019), 160–87.
47. *See* X. Seuba, 'The Relevance of the Principles for Intellectual Property Provisions in Bilateral and Regional Agreements vis-à-vis European Preferential Trade Agreements', 44 *IIC* (2013), 943.
48. *See*, in detail, X. Seuba, 'Intellectual Property in Preferential Trade Agreements: What Treaties, What Content?', *The Journal of World Intellectual Property* (2013); and Seuba, *supra* note 1, 122–30.

One of the major changes following the TRIPS Agreement is the regulation of intellectual property enforcement in the digital domain. Since the adoption of the WIPO internet treaties in 1996,[49] PTAs have included an obligation to ratify treaties related to digital enforcement.[50] In other cases, treaties not only legislate by reference but also directly regulate the digital enforcement measures to be adopted and address in particular anti-circumvention of effective technological measures and electronic rights management information.

As regards border enforcement, numerous treaties contain measures that potentially affect goods protected by intellectual property rights. These are measures of a general nature, however, such as the inspection of goods entering the country. However, many other treaties regulate the specific relationship between intellectual property rights and border measures. Fundamentally, these treaties expand both the categories of intellectual property rights – possibly all of them – and the border situations that are the object of control: importation, exportation and transit.

The diversity existing across PTAs regulating intellectual property enforcement makes it impossible to generalise about the content of the general provisions specifically targeting these enforcement measures. Probably the only valid generalisation is that, in the majority of cases, there is no section on general provisions for intellectual property enforcement. The PTAs promoted by the United States and the European Union are an exception, however, as they often enshrine general principles and understandings on how enforcement should be implemented, and coincide in aspects such as mandating ex officio action in the context of border and criminal enforcement, or requiring final decisions on the merits of a case be made in writing. Three areas stand out: the provision of more extensive protection,[51] the inclusion of fair trial guarantees[52] and references to resource-allocation.[53]

49. The WIPO 1996 Copyright Treaty and Performances and Phonograms Treaty are commonly known as the 'WIPO internet treaties'. The TRIPS Agreement was outdated in this particular domain as soon as it entered into force, since it did not address enforcement on the internet. The WIPO internet treaties require States to 'ensure that enforcement procedures are available under their law so as to permit effective action against any act of infringement of rights covered by this Treaty, including expeditious remedies to prevent infringements and remedies which constitute a deterrent to further infringements'. These treaties codified the first attempts to respond to online infringement of intellectual property rights, in particular copyright, which were made by means of technological protection measures against unauthorised access and copying, as well as electronic rights management information.
50. *See* for instance EU-Chile FTA and EIA (2003/2005); EU-CARIFORUM States FTA and EIA (2008).
51. Agreements concluded by the Unites States commonly mention the possibility of providing more extensive enforcement of intellectual property rights under its law than required by the treaty, providing that 'the more extensive protection does not contravene' the agreement itself. This is reminiscent of the construction of Article 1.1 of the TRIPS Agreement, generally presented as the provision limiting the ever-increasing protection of intellectual property rights.
52. Due process and fair trial standards are also commonly mentioned in bilateral treaties promoted by the United States in the context of intellectual property enforcement articles. In some cases, the incorporation of due process principles is made in general terms. On other occasions, however, only specific aspects relating to due process are mentioned. ACTA, the TPP and more recent European trade agreements have improved references to fair trial principles in international agreements relating to intellectual property rights.
53. TRIPS Article 41.5 states that nothing in the agreement 'creates any obligation with respect to the distribution of resources as between enforcement of intellectual property rights and enforcement of law in general'. Some PTAs have tried to make sure that references of this type

D. CURRENT CHALLENGES AND THE WAY FORWARD

I. How Artificial Intelligence Transforms Intellectual Property Enforcement

When considering present technological disruption, TRIPS articles seem to pertain to a world that is vanishing and is giving way to a very different reality. Fuelled by a profusion of digitised data and rapidly advancing computational processing power,[54] artificial intelligence techniques and functional applications[55] give rise to unprecedented opportunities for innovation and creativity, and also bring about important challenges to intellectual property basic principles, including in the area of enforcement.[56] Three major areas stand out.

First, the use of artificial intelligence techniques to generate innovative and creative products has prompted discussions concerning the need, extent and legal grounds of intellectual property protection of products developed thanks to artificial intelligence.[57] Secondly, regarding the means that enable creation and innovation, the intellectual property protection of artificial intelligence techniques and functional applications *per se* has skyrocketed in recent years.[58] Thirdly, the use of artificial intelligence, big data and distributed ledger technologies also impacts intellectual property enforcement. The increase of available information and the changes in the

---

do not impact on the actual respect of substantive rights. Hence, in some PTAs it is stated that 'Parties understand that a decision that a Party makes on the distribution of enforcement resources shall not excuse that Party from complying with the provisions of this Chapter'. *See*, Seuba, *supra* note 1, 128.

54. WIPO, *Artificial Intelligence*, WIPO Technology Trends, Geneva: WIPO, 2019, p. 13.
55. Artificial intelligence techniques include machine learning, deep learning, fuzzy logic, logic programming, neutral networks, latent representation and unsupervised learning. Artificial intelligence functional applications include computer vision (including image recognition and biometrics), natural language processing (including semantics and sentiment analysis), speech processing (speech-to-speech and speaker recognition), robotics, control methods. *See* WIPO, *ibid.*, p. 31.
56. On policy issues, *see* the interview to the Director General of WIPO, Francis Gurry, *WIPO Magazine*, September 2018, available at https://www.wipo.int/wipo_magazine/en/2018/05/article_0001.html (accessed June 2019). WIPO has also made available a website on 'Artificial Intelligence and Intellectual Property' with information and practical resources, available at https://www.wipo.int/about-ip/en/artificial_intelligence/ (accessed May 2020).
57. As H. Pihlajamaa emphasises, artificial intelligence poses challenges to inventorship and ownership, patent eligibility, assessment of inventiveness, and sufficiency of disclosure. *See* H. Pihlajamaa, *Legal Aspects of Patenting Inventions Involving Artificial Intelligence (AI)*, presentation available at https://www.epo.org/news-issues/issues/ict/artificial-intelligence.html (accessed July 2019). A vast body of literature already addresses these challenges. *See* T. L. Butler, 'Can a Computer be an Author - Copyright Aspects of Artificial Intelligence', 4(4) *(Comm/Ent): A Journal of Communications and Entertainment Law* (1981–1982), 707–48; A. Lauber-Rönsberg, S. Hetmank, 'The concept of authorship and inventorship under pressure: Does artificial intelligence shift paradigms?', 14(7) *Journal of Intellectual Property Law & Practice* (2019), 570–79; R. Abbott, 'I Think, Therefore I Invent: Creative Computers and the Future of Patent Law', 57(4) *Boston College Law Review* (2016); N. Shemtov, *A Study on Inventorship in Inventions Involving AI Activity* (EPO, Munich, 2019).
58. P. Cupitt, 'Patenting Artificial Intelligence at the European Patent Office', *CIPA Journal*, April 2019.

techniques used to make such information useful impact fundamental aspects of intellectual property enforcement. These changes revolve around three concepts: authority, automation and centralisation.

A substantial change concerns the authority in charge of law enforcement, since public institutions have delegated to private entities enforcement functions they usually exercised.[59] A telling example is that of online intermediaries,[60] which have acquired a central role in managing behaviour in the digital environment.[61] From free speech to access to information, digital behaviour is mediated by search engines, websites and social networks. Their power expands to intellectual property enforcement, since online intermediaries not only identify infringement but also produce the information regarding the infringing activity, the infringers, the channels of commerce and its financial aspects.[62] Intermediaries also use algorithms to remove allegedly infringing content upon notice of an infringement, and also to *ex ante* monitor, filter, block and disable access to content automatically flagged as infringing.[63]

Privatisation leads to the convergence of law enforcement and adjudication powers.[64] Private stakeholders that identify infringing products also apply the corresponding sanctions: from destroying infringing goods to cutting access to the internet. The conventional way of functioning has been drastically altered. Customs officials, police and judges had always been part of the enforcement process, which encompasses a variety of interrelated activities. However, the substitution of these

59. *See* examples at F. Mostert, *Study on approaches to online trademark infringements*, 31 July 2017, WIPO/ACE/12/9 REV. 2, 9-12.
60. G. Frosio, 'Why Keep a Dog and Bark Yourself? From Intermediary Liability to Responsibility', 25(1) *Oxford International Journal of Law and Information Technology* (2017), 1–33; European Commission Communication on Online Platforms and the Digital Single Market Opportunities and Challenges for Europe, COM(2017)555 final, 28 September 2017. On the responsibility of intermediaries themselves, *see*, K. Weatherall, *Internet Intermediaries and Copyright. A policy paper produced for the Australian Digital Alliance*, available at https://www.aph.gov.au/DocumentStore.ashx?id=79110429-08ee-4b3b-8219-85071c8c0cee&subId=563534 (accessed March 2020); E. Rosati, 'The CJEU Pirate Bay Judgment and Its Impact on the Liability of Online Platforms', 39(12) *EIPR* (2017), 737; J. Ginsburg, J.A. Budiardjo, 'Liability for Providing Hyperlinks to Copyright-Infringing Content: International and Comparative Law Perspectives', 41(2) *Columbia Journal of Law and the Arts* (2018), 153.
61. M. Perel, N. Elkin-Koren, 'Black Box Tinkering: Beyond Transparency in Algorithmic Enforcement', 69 *Florida Law Review* (2017), 190. This is a power that platforms do not necessarily wish to have. Google 'didn't ask to be the decision maker' on deletions, Google's Executive President Eric Schmidt said. *See* A. White, 'Google EU Ruling Response Vetted as Complaints Pile Up - Bloomberg', 18 September 2014, available at http://www.bloomberg.com/news/articles/2014-09-18/google-eu-rulingresponse-vetted-as-complaints-pile-up (accessed August 2019).
62. For instance, Chinese giant Alibaba leads the use of big-data analytics and machine learning and sets a cutting-edge standard in the area. Alibaba automated systems flag a product as counterfeit. Next, the system pools financial and commercial information and identities counterfeiters, and probably the manufacturing site and movement of funds. *See* Alibaba, *Alibaba Intellectual* Property Rights *Protection Handbook*, available at https://ipp.alibabagroup.com/infoContent.htm?skyWindowUrl=notice/handbook-en (accessed May 2020).
63. *See* a list of authors and works that have discussed the function internet intermediaries as gatekeepers at M. Perel, N. Elkin-Koren, 'Accountability in Algorithmic Copyright Enforcement', 19 *Stanford Technology Law Review* (2016), 480 (*see also* 485).
64. *Ibid.*, 481.

actors by private operators gives rise to the concentration of functions in the hands of a single actor that thereby becomes prosecutor, judge and executioner. While this may certainly enhance efficacy and may be the adequate response to the volume of current trade, it also raises concerns from the point of view of independence, accountability[65] and fair trial standards.

A second and related phenomenon concerns automation, that is, the fact that machines themselves implement the law. Computers use machine learning techniques to derive legal consequences, implement orders and reach conclusions from a database of primary sources.[66] In addition to automated processes that apply to all branches of the law, there are *sui generis* types of automation applicable to intellectual property. For instance, machines may respond to copyright-based internet takedown requests, and machines may also determine the existence of trademark infringement thanks to image recognition.[67] The changes brought by artificial intelligence do not merely impact the online environment but also the manner in which judges adjudicate intellectual property cases, lawyers practise intellectual property law and authorities, including customs authorities, identify infringement. While due process concerns arise,[68] many start-ups have developed applications that are transfiguring law practice,[69] in particular those that enable the automation of time-consuming processes, such as conducting research, writing memos, undertaking due diligence and collecting evidence.[70] Automation of the law is promoted invoking practical advances in terms of efficiency, savings, consistency in applying legal doctrines and law harmonisation.[71]

---

65. *Ibid.*, 477.
66. S. Morse, 'Government-to-Robot Enforcement', 696 *Public Law and Legal Theory Research Paper Series*, The University of Texas School of Law, available at https://papers.ssrn.com/sol3/JELJOUR_Results.cfm?form_name=journalbrowse&journal_id=184028 (accessed May 2020)
67. For instance, in 2014 WIPO added image-search to its Global Brand Database, allowing users to search for visually similar trademark from among the millions of images in the collection. WIPO, *WIPO Launches Unique Image-Based Search for Trademarks, Other Brand Information*, 12 May 2014, PR/2014/760, https://www.wipo.int/pressroom/en/articles/2014/article_0007.html (accessed July 2019). Private developers have brought to the market applications that allow conduct of similar analyses, among them, *TrademarkNow, TrademarkVision, MikeTM Suite* and *LawPanel's Aila*. Other applications allow fakes to be identified just by scanning with a phone device. This is for instance the case for *Entrupy* and *Goat*.
68. D. K. Citron, F. Pasquale, 'The Scored Society: Due Process for Automated Predictions', 89(1) *Washington Law Review* (2014), 1–34.
69. B. Rubin, 'Legal Tech Startups Have a Short History and a Bright Future', *TechCrunch*, 6 December 2014, available at http://techcrunch.com/2014/12/06/legal-tech-startups-have-ashort-history-and-a-bright-future/ (accessed July 2019); M. McKamey, 'Legal technology: artificial intelligence and the future of law practice', 22 *Appeal*, 57; E. A. Rayo, 'AI in Law and Legal Practice – A Comprehensive View of 35 Current Applications', *Techemergence*, 29 November 2017, available at https://www.techemergence.com/ai-in-law-legal-practice-current-applications/ (accessed May 2020).
70. M.R. Grossman, G. Cormack, 'Technology-Assisted Review in E-Discovery Can Be More Effective and More Efficient Than Exhaustive Manual Review', XVII(3) *Richmond Journal of Law & Technology* (2011) 11; D. Garcia, 'Preparing for Artificial Intelligence in the Legal Profession', *Practice Trends, The Lexis Practice Advisor Journal*, 6 July 2017, available at https://www.lexisnexis.com/lexis-practice-advisor/the-journal/b/lpa/archive/2017/06/07/preparing-for-artificial-intelligence-in-the-legal-profession.aspx (accessed May 2020).
71. Perel and Elkin-Koren, *supra* note 63, 477. A more critical and analytic view on the phenomenon, D. Remus, F.S. Levy Frank, 'Can Robots Be Lawyers? Computers, Lawyers, and the Practice

A third change relates to centralisation. Under this term reference is made to the fact that a single action – writing a bit of software code – produces legal decisions for many individuals at once.[72] These are decisions that, previously, required an individualised procedure.[73] Until recently, enforcement was human-driven, dynamic, public and individualised. Public authorities enforcing intellectual property – judges, customs officials and police – were 'just' humans. Similarly, intellectual property could not be understood as an automated process, but as a process of weighing and balancing competing rights and interests,[74] a process taking place in an individualised fashion in public settings and administered either by judicial or administrative authorities. These features contrast with a new situation where enforcement mechanisms are automated, centralised and privatised, and big players take the place of public authorities.

II. A Contextualised Reading of Intellectual Property Enforcement

As noted in the introduction to this chapter, enforcement describes an action, not a preset state of things, a pre-established outcome or a situation where a homogeneous implementation of the same norms exists. Intellectual property enforcement is hence better understood as a process, a weighing and balancing process for the implementation of intellectual property rights. Such an understanding has major consequences in different contexts, including intellectual property adjudication and the estimation of intellectual property rights' economic value and impact on welfare.

While the right to exclude is the most visible aspect of intellectual property entitlements, under an instrumentalist understanding of intellectual property law[75] exclusion is just a mechanism for the fulfilment of broader policy goals. Other rights, remedies, processes and institutions are of relevance to fulfil those goals and are also taken into account in the weighing and balancing process to enforce intellectual property rights. Contextualisation within the broader legal framework,

of Law', 27 November 2016, available at SSRN: https://ssrn.com/abstract=2701092 or http://dx.doi.org/10.2139/ssrn.2701092; A. Marwaha, 'Seven Benefits of Artificial Intelligence for Law Firms', *Law Technology Today*, 13 July 2017, available at www.lawtechnologytoday.org/2017/07/seven-benefits-artificial-intelligence-law-firms/ (accessed May 2020).

72. Morse, *supra* note 66.
73. As Lessig stated in his acclaimed 2000 piece, in the age of cyberspace the 'regulator is code – the software and hardware that make cyberspace as it is. This code, or architecture, sets the terms on which life in cyberspace is experienced. It determines how easy it is to protect privacy, or how easy it is to censor speech.' L. Lessig, 'Code Is Law. On Liberty in Cyberspace', *Harvard Magazine*, 1 January 2000, https://harvardmagazine.com/2000/01/code-is-law-html (accessed May 2020).
74. The same applies to other legal domains. For instance, the WTO Appellate Body has noted 'In sum, determination of whether a measure, which is not 'indispensable', may nevertheless be 'necessary' within the contemplation of Article XX(d), involves in every case a process of weighing and balancing a series of factors which prominently include the contribution made by the compliance measure to the enforcement of the law or regulation at issue, the importance of the common interests or values protected by that law or regulation, and the accompanying impact of the law or regulation on imports or exports.' Appellate Body Report, *Korea –Various Measures on Beef*, WT/DS161/AB/R, 11 December 2000, para. 164.
75. P. Drahos, *A Philosophy of Intellectual Property* (ANU eText, 2016), 231–65.

and due consideration of public interest, fundamental rights, competition and free trade principles, are key in that operation.

The weighing and balancing process to enforce intellectual property rights goes hand in hand with legal concepts such as judicial discretion and flexibility. The former is a traditional legal principle, while the latter is a loose term that alludes to the margin of space within intellectual property norms and how states and other relevant stakeholders can make use of it. Far from leading to arbitrary outcomes or to a weakened protection of intellectual property rights, judicial discretion and flexibility are key tools to reaching and enforcing fair and equitable decisions in light of what is prescribed by the law and the circumstances of the case. In light of this contextualised approach to intellectual property enforcement, it comes as no surprise that debates in the area of enforcement connect closely to debates revolving around substantive intellectual property norms. The balance between the interests of right holders and the broader interests of society is the chief concern of authorities. Access to information and to vital products, for instance, are among the topics that both substantive and enforcement norms alike influence.

In the majority of cases, norms integrating the global regime for the enforcement of intellectual property rights leave national authorities ample space for adjustment and for 'creative and forward-looking implementation'.[76] This is particularly the case of TRIPS. Even if the drafting of international rules is frequently vague and may lack balance, authorities can still adjust intellectual property enforcement norms so as to guarantee an efficient, fair and balanced enforcement. The combination of comparative intellectual property law and fundamental rights is the most productive approach for that purpose, within the framework of broader policy goals and general principles of law – notably the principle of proportionality.

In the weighing and balancing process for the civil enforcement of intellectual property rights, the rights to privacy and due process – notably the principle of equality of arms – are of relevance when it comes to evidence and measures for the preservation of evidence. Likewise, due process – particularly the right to be heard – and equity considerations are central to the award of interim injunctions. In its turn, broader societal interests – including fundamental rights – may determine the award of a final injunction, while proportionality and due process considerations also shape the award of damages and corrective measures. When it comes to border enforcement, the rationale is similar to that of interim and final injunctions, thus it is crucial considering its impact on due process – notably the right to be heard and the principle of equality of arms – and on equity and fundamental rights beyond the country of customs procedures. Finally, criminal enforcement must be designed and applied under the principles of proportionality, legal certainty and procedural justice.

Twenty-five years since the adoption of TRIPS, and while its provisions still provide a sound and useful framework, they need to be considered in light of current tools and technological and political developments.

Economic analysis of intellectual property enforcement may play a relevant role in the design of future norms. The scale and impact of intellectual property infringement are among the central topics of interest of policymakers. It could not

76. P. Roffe, *Intellectual Property Provisions in Bilateral and Regional Trade Agreements: The Challenges of Implementation* (CIEL, 2007), 11.

be otherwise, given the economic, scientific and cultural relevance of intellectual property. Economic analysis is helpful to both designing and implementing enforcement norms. In the first case, quantification of all relevant factors, costs and impact on welfare, gives a sense and a guide for normative action. In the second case, economic impact is closely related to fundamental legal principles impacting remedies, such as proportionality and unjust enrichment – a principle for instance that puts a cap on damage awards.

Present and prospective scenarios must also consider digitalisation and the current process of automation, centralisation and delegation of authority in intellectual property enforcement. The expansion of automated algorithmic enforcement, the application of big data analytics to the enforcement of intellectual property rights, the applications of blockchain to intellectual property enforcement, and the development of devices that automatically enforce intellectual property, are all meant to boost the efficiency of intellectual property enforcement. At the same time, and in the same way that artificial intelligence challenges traditional concepts of authorship and inventorship, it also raises profound challenges to the concept of enforcement – largely based on the centrality of human intervention – and obliges reflection on accountability authority, and due process.

Finally, most observers predict a prolonged stalemate of multilateralism and the unremitting advancement of bilateralism and plurilateralism, including in the intellectual property enforcement domain. While such a situation is possible, so is a shared understanding on enforcement. While international debates on enforcement have been frequently polarised, States at different levels of socio-economic development and with different legal traditions share fundamental principles of balance and fairness, and also profess similar respect to fundamental rights of chief relevance regarding enforcement. It is consequently possible to advance an agenda for multilateral, or at least parallel, normative action in the area of enforcement if the foundations of such an agenda are identified: a common understanding of the systemic role of enforcement in the broader legal system, the fundamental principles of balance and fairness, and the guidance and limits resulting from fundamental rights entitlements.

CHAPTER 9

The TRIPS Agreement and WTO Dispute Settlement: Past, Present and Future

Peter Van den Bossche

A. INTRODUCTION

In 2020, the WTO Agreement on Trade-Related Aspects of Intellectual Property Rights ('TRIPS Agreement') marked its twenty-fifth anniversary. There was, however, little reason for celebration. The COVID-19 pandemic had plunged the world economy into an unprecedented crisis. In April 2020, the IMF predicted that global GDP would contract by as much as 3 per cent in 2020,[1] and the WTO forecast that the volume of world trade would decline in 2020 between 13 and 32 per cent depending on the how long the health crisis would last and how governments would respond to the economic impact of the crisis.[2] Even the decline under the best-case '13 per cent' scenario would still be the steepest decline on record.[3] However, global trade and the multilateral trading system, of which the TRIPS Agreement is one of the pillars, was in crisis already before any of us had heard of the new coronavirus or considered 'social distancing' a civil duty (rather than deviant behaviour). Global trade in goods declined in 2019 by 3 per cent in value terms and global trade in commercial services grew by a paltry 2 per cent only.[4] In its latest *Report on Trade and Investment Barriers*, the European Commission found that in 2019 the overall number of trade barriers kept increasing and noted that 'protectionism has become ingrained in trade relations

1. *See* https://blogs.imf.org/2020/04/14/the-great-lockdown-worst-economic-downturn-since-the-great-depression/. In May 2020, the World Bank predicted a contraction of global GDP in 2020 of 5.2 per cent. *See* https://www.worldbank.org/en/publication/global-economic-prospects.
2. *See* https://www.wto.org/english/news_e/pres20_e/pr855_e.htm.
3. In June 2020, the WTO estimated that the 2020 decline in global trade was 'unlikely' to reach the worst-case '32 per cent' scenario projected in April 2020. *See* https://www.wto.org/english/news_e/pres20_e/pr858_e.htm.
4. *See* https://timeseries.wto.org.

with many partners'.[5] There are multiple causes for this development in international trade but the dramatic shift in the trade policy of the United States since 2017 has arguably been the most important among them. The multilateral trading system and its principal institution, the WTO, have for almost four years now been under direct attack from the United States, which under the Trump Administration evolved from the 'champion' of the system to its 'demolisher-in-chief'. Since Donald Trump assumed the US presidency in January 2017, populist economic nationalism and protectionism have become the main features of US trade policy. The benefits for the United States of a rules-based multilateral trading system and of membership of the WTO have been openly and repeatedly questioned by both President Trump and members of the US Congress.[6] Among the most destructive actions taken by the United States against the rules-based multilateral trading system and the WTO is its frontal attack on the WTO dispute settlement system and in particular appellate review under the system by the WTO Appellate Body. As a result of the US obstruction of the appointment of new Appellate Body judges, the Appellate Body has been paralysed since December 2019 and the WTO dispute settlement system been seriously undermined. In this chapter, we will examine: (1) the core features of the WTO dispute settlement system; (2) the performance of the WTO dispute settlement system in TRIPS disputes; (3) the current crisis of WTO dispute settlement; and (4) the impact of that crisis on the application and enforcement of the TRIPS Agreement.

B. THE WTO DISPUTE SETTLEMENT

The establishment of the WTO in January 1995, as a result of the successful conclusion of the Uruguay Round negotiations (1986–1993), has been considered 'the most dramatic advance in multilateralism since the inspired period of institution building in the late 1940s'.[7] Together with the establishment of the WTO, new and/or stronger multilateral rules on trade in goods and services and on the protection of intellectual property were also adopted. The singular most important achievement of the Uruguay Round negotiations was, however, the creation now a new two-stage system for compulsory and binding dispute settlement, provided for in the Understanding on Rules and Procedures for the Settlement of Disputes, commonly referred to as the Dispute Settlement Understanding or DSU, attached to the WTO Agreement as Annex 2. The DSU is to ensure the compliance and, if necessary, enforce compliance, of WTO Members with their obligations under WTO law, including the obligations under the TRIPS Agreement. In fact, the possibility of ensuring compliance with the TRIPS

5. *See* European Commission, Report from the Commission to the European Parliament and the Council on Trade and Investment Barriers, 1 January 2019 – 31 December 2019, COM(2020) 236 final, dated 15 June 2020.
6. *See* e.g. https://www.cnbc.com/2018/08/30/trump-threatens-to-withdraw-from-world-trade-organization.html (on President Trump's statement that the US would withdraw from WTO if it 'did not shape up'); and https://www.hawley.senate.gov/senator-hawley-introduces-joint-resolution-withdraw-wto (on the joint resolution to withdraw from the WTO introduced by Senator Josh Hawley).
7. *See* Report of the Consultative Board to the Director-General Supachai Panitchpakdi, *The Future of the WTO: Addressing Institutional Challenges in the New Millennium* ('Sutherland Report') (WTO,2004), para. 1.

Agreement through WTO dispute settlement was considered a major step forward in international intellectual property law and an important reason for making the TRIPS Agreement part of WTO law.

The WTO dispute settlement system is based on the dispute settlement system of the1947 General Agreement on Tariffs and Trade (GATT 1947). The latter system evolved between the late 1940s and the early 1990s from a system that was primarily a power-based system of dispute resolution through diplomatic negotiations, into a rules-based system of dispute resolution through adjudication. The WTO dispute settlement system is a further leap forward in the process of progressive 'judicialisation' of the resolution of international trade disputes. As discussed below, since January 1995, the WTO dispute settlement system has been widely used and its 'output', in terms of the number of dispute settlement reports, has been remarkable. Both developed and developing country Members have frequently used the system to resolve their trade disputes, including disputes on politically very sensitive issues.

The jurisdiction of the WTO dispute settlement system is compulsory, exclusive and contentious in nature. Furthermore, it is very broad in scope. It covers disputes arising under all but two WTO agreements, including the *TRIPS Agreement.*[8] In principle, any act or omission attributable to a WTO Member can be a measure that is subject to WTO dispute settlement. Note that measures that can be subject to WTO dispute settlement include action or conduct by private parties attributable to a Member; measures that expired or were withdrawn during the proceedings and are thus no longer in force; legislation as such (as opposed to the actual application of this legislation in specific instances); unwritten norms or rules of Members, including practices or policies which are not set out in law; and measures by regional and local authorities. Access to the WTO dispute settlement system is limited to WTO Members. A WTO Member can have recourse to the system when it claims that a benefit accruing to it under one of the covered agreements is being nullified or impaired (Article 3.1, 26 DSU and Article XXIII of the GATT 1994). A complainant will almost always argue that the respondent violated a provision of WTO law and file a violation complaint. If the violation is shown, there is a presumption of nullification or impairment of a benefit (Article 3.8 DSU). Alternatively, but never done with success to date, a complainant can file a non-violation complaint and claim that a benefit accruing to it is being nullified or impaired as a result of the application by a Member of any measure, whether or not it conflicts with any provision of WTO law. Note, however, that no non-violation complaints can be brought under the *TRIPS Agreement.*[9] Non-governmental organisations, industry associations, companies or

---

8. Only disputes arising under the *Trade Policy Review Mechanism and the Plurilateral Agreement on Trade in Civil Aircraft do not fall within the* jurisdiction of the WTO dispute settlement system. *See* Appendix 1 DSU.
9. There was strong resistance from developing countries during the Uruguay Round negotiations against inclusion of non-violation complaints as a cause of action under the TRIPS Agreement, as they were concerned that this would create the possibility to extend the protection of the TRIPS Agreement beyond that specified in its provisions. For this reason, Article 64.2 of the TRIPS Agreement provided that, for a period of five years from the entry into force of the WTO Agreement, no non-violation complaints could be brought under the TRIPS Agreement. This 'moratorium' has been extended multiple times and still applies today, as Members have been unable to agree, pursuant to Article 64.3 of the TRIPS Agreement, on the scope and modalities for non-violation complaints.

individuals have no direct access to the WTO dispute settlement system. However, disputes, including TRIPS disputes, are usually brought to the WTO for resolution at the instigation of companies and industry associations. They lobby their (or a) government to initiate WTO dispute settlement proceedings and can thus be said to have 'indirect access' to the system.

The prime objectives of the WTO dispute settlement system are to provide security and predictability to the multilateral trading system (Article 3.2 DSU) and to settle disputes between WTO Members promptly (Article 3.3 DSU). WTO dispute settlement has six key features, which in addition to the compulsory and exclusive jurisdiction of the WTO dispute settlement system and the process of WTO dispute settlement contribute to, and explain, the importance and success of WTO dispute settlement to date discussed below. Some of these features set apart the WTO dispute settlement system from other international dispute settlement mechanisms. These features also may offer an explanation for the use made of the WTO dispute settlement system for the resolution of TRIPS disputes.

First, the WTO dispute settlement system is a single, comprehensive and integrated dispute settlement system. The rules of the DSU apply to all disputes arising under the covered agreements (Article 1.1 DSU). Article 64.1 of the TRIPS Agreement explicitly confirms that the DSU applies to any TRIPS dispute. A number of these covered agreements, including the TRIPS Agreement, provide, however, for some special and additional rules and procedures 'designed to deal with the particularities of dispute settlement relating to obligations arising under a specific covered agreement' (Article 1.2 and Appendix 2 DSU). An example of such special and differential rule is the exclusion, already noted above, of non-violation complaints in TRIPS disputes (Article 64.2 and 3 of the TRIPS Agreement).

Second, the DSU provides for several methods to settle disputes between WTO Members: consultations or negotiations (Article 4 DSU); adjudication by panels and the Appellate Body (Articles 6–20 DSU); arbitration (Articles 21.3(c), 22.6 and 25 DSU); and good offices, conciliation and mediation (Article 5 DSU). Of these methods, arbitration under Article 25 and good offices, conciliation and mediation under Article 5 have only played a marginal role. In all WTO disputes, including TRIPS disputes, Members had recourse to consultations (Article 4 DSU), and, if those were unsuccessful, adjudication (Articles 6 to 19 DSU). As discussed below, however, some WTO Members are currently resorting to arbitration under Article 25 to address the current crisis of WTO dispute settlement.

Third, pursuant to Article 23 DSU, Members must settle disputes with other Members over compliance with WTO obligations through the *multilateral* procedures DSU, rather than through *unilateral* action. Concerns regarding unilateral action taken by the United States in the late 1980s and early 1990s, also in disputes regarding the protection of intellectual property rights, were the driving force behind the Uruguay Round negotiations on dispute settlement, which eventually resulted in the DSU. The recent return of the United States to unilateral action is at the core of the current crisis of the WTO dispute settlement system.

Fourth, the WTO dispute settlement system prefers Members to resolve a dispute through consultations, resulting in a mutually acceptable solution, rather than through adjudication (Article 3.7 DSU). In other words, the DSU prefers parties *not* to go to court, but to settle their dispute amicably out of court. As discussed below, a high number of TRIPS disputes are resolved through consultations and do not proceed to the adjudication stage of the WTO dispute settlement system.

Fifth, the WTO dispute settlement system serves not only 'to preserve the rights and obligations of Members under the covered agreements', but also 'to clarify the existing provisions of those agreements' (Article 3.2, second sentence, DSU). The scope and nature of this clarification mandate is, however, explicitly circumscribed. Panels and the Appellate Body are precluded from adding to or diminishing the rights and obligations of Members (Article 3.2, last sentence and 19.2 DSU). The DSU does not condone judicial activism. For panels and the Appellate Body to stay within their mandate to clarify existing provisions and not stray into judicial activism, it is therefore important that they interpret and apply the provisions concerned correctly, i.e. in accordance with customary rules of interpretation of international law, as codified in Articles 31 and 32 of the Vienna Convention on the Law of Treaties (Article 3.2, second sentence, DSU).[10] As discussed below, at the very heart of the current crisis of WTO dispute settlement is the criticism of the United States that the WTO Appellate Body engaged in judicial activism and, through erroneous interpretation of the WTO agreements, added obligations to which the United States never agreed.

Sixth, the DSU provides for three types of remedy for breach of WTO law: one final remedy, namely, the withdrawal (or modification) of the WTO-inconsistent measure; and two temporary remedies which can be applied awaiting the withdrawal (or modification) of the WTO-inconsistent measure, namely, compensation *and* suspension of concessions or other obligations (commonly referred to as 'retaliation') (Article 3.7, 21 and 22 DSU). A measure which was found to be WTO-inconsistent must be withdrawn immediately or, if that is impracticable, within a 'reasonable period of time'. However, when the offending party fails to do so, and the parties are subsequently unable to agree on compensation for the harm that will result from the lack of compliance, the original complaining party may request authorisation from the DSB to retaliate against the offending party by suspending concessions or other obligations with respect to that offending party. Retaliation, often in the form of a drastic increase in the customs duties on strategically selected products, puts economic and political pressure on the offending party to withdraw (or modify) its WTO-inconsistent measure(s). Subject to certain conditions, the retaliation may take the form of the suspension of obligations under agreements other than those with regard to which a violation was found in the underlying dispute (i.e. cross-retaliation). Note that in a number of disputes which did not relate to the TRIPS Agreement, the complainant was authorised to retaliate against the non-complaining respondent by suspending obligations under the TRIPS Agreement.[11] To date, Members applied retaliation measures in only four cases, while the number of disputes in which the

10. Pursuant to Articles 31 and 32 of the Vienna Convention on the Law of Treaties, panels and the Appellate Body interpret provisions of the covered agreements in accordance with the ordinary meaning of the words of the provision in their context and in light of the object and purpose of the agreement involved; and, if necessary and appropriate, they have recourse to supplementary means of interpretation.
11. *See* e.g. in *EC – Bananas III*, Ecuador and in *US – Gambling* Antigua and Barbuda were authorised to retaliate by suspending obligations under the TRIPS Agreement vis-à-vis the European Union and the United States respectively. Neither country, however, made use of this possibility. In *United States – Upland Cotton*, Brazil was also authorised to retaliate by suspending obligations

DSB authorised Members to do so was significantly higher. The effectiveness and/ or appropriateness of retaliation - which is by definition trade destructive - as a temporary remedy for breach of WTO law is the subject of debate.

Among the institutions involved in WTO dispute settlement one must distinguish between a political institution, the Dispute Settlement Body (DSB), and two independent, judicial-type institutions, the dispute settlement panels and the Appellate Body. The DSB, which is composed of all WTO Members, administers the dispute settlement system (Article 2 DSU). It has the authority to establish panels, adopt panel and Appellate Body reports, and authorise retaliation in case of non-compliance (Article 6.1,16.4, 1714 and 22.6 DSU). It takes decisions on these important matters by *reverse consensus*.[12] As a result, the DSB decisions on these matters are quasi-automatic. However, on all other matters, including the (re-)appointment of Appellate Body judges, the DSB takes decisions by consensus and each Member thus has a veto right (Article 2.4 DSU). As explained below, this consensus requirement has resulted in the paralysis of the Appellate Body since December 2019.[13] Notwithstanding its importance in WTO dispute settlement, the actual adjudication of disputes brought to the WTO is not done by the DSB, but done, at the first-instance level, by dispute settlement panels and, at the appellate level, by the Appellate Body. Panels are *ad hoc* bodies established for the purpose of adjudicating a particular dispute and are dissolved once they have accomplished this task. A panel is established by the DSB but the parties decide on the composition of the panel by mutual accord. If they fail to do so within 20 days after the establishment of the panel, either party can ask the Director-General of the WTO to appoint the panellists (Article 8.7 DSU). As a rule, panels are composed of three well-qualified governmental and/or non-governmental individuals, who are not nationals of the parties or third parties to the dispute (Article 8.1 DSU). The *ad hoc* composition of panels allows for the appointment of panellists with specific expertise in the subject matter of the dispute concerned. In panels dealing with TRIPS disputes, some of the panellists thus clearly had extensive expertise in intellectual property law and were undoubtedly appointed for that reason.[14] The task of the panel with regard to the disputed measure is to undertake neither a *de novo* review nor a deferential review, but 'to make an objective assessment of the matter before it, including an objective assessment of the facts of the case and the applicability of and conformity with the relevant covered agreements' (Article 11 DSU). As the trier of facts, a panel must base its findings on a sufficient evidentiary basis on the record; must treat evidence in an 'even-handed' manner; and should not disregard evidence that is relevant to the case of one of the parties. Panels may

---

under the TRIPS Agreement vis-à-vis the United States and, in that case, the threat of such suspension, did have a significant impact on the resolution of the dispute. *See* below, p. 266.

12. A decision is taken by *reverse consensus* unless there is a consensus among Members not to take the proposed decision. For example, a decision to establish a panel at the request of the complainant is taken by the DSB unless the latter decides by consensus not to establish the panel. It is clear that the complainant requesting the establishment of a panel is very unlikely to join the consensus not to establish the panel.
13. *See* below, p. 267.
14. Note, however, that, as discussed below, disputes in which claims of inconsistency with the *TRIPS Agreement* were raised, often also concerned claims of inconsistency with other WTO agreements, and thus required panelists with broader expertise.

exercise judicial economy; they need only address (but at the same time are required to address at least) those claims which must be addressed in order to resolve the matter at issue in the dispute. A panel report must, at a minimum, set out the findings of fact, the applicability of relevant provisions and the basic rationale behind any findings and recommendations it makes (Article 12.7 DSU). Where a panel concludes that a Member's measure is inconsistent with WTO law, it shall recommend that the Member concerned bring that measure into conformity with WTO law (Article 19.1 DSU). The recommendations and rulings of the panel become legally binding when they are adopted – by reverse consensus – by the DSB.

The Appellate Body is a permanent international tribunal of seven judges appointed by the DSB for a term of four years (renewable once) (Article 17. 1 and 2 DSU). The Appellate Body shall comprise 'persons of recognized authority, with demonstrated expertise in law, international trade and the subject matter of the covered agreements generally' (Article 17.3 DSU). Note that of all judges who served on the Appellate Body to date, only one, Mr. A.V. Ganesan, had extensive prior expertise in international intellectual property law.[15] Appellate Body members must be independent and impartial, avoid direct and indirect conflicts of interest and respect the confidentiality of proceedings (Article 17.3 DSU and Rules of Conduct for the DSU). The Appellate Body hears and decides appeals in divisions of three of its Members (Article 17.1 DSU). Only parties to the dispute can appeal a panel report (Article 17.4 DSU). An appeal is limited to issues of law covered in the panel report and legal interpretations developed by the panel (Article 17.6 DSU). Issues of fact cannot be appealed. However, the treatment of the facts or evidence by a panel may raise the question of whether the panel has made an objective assessment of the facts as required under Article 11 DSU. This is a legal issue and can therefore be examined by the Appellate Body. As explained below, this is, however, contested by the United States. The Appellate Body may uphold, modify or reverse the legal findings and conclusions of the panel that were appealed (Article 17.13 DSU). On occasion, the Appellate Body has also – in the absence of the authority to remand a case to the panel – felt compelled to 'complete the legal analysis' on issues not addressed by the panel. It has done so in order to provide a prompt resolution of the dispute.

The WTO dispute settlement process may – and often does – entail four major steps: (1) consultations; (2) panel proceedings; (3) appellate review proceedings; and (4) implementation and enforcement. The four-step WTO dispute settlement process has six features that are particularly noteworthy, partly because they distinguish WTO dispute settlement – in both positive and negative ways – from other international dispute settlement mechanisms. These six features are: (1) the short time frame for each of the steps in the process; (2) the confidentiality and resulting lack of transparency of the process; (3) the burden of proof in WTO dispute settlement proceedings, which is on the party that asserts the affirmative of a particular claim or defence; (4) the important role of private legal counsel in representing parties in WTO dispute settlement; (5) the acceptance and consideration by panels and the Appellate Body of *amicus curiae* briefs; and (6) the obligation on Members to act in good faith in WTO dispute settlement proceedings, and the obligation on panels

15. Mr. A.V. Ganesan served as India's chief negotiator on the *TRIPS Agreement* during the Uruguay Round.

and the Appellate Body to ensure due process in these proceedings. Several of these procedural features have given raise to controversy. Most developing countries strongly object to the Appellate Body's case law on the acceptance and consideration of *amicus curiae* briefs, and, as discussed below, the United States severely criticises the Appellate Body for exceeding, without the agreement of the parties, the mandatory, but often totally unrealistic, 90-day timeframe for appellate review.

C. PERFORMANCE OF THE WTO DISPUTE SETTLEMENT SYSTEM IN TRIPS DISPUTES

Overall, the WTO system for resolving trade disputes between WTO Members has been a remarkable success. In 1996, Director-General Renato Ruggiero referred to the WTO dispute settlement system as the 'jewel in the crown' of the WTO. Such praise was in this second year of the system probably premature, but it would soon, and this for many years, prove to be justified. Between 1995 and 2019, 593 disputes were brought to the WTO for resolution.[16] While the United States and the European Union were the most frequent complainants, developing country Members made frequent use of the WTO dispute settlement system to challenge the WTO consistency of trade measures of other Members. In a number of years developing country Members brought more disputes to the WTO than developed country Members.[17] The United States and the European Union have not only been the most frequent complainants, also more than any other Member they were respondents, albeit that the European Union in this respect is a distant second. The rate of compliance with rulings of WTO dispute settlement panels and the Appellate Body has been consistently very high. Note, however, that the United States has consistently failed to comply with a number of rulings which required it to withdraw or amend WTO-inconsistent measures.

Of the 593 disputes brought to the WTO between 1995 and 2019, i.e. of the disputes in which consultations between the parties were initiated during this period, 41, or 7 per cent, concerned obligations under the TRIPS Agreement.[18] The United States was by far the most frequent complainant in TRIPS disputes (18), followed by the European Union (8). The United States initiated almost 50 per cent of all TRIPS dispute proceedings. Other WTO Members were complainants in TRIPS disputes only once or twice. The European Union (7) was more than any other Member the respondent in TRIPS disputes, followed by Australia (5) and the United States (4). Contrary to what developing country Members had feared, there was definitely no tsunami of TRIPS disputes brought to the WTO by developed country Members against developing country Members. In fact, in only 13 of the 41 disputes were the respondents developing country Members.[19] Most TRIPS disputes were initiated in the early years of the WTO, i.e. in the period from 1996 to 2000 (23) but there was

16. *See* http://worldtradelaw.net/databases/searchcomplaints.php. To date, only two disputes were brought to the WTO in 2020.
17. *See* http://worldtradelaw.net/databases/complaintsclassification.php.
18. For data on the consultations initiated between January 1995 and December 2019, *see* http://worldtradelaw.net/databases/searchcomplaints.php. Note that none of the consultations initiated in 2020 concerned TRIPS matters.
19. China (3), Indonesia (2), Argentina (2), India (2), Pakistan (1), Turkey (1), Cuba (1), and Brazil (1).

a recent peak in the years 2017–2019 (8). The TRIPS provisions most as issue in the disputes in which consultations were initiated concerned (in order of importance) the domestic enforcement of IPRs, patents, trade marks, copyright and the national treatment obligation. Note the relatively low number of TRIPS disputes brought to the WTO (7 per cent of all WTO disputes). It has been suggested that some of the core features of WTO dispute settlement explain this relatively low number of TRIPS disputes brought to the WTO for resolution.[20] As discussed above, only WTO Members, and not the IP holders themselves can bring a TRIPS dispute to the WTO, and while IP holders may be successful in lobbying a WTO Member to do so, their efforts in this respect are often likely to fail. Also, only measures by a WTO Member (or measures attributable to it) can be challenged in WTO dispute settlement. IP infringements by private operators cannot, whereas these infringements are probably what IP holders are most concerned about. Moreover, the remedies available under the DSU offer little comfort to the winning complainant, as these remedies are only prospective. Past economic harm caused to the IP holder as a result of a TRIPS-inconsistent measure is not compensated. Future economic harm can be compensated but such compensation is of little interest to IP holders because is normally is in the form of a reduction of trade barriers on other products or services. In only one TRIPS dispute, *US – Section 110(5) Copyright Act,* the United States paid the European Union, the complainant (and thus presumably the EU IP holders) EUR 1.2 million per year for a period of three years, as compensation for its continuing non-compliance with the ruling in this case. Such award of monetary compensation is, however, very exceptional. As discussed below, the retaliation measures which a complainant may be authorised to take vis-à-vis a respondent who fails to comply with a ruling, is also of little help to the IP holder. Finally, note that in practice WTO dispute settlement proceedings, while short in comparison with the proceedings of other international courts and tribunals, may take too much time for IP holders to find them an attractive response to specific instances of breach of TRIPS obligations.

In addition to the relatively low number of TRIPS disputes brought to the WTO for resolution, one should note that in 45 per cent of these disputes, consultations were 'successful' in the sense that the dispute did not proceed to the next stage in the WTO dispute settlement process, namely panel proceedings.[21] This may be because the complainant and the respondent reached a mutually agreed solution to the dispute or because the complainant (and/or the IP holders initially lobbying for proceedings to be initiated) decided not to pursue the case further. Note that this percentage of 'successful' consultations (45 per cent) is significantly higher than the overall 'success' rate of consultations (20 per cent). In addition to the reasons already mentioned above for the low number for TRIPS disputes, the high rate of successful consultations may also be explained by the fact that in a number of TRIPS disputes the TRIPS obligations were very clear and the TRIPS inconsistency quite obvious. In those disputes, the initiation of formal consultations by the complainant was all

20. *See* e.g. J. Pauwelyn, 'The Dog that Barked But Didn't Bite: 15 Years of Intellectual Property Disputes at the WTO' (November 2010), available at https://papers.ssrn.com/sol3/papers.cfm?abstract_id=1708026.

21. *See* http://worldtradelaw.net/databases/searchcomplaints.php and http://worldtradelaw.net/databases/wtopanels.php.

that the respondent needed as 'encouragement' to either withdraw or modify the TRIPS inconsistent measure.

To date, TRIPS disputes that did proceed to the panel stage resulted in 13 panel reports.[22] In total, WTO disputes between 1995 and 2019 resulted in 258 panel reports. Only 5 per cent of these reports concern TRIPS disputes. Not surprisingly, the United States (6) and the European Union (4) were most frequently the complainants in disputes that resulted in panel reports. The most frequent respondents were the United States and Australia (each 4) and China, India and the European Union (each 2).[23] Most of the 13 panel reports were issued in the period between 1998 and 2000 (7). There are currently two TRIPS disputes pending before a panel.[24] The TRIPS provisions most at issue in panel reports concerned (in order of importance) trade marks, the national treatment obligation, geographical indications, and the enforcement of IPRs.

Of the 13 panel reports in TRIPS disputes circulated to date, four were appealed to the Appellate Body and resulted in Appellate Body reports.[25] The appeal rate of 41 per cent is considerably lower than the normal appeal rate of 68 per cent.[26] Only 2 per cent of the 145 Appellate Body reports circulated to date concerned TRIPS disputes.[27] The Appellate Body has had very few occasions to clarify TRIPS provisions pursuant its mandate under Article 3.2 DSU. The TRIPS provisions at issue in these Appellate Body reports concerned trade marks, patents, the enforcement of IPR, and the protection of existing subject matter. It has been suggested that the reason for the low appeal rate of panel reports is that TRIPS panels, more than other panels, are 'carefully balanced giving something to each side which neither side was willing to risk on appeal' and that 'parties may also be apprehensive of involving the Appellate Body whose rulings ... carry more weight and set a deeper precedent than panels'.[28]

22. In reverse chronological order: *Saudi Arabia – IPR* (DS567) (complaint by Qatar); *Australia – Tobacco Plain Packaging* (DS435, DS441) (complaints by Honduras and Dominican Republic); *Australia – Tobacco Plain Packaging* (DS458, DS467) (complaints by Cuba and Indonesia); *China – IP Rights* (DS362) (complaint by the United States); *EC – Trademarks and Geographical Indications* (DS290) (complaint by Australia); *EC – Trademarks and Geographical Indications* (DS174) (complaint by the United States); *US – Section 211 Appropriations Act ('Havana Club')* (DS176) (complaint by the European Communities); *US – Section 110(5) Copyright Act* (DS160) (complaint by the European Communities); *Canada – Patent Term* (DS170) (complaint by the United States); *Canada – Pharmaceuticals Patents* (DS114) (complaint by the European Communities); *India – Patents* (DS79) (complaint by the European Communities); *Indonesia – Autos* (DS54, DS55, DS59, DS64) (complaints by European Communities, Japan and the United States); and *India – Patents* (DS50) (complaint by the United States).
23. Note that the numbers between brackets refer to the number of disputes which resulted in panel reports, not to the number of panel reports.
24. *UAE – Trade in Goods and Services*, and IP (DS526) (complaint by Qatar) and *China – IP Rights* (DS542) (complaint by the United States).
25. In reverse chronological order: *Australia – Tobacco Plain Packaging* (DS435, DS441) (complaints by Honduras and Dominican Republic); *US – Section 211 Appropriations Act ('Havana Club')* (DS176) (complaint by the European Communities); *Canada – Patent Term* (DS170) (complaint by the United States); *Canada – Pharmaceuticals Patents* (DS114) (complaint by the European Communities); and *India – Patents* (DS79) (complaint by the European Communities). It is at present unclear whether the panel report in *Saudi Arabia – IPR* (DS567) (complaint by Qatar), which was circulated on 16 June 2020, will be appealed.
26. *See* http://worldtradelaw.net/databases/appealcount.php.
27. *See* http://worldtradelaw.net/databases/abreports.php.
28. Pauwelyn, *supra* note 20, at 44.

As regards the implementation of, and compliance with, panel and/or Appellate Body rulings, the reasonable period of time for implementation could not be agreed upon by the parties and was set by an arbitrator in three TRIPS disputes.[29] As already discussed above, in one TRIPS dispute, the level of compensation for future harm caused by the TRIPS-inconsistent measure was determined by arbitration under Article 25 DSU, and to date this has been the only use ever made of Article 25 DSU.[30] DSB authorisation to retaliate because the respondent failed to comply was requested in that same dispute, but this request was subsequently not further pursued in spite of the continued failure to comply. In this and one other TRIPS dispute, there was been long-standing failure to comply with the rulings and recommendations of the panel and the Appellate Body.[31] In both disputes the United States was the respondent failing to comply.

In sum, while some WTO Members have often claimed that other Members systematically act inconsistently with their obligations under the TRIPS Agreement, compared to other WTO agreements, few TRIPS disputes were brought to the WTO and when they were brought, more often than other WTO disputes they were not pursued to the end. More use of the WTO dispute settlement system would have allowed for the rules-based resolution of specific TRIPS disputes between WTO Members, rather than see these disputes fester, be politicised and affect negatively the relations between the Members concerned. More use of the WTO dispute settlement system would also have allowed for the clarification of existing TRIPS provisions and for the development of WTO intellectual property law. While the WTO dispute settlement system definitely made a more significant contribution to the development of the law of WTO agreements apart from the TRIPS Agreement, this does not mean that the WTO dispute settlement had no impact on the development of WTO IP law over the past 25 years. Among the disputes noteworthy here are *India – Patents* (DS50) (1998), *Canada – Patent Term* (DS170), *US – Section 211 Appropriation Act ('Havana Club')* (DS 176), *EC – Trademarks and Geographical Indications* (DS174, DS290), *China – IP Rights* (DS362), and *Australia – Tobacco Plain Packaging* (DS435, DS441, DS458, DS467).

29. In reverse chronological order: *US – Section 110(5) Copyright Act* (DS160) (complaint by the European Communities) (reasonable period of time for implementation: 12 months); *Canada – Patent Term* (DS170) (complaint by the United States) (reasonable period of time for implementation: 10 months); *Canada – Pharmaceuticals Patents* (DS114) (complaint by the European Communities) (reasonable period of time for implementation: 6 months). *See* http://worldtradelaw.net/databases/rptawards.php.

30. In *US – Section 110(5) Copyright Act* (DS160) (complaint by the European Communities), the arbitrator determined the compensation required to be EUR 1.2 million per year. As noted above, the United States paid the European Communities this amount for three years and then halted the payments without having complied with the rulings in this case.

31. *US – Section 211 Appropriations Act ('Havana Club')* (DS176) (complaint by the European Communities); and *US – Section 110(5) Copyright Act* (DS160) (complaint by the European Communities).

D. THE CRISIS OF WTO DISPUTE SETTLEMENT

As noted above, the WTO dispute settlement system is currently in crisis, but while this crisis is now acute and existential, it has been looming for many years. Even during the early years of WTO dispute settlement, there were a number of crisis moments, for example in 1997 in the context of the *US – Helms Burton* dispute regarding the jurisdiction over disputes in which national security was invoked; in 1999 in the context of the *EC – Bananas III* dispute regarding the sequencing of the Article 21.5 DSU compliance procedure and the Article 22.6 DSU procedure for DSB authorisation for retaliation; and in 2001 in the context of the *EC – Asbestos* dispute regarding the acceptance and consideration of *amicus curiae* briefs.[32] Also, in the context of the DSU review (1998–1999) and the DSU reform negotiations in the context of the Doha Round negotiations (2001-), WTO Members, while expressing general satisfaction with the WTO dispute settlement system, tabled dozens of proposals for change.[33] As from 2005 onwards, the WTO dispute settlement system became gradually ever more the victim of its own success. First, the dispute settlement workload grew steadily, in particular due to the increasing number of claims of inconsistency raised in each dispute and the rising complexity of the measures challenged and the legal arguments made. However, the resources made available did not keep track with this growing workload. Secondly, the institutional imbalance between the successful judicial branch of the WTO and its mostly ineffective legislative branch became ever more apparent and made WTO Member seek changes to WTO law through litigation rather than negotiation. This development brought with it the perception of, if not the danger of, judicial activism by WTO panels and, in particular, the Appellate Body. Thirdly, certainly since 2010, some WTO Members, and in particular the United States, have adopted an ever more antagonistic discourse against the Appellate Body whenever the latter's rulings were unfavourable. Fourthly, some WTO Members, and again in particular the United States, undermined the independence and impartiality of WTO adjudicators by *inter alia* blocking the reappointment of Appellate Body members who were seen as not having 'served' US interests sufficiently (Jennifer Hillman of the United States in 2012) or were seen as having ruled against the United States (Seung Shang of Korea in 2016). The current crisis of the WTO dispute settlement system was thus already looming for some time.

It was, however, only under the Trump Administration that the crisis of WTO dispute settlement became acute. As from the summer of 2017, the United States has obstructed the process of appointment or re-appointment of Appellate Body members because, as it repeatedly stated, it has serious 'concerns' regarding the functioning of the Appellate Body. The United States accuses the Appellate Body of judicial overreach as well as blatant disregard for its procedural and institutional rules.[34] As to the alleged judicial overreach, the United States accuses the Appellate

32. *See* P. Van den Bossche & W. Zdouc, *The Law and Policy of the World Trade Organization* (4th edn., Cambridge University Press, 2017), 622, 290–91, and 260–64.
33. *See ibid.*, pp. 294–96.
34. *See* US President's 2018 Trade Policy Agenda, p. 22 ff, at https://ustr.gov/about-us/policy-offices/press-office/reports-and-publications/2018/2018-trade-policy-agenda-and-2017; and United States Trade Representative, *Report on the Appellate Body of the World Trade Organization*, February 2020, at https://ustr.gov/sites/default/files/Report_on_the_Appellate_Body_

Body, *first*, of judicial activism, i.e. of creating, through erroneous interpretations of WTO provisions, obligations the United States had never agreed to; *secondly*, of rendering advisory opinions in that the Appellate Body ruled on issues that were not necessary to rule upon to resolve the dispute at hand; *thirdly*, of reviewing factual findings of the panel and in particular findings on the meaning of domestic law, which fall outside the Appellate Body's mandate under Article 17.6 DSU; and *fourthly*, of considering its case law as having binding precedential value. As to the alleged disregard for procedural and institutional rules, the United States objects in particular to the Appellate Body exceeding the mandatory 90-day timeframe for appellate review without the explicit agreement of the parties, and to allowing, pursuant to Rule 15 of the Working Procedures for Appellate Review, out-going Appellate Body members to complete the disposition of appeals which were assigned to them before the end of their term in office. With the exception of the last concern, the United States had also voiced the same or very similar concerns regarding the functioning of the Appellate Body under the Obama and George W. Bush Administrations. However, the Trump Administration, by blocking the (re-)appointment of Appellate Body judges, transformed these 'concerns' into an existential crisis of the Appellate Body. On 11 December 2019, the number of Appellate Body judges in office fell below the minimum of three. Of the seven Appellate Body judges in mid-2017, only Ms. ZHAO Hong of China was left, after the terms of Amb. Ujal Bhatia Singh of India and Mr. Thomas Graham of the United States had come to an end. As from 11 December 2019, the Appellate Body could no longer hear any new appeals and of the 12 appeals pending at that time, it was only allowed to complete the disposition in three.[35] The paralysis of the Appellate Body severely undermines the whole WTO dispute settlement system as it may be expected that parties losing a case at the panel stage will appeal the unfavourable panel report to the paralysed Appellate Body - an action referred to as appealing into the void - and will thus prevent the panel report from being adopted by the DSB and becoming legally binding. For almost 25 years, the WTO dispute settlement system was a glorious experiment with the rule of law in international trade relations. Unless an agreement is reached on how to address the United States' concerns regarding the functioning of the Appellate Body, this experiment has sadly come to an end. In search of such agreement, no less than 22 WTO Members and the African Group have, since November 2018, tabled, either individually or jointly, position papers with proposals to address the US concerns regarding the functioning of the Appellate Body.[36] Some of these position papers, such as the Communication

---

of_the_World_Trade_Organization.pdf. *See also* the statement by the United States at the DSB meetings on 22 June 2018 concerning Article 17.5 DSU and the 90-day timeframe for appellate review, on 27 August and 26 September 2018 concerning Article 17.6 DSU and appellate review of panel findings of fact, including on the meaning of domestic law; and on 29 October 2018 concerning the issuance of advisory opinions on issues not necessary to resolve a dispute.

35. The disposition of these three appeals was completed pursuant Rule 15 of the Working Procedures of Appellate Review. The Appellate Body Report in the last of these three appeals, *Australia — Tobacco Plain Packaging* (DS435 and DS441), was circulated on 9 June 2020. As discussed above, this report addressed *inter alia* a number of TRIPS issues.

36. *See* Communication from the European Union, China, Canada, India, Norway, New Zealand, Switzerland, Australia, Republic of Korea, Iceland, Singapore and Mexico and Montenegro to the General Council, WT/GC/W/752/Rev. 2, dated 11 December 2018; Communication from the European Union, China, India and Montenegro to the General Council, WT/GC/W/753, dated

from the European Union, China, Canada, India, Norway, New Zealand, Switzerland, Australia, the Republic of Korea, Iceland, Singapore, Mexico and Montenegro of 10 December 2019, were rather 'sceptical' about the legitimacy of the concerns raised by the United States and made proposals which safeguarded the key features of WTO appellate review.[37] Other position papers, such as the Communication from Brazil, Paraguay and Uruguay of 25 April 2019, were much more sympathetic to the US concerns and altered some key features of WTO appellate review. Almost all WTO Members were, and still are, of the view that whatever legitimate concerns the United States might have regarding the functioning of the Appellate Body, these concerns did not justify the obstruction of the appointment process, which resulted in the paralysis of the Appellate Body and the undermining of the whole WTO dispute settlement system. WTO Members repeatedly, and in growing numbers, called upon the United States to allow for the appointment of new Appellate Body Members. At the meeting of the DSB on 29 June 2020, 122 WTO Members called on the DSB to take immediately the decision to unblock the appointment process.[38]

In December 2018, the WTO General Council appointed Amb. David Walker of New Zealand as 'Facilitator' to resolve the differences among WTO Members on the functioning of the Appellate Body in order to allow for the unblocking of the appointment process.[39] Over the next 10 months, Amb. Walker, who was also elected as DSB Chair in early 2019, met with WTO Members, in small groups and in open-ended informal meetings to discuss the proposals for reform tabled and seek a way out of this crisis. The United States, however, did not table any reform proposal and, reportedly, did not even engage in the discussions but only sent a junior diplomat to take notes. Based on the proposals made by Members and the extensive discussions on these proposals, Amb. Walker on 15 October 2019 submitted to the General Council a Draft Decision on the Functioning of the Appellate Body. [40] This

26 November 2018 and WT/GC/W/753/Rev., dated 11 December 2018; Communications from Honduras to the General Council, , WT/GC/W/758, dated 21 January 2019, WT/GC/W/759, dated 21 January 2019, WT/GC/W/760, dated 29 January 2019, and WT/GC/W/761, dated 4 February 2019; Communication from the Separate, Customs Territory of Taiwan, Penghu, Kinmen and Matsu to the General Council, WT/GC/W/763/Rev., dated 8 April 2019; Communication from Brazil, Paraguay and Uruguay to the General Council, WT/GC/W/767/Rev. dated 25 April 2019; Communication from Japan, Australia and Chile to the General Council, WT/GC/W/768, dated 18 April 2019, and WT/GC/W/768/Rev., dated 26 April 2019; Communication from Thailand to the General Council, WT/GC/W/769, dated 26 April 2019; and Communication from the African Group to the General Council, WT/GC/W/776, dated 26 June 2019. *See also*, more generally, European Commission, *Concept Paper on WTO Modernisation*, Part 3 on Future EU Proposals on Dispute Settlement, dated 20 September 2018; and Communication from Canada, *Strengthening and Modernizing the WTO: Discussion Paper*, Theme 2: Safeguarding and Strengthening WTO Dispute Settlement, JOB/GC/201, dated 21 September 2018.

37. On the US reaction to the Communication from the EU, China, Canada, India and others, *see* Statements by the United States at the Meeting of the WTO General Council on 12 December 2018 (agenda items 7 and 8). https://geneva.usmission.gov/2018/12/12/statements-items-7-and-8-by-the-united-states-at-the-meeting-of-the-wto-general-council/.
38. *See* Proposal on Appellate Body Appointments, WT/DSB/W/609/Rev. 18, dated 19 June 2020.
39. *See* https://www.wto.org/english/news_e/news19_e/gc_18jan19_e.htm.
40. General Council, Informal Process on Matters related to the Functioning of the Appellate Body – Report by the Facilitator, H.E. Dr. David Walker (New Zealand), JOB/GC/222, dated 15 October 2019, Annex.

Draft Decision aimed at 'seeking workable and agreeable solutions to improve the functioning of the Appellate Body', in the hope to avoid the paralysis of the Appellate Body as from December 2019.[41] The Draft Decision *inter alia* addressed:

(1) the US concern regarding judicial activism, by stating that pursuant to Articles 3.2 and 19.2 DSU, Appellate Body rulings 'cannot add to or diminish the rights and obligations provided in the covered agreements';
(2) the US concern regarding binding precedent, by stating that precedent is 'not created through WTO dispute settlement proceedings', but that consistency and predictability in the interpretation of WTO law is 'of significant value to Members';
(3) the US concern regarding advisory opinions rendered by the Appellate Body, by stating that the latter may only address issues raised by the parties to the extent necessary to resolve the dispute;
(4) the US concern regarding appellate review of findings on the meaning of municipal law, by stating that the meaning of municipal law is to treated as a matter of fact and therefore, pursuant to Article 17.6 DSU, not subject to appellate review;
(5) the US concern regarding the 90-day timeframe for appellate review, by stating that, pursuant to Article 17.5 DSU, the Appellate Body is obligated to issue its report within 90 days of the notice of appeal and that this timeframe can only be extended with the agreement of the parties; and
(6) the US concern regarding the Rule 15 of the Working Procedures for Appellate Review, by deciding that only the DSB can authorise outgoing Appellate Body members to complete the disposition of an appeal after the expiry of their term in office, if and when the oral hearing in the appeal took place prior to the expiry.

The Draft Decision was a carefully constructed compromise between the Members engaged in the discussions on the functioning of the Appellate Body, which preserved the core features of the WTO appellate review. However, the hope that the Draft Decision would allow the WTO to avoid the paralysis of the Appellate Body as from 11 December 2019 was very short-lived. On the same day as the Draft Decision was submitted, the United States rejected most of the 'solutions' reflected in the Draft Decision. According to the United States, there was no agreement on how to ensure that the limitations imposed by the DSU on the Appellate Body are respected in the future and what the consequences are for continued failure to adhere to these limitations.[42] Subsequently, the impasse was complete and the paralysis of the Appellate Body on 11 December 2019 unavoidable. At the meeting of the General Council on 3 March 2020, Amb. Dennis Shea of the United States declared that by repeatedly failing to interpret the WTO agreements consistent with the text of those agreements, 'the Appellate Body has undermined a rules-based trading system by persistently

41. *Ibid.*, para. 1.22.
42. Statement by Amb. Dennis Shea (United States) at the WTO General Council meeting on 15 and 16 October 2019 on *Informal Process on Matters Related to the Functioning of the Appellate Body – Report by the Facilitator* https://geneva.usmission.gov/2019/10/15/statements-by-the-united-states-at-the-wto-general-council-meeting/.

breaking those rules'.[43] Amb. Shea emphasised again that the United States has been raising its concerns regarding the functioning of the Appellate Body for many years, but that the problem 'has only worsened as too many WTO Members have remained unwilling to do anything to rein in' the Appellate Body's disregard for WTO rules.[44] According to the United States, the current crisis can only be overcome and reform of the WTO dispute settlement system achieved, if WTO Members recognise and 'come to terms with the failings of the Appellate Body'.[45] The United States insists that WTO Members 'engage in a deeper discussion of the why the Appellate Body has felt free to depart from the role Members assigned to it'.[46]

However, many other Members, including the European Union, China, India and Canada, disagree that the Appellate Body systematically engaged in judicial overreach and demonstrated intentional disregard for procedural and institutional rules.[47] At the General Council meeting of 9 December 2019, two days before the Appellate Body became paralysed, Amb. Joao Aguiar Machado of the European Union stated that 'the EU wishes to emphasise that [the Appellate Body] has served well all Members in an independent, highly professional and, given the circumstances, very efficient manner. The European Union, therefore, would like to commend all the present and past members of the Appellate Body on their work, as well as the staff working on the Appellate Body's secretariat'.[48] The United States' position on the functioning of the Appellate Body reflects: (1) its strong and ideologically charged disagreement with Appellate Body case law which restricts the ability of the United States to protect its domestic industry from import competition; and (2) its wish to return to a pre-WTO situation in which it could use its economic and other power to 'resolve' trade disputes with trading partners. On 17 June 2020, during briefings to the US House Ways and Means Committee and Senate Finance Committee, Amb. Robert Lighthizer, the United States Trade Representative, reportedly said that 'he would be content if the AB is never restored, arguing that the WTO members need to talk about a new dispute settlement system' and that 'he believes the original

43. Statement by Amb. Dennis Shea (United States) at the WTO General Council meeting on 3 March 2020 on the USTR Report on the Appellate Body of the World Trade Organization (item 11), https://geneva.usmission.gov/2020/03/03/statements-by-ambassador-dennis-shea-at-the-march-3-2020-general-council-meeting/.
44. *Ibid.*
45. *Ibid.*
46. *Ibid.*
47. *See* e.g. Statement by Amb. Joao Aguiar Machado (European Union) at the WTO General Council meeting on 15 and 16 October 2019 on *Informal Process on Matters Related to the Functioning of the Appellate Body – Report by the Facilitator* https://eeas.europa.eu/delegations/world-trade-organization-wto/68955/eu-statement-ambassador-jo%C3%A3o-aguiar-machado-general-council-meeting-15-and-16-october-2019_en; and Statement by Amb. ZHANG Xiangchen (China) at the WTO General Council meeting on 15 & 16 October 2019 on *Informal Process on Matters Related to the Functioning of the Appellate Body – Report by the Facilitator* http://wto2.mofcom.gov.cn/article/chinaviewpoins/201910/20191002905004.shtml.
48. Statement by Amb. Joao Aguiar Machado (European Union) at the WTO General Council meeting on 9 December 2019 on *Informal Process on Matters Related to the Functioning of the Appellate Body – Report by the Facilitator and Draft Decision on the Functioning of the Appellate Body*, WT/GC/W/791, item 11, https://eeas.europa.eu/delegations/world-trade-organization-wto/71695/eu-statement-ambassador-joão-aguiar-machado-general-council-meeting-9-december-2019_en?utm_source=dlvr.it&utm_medium=twitter.

(GATT) non-binding system that encouraged countries to work out their disputes was better'.[49] Amb. Lighthizer seems unwilling to recognise that the WTO dispute settlement system was established because the GATT dispute settlement system no longer worked as from the late 1980s and that the United States' recourse at that time to unilateral, power-based 'resolution' of trade disputes already when the United States was in all respects still a much more powerful nation, had become unacceptable to its trading partners and detrimental to international trade relations.

On 24 January 2020, in the margin of the 2020 World Economic Forum in Davos, Switzerland, the ministers of 17 WTO Members announced that, while they remain committed to finding a solution to the Appellate Body crisis, they would work together 'towards putting in place contingency measures that would allow for appeals of WTO panel reports in disputes among themselves'.[50] They instructed their officials to 'expeditiously finalise work' on a multi-party arrangement for appeal arbitration under Article 25 DSU. In 2019, the European Union had already made bilateral arrangements for appeal arbitration under Article 25 DSU with Canada and Norway, under which former Appellate Body members would act as appellate arbitrators.[51] Article 25 DSU provides for 'expeditious arbitration within the WTO as an alternative means of dispute settlement' and had been resorted to but once since 1995.[52] Probably faster than anyone had expected, but clearly reflecting the desire to preserve a credible WTO dispute settlement system, on 27 March 2020 16 WTO Members announced that they had reached an agreement on the Multi-Party Interim Appeal Arbitration Arrangement under Article 25 of the DSU (MPIA), which became effective on 30 April 2020, when it was notified to the DSB.[53] The MPIA is a valiant attempt to save what can be saved of the WTO dispute settlement system. However, it is but, and should not be more than, a temporary substitute for appellate review by the Appellate Body. At present, 21 WTO Members are party to the MPIA, including Brazil, Canada, China, the European Union and Mexico, i.e. five of the ten most frequent users of the WTO dispute settlement system. The number of parties to the MPIA is expected to increase further and it should be noted that also WTO Members who are not MPIA parties may resort on an *ad hoc* basis to appeal arbitration under the MPIA. Parties to the MPIA agree not to appeal panel reports to the paralysed Appellate Body (i.e., agree not to appeal panel reports into the void), but will resort to appellate arbitration under Article 25 DSU. The MPIA appeals will be heard by three arbitrators randomly selected from a fixed pool of ten arbitrators. To the extent that the procedures followed under the MPIA will mimic appellate review by the Appellate Body – and that is the stated intention – the MPIA may serve

49. *See Washington Trade Daily*, 18 June 2020, www.washingtontradedaily.net.
50. *See* https://trade.ec.europa.eu/doclib/docs/2020/january/tradoc_158596.pdf.
51. *See* for the EU/Canada Arrangement, https://trade.ec.europa.eu/doclib/docs/2019/july/tradoc_158273.pdf, and for the EU/Norway Arrangement, https://trade.ec.europa.eu/doclib/docs/2019/october/tradoc_158394.pdf.
52. *See* Award of the Arbitrators, *US – Section 110(5) Copyright Act (Article 25)*, circulated 9 November 2001, referred to above.
53. Statement on a Mechanism for Developing, documenting and Sharing Practices and Procedures in the Conduct of WTO Disputes, Addendum, JOB/DSB/1/Add. 12, dated 30 April 2020, https://trade.ec.europa.eu/doclib/docs/2020/april/tradoc_158731.pdf. Note that the 17 WTO Members which in January 2020 committed themselves to working towards an appeal arbitration arrangement, only Korea did not, and still is not, a party to the MPIA.

the parties thereto well as long as the Appellate Body is paralysed. The nominations made for the pool of MPIA arbitrators justify this hope. However, it remains to be seen how the MPIA will work in practice. On 3 June 2020, Australia and Canada in *Canada – Sale of Wine* (DS 537), Mexico and Costa Rica in *Costa Rica – Avocados* (DS524), and Brazil and Canada in *Canada – Aircraft* (DS522) notified the DSB that they have agreed – under the MPIA – to Procedures for Arbitration under Article 25 DSU.[54] However, on 5 June 2020, the United States reportedly wrote to DG Acevêdo objecting to the MPIA, which was referred to as a 'China-EU arrangement' and was said to create an 'ersatz' Appellate Body 'exacerbating the erroneous WTO appellate practice rather than reforming it'. According to the United States, the WTO Members that are parties to the MPIA have no right to use any WTO financial or staff resources on arbitration under the MPIA or instruct the Director-General to do so.[55]

E. IMPACT OF WTO DISPUTE SETTLEMENT CRISIS ON THE TRIPS AGREEMENT

To date, the United States has not raised any of its concerns regarding the Appellate Body, whether regarding the latter's judicial overreach or its disregard for procedural and institutional rules, in the context of Appellate Body reports which dealt with TRIPS issues.[56] As noted above, the Appellate Body since 1995 has circulated reports dealing with TRIPS issues in a mere four disputes. In two of these disputes, the United States was the complainant: *India – Patents* (1998) and *Canada – Patent Terms* (2000). In both cases, the Appellate Body found in favour of the United States and the latter therefore obviously did not consider the Appellate Body to be guilty of any form of judicial overreach. The Appellate Body was also able to complete the appellate review proceedings in these relatively small appeals within the mandatory 90-day timeframe.[57] In a third dispute, the United States was the respondent: *US – Section 211 Appropriation Act ('Havana Club')* (2002), and while the Appellate Body ruled on a number of claims against the United States, the latter has not included these rulings in its list of examples of judicial overreach.[58] This report was circulated on day 90. In the fourth dispute in which the Appellate Body circulated a report dealing with TRIPS issues, *Australia – Tobacco Plain Packaging,* circulated on 9 June 2020, the United States was not a party, but, as one might expect, an active third party. As this Appellate Body report has not yet been discussed in the DSB, it remains to be seen how the United States will respond to this report and whether it will raise any of its concerns regarding the functioning of the Appellate Body. The appellate review

54. *See* e.g. WT/DS537/15, dated 3 June 2020.
55. *See also* Bryce Baschuk, *U.S. Pledges to Block Funding for EU's WTO Appellate Body Proxy*, Bloomberg Law, 12 June 2020, https://news.bloomberglaw.com/international-trade/u-s-pledges-to-block-funding-for-eus-wto-appellate-body-proxy.
56. It may still do so with regard to the Appellate Body report in *Australia – Tobacco Plain Packaging*, which was circulated on 9 June 2020.
57. Note that the Appellate Body report in *India – Patents (1998)* was circulated 65 days after the notice of appeal.
58. *See* United States Trade Representative, *Report on the Appellate Body of the World Trade Organization*, February 2020, at https://ustr.gov/sites/default/files/Report_on_the_Appellate_Body_of_the_World_Trade_Organization.pdf.

proceedings in that case took 691 days, rather than 90 days, and the parties were not asked for their agreement to exceed the mandatory 90-day timeframe.

The fact that the United States has, to date, not explicitly raised concerns regarding Appellate Body reports addressing TRIPS issues is, however, of little importance to TRIPS dispute resolution. In the absence of a fully functional WTO dispute settlement system, TRIPS disputes may remain unresolved, may fester, and may trigger unilateral retaliation of WTO Members adversely affected by the alleged TRIPS-inconsistent measures. Also, in the absence of a fully functional dispute settlement system and, in particular, in the absence of an active Appellate Body, there will be no further clarification of TRIPS provision, and thus no further development of WTO IP law, through adjudication. The long-term impact of the crisis of the WTO settlement system will be for the WTO IP law no less harmful than for other fields of WTO law.

POST-SCRIPTUM

In January 2021, Joe Biden succeeded Donald Trump as US president. While the Biden administration has in many areas reversed the policies pursued by the Trump administration, changes in US trade policy have been minor so far. Note in this regard that Joe Biden, as the Democratic presidential candidate, claimed that 'economic security is national security', promised to create millions of manufacturing jobs, pledged to reverse America's dependency on China, announced his intention to strengthen 'Buy American' rules, and did not voice any support for a rules-based WTO dispute settlement system.

Index of Cases

Mexico – Taxes on Soft Drinks (2006)	Appellate Body Report, *Mexico – Tax Measures on Soft Drinks and Other Beverages*, WT/DS308/AB/R, adopted 24 March 2006	42
Peru – Agricultural Products	Appellate Body Report, *Peru – Additional Duty on Imports of Certain Agricultural Products*, WT/DS457/AB/R and Add.1, adopted 31 July 2015	49
	Panel Report, *Peru – Additional Duty on Imports of Certain Agricultural Products*, WT/DS457/R, circulated 27 November 2014	
Russia – Traffic in Transit	Panel Report, *Russia – Measures Concerning Traffic in Transit*, WT/DS512/R, adopted 26 April 2019	245
Saudi Arabia – IPRs	Panel Report, *Saudi Arabia – Measures Concerning the Protection of Intellectual Property Rights*, WT/DS567/R, report circulated 16 June 2020, under appeal 28 July 2020	245, 266
Sweden – Intellectual Property Rights (United States)	*Sweden – Measures Affecting the Enforcement of Intellectual Property Rights*, WT/DS86 mutually agreed solution 2 December 1998	246
Turkey – Textiles	Appellate Body Report, *Turkey – Restrictions on Imports of Textile and Clothing Products*, WT/DS34/AB/R, adopted 19 November 1999	49
United Arab Emirates – Goods, Services and IP rights	*United Arab Emirates – Measures Relating to Trade in Goods and Services, and Trade-Related Aspects of Intellectual Property Rights*, Panel composed 3 September 2018	266
US – 1916 Act (2000)	Appellate Body Report, *United States – Anti-Dumping Act of 1916*, WT/DS136/AB/R, WT/DS162/AB/R, adopted 26 September 2000	42
US- Clove Cigarettes (2012)	Appellate Body Report, *United States – Measures Affecting the Production and Sale of Clove Cigarettes*, WT/DS406/A/R, adopted 24 April 2012	204
US – Gambling (2005)	Appellate Body Report, *United States – Measures Affecting the Cross-Border Supply of Gambling and Betting Services*, WT/DS285/AB/R, adopted 20 April 2005	61, 261
	Panel Report, *United States – Measures Affecting the Cross-Border Supply of Gambling and Betting Services*, WT/DS285/R, adopted 20 April 2005, as modified by Appellate Body Report WT/DS285/AB/R	

Subject Index

D

E

H

I

U

IEEM SERIES ON INTERNATIONAL INTELLECTUAL PROPERTY LAW

1. Intellectual Property in the Digital Age – Challenges for Asia
   Christopher Heath and Anselm Kamperman Sanders (eds.)
   Published by Kluwer Law International 2001
   ISBN 90-411-9847-4

2. Intellectual Property in the Bio-Medical Age – Challenges for Asia
   Christopher Heath and Anselm Kamperman Sanders (eds.)
   Published by Kluwer Law International 2003
   ISBN 90-411-9926-8

3. New Frontiers of Intellectual Property Law
   Christopher Heath and Anselm Kamperman Sanders (eds.)
   Published by Hart Publishing 2005
   ISBN 978-1-84113-538-0

4. Intellectual Property and Free Trade Agreements
   Christopher Heath and Anselm Kamperman Sanders (eds.)
   Published by Hart Publishing 2007
   ISBN 978-1-84113-801-5

5. Spares, Repairs and Intellectual Property Rights
   Christopher Heath and Anselm Kamperman Sanders (eds.)
   Published by Kluwer Law International 2009
   ISBN 978-90-411-3136-2

6. Landmark Intellectual Property Cases and Their Legacy
   Christopher Heath and Anselm Kamperman Sanders (eds.)
   Published by Kluwer Law International 2011
   ISBN 978-90-411-3343-4

7. Intellectual Property Liability of Consumers, Facilitators and Intermediaries
   Christopher Heath and Anselm Kamperman Sanders (eds.)
   Published by Kluwer Law International 2012
   ISBN 978-90-411-4126-2

8. Employees, Trade Secrets and Restrictive Covenants
   Christopher Heath and Anselm Kamperman Sanders (eds.)
   Published by Kluwer Law International 2017
   ISBN 978-90-411-8379-8

9. Intellectual Property Rights as Obstacles to Legitimate Trade?
   Christopher Heath, Anselm Kamperman Sanders and Anke Moerland (eds.)
   Published by Kluwer Law International 2018
   ISBN 978-94-035-0330-1

10. Intellectual Property and International Dispute Resolution
Christopher Heath and Anselm Kamperman Sanders (eds.)
Published by Kluwer Law International 2019
ISBN 978-90-411-9097-0

11. Intellectual Property and the Fourth Industrial Revolution
Christopher Heath, Anselm Kamperman Sanders and Anke Moerland (eds.)
Published by Kluwer Law International 2020
ISBN 978-94-035-2212-8

12. 25 Years of the TRIPS Agreement
Christopher Heath and Anselm Kamperman Sanders (eds.)
Published by Kluwer Law International 2021
ISBN 978-94-035-2883-0

www.ingramcontent.com/pod-product-compliance
Lightning Source LLC
Chambersburg PA
CBHW071330230926
51849CB00002B/354
9789403528830